Late Life Jazz

LATE LIFE JAZZ

The Life and Career of Rosemary Clooney

Ken Crossland

and

Malcolm Macfarlane

OXFORD
UNIVERSITY PRESS

OXFORD
UNIVERSITY PRESS

Oxford University Press is a department of the University of Oxford.
It furthers the University's objective of excellence in research,
scholarship, and education by publishing worldwide.

Oxford   New York
Auckland   Cape Town   Dar es Salaam   Hong Kong   Karachi
Kuala Lumpur   Madrid   Melbourne   Mexico City   Nairobi
New Delhi   Shanghai   Taipei   Toronto

With offices in
Argentina   Austria   Brazil   Chile   Czech Republic   France   Greece
Guatemala   Hungary   Italy   Japan   Poland   Portugal   Singapore
South Korea   Switzerland   Thailand   Turkey   Ukraine   Vietnam

Oxford is a registered trade mark of Oxford University Press
in the UK and certain other countries.

Published in the United States of America by
Oxford University Press
198 Madison Avenue, New York, NY 10016

© Oxford University Press 2013

Library of Congress Cataloging-in-Publication Data
Crossland, Ken, author.
Late life jazz : the life and career of Rosemary Clooney / Ken Crossland & Malcolm Macfarlane.
    pages   cm
Includes bibliographical references and index.
Discography: pages.
ISBN 978-0-19-979857-5 (hardback : alk. paper)
1. Clooney, Rosemary. 2. Singers—United States—Biography.
I. Macfarlane, Malcolm, 1942– author. II. Title.
ML420.C58C76   2013
782.42164092—dc23
[B]
2012051013

9 8 7 6 5 4 3 2 1

Printed in the United States of America
on acid-free paper

CONTENTS

FOREWORD

There are many singers who have graced our lives with legacies that will live on, but I daresay not one of them was ever as joyful to be around nor as special as Rosemary Clooney.

There was something about Rosemary that gave those near her a heightened sense of being alive when they were in her presence. That palpable joy she created was just one of her many gifts, and whenever I was with her it was exciting as I never knew what the day would bring, other than something unexpected. She was exceedingly smart, kind, incisive, tender, tough, playful, gossipy, spiritual, and above all practical. She would "cut to the chase" and didn't like to waste time. Too much of it had been squandered years before when she had her nervous breakdown and she was mindful that time was precious, whether it was used for work, play, or introspection.

She lived a large, full life and saw with equal clarity the tragedy and triumph it offered. And Lord was she witty, I mean the laugh out loud kind of wit, as humor was an antidote for the sad stuff. Rosemary could also be moody, and on certain days one look told you it was best to keep your mouth shut or you'd surely be hit with a zinger. Yet even at her most irascible, the wit never foundered. She managed to speak her mind forcefully but you always knew she loved you, and underneath it all dwelt the ultimate earth mother. She made friends so easily that she couldn't keep up with them all. Once while flying back to Beverly Hills from New York she met a young television host who had fallen out of favor. By the time she arrived in Los Angeles they had exchanged numbers and she invited him to visit her home. When she reported to her kids that she invited her new friend over for dinner, they cried in unison "Oh no mother, not him!" But she couldn't help it; everybody wanted to be her friend.

If she had never sung a note she would have remained a beloved soul to those around her, but the gift of her voice communicated directly to the hearts of millions and made her a star. When Rosemary sang, it was transcendent, deeply soulful, and it all seemed to pour out so easily, even at an early age. People didn't know it was a lifetime of hard experience that made her songs so real, so conversational, especially in the latter days. As her voice slowly lost its fluidity over the last decade, her interpretive powers grew and grew. The loss of range didn't bother her and she was circumspect about it. She would test her voice with a single note and say "it's there," and if it wasn't up to snuff, she still accepted whatever she had and gave a brilliant show anyway. Through the years Rosemary had two voices and two distinct careers and would later dismiss the earlier performances saying she didn't understand "those songs" then as she did now. So one day I challenged her by playing a searingly sad recording of "I'll Be Around," made when she was 23. When it was over she quietly said, "Well, I did understand some things then." Another time she listened with me as I played a favorite early recording that she had forgotten. On the old record she effortlessly hit a soaring high note, and her response was one of mock irritation exclaiming "Well, aren't you too cute." She no longer clung to the seriousness of youth and had to comment on her earnest bravado.

Singing with her was a dream come true and I never imagined that one day I would collaborate with her, for she was my favorite female voice. When I listened to her during my formative years I sometimes projected thoughts of what she must be like as a person, and then one day, years later, there I was seated in her living room rehearsing a song. She was supportive and nurturing and gently made suggestions about how to make our duets better. We were rehearsing in the same room where she had sung with Bing Crosby, and it was at times an almost surreal, heady experience. After a few successful shows, we discovered that we were very comfortable together onstage. One night after a particularly solid show, she stated that the only other person with whom she ever felt such ease onstage was Bing himself. If only I could have sung anywhere near the way Bing sang with her! They were the most natural vocal duo I ever heard and they will never be bettered.

Every day I think about her. As time passes she grows stronger in memory, unlike others who have strangely faded away. The day of her funeral was numbingly hard. Being a person who fervently believes in an afterlife and that the soul goes on should have given me more comfort on some level. Yet the thought that I would never again be able to call her and share a story, a laugh, or hear a few comforting words had finally become irrevocably real. Though I didn't know it, the hardest part was yet to come. It happened as we made the final journey to her resting place, a trip that took about 25 minutes from the church to the cemetery. Along the route, lining the rural roads, were people everywhere: standing, watching, crying, silently paying tribute to one who deeply mattered in their lives. There were laborers in overalls, waitresses in uniforms, ruddy-faced farmers, men in business suits, pastors, postmen, children, mothers, fathers, grandparents . . . just people. People who had stopped their work in midday to say goodbye; and they were all her people. She had touched their lives, and they had lost a member of their family. Such an unexpected demonstration of mass devotion caused a backlog of tears to flow and I thought about how much she would have loved knowing that they were all there. After all, the thing she most wanted was to put something good in the world and make a difference, and what more significant proof would ever exist to show what a difference she had made?

Michael Feinstein, Los Angeles, October 2011

Late Life Jazz

Introduction

The 21st-century world of show business is very familiar with the name "Clooney." Few of Hollywood's present aristocracy can match the success that actor, producer, director, and screenwriter, George Clooney, has enjoyed in the first years of the new millennium. Time was, however, when the Clooney name was represented by an altogether different show business figure. Rosemary Clooney—George's aunt—sustained one of the most remarkable and enduring careers in show business, from her professional singing debut in 1945 to her final concert appearance in December 2001. Starting as a band singer with her sister, Betty, Rosemary quickly became an international star. Her own labeling was more modest. "Girl Singer" was the only title she ever used. Hollywood soon beckoned the sweet-voiced, svelte, honey-blonde girl from Kentucky. She met its call as the female lead and love interest for Bing Crosby in the iconic *White Christmas* in 1954. On television, she hosted her own weekly show and as Eisenhower's decade progressed, Rosemary came to epitomize the American dream. A Hollywood marriage to actor, José Ferrer, and a fast-growing family only served to enhance the apparent richness of her life in the land of milk and honey. The small-town girl who sang with the laugh in her voice had made it to the top.

But not everything was as it seemed. The 1960s found the show business marriage going sour. The Ferrers became fodder for the divorce court reporters. The hit records had long since dried up, and by the time she stopped producing babies, Hollywood had moved on from the girl-next-door musicals. Rosemary took refuge in prescription medication and politics. When an assassin cut down her friend, Robert F. Kennedy, as Rosemary looked on, her life went into tailspin. A few weeks later, it crashed dramatically down to earth on the stage of a Reno nightclub. Long years of mental health therapy followed. Professional oblivion dawned.

That Rosemary came back was in itself remarkable. That she was able to do so in a way that artistically outshone her first career was astounding. Few, if any, performers have achieved such an artistic juxtaposition. Once dismissed as a voice only for Mitch Miller's novelty songs and gimmicky recordings, Rosemary now became the interpreter par excellence of the American popular song. Cowbells and harpsichords made way for an ensemble that comprised America's finest jazz musicians. Not everyone, not even Rosemary herself, thought that she had become a jazz singer, but when asked if there was a finer exponent of vocal timing, rhythmical appreciation and lyrical interpretation, few could name anyone better. "That's jazz," her friend and mentor, Bing Crosby, once sang and to many, it was.

Now, a decade and more after her death, the question of how Rosemary Clooney will be remembered is apposite. History often claims 20/20 hindsight, but left to its own devices can make mistakes. Anyone using Billboard's pop music charts for an assessment of Miss Clooney's career would conclude that she enjoyed a four-year spell of popularity, excelled as a singer of trite ditties, but was never heard of again once the world spun its first Elvis Presley record. After the success of White Christmas in 1954, her movie career sank without a trace. And anyone scanning the library shelves would find two autobiographies that, like any self-penned memoir, were more about opinions and memories than objectivity and fact. Neither represents the historical chronicle that her career deserves. More recent studies of the art of popular singing have begun to redress the balance, yet the complete story of her career remains to be told.

Rosemary Clooney was arguably the most versatile popular singer in history. She marched to Mitch Miller's beat while breaking new ground with Duke Ellington for the first genuine pop-jazz collaboration. She could count rockabilly, country and western, pop, jazz, hymns, lullabies, Christmas songs, mambo rhythms, and barbershop harmony among her repertoire. She could schmaltz and schmooze with Crosby in one scene in White Christmas, and become a sultry siren in the next. Duet partnerships with the vocal aristocrats such as Crosby, Sinatra, Tony Bennett, and Perry Como stood alongside knockabout collaborations with the likes of Gene Autry, Marlene Dietrich, and Guy Mitchell. What other singer stood toe-to-toe with jazz legends such as Ellington, Benny Goodman, Harry James, Count Basie, and Nelson Riddle and then, years later, could act as a pied piper for a new generation that included John Pizzarelli, John Oddo, Scott Hamilton, and Warren Vaché? Late Life Jazz provides the first full, objective record of the career of Rosemary Clooney. It seeks to present material drawn from contemporary accounts of her life and music making alongside more recent, retrospective opinion, including our own. In this book, we seek to offer a definitive chronicle and critical appraisal of the life and career of a remarkable lady, one who was proud to be "George's aunt," but who was also so much more.

CHAPTER 1

Kentucky, Sure as You're Born

When Rosemary Clooney assembled an album of songs to mark her 50th anniversary in show business, she asked her brother Nick to write a sleeve note. Looking down the playlist, the TV talk show host and journalist raised an eyebrow at the opening selection. "'Danny Boy?' Why 'Danny Boy?'" he asked his elder sister in a call to her at home on the West Coast. A few months later, Terry Gross, interviewing Rosemary for *Fresh Air* on National Public Radio, asked the same thing. Her answer to Gross was typical Clooney—direct, quick-witted, and brutally frank. "It got the Irish song out of the way," she said. "'Why didn't you do an Irish song, Rosemary? An Irish song would have been nice on the album.' You know how many times I've heard that?"[1] But the answer she gave to her brother was more thoughtful. "Well," she said, "it's sort of the beginning of everything."[2] The younger Clooney knew immediately what his sister meant. He was in Kentucky, she in California, but both of them knew that spiritually, their homeland was the glens and valleys that Rosemary sang about in every rendition of the Irish American anthem. It had been a long journey.

The home-leaving lyrics for "Danny Boy" were penned by Frederic Weatherly in 1910. Fifty years before, Rosemary Clooney's great-grandparents-to-be, Nicholas Clooney and Bridget Byron, had made their separate ways across the Atlantic Ocean. Nicholas was born in County Kilkenny, Ireland, in 1830 and was in his mid-20s when he made the crossing. Bridget, at 19, was six years his junior when she emigrated to the United States in 1855. They came for one reason alone—survival. Ireland was starving. The staple diet of the island was the potato, and one acre of the crop would feed an Irish family for a year, as it had done for centuries. But in 1845, the potato crop rotted within days of being taken from the ground. The blight continued into the next year and the years beyond. It became one of the greatest humanitarian tragedies of the 19th century. Famine, disease, and eviction followed quickly in the wake of the crop failure. From 1847 to 1850, between one fifth and one sixth of the Irish population died each year, either from starvation or consequential diseases such as cholera. In 1851, the population of Ireland stood at 6.5 million. Without the famine, the Census Commissioners estimated that the figure would have exceeded 9 million. The choice for the Irish was stark; stay home and likely die or take a chance on the sea crossing. By the end of 1854, 2 million Irish—one quarter of the population—had opted for the voyage across the Atlantic. They came first in sailing ships, enduring a harrowing six weeks at sea, mostly below deck and often in conditions more suited to the transportation of animals than human beings. One in every hundred who left Ireland failed to survive the voyage. Steam replaced sail during the 1850s, and though the crossing conditions eased, life for those who made it to the New World was often little better than what they had left behind.

The first wave of Irish immigrants to the United States had arrived earlier in the century and had been skilled laborers, in demand for the turnpike and canal projects across the eastern United States. The famine refugees, however, were uneducated and unskilled. Shantytowns grew up, with houses that were little more than huts and sanitation almost nonexistent. Racial discrimination was rife. "No Irish" was a common sign posted where men stood in line for work. Often, it was the womenfolk who came first, paying for the passage by taking work as indentured domestic servants. The price of the Atlantic crossing was a period of servitude. Irish maids were so predominant that they became known as "biddies," a derivation from the most common Irish female name, Bridget. Once settled, husbands and sons would join them.

Nicholas Clooney and Bridget Byron settled separately in Mason County, Kentucky, and eventually became man and wife there on May 24, 1862. Boston and New York had become the primary locations for Irish settlers, but Kentucky had provided a home for both Scottish and Irish immigrants since the time of the American Revolution. The first settlers were Protestants, before a more Gaelic influx began in the first decades of the 1800s. By 1839, the *Covington Western Globe* was reporting that Irish navvies were the major workers for new infrastructure projects such as the Covington & Lexington Turnpike.[3] Railroad expansion quickly followed, although until 1845, the influx of immigrants from Ireland was still little more than a trickle.

When he came to the United States, Nicholas Clooney first lived as a lodger with the Knox family, who were also recent arrivals from Ireland.

The Knox's home was in Maysville, Kentucky, on the Ohio River. Maysville dated back to 1784 when a settlement known as Limestone was established, just where Limestone Creek flowed into the Ohio River. Within three years, Limestone had become Maysville, named for John May, one of the founders of the state of Kentucky. Situated 400 miles downstream from Pittsburgh, Maysville marks the northern boundary of the state, 60 miles northeast of Lexington and approximately the same distance southeast of Cincinnati. Some 10 miles away sits the town of Mayslick, also named for a member of the May family, John's brother, William. Mayslick provided a home for two other Irish families who had forsaken their homeland. The Sweeneys had arrived among the first wave of Irish immigrants while the Guilfoyles were part of the post-famine influx. When a Sweeney married a Guilfoyle, the union produced a son who would grow up to be Rosemary Clooney's maternal grandfather.

Nicholas and Bridget Clooney raised seven children, the sixth of whom, Andrew Bartholomew Clooney, was to become the most influential figure in Rosemary Clooney's early life. He was born on June 25, 1874, and as a first-generation American, quickly set about exploiting the opportunities that the United States offered. Quick and smart, Andrew Clooney flirted with a career in the law before settling for a role as a small town watchmaker and jeweler, working from a first-floor store on Maysville's Market Street. Andrew Clooney's passion was politics. He founded a free newspaper in Maysville and his left-of-center views anticipated Franklin Roosevelt's New Deal radicalism by a generation. "Closer to libertarianism than we would like" was Nick Clooney's recollection of his grandfather. One of Nick's earliest childhood memories was of his grandfather being forcibly held down for a typhoid shot during the 1937 Ohio flood. "He regarded it as an invasion of his body," Clooney said.[4] Andrew Clooney's involvement in local politics saw him serve two terms as the Democratic mayor of Maysville in the 1930s, later also acting as a city commissioner at the time of the flood. His grandchildren adored him. They loved the trinkets and goodies that he collected during his mayoral duties and would bring home for them as much as they loved the warmth and humor of his personality. A tall, elegant man with a bush of white hair, Andrew B. Clooney told bedtime stories to his grandchildren and created within them a warm sense of love and reassurance. "He never talked to us like children," said Nick. "He talked to us as if we were adults."[5]

Andrew Clooney's wife was not part of the Kentucky Irish heritage. She was Crescentia Koch, the daughter of a Huguenot family originally from Alsace-Lorraine on the French-German border. Their arrival on the banks of the Ohio had preceded even that of Rosemary's Irish ancestors.

The Kochs quickly Anglicized their names. Crescentia soon became Cynthia (although her grandchildren always called her Molly), while her pronunciation of her surname usually came out as "Cook" rather than its German-sounding derivation. The Kochs had grand ideas for their daughter, and a union with an Irish shopkeeper with dangerous political leanings was hardly the marriage they had in mind. As she shared this frustrated ambition, it found an outlet in her personality. Cynthia's grandchildren found her a distant and materialistic woman, whose attempts to convey love and affection came across as superficial and false. She was "a Southern belle," Rosemary recalled in 1956, who "knew all the feminine things—perfume, music, how to paint a tray or square a canvas with violets and roses. She was just born to please a man," she said.[6] Nick Clooney recalled his grandmother as an elitist woman, gifted and talented, but angry and frustrated that her talents—and her husband's—had not taken them further up the social ladder. Nevertheless, the marriage between the Clooney and Koch offspring was a sound one. It produced two children, a daughter, Olivette born in 1900, and a son Andrew Joseph Clooney, born on October 13, 1902. Andrew J. Clooney became Rosemary's father.

Rosemary's mother, Frances Guilfoyle, was the eventual product of the marriage of Cornelius Guilfoyle to Rosanna Sweeney in Mayslick on August 26, 1869. The marriage produced 11 children. The third eldest was Michael Guilfoyle, born in 1874, who became Rosemary's grandfather. His wife, Martha Adelia (Ada) Farrow was the daughter of a failed pioneer farmer who had taken his family out west to Kansas in a covered wagon, only to be driven back east by the first harsh winter. Along with Andrew B. Clooney, Ada Guilfoyle would become the other dominant influence on the early life of her granddaughter Rosemary. Michael and Ada married in 1904 and had nine children, including Frances Guilfoyle, Rosemary's mother. When Michael Guilfoyle died in the street of a brain aneurysm in 1928, Ada Guilfoyle was left with the challenge of raising the family on her own.

The character of her daughter, Frances, and the man she had chosen as her husband, Andrew J. Clooney, multiplied that challenge. He had inherited none of his father's drive and ambition and soon settled into a life of shiftless vagabondage. Rosemary later wrote that her father had decided even before she was born that "his dreams were submerged at the bottom of a bottle."[7] "Daddy spent a lot of time in various saloons in Maysville," she said. "There weren't too many, but there were enough for him."[8] Andrew Clooney fathered his first child, a son, also called Andrew, in 1921. The child's mother, Annie Elsie Ennis, took the Clooney surname and at her death in 1929, was described as a widow, although no record can be traced of their marriage or divorce. Married or not, they had separated some time before Ennis's death. By then Andrew J. Clooney was undeniably married to Frances Guilfoyle. That wedding took place in St. Patrick Church in Maysville on August 15, 1928, at which time Andrew and Frances were already the parents of a daughter. The baby, registered under the name of Rose Marie Clooney, had been born in Maysville on May 23, 1928.[9] Her accepted Christian name soon became Rosemary, although friends referred to her as "Rose" throughout her life.

Andrew Clooney was 25 years old and his new wife 19 when they set out on married life. It was a union built on shifting sands. Rosemary later described it as being "like a soap opera,"[10] characterized by frequent separations. The pattern continued throughout Rosemary's childhood, although her mother and father were reunited often enough to produce two more children, Elizabeth Anne (Betty) in 1931 and Nicholas (Nick) three years later. Rosemary's memories of her childhood were often colored with bitterness. While her father could usually be found in a saloon bar, she remembered her mother as being more interested in selling ready-to-wear clothing than raising children. Frances Clooney was not the first woman to put her career ahead of her children, but in Kentucky in the 1930s, it was an unusual trait. She was "a natural saleswoman, garrulous and born with the gift of making people feel important," Nick Clooney said of his mother.[11] Rosemary eventually came to see some of the same characteristics in her sister, Betty. The pushiness, the eye for an angle, and the ability to close a sale were essentials on the bottom rung of the show business ladder, and it was Betty who used them to gain the girls' first foothold. The lifestyle of their parents, however, did nothing to create a stable home environment for the three Clooney children. "I don't think Betty and I and Nicky spent more than two weeks in the same house with them," Rosemary said.[12] The consequence was that the wider Clooney and Guilfoyle families—aunts, uncles, but more especially their respective grandparents—essentially raised the three children, who grew up like orphans.

The town of Maysville where Rosemary Clooney was born had a population of 6,500 at the census that came two years after her birth. The population had tripled in size in the 100 years since the town had attained city status, but it was a growth rate that was only one fifth the national average. What increase there was came largely from expansion of the city's boundaries. Despite Kentucky's reputation as an early home for the first wave of Irish immigration, the flood of other nationalities into the United States around the turn of the 20th century largely passed by the Ohio townships. Maysville owed its origins to the Ohio River and had soon developed into a thriving port, an outlet for the export of hemp and tobacco, but it was slow, organic growth, hardly likely to radically alter the makeup and character of the town. A wrought-iron industry later developed in the town, but at the time of Rosemary's birth, Maysville remained a predominantly agricultural settlement where tobacco was king. Even into the 1980s stockyards could still be found close to the center of the town itself.

Rosemary's earliest memory of a place she could call home was the apartment that her grandpa and Grandma Clooney kept above the jeweler's shop on Market Street. It was, she later said, a stylish house where she and Betty experienced the sensation of being loved for the first time in their lives. Andrew Clooney senior was quick to involve his granddaughters in his political activities, persuading them to sing at fund-raising events and taking them along to the public meetings that were a regular part of his life. He also promoted Rosemary's friendship with a black girl, Blanchie Mae Chambers, whose mother worked as a maid at the Central Hotel in town. It provided Rosemary with her first experience of the racial segregation that dominated the South, and her grandfather's rebuttal of it stayed with her all her life. Blanchie Mae remained a lifelong friend, and pointedly, when Rosemary returned to Maysville for a triumphant motorcade procession in 1953, it was her childhood friend who sat alongside her, although even then, she had to be passed off as her maid.

This first, brief period of stability in the early life of Rosemary Clooney came to an abrupt end in 1939 with the death of her paternal grandmother, Cynthia. Despite acknowledging that she had always been her grandmother's favorite, Rosemary felt no sense of loss. "I remember thinking 'I should be feeling more than I am feeling,'" she said later.[13] What loss Rosemary—and her siblings—did feel came because their grandmother's death also took them away from the grandfather they loved. In 1937, two years before Cynthia's death, Maysville along with countless other towns along the length of the Ohio River, had been consumed by one of the worst floods in history. Despite Canute-like tones of defiance, Andrew B. Clooney had seen his business premises devastated. His spirit broken by the flood and then by the loss of his wife, he was in no position to look after three grandchildren on his own.

The solution was for the Clooney children to move in with the Guilfoyles. Their new home with their grandmother Guilfoyle was on West Third Street. Life there could not have been more different from living with their late grandmother Clooney. The two women were like chalk and cheese, and despite a shared interest in the children that their two offspring had neglected, their relationship had never passed beyond the formality of "Mrs. Clooney" and "Mrs. Guilfoyle." But where Cynthia Clooney was refined and formal, Ada Guilfoyle was a practical woman of great strength, warmth, and love. Her youngest child was only three years older than Rosemary and the addition of three grandchildren meant that the family she now supported had expanded to 12. Having grown up on a farm and then taught school, Ada Guilfoyle seemed to possess all the skills necessary to raise a large family. She supplemented her time around the house by working nights as a practical nurse. Even when the children had flown the nest, Grandma Guilfoyle could be called upon to go the extra mile. Once when Rosemary was touring with the Tony Pastor orchestra, the entire band descended on the Guilfoyle household with no warning. She killed, dressed, and cooked 22 chickens to feed her houseguests. "Best Southern fried chicken I ever tasted," said Gene Cipriano, one of the band members who shared in the feast.[14]

Perhaps the only common ground between the Clooneys and the Guilfoyles was their shared love of music. Her grandfather's apartment had boasted a fine piano among its furnishings, plus a radio set. Rosemary's father had an excellent singing voice and his sister Olivette led a small band that played for parties at the local country club. Rosemary's grandfather Guilfoyle had been known for his love of dancing, but it was his daughter Ann—Rosemary's aunt—who had the most significant musical influence on the young Rosemary. Ann Guilfoyle had started to build a career as a nightclub singer, working in Lexington at several clubs and often performing with some of the touring bands that passed through town. Nick Clooney recalled his Aunt Ann as a glamorous figure, always well dressed, smelling of the most expensive perfume and the first to have anything that came on the market that might seem cool. "She always had a new car," he said, "despite being a terrible driver."[15] Her show business lifestyle led to frequent confrontations with her mother, Ada, whose attempts to rein back her daughter were validated when Ann died tragically from an accidental drugs overdose at the age of 25. Her life—and death—provided Rosemary with her first exposure to the light and darker sides of the show business world.

With such a heavy musical influence from both sides of the family, it was no surprise that Rosemary started singing almost as soon as she learned to talk. Her stage debut came just before her third birthday when her aunt Olivette arranged for her to sing "When Your Hair Has Turned to Silver" on the stage of the Russell Theater, Maysville's downtown movie house. Not long after, Rosemary was singing "Home on the Range" at one of her grandfather's political gatherings and her first review came in 1933 when the *Middlesboro Daily News* reported that she had sung three songs at the conclusion of Maysville's centenary dinner in the Central Hotel.[16] She was still only five years old but music, it seemed, was in her blood.

It wasn't just music. It was apparent from Rosemary's stage debut in 1940 that she was also born with a natural stage presence. The occasion was a St. Patrick's High School production of *Snow White and the Seven Dwarfs*. Rosemary had set her heart on playing the part of Snow White, opposite her cousin and would-be beau, Joe Breslin. In the end, Rosemary had to settle for the part of the witch, a role that she nevertheless played with considerable relish. A fellow cast member, Marion Byron Gilligan, remembered with a shiver Rosemary's hideous laugh as she handed the poison apple to Snow White, an unsuspecting Rose Marie Tierney. Another classmate, Wanda Ring Anderson recalled a memorable footnote to the same scene. Just as the witch offered the apple, her taped-on nose fell off, landing right in her basket. Without missing a beat, Rosemary went on with her lines. "She stole the show even then. She was a regular comedienne," Wanda said.[17]

The *Snow White* production marked the end of Rosemary's years in Maysville, at least for the time being. Later that year, her uncles George and Chick opened a filling station business in Ironton, Ohio, and the entire Guilfoyle family moved the 73 miles to join them. It proved to be an unlucky town. During their time there, Chick was injured in an accident, his sister Christine developed a brain tumor, and their sister Ann succumbed to a drug overdose. When the filling station business failed, the family moved to Cincinnati, where George took a job for the Baldwin Piano Company. Briefly the family all lived on Fairfax Avenue in Cincinnati, and Rosemary attended Withrow High School. It wasn't long, however, before they were on the move again, this time to Indian Hills Road, where Grandma Guilfoyle took over an old farmhouse. It would be the last of the homes that the Clooney children would share with one of their grandparents.

Andrew and Frances Clooney were still, at best, intermittent presences in the lives of their three children. Frances had by now moved on from her job as a sales clerk in the dress store, first to a store manager position and then into a traveling sales job with the Lerner dress company. She loved the job and life on the road. Each week, she would send a $5 bill back home to her children in Cincinnati, but the postmark on the envelope was the closest the kids came to knowing their mother's precise whereabouts. Things changed yet again in 1942, however, when the divorce that had long seemed inevitable finally became a reality. The newly single Frances Clooney returned home, taking an apartment on Clinton Springs Avenue in Cincinnati. It was to be only a brief return. Within weeks, she announced that she planned to remarry and that her husband-to-be, Bill Stone, was a sailor in California. Worse still, she was taking Nick with her to California, but leaving Rosemary and Betty in Kentucky. She told the girls that she would send for them once she was settled on the West Coast, but the promise was like all the others that the girls had heard before—hollow and unfulfilled. When the day came, the tearful sisters could only watch as their mother disappeared once more, this time waving to them through the back window of a cab that carried her and their younger brother to the railroad station. They saw neither of them again for two years. It was a traumatic separation for all three children, especially Nick. "I knew my sisters far better than I knew either of my parents," he said.[18]

Frances Clooney's departure was followed by another surprising twist in the lives of Rosemary and Betty. As one parent rode out of town, the other made a surprise return. Seemingly reformed and chastened by his now sole responsibility for his daughters, Andrew Clooney junior managed to kick his drinking habit and found a job with the Wright Aeronautical defense plant in Cincinnati. He took an apartment on Elberon Avenue and the girls moved in with him. For a time, life was good. The job paid decent money and better still, most of it came home with Andrew at the end of the week. At a time when most Americans had shifted their focus to the war in Europe and the Pacific, Rosemary and Betty found that wartime offered them a brief interlude of domestic stability. They were able to get to know their father almost for the first time, sharing their musical interests with him, singing, and debating the merits of Bing Crosby and Frank Sinatra, heard on records on the jukebox in the Fountain Square drugstore. It seemed too good to last, and it was. Andrew Clooney's spell on the wagon lasted almost as long as America's involvement in the war in Europe, but by the time VE Day arrived in May 1945, his old habits had returned. Earlier that year, he had returned home just long enough to gather up the defense bonds that he had saved through the war and disappear in a cab, taking the savings with him. Rosemary and Betty, still only 16 and 13 years of age, were left alone. It was time to start looking after themselves.

The question was how? Both girls were still of school age[19] and had no prospects of earning enough money outside school to buy food and keep a roof over their heads. They made a few cents here and there collecting deposits on empty bottles but it was nothing more than pin money for two teenage girls. They knew, however, that they could sing, and the saleswoman's genes that Betty had inherited told her that if they could get the right people to hear them, they could make enough money to live. The right people, she said, could be found downtown at Station WLW in Cincinnati. Self-proclaimed as "The Nation's Station," WLW had first taken to the airwaves in 1922 with one of the most powerful broadcast transmitters of any American station. Its 500-kilowatt output was capable of reaching listeners as far away as Canada and South America. WLW was primarily a music station; better still, it ran open auditions every Thursday evening. The sisters decided to try their luck. It was only as they sat and waited for their turn that the girls had their first experience of stage fright. "When our names were called out," Betty Clooney later recalled, "we suddenly realized how scared we were, even Rosie, on whom I counted for support." The girls sang "Hawaiian War Chant," an authentic Hawaiian song (but not a war chant) that dated back to the 1860s and had enjoyed a late '30s revival, courtesy of English lyrics by Ralph Freed. Tommy Dorsey's band had a hit record with the tune, and while the girls didn't know all of the Hawaiian lyrics that were interspersed through the song, they took a chance that no one else did either. To fill the gaps, they added some Hawaiian sounding 'ee's' and 'ooh's' and got away with it. "They asked us up to do another," said Betty. "Then the program director came out of the control room and said that if we would take some lessons in mike technique, they could use us."[20] The contract was worth $20 per week, a small fortune to the girls.

A 56-second acetate of the girls' second song from their audition, a cover of the King Cole Trio's recording of "Straighten Up and Fly Right," provides the first evidence of how the young Clooney sisters sounded as they set out on their new career. There were many similarities about their voices. Both had near perfect pitch, and unsurprisingly, approached the phrasing of a song almost identically. In their upper registers, the voices were so similar that, even 65 years later, it is difficult to distinguish between them. What differences there were came from the fact that Betty sang a little lower than Rosemary and lacked some of the granularity that would become such a trademark of her older sister. Both agreed that Rosemary was the natural lead singer for the partnership, with Betty's superior ear for harmony making her a perfect foil. The same could not be said about their physical appearance. Each girl had inherited their mother's dark coloring, but Rosemary had transformed herself into an elegant blonde from an early age. Betty had more of her mother's facial characteristics as well as her coloring, including a longer, thinner face. Closer examination of their nose and mouth features would reveal a likeness, but from a distance, it was the way they sounded rather than how they looked that told the audience that this was a natural sister act.

With a contract in their pocket, the girls now felt confident about their ability to pay their own way. They approached their Aunt Jean, their mother's sister, about moving in with her branch of the Guilfoyle family in suburban Cincinnati. She said yes, and even when their father returned home whistling "Kentucky Babe" (a sign of sobriety, Rosemary later recalled), the girls decided to stay put. Once bitten, twice shy. They enrolled at the Our Lady of Mercy Academy in downtown Cincinnati, close to station WLW, where they quickly became regular features on two shows. First, they worked on *Crossroads Café*, an afternoon show that featured host Rita Hacket and a big band in the studio, before moving on to a late night show. *Moon River* was the station's flagship offering, 30 years before Johnny Mercer would immortalize the title in an Academy Award-winning song. The show aired between 11:30 and midnight every night, commercial free to maintain a restful ambience.

The girls were true to their commitment to take some music and singing lessons and were soon picking up other work around the city. They sang with a band led by a boy named Billy Petering, playing high school dances and other local festivals. Petering became Rosemary's first serious beau. Then a local bandleader named Barney Rapp heard them on the radio and hired the girls to sing with his bigger ensemble. The Rapp band primarily played music for dancing but provided a home to a succession of up-and-coming vocalists, including a young blonde singer from Cincinnati called Doris Kappelhoff. It was Rapp who was credited with changing her name to Doris Day after hearing her sing "Day by Day." Rapp had started his career in New England before moving to Ohio, where he played and broadcast from hotels and nightclubs as well as making records on the Victor label. The Clooney girls became his regular singers and this, together with their radio work meant that they were soon taking home over $100 every week—each. It was a world away from the hand-to-mouth existence that had characterized much of their earlier lives.

The nine months that the girls spent singing with the Barney Rapp band gave them their first real experience of show business. They played some big clubs in Cincinnati, including the Beverly Hills Supper Club and the Castle Farms Club, where the Paul Whiteman orchestra had played in the '20s. Rapp also doubled as an agent for the sisters, providing them with bookings with other bands such as Clyde Trask's orchestra. It was Rapp's role as a work-finder that was ultimately to prove his most significant contribution to the career of Rosemary Clooney. One day, early in 1946, Rapp ran into an old buddy named Charlie Trotta, trumpet player, sometime vocalist, and road manager for the much bigger Tony Pastor outfit. "Tony wants a new girl singer," Trotta told him, "got any ideas?" Rapp's reply was to the point. "A girl singer?" he said. "I can do better than that. I can find him two."

CHAPTER 2

The Clooney Sisters

Tony Pastor boasted a musical pedigree that ran solidly through the halcyon years of American big band swing. Born in Middletown, Connecticut, in 1907, Pastor began playing the saxophone at the age of 16. Growing up in nearby New Haven and playing with the John Cavallaro band, Pastor met and befriended a young clarinetist named Artie Shaw. The elder of the two friends by three years, Pastor became something of a role model for the young Shaw, who, for a time, seemed happy to take on the role of bag carrier for him. Soon, the two musicians were playing together, first with Irving Aaronson and his Commanders and then with Austin Wylie's orchestra. Shaw though, was a driven man. It wasn't long before he had formed a band of his own and when he did, in 1936, Pastor was a natural selection as the saxophonist.

The Shaw band was not the overnight success that its leader expected, and he experimented with several different instrumental combinations before finally breaking through with a recording of "Begin the Beguine." The strain of leading the band and keeping his own ambition in check took its toll, however, and Shaw suffered the first of several collapses in 1938. Nevertheless, it was still a surprise when, a year later, he suddenly quit the band, leaving it to carry on without him. The band members looked to Pastor to take over as leader but he too had other plans. Although his first attempt at leading his own band in the early 1930s had not gone well, he too retained the ambition to step out on his own. Boston agent Cy Shribman had already offered backing to Pastor if he chose to make a break from Shaw, and the demise of the Shaw band offered the opportunity that he had been waiting for. With Shaw's musicians talking vaguely about setting up a cooperative, Pastor decided that his time had come. "I had a chance to go out with my own band, so who needed a whole band of partners?" he said.[1]

Pastor's musical credentials came from the mellow tone of his tenor sax playing, although it was his exuberant singing style that came to define his new band's personality. Strongly influenced by Louis Armstrong's vocals, Pastor's exaggerated phrasing and croaky voice complimented his bright and bouncy personality. "Short and round, good-humored and easygoing" was Rosemary Clooney's later summation of him.[2] As well as his solo vocals, Pastor was also a regular duettist, sharing the microphone with Johnny McAfee, who also led the sax quintet in the band, plus a succession of girl singers that included Dorsey Anderson, Eugenie Baird, and Virginia Maxey. It was the latter's departure in 1946 that created the vacancy that the Clooney Sisters would fill.

The Pastor audition came without any warning for Rosemary and Betty, so much so that they were out swimming when Barney Rapp tracked them down and told them about his conversation with Charlie Trotta. "They were just a couple of fresh-looking kids when we hired them," Trotta later recalled. "They were doing a local radio show after school when they came to sing for me. They'd come straight from swimming. Their hair wasn't combed. They had on flat-heeled shoes and no stockings. There was no piano, but they sang a full arrangement of 'Patty Cake, Patty Cake Baker's Man' without missing a note."[3] Pastor was immediately taken by them. "They were smart kids, but they were only babies," he told George T. Simon years later. "They had good ears and some corny arrangements of their own. But Ralph Flanagan, who was writing for us, gave them some good new arrangements."[4]

Rosemary and Betty signed a five-year contract on November 30, 1946, appointing Rapp and Trotta as their "exclusive business managers, personal representatives and advisors," and granting them 10% commission on their earnings. Their Uncle George (Guilfoyle) countersigned the deal as their "duly appointed and acting guardian." The agreement provided the Clooney Sisters with a conduit into Pastor's band and an entirely new way of life. Pastor's outfit was the ultimate road band. Although a regular on the airwaves and a not infrequent visitor to the recording studio, the band made its money from clambering aboard a bus and heading from town to town. One estimate was that the band traveled a million miles throughout the United States during the 1940s.[5] Life for a singer with a traveling band wasn't easy. Usually, the band's arrangements were written to a dance tempo, with the singer often the last to see them. Equally, the singers were expected to handle just about any type of material—ballads, up-tempo swing, and novelty—again with little chance to rehearse their numbers before they were called on for their turn at the microphone. For a girl singer, there were other complications. Among them were where to change, where to do makeup, and not least, how to deal with a succession of musicians with an eye to some extracurricular activity. The list of girl singers who wound up marrying a member of the band they toured with was a long one. The list of affairs and one-night stands was longer still.

How to protect Rosemary and Betty from the wolf-trap that they were about to enter was a pressing question for the Clooney and Guilfoyle families. The answer came in the form of Uncle George who agreed to travel with the band and act as the girls' chaperone. "No nun in a Catholic convent took better care of her girls than Uncle George did of us—often to our total frustration," Rosemary later recalled.[6] Gene Cipriano and Henry Riggs Guidotti, sax player and drummer, respectively, in the band, recalled that the chaperoning was highly effective. "They were squeaky clean," said Riggs. "The only time we ever saw them was on stage, on rehearsal, or on the bus."[7] Cipriano remembered Uncle George as an ever-present figure, who made sure that his two nieces were regular Sunday churchgoers and wholesome eaters. "They were hooked on mushroom omelettes," he said.[8] "Hooked" was an operative word in the Pastor band. Soft drug use was rife. "We were pretty high above the ground most of the time," Henry Riggs said, a reference to the widespread use of marijuana among the musicians. Looking back almost 50 years later, Rosemary Clooney concurred. "They were on everything but roller skates," she said.[9]

The sisters' debut with the Pastor orchestra came on July 10, 1946, at the Marine Ballroom on the Steel Pier in Atlantic City. Wearing plaid taffeta gowns crafted by Grandma Guilfoyle, the girls took a deep breath, looked at each other, and stepped onto the bandstand. Their opening duet[10] went over well, but Rosemary soon found trouble with the solos that Pastor had handed her. None of them had been scored in the right key for her and when she reached for a high note in the first one, her voice broke into a comical, discordant croak. "In my mind I was already on the train back to Cincinnati, and I wanted to cry. But before all those people?" she told an interviewer a few years later. Instead of crying, Rosemary smiled at the 3,000 faces looking at her from the ballroom floor and received a heartening roar of applause. Next time she hit the note right on the nail. "It was easy then," she said. "I knew they were with me."[11]

The girls soon fell in with the band's summer touring schedule, traveling throughout the Ohio valley and beyond. In late August 1946, the band played a week at Orsatti's Casino, New Jersey, before heading into New York City. It was Rosemary's first taste of Manhattan and also her first experience of entering a recording studio. The recordings that the band made during the visit were for the little-known Cosmo Records and featured several songs from the 1946 Disney hit movie *The Song of the South*. The Clooney Sisters appeared on five of the songs, although on four of them, their role was no more than as backing vocalists to Pastor himself. The fifth record was different and featured Rosemary in a duet with Pastor on the film's romantic ballad, "Sooner or Later." This time, the lead vocal went her way with the bandleader playing the supporting role. Rosemary's husky, almost whispered rendition was a world away from the cheeriness of "Zip-A-Dee-Doo-Dah" and announced the arrival of a serious female vocalist. *Billboard* said that Pastor and Clooney "made a fetching romantic twosome,"[12] although it was another review that stuck in Rosemary's mind. It said Rosemary's vocal was "the nearest thing to Ella Fitzgerald that we've ever heard."[13]

Through the autumn and into the winter of 1946, the Pastor band played up and down the eastern states, broadcasting on Saturday nights over station WCAE in Pittsburgh before returning to New York for a pre-Christmas booking at the New York Paramount. For Rosemary and Betty, the excitement of just being in New York was the predominant memory that they held of that time, far outstripping any musical or career landmarks that New York might have offered. Working at the Paramount gave Rosemary the opportunity to stand in the footprints of her idol, Frank Sinatra, at the theater that had marked the beginning of his bobby-sox era in 1943. For Rosemary, these early visits to New York marked the start of a love affair with the city that would last for the rest her life.

The year 1947 brought more miles and more one night stands for the band, but Rosemary soon gained sufficient prominence to merit a solo turn at the microphone, in addition to the Clooney Sisters' normal spot. She had also managed to escape from the watchful eye of Uncle George long enough to start an affair with the band's guitarist, Milt Norman. It lasted several months until Uncle George – and Pastor – found out. The affair was exposed during the band's lengthy sojourn in California during the summer of 1947, an itinerary that included an extended spell at the Hollywood Palladium, some filming for Columbia Pictures, and recording dates under a new contract with Columbia Records. Pastor fired Norman as soon as he found about the affair, although the guitarist had planned to leave the band in California anyway. Norman hoped to persuade Rosemary to stay with him, but when she came to do her solo spot on the recording session, she had already decided that the affair had no future. When Norman played the lilting opening bars to "I'm Sorry That I Didn't Say I'm Sorry (When I Made You Cry Last Night)," Rosemary looked across from the microphone, knowing how prophetic the lyric had become. It would not be the last time that Rosemary Clooney would find herself in a recording studio, voicing a lament to a lost love. Whether it was the tears she was holding back or simply her innate ability to read a lyric, Rosemary delivered a vocal that was full of emotion, singing in a voice that was barely above a whisper. The style anticipated the half-spoken delivery that characterized Marilyn Monroe a decade later. The result was striking. Columbia promoted the disc heavily, and America's new emperors of the airwaves, the disc jockeys, gave it play after play.

The ballad aside, the June 5 recording session was otherwise notable for requiring Rosemary to adopt a false accent for the first time, something that would soon become commonplace once she came under the influence of Mitch Miller. The phony-Italian accent, however, was for the future. This time, Rosemary was called upon to handle a piece of Irish brogue before moving onto a Caribbean calypso. The Irish accent was needed for "My O'Darlin' My O'Lovely My O'Brien," although there was precious little about it that her great-grandparents would have recognized as authentic. The dose of West Indian was equally unconvincing on "Bread and Butter Woman," which *Billboard* dismissed as a "weak calypso styled ditty" when it eventually saw release, some two years after it was recorded.[14]

Alongside the Columbia recording contract, the Pastor band could also boast radio and film credits. CBS radio hooked up with the band during its time at the Hollywood Palladium to broadcast *One Night Stand*, a show that featured the Pastor orchestra along with another guest band that joined the show from a remote location. Described by announcer Bill Ewing as a "lush thrush," Rosemary took solo spots with such songs as "That's My Desire," while also joining Pastor for more boisterous numbers such as "A Rainy Night in Rio" and "Moving Along." *Billboard* reviewer Alan Fischter was at the Palladium for one of the shows and wrote that the Clooney Sisters "pass the eye-and-ear test with plenty to spare."[15] On the screen, the band appeared in *Two Blondes and a Redhead* as well as starring in one of Universal's "name band" shorts. Both movies were filmed during their stay on the West Coast in the summer of 1947. The "name band" movies were typically one-reelers, built around a single band and often filmed in a single day. Typically, the films ran to a budget of around $10,000, most of which was eaten up by the band's fee. It was the Pastor short—production number 2312—that offered Rosemary her first big screen appearance: Rosemary and Betty reprising their Barney Rapp audition piece on "Hawaiian War Chant." In another scene, set in a picture house, Rosemary cuddled up to her boss for an unctuous romantic duet called "Movie Tonight," notwithstanding the age difference between them that made Pastor old enough to be her father.

The Hollywood retreat over, it was back on the road for the Clooney Sisters. Saltair in Utah, Lubbock in Texas, and Sheboygan in Wisconsin were but three of dozens of other anonymous locations where the band played one-nighters.[16] From September 1947, however, the band's priorities changed. The record industry was bracing itself for another strike by the American Federation of Musicians (AFM). Just as he had done in 1943, union president James C. Petrillo was threatening to bar his members from entering a recording studio. The 1943 dispute had centered on royalty payments and had taken the music business by surprise. It lasted over a year and the big record companies saw their outputs dry up to a trickle for the duration of the ban. Five years later, the issue was similar, although Petrillo also had a new piece of labor legislation, the Taft-Hartley Labor-Management Relations Act, in his sights. This time, the big companies were determined that they would be ready. They began stockpiling. It wasn't just the bands who were affected. The strike precluded any musician from accompanying a solo vocalist in the studio. The response of the major labels was to have all their contracted artists in the studios as much as they could before the cessation began.

A band such as Tony Pastor's was firmly in the middle of the dispute and in the last three months of 1947, they made several visits to the studios in New York to add to their pile. The sessions offered Rosemary some good solo opportunities, although ironically, it was a song recorded and stashed away for over 15 months that came to be regarded as a milestone in her recording career. "Grieving for You" dated from 1920 and began life as a ragtime piano roll. Rosemary had started singing it early in her tenure with Pastor. Drummer Henry Riggs recalled her singing it at the Oriental Theater in Chicago in one of her first solo spots. Such was the emotion in Rosemary's rendition, said Riggs, that the audience received the song in stunned silence for 10–15 seconds before leaping to their feet and roaring their approval. Riggs was amazed, he said, that "this little girl could sing with so much passion."[17]

By the time Rosemary recorded it more than a year later, it was apparent that she had learned much from her apprenticeship as a band singer. Just as her idol Frank Sinatra credited Tommy Dorsey's trombone as giving him a model for breath control, Tony Pastor's tenor sax styling was clearly influencing the young girl singer, a point that *Billboard* picked up in its January 1949 review of the disc. "Rosemary Clooney delivers an intriguingly hushed vocal in a style reminiscent of her boss's tenor sax offerings," it said.[18] When the disc was finally released, late in 1948, it reached #11 in *Billboard*'s disc jockey chart, staying there for five weeks.

Despite having been with Tony Pastor for little more than a year, it was apparent that one of the Clooney Sisters was developing her vocal skills faster than the other. It was not surprising. Most singing groups—Paul Whiteman's Rhythm Boys which spawned Bing Crosby, Dorsey's Pied Pipers (Jo Stafford), even another sister act, the Boswell Sisters (Connee Boswell)—had seen one of its members develop ahead of the rest. It was also the case that most of the enduring sister acts had been threesomes rather than doubles. The Andrews Sisters, the Fontane Sisters, and the McGuire Sisters were the most notable contemporaries of the Clooneys, but all were trios who traded on the greater harmonic interplay that three voices offered over two. It wasn't until the emergence of the Bell Sisters in the early 1950s that American music saw a sister duo successfully strike out alone. Rosemary's fictional partnership with Vera-Ellen to create "the Haynes Sisters" for the 1954 movie *White Christmas* implied that the twosome model was more common than was actually so.

Solo stardom was beckoning, but as 1948 dawned, there were still thousands of miles to be traveled on the band bus. The remoteness of their lifestyle had been brought into sharp focus in November 1947 when Rosemary and Betty had stepped off the bus in a nondescript country town somewhere in middle America to be told offhandedly that there had been a phone call at the hotel. Andrew B. Clooney—"papa"—had passed away suddenly at the age of 73. There was no opportunity even to get home for the funeral. Rosemary and Betty found their own way of paying their respects before the Pastor circus rolled on once more. Rosemary was by now featured prominently, interspersing novelty duets with Pastor alongside more serious ballads such as "You Started Something." There were two clear styles to her singing: the hushed, slightly nasal sound of her solos contrasting with full-throated (and often phony-accented) delivery of the more comedic duets. The ability to adapt her style at the drop of a hat was an early indication of the versatility that would characterize her work during the next decade.

The Pastor band would prove to be one of the most durable of American touring ensembles, but it was part of a dying race. The heyday of the big bands had come during the years leading up to World War II, but after 1942, their popularity had started to slide. There were many reasons, although the loss of musicians to the draft, the AFM strike of 1943, and the shift in musical tastes toward the singers were the primary ones. After the war, Benny Goodman, Woody Herman, Harry James, Tommy Dorsey, Les Brown, and others all folded their ensembles within weeks of one another. In their place, their former singers—Peggy Lee, Frances Wayne, Helen Forrest, Jo Stafford, and Doris Day—set out on their own. Pastor stayed on the road longer than most before finally settling in Las Vegas in 1957. "I got in on the very last good days of the big band business," Rosemary said in 1961.[19]

The band might keep on touring but there was little Tony Pastor could do to stop his girl singer from overtaking him as the main attraction. In February 1948, she appeared in a solo spot on *Arthur Godfrey's Talent Scouts* on CBS radio. By now, Uncle George's role had extended to that of manager as well as chaperone and he was instrumental in gaining the opportunity for her. Rosemary sang a ballad called "Golden Earrings" and it was enough to earn her a tie for first prize. A young Italian American singer called Joe Bari came third. Within a few years, he, now named Tony Bennett—and Rosemary would stand together on the front line of Mitch Miller's assault on the popular music charts, and some would say, on his assault on good taste and quality in popular song. Later still, Bennett and Clooney would compete in the same category for the prestigious Grammy Award, always with the same result. When Rosemary looked back on her 1948 triumph, it was, she wrote, "the only time I ever won anything against Tony Bennett."[20] Bennett himself recalled their encounter as part of his concert performances in 2010. "Rosemary Clooney and me were the American Idols of the 1950s," he told audiences. "She was my sister in show business."[21]

The first public indication that Rosemary would leave the Pastor band to pursue a solo career was a *Billboard* report in November 1948, which said that after the band's current engagement in New York, she would step out alone. Accurately, if prematurely, the report indicated that Rosemary's solo career would be overseen by New York agent, Joe Shribman, the nephew of Tony Pastor's original backer, Cy Shribman. Joe was also the main agent for the Pastor band in New York. "When Rosemary heard Shribman and Charlie Trotta talk about her as a solo talent," Nick Clooney recalled, "it sparked her ambition." It also sparked a difficult time in the lives of everyone affected by the potential breakup of the Clooney Sisters. Pastor's drummer, Henry Riggs recalled that the deal to take Rosemary out on her own was done without Pastor's knowledge. "Charlie Trotta and Joe Shribman cut Tony Pastor out of Rosie's contract," he said. "It broke Tony's heart."[22] The deal would also cut Uncle George out of Rosemary's career, although until she reached her 21st birthday, his consent was still needed to any new contractual arrangement. With that date still six months away, *Billboard* was forced to backtrack on its scoop and was soon reporting that the Clooney Sisters had returned to the Pastor fold.[23]

That meant another winter on the road. In December alone, the band traveled over 1,500 miles—from Clear Lake, Iowa, to Madison, Wisconsin, then onto Monessen, Pennsylvania, and then a 483 mile slog to Hartford, Connecticut—all the stops coming within days of each other. Into 1949, an extended engagement in New York offered some respite as well as the opportunity to try out a new medium. Television had first reared its head in 1939, only to find its progress halted by America's entry into World War II. Ten years later, America found itself enjoying an affluent peace and television was one of the main beneficiaries. At first, its growth curve was far from spectacular. At Christmas 1948, the US population was approaching 150 million, yet there were only 350,000 television sets in use. Twenty-seven television stations were on the air. Most of these—and 75% of the sets—were around the New York metropolis. Within a year, the number of sets had jumped to 2 million, and in another 12 months was up to 8 million.[24] From then on, television became an unstoppable bandwagon.

Led by Perry Como and Milton Berle, singers and comedians were for-saking the script-in-the-hand microphone of the radio station for the chance to populate the small box in the corner of the living room. Rose-mary's girl-next-door image would ultimately prove to be more successful on television than on the big screen of Hollywood. Her TV debut came in March 1949 when she joined a lengthy list of jazz musicians as a guest on two editions of *Eddie Condon's Floor Show* on NBC. Condon's shows were live, half-hour affairs, loosely based on his New York jazz club. His guest list featured the great and the good of American jazz, as well as his regular New York cronies. Rosemary's first appearance on March 5, 1949, offered her only one song – "Way Down Yonder in New Orleans"—but marked her first real association with American jazz.

If 1949 was a year of growth for the television business, it also was a year of unanticipated crisis for the recording industry. In 1947—the year before Petrillo's second AFM strike—the record companies had witnessed their best ever year, with sales grossing over $200 million and sales of record players reaching 3.5 million. During that year, 375 million records had been pressed and nobody saw the hiatus of 1948 as anything more than a temporary hitch. With their stockpiles of recordings more than cov-ering the gap left by the musicians' action, the big labels were still pushing out their 1947 recordings into 1949 and beyond. What they failed to see was that the 18-month-old, shrink-wrapped diet they offered had not kept pace with what the public wanted to hear. It was, wrote music business historian Russell Sanjek, "too large an output, too startlingly alike."[25] Sales plummetted and at many of the big labels, the top executives were the first casualties.

None of this was apparent to Rosemary and the musicians she worked with on her final two sessions with the Pastor band in New York in March 1949. Most attention focused on the fact that Pastor, knowing that he would lose his star vocalist once the month of May turned, offered her the opportunity to put her name above that of the band for the first time on a song called "Bargain Day." Although a landmark in billing terms, Rosemary's first accredited solo disc was pure 1940s, a plaintive lyric sitting atop a conventional melodic structure. Rosemary's full-throated vocal was dictionally perfect but lacked the pathos she had displayed on "Grieving for You" some 18 months previously. Ironically, it was another song from the same session that offered a better beacon for her immediate future. The Clooney Sisters backed a Pastor vocal on "A-You're Adorable." The disc ran a poor second to the hit version by Perry Como and the Fontane Sisters but was a forerunner of the coming decade's appetite for novelty songs. No one, not even Como himself, would be more associated with the decade's appetite for tackiness than Rosemary Clooney.

With her 21st birthday approaching, there was no question now that Rosemary would go solo as soon as she could take matters into her own hands. Seeing potential in both his nieces, Uncle George had begun talking to Joe Shribman about solo careers for both girls. Shribman, however, saw George Guilfoyle as an amateur in a professional world and convinced Rosemary that he and Trotta were the men to lead her to the Promised Land. Matters came to a head when they delivered that message to Uncle George. It was a difficult conversation, carried out with Rosemary in the room. Guilfoyle refused to believe it unless he heard it from Rosemary herself. When he asked her to her face if she believed that he would be a burden, her answer was unequivocal. "Yes," she said.[26]

Rosemary's decision to go solo marked the end of the road for Betty Clooney too. In years to come, Betty was often portrayed—particularly by Rosemary—as a figure of virtuous self-sacrifice. "She wanted me to have a chance; she wanted me to go to New York and knew that we could not do that as a sister act," Rosemary said in a TV interview later in her career.[27] There were other explanations offered too—that Betty was fed up with the touring regime or that, being the younger of the sisters by three years, she had missed out on her teenage years and wanted to fill that gap in her life. There were elements of truth in these stories, but no more. Nick Clooney said that his younger sister always knew that vocally, she did not have the goods to match her elder sibling. "She was a world class singer," he said but when the chips were down, "there were four notes that Rosemary could hit that Betty couldn't." The idea though, that Betty Clooney's performing ambitions had been fulfilled by the brief period with the Pastor Band and that she was keen to go home to recapture her lost youth was, said Nick, "all baloney."[28] Betty's driven nature was never likely to be satisfied with a brief taste of show business, most of it spent on a bus traveling the highways and byways of North America. Nevertheless, the split came and Betty had little option but to return home to Cincinnati. She continued to perform, appearing on local television, and in the early '60s she was a regular on

NBC's *Today* show. She recorded for the Cincinnati-based King Records and Decca's subsidiary Coral without ever matching the hit stream of her older sister. Rosemary's decision to go solo caused no lasting damage to the relationship between the sisters, but it was only in later life that she revealed the angst that it had caused her. "It bothered her for the rest of her life," Nick Clooney said.[29] The closest Rosemary came to acknowledging it came in her 1997 interview with Terry Gross, who asked her how she had felt, leaving Betty. Rosemary's answer was a compassionate statement of irresistible ambition. "I felt sad; I felt grateful," she said, "and I went."[30]

Rosemary's timing was ultimately dictated by nothing more than an accident of birth but could not have worked more to her advantage. Columbia Records was one of the first among the major disc-makers to look for new talent to lead them into the 1950s. They cast their net widely. When they hauled it in, they found it contained a young girl singer from Kentucky and a classically trained oboist from Rochester, New York. Rosemary Clooney was about to meet Mitch Miller.

CHAPTER 3

Come On-a My House

Rosemary Clooney signed a solo contract with Columbia Records on May 24, 1949, the morning after her 21st birthday. She would remain with the label for nine years and record over 250 commercial sides, displaying a versatility in material that few artists, before or since, have matched. Her repertoire included children's songs, Christmas songs, country and western, and ballads from the Great American Songbook, while her disc partners ranged from Benny Goodman through Frank Sinatra to Marlene Dietrich. Her recorded output led to 20 separate appearances in *Billboard*'s weekly record charts, with four number ones and a further three Top Ten hits.[1] These included timeless ballads such as "Hey There" and "Tenderly," lilting country songs such as "Beautiful Brown Eyes" and "Half As Much," and jazz standards in the form of "Memories of You." Yet for all the quality in that list, Rosemary Clooney's 1950s reputation is all about phony-accents, nonsense lyrics, and banal melodies. "Mambo Italiano," "Botch-A-Me (Ba-Ba-Baciami Piccina)," and above all else, "Come On-a My House" defined the sound of Rosemary Clooney in the '50s and the two decades beyond. The emergent songbird from Kentucky became the queen of the novelty songs but on her head, she wore a crown of thorns. It would take over 25 years for her artistic reputation to fully recover.

The man who engineered the deal to take Rosemary to Columbia was Manie Sachs,[2] head of Artists & Repertoire (A&R). Sachs started life as a salesman in the dress business, the same industry as Rosemary's mother. When he moved into the music industry, it was his interest in sales and marketing rather than an inherent musicality that inspired him. Nevertheless, he rose to become one of the biggest and most influential people in the business. He made his name at Columbia Records, before leaving to become vice-president of RCA in 1950. When he first joined Columbia in 1939, it was on the back of a family investment. Columbia Records was part of the wider CBS family. The brand had been one of the founding fathers of the American recording industry but had fallen on hard times during the Depression, so much so that by the time CBS chief William S. Paley reacquired it in 1936, the name was almost defunct. Paley set about restoring Columbia Records to its former glory and Sachs played a key role. He brought names such as Harry James, Dinah Shore, and Doris Day to Columbia and when he added a young Frank Sinatra to the roster, the turnaround was complete.

By the time Sachs signed Rosemary Clooney in 1949, change was on the horizon once again. With sales dropping through the floor, it seemed that every A&R manager worked in an office with a permanently revolving door. One of the first—and least expected—casualties was Eli Oberstein at RCA. Oberstein was another industry giant, but reputations, it seemed, counted for nothing. When RCA went looking for a replacement, they turned to Manie Sachs, making him an offer that he couldn't refuse.[3] Sachs's departure left a vacancy at Columbia. Executive VP and head of classical records, Goddard Lieberson, remembered a classmate from his days at the Eastman School of Music in Rochester, New York. His name was William Mitchell ("Mitch") Miller.

Miller was an unlikely choice for the simple reason that his DNA seemed rooted in classical music. After graduating from Eastman, Miller moved to New York. His instrument was the oboe. It was a specialty that worked in his favor, the laws of supply and demand usually working on his side. Miller worked with various classical orchestras as well as joining some of the CBS radio ensembles (he was in the band that had orchestrated Orson Welles's iconic *War Of The Worlds* broadcast in 1938). The move from the orchestra pit to the control booth came in 1947 when he joined Keynote Records as head of classical A&R. When Mercury Records acquired Keynote soon after, Miller found himself in unfamiliar territory. Assigned to a role in Mercury's pop music division, it proved to be the making of the man. Miller quickly signed Frankie Laine and Patti Page but more significantly, set about changing the way pop records were made, utilizing every possible type of sound that he could think of. Laine's vocals were soon set to the accompaniment of galloping hooves and cracking whips. It heralded a sea change in the recording business and it was this that attracted the attention of Goddard Lieberson.

Sixty years after Mitch Miller's arrival at Columbia, he remains one of the most controversial figures in American music history. Supporters and detractors alike, however, all on agree on one thing: Mitch Miller transformed the role and the importance of the record producer in the music-making process like no one before or since. Rhythm and blues writer-cum-producer Jerry Wexler's perspective was that "they should build a statue to Mitch Miller at 57th and Broadway. . . . He was the first great record producer in history."[4] Jazz critic Will Friedwald, in a 2010 obituary after Miller's death at the age of 99, supported Wexler's view. Miller, he said, "virtually invented the job of the pop-music producer," going on to observe that "as singers replaced the big bands as the focal point of pop, the producers—formerly known as A&R (artists and repertoire) men—took over from the bandleaders as the industry's decision makers and power brokers. By the start of the rock era, Miller had set an example that every music-world mover and shaker to come, from Phil Spector to Quincy Jones, Berry Gordy and even Simon Cowell, has emulated."[5]

Miller's great gift was being able to anticipate what record buyers wanted. The disastrous sales figures for the last years of the 1940s proved that this was no longer the sentimental music of World War II or even the big band swing that had dominated the music scene a decade before. America in the '50s was embracing a new world of modernity and ease and was looking forward, not back. The message was one of change. Miller read the mood better than anyone else and realized that artistic purity counted for nothing. That was something to leave to his classical music colleagues. "If it sounds right, it's right," he said in a 2004 interview.[6] His interest was all about the production and the sound that he could create in the studio, using every possible tool available to him. Reputations held as little merit for him as did artistic purity. Whether his singer was Tony Bennett, Rosemary Clooney, or even Frank Sinatra mattered not a jot. In commercial terms, the approach worked but success came at a price. To this day, some music critics and historians have never forgiven him. "Under Miller's influence, normal voices took on awesome, doom-filled proportions," wrote *New York Times* music critic John S. Wilson, "gunned up by echo chambers, multiple taping and the endless use of sound gadgetry."[7] Others blamed him for the musical wasteland that became '50s America. "A Sherman-like crusade in the 1950s on behalf of banality," said another obituarist.[8]

Mitch Miller transformed careers, none more so than that of Rosemary Clooney. "Nothing much happened to me until I met Mitch," she said later.[9] It was true. Moving to New York, she had taken a small, one-bed apartment close to West 57th Street. Her contract with Columbia was a start, but it was hardly megabucks. The deal paid her $50 a side but with a guarantee of only eight sides a year and a net royalty of three cents per record sold. Her first singles appeared on Columbia's cut-price Harmony label, retailing at

49 cents. For her debut release, Columbia paired a Bob Merrill-Monty Nevins song "Lover's Gold" with an early Hal David composition, "The Four Winds and the Seven Seas." That disc made no impact but the early signs of chart success came with a song that Rosemary recorded at her next session on September 14, 1949. "The Kid's a Dreamer" was picked up and pushed hard by Philadelphia disc jockey Doug Arthur. Local sales of 65,000 gave Rosemary a minor hit. It was the first Rosemary Clooney record to bring her voice to a wider audience, although it owed its success to the power of promotion, Rosemary's singing being little more than an exercise in clinical vocal precision. Confidence was building, however, and by the summer of 1950, she was beginning to find the relaxed casualness that would become a trademark. "Why Fight the Feeling," an early collaboration with arranger Percy Faith in June 1950, was an example. *Billboard*, said it was "done with conviction" ahead of Faith's "delicate and lively" scoring.[10]

With the regular paycheck from Tony Pastor a thing of the past, Rosemary needed more than just Columbia record dates to keep her solvent. Joe Shribman proved to be an enterprising agent, finding plenty of one-night bookings in New York and surrounding cities as well as lining up a regular diet of radio and TV appearances. Rosemary's radio spots included one of the many popular musical quiz shows, *Sing It Again* on CBS radio plus a more regular spell as guest on Vaughn Monroe's *Camel Caravan* show. Radio bookings were fine but it was television, especially in New York, that had everybody talking. Rosemary made her national TV debut on Ed Sullivan's *Toast of the Town* show on Christmas Day 1949, a noteworthy debut although Sullivan's show had not yet attained its instant passport-to-stardom status that it would acquire in the '50s. Rosemary sang two songs, "A Dreamer's Holiday" and "Why Don't You Haul Off and Love Me," the latter with a set of country and western dancers that anticipated the type of setting she would use in her own shows during the '50s. Singing with greater expression and a fuller voice than on her records of the time, Rosemary's expressive face, perma-smile, and seductive off-the-shoulder dress sent a clear message that here was a star in the making.

Other shows included *The Morey Amsterdam Show* and *Robert Q's Matinee*—where Rosemary first met her future husband, José (Joe) Ferrer—plus another competition show, *Songs for Sale*, on which Rosemary shared the spotlight once more with Tony Bennett. The show was purportedly an opportunity for amateur songwriters to have Clooney or Bennett perform their songs in front of a panel of experts who would rate their chances. In practice, it was more about promoting the members of the panel than opening the door to new talent. But, as one reviewer said, "it didn't matter. With the one exception, there were very good reasons why these songs had never been published."[11] Tony Bennett concurred. The songs, he said, were "consistently mediocre."[12] What's more, wrote Bennett, the time constraints on the show meant that he and Rosemary were seldom able to learn the songs in time for the live show and had to rely on cue cards for the lyrics. Rosemary's brother Nick, who spent the summer of 1950 rooming with his sister in New York, recalled that matters were made worse by the fact that neither of the two singers could read music and had to try and memorize the melodies. "I remember well the look of horror on the faces of some of the songwriters as the melodies they had labored over became unrecognizable on national TV," he wrote.[13]

Back in the Columbia studios (the one-time Adams Memorial Presbyterian Church) on New York's East 30th Street, Rosemary was developing her first niche specialty. Songs for kids were a big part of the disc market in the early '50s and all the big labels gave them significant attention. Indeed, for the Hollywood-based Capitol Records, children's songs accounted for one third of its revenue. The artistic challenge of producing a record targeted at juvenile ears sat comfortably with Rosemary. "The arrangements can be cute, but your diction has to be perfect," she said. "Kids have to understand every single word, because you're telling them a story and they insist on hearing it. Never sing down to children. If you do, they recognize it and can't stand it."[14] Rosemary was also conscious that most kids' records featured a male voice. "Children won't buy most women's voices," she said "because mothers are around the house every day and discipline comes from mothers. Sing it like you're a man with a feminine voice," was her tip.[15] It worked. Rosemary produced a string of successful children's records, culminating in "Suzy Snowflake" which sold a quarter of a million copies in 1951. By 1955, Rosemary's children's titles had notched up sales of over 1 million for Columbia.

Rosemary was well aware that one of her stablemates at Columbia was her idol, Frank Sinatra. Nevertheless, a call from Joe Shribman in April 1950 came as a total shock. "Sinatra wants to make a record with you," he told her. It was a dream come true although Rosemary soon discovered that Sinatra's request was anything but the endorsement she craved. Sinatra needed a duet partner to promote a song that he had co-authored called "Peachtree Street," a forgettable song about the main street of Atlanta, Georgia. He told Manie Sachs that he wanted Dinah Shore, Columbia's #1 female vocalist on the disc with him. Shore turned him down, saying the song was so bad that she wanted nothing to do with it. Sinatra threw a temper and, as a rebuff to Shore, asked Sachs for the name of the last girl singer that he had signed. That, Rosemary later explained, was how her dream duet came about. Although the two of them gave a lively performance,

Dinah Shore's assessment turned out to be correct. "When 'Peachtree Street' hit the stores, it was dead on arrival," Rosemary later wrote.[16] There were other duets with Sinatra before he left the label, including the inane "Love Means Love" and an even worse catalog song, "Cherry Pies Ought to Be You," but both suffered the same fate as "Peachtree." It was the beginning of two uneasy relationships, Rosemary's with Sinatra and Sinatra's with his record label. A year later, during her Las Vegas debut at the Thunderbird, Sinatra had been working down at the Desert Inn and used his time on stage to rubbish Rosemary's early recordings. "The worse fake accent I ever heard," he said.[17] Sinatra's venom, wrote James Kaplan, was directed at Mitch Miller rather than Rosemary, but she nevertheless took it as an affront (as did Miller who "exploded," said Kaplan, when the comments were fed back to him.)[18]

By the time "Peachtree Street" hit the shops, Manie Sachs had departed for RCA and in his place sat the goateed Mitch Miller. One of his first recruits was a young singer from Detroit, Michigan, called Al Cernik, the son of Croatian immigrants. Renaming him Guy Mitchell ("my name is Mitchell and you seem to be a nice guy, so we'll call you Guy Mitchell" goes the apocryphal story), Miller quickly paired him with Rosemary for four duets, including two songs from the new Irving Berlin musical *Call Me Madam*, "You're Just in Love" and "Marrying for Love." The resulting single reached #24 in *Billboard*, a creditable showing for two newcomers who bested competition from more established names, including collaborations between Dinah Shore and Russell Nype, and Dick Haymes and Ethel Merman.[19]

Mitch Miller's uncompromising approach to changing the sound that buyers would hear on a Columbia record resulted in a series of battles royal, none more so than that between him and his star vocalist, Frank Sinatra. When Sinatra refused point blank to record two songs that Miller pushed in his direction, a split became inevitable. Miller took the songs instead in the direction of Guy Mitchell and both "The Roving Kind" and "My Heart Cries for You" became massive hits. The success further accentuated Miller's self-confidence, not that it was needed. Other singers too found the new regime hard to take. Tony Bennett subsequently described his relationship with Miller as being almost a permanent state of war, with compromises being made all the time by one side or the other about the songs he recorded. Rosemary's musical instincts had her firmly in the Sinatra and Bennett camp although her desire for success meant she was less likely to dig her heels in the way Sinatra had. What's more, her first exposure to Miller had brought no indication that he was a musical revolutionary. She had first met him toward the end of her days with the Pastor band. Miller, then on the lookout for new talent for Mercury Records, had complimented her on "Grieving for You." "Nice sounds" he said. Interviewed in 1955, Miller remembered that first encounter. "I was alerted by Rosie's voice in "Grieving for You" right away. It had depth and heart," he said.[20]

Rosemary's first session with Miller in January 1951 produced an immediate success. Miller had heard a new country song, first sung by Alabama's guitar-based Delmore Brothers, called "Beautiful Brown Eyes." As it was a plaintive country song, Miller went to work in his classic big production style, multitracking Rosemary's vocal and throwing in a big echo chamber for good measure. The results were astounding. The disc sold 400,000 copies and put Rosemary on the cover of *Downbeat*. It also brought her an improved contract, with royalties up to 5% and a guarantee of $250,000 over five years. "Beautiful Brown Eyes" reflected Miller's open door policy toward the material that he would use. He cast his net far and wide. Crossovers and covers were consistent parts of the repertoire that Miller gave his artists, although it was his affinity for nonsense and novelty songs that usually defined the battle lines.

None more so than "Come On-a My House." The song that would become indelibly linked to the name of Rosemary Clooney for the rest of her career was written in 1939 by two cousins, dramatist and author William Saroyan and Ross Bagdasarian, who later used the stage name of David Seville when he became the man behind Alvin and the Chipmunks. Saroyan was an Armenian American and took the idea for the melody from an old Armenian folk song. The song wasn't new—the two cousins had recorded it for Coral Records in 1939. It came to Miller's attention through a demo record by Kay Armen. Miller had in mind an arrangement behind Rosemary that centered on a harpsichord, a keyboard relic more usually associated with Bach than the world of pop. When he explained this to Rosemary and played her the demo, she was aghast. "I don't think it's for me," she told him. Miller's response, she said later, was patient but ultimately, forthright. After briefly attempting to persuade her of the commercial potential of the song, Miller decided on a different approach. "Let me put it this way. You show up tomorrow or you're fired!" he told her. In later years, Rosemary would dine out on that story, but without any sense of malice. "Truthfully, all I ever wanted in those days was a hit. I wanted terribly to be a success," she told *Stereo Review* in 1981.[21] "You get so pompous when you're young," she told interviewer Diane Sawyer 10 years later. "I took myself so seriously. Mitch was trying to put it in a nice way. But when he said I'd be fired, I understood that."[22] Despite her willingness to fall into line, the relationship between Rosemary and Miller was never an easy one. Singer Michael Feinstein thought that Rosemary had never really liked Miller—"he was a vulgar man. He had a dark soul,"[23] Feinstein said, although Rosemary's manager in the final years of her career, Allen Sviridoff, thought that the relationship mellowed over time. "I worked with them together in the eighties half a dozen times and I never saw any signs of Rosemary not liking him," he said.[24]

Rosemary did show up to record "Come On-a My House" but in a bizarre twist, the key instrument, the harpsichord, failed to arrive. Rosemary and the musicians hung around for a couple of hours but when it was apparent that Miller's piece de resistance was not going to appear, she asked Stan Freeman, booked on the date to play the missing keyboard, what else he knew. Opening up the piano, Freeman played an elegant introduction to Alec Wilder's "I'll Be Around" to which Rosemary added an exquisite vocal that showcased "her purity of line, nuance of lyric, musical taste and rhythmic instincts."[25] A hastily improvised arrangement to "The Lady Is a Tramp" followed, with Rosemary singing to the backing of a freely swinging jazz trio for the first time in her recording career, prefacing her later Concord style by some 25 years. The two recordings might have been little more than fillers at the time they were made and indeed lay dormant in Columbia's vaults for four years before tiptoeing onto a 1955 compilation long player. Nevertheless, they were landmarks in the developing maturity of Rosemary's art.

One day later, Stan Freeman moved over from the piano to lay his fingers on the now-delivered harpsichord and Rosemary got to work on Miller's magnum opus. Without the first idea of what an Armenian accent would sound like, she reverted to the Italian-American dialect that was so familiar from her Tony Pastor days. Miller was happy as long as the accent sounded vaguely European, although Rosemary also found that, despite his platitudes about "the sound," Miller paid attention to detail. Rosemary was uncertain about the hidden meaning in Saroyan's lyric. Was the invitation she was giving to "Come On-a My House" a euphemism for sex? Was that the interpretation she should give? Taking time out from arranging the layout of the studio to maximize the impact of the harpsichord, Miller took the young singer aside for a word of advice. "This song could be taken as 'come and have sex,' but what you're looking for is marriage," he told her. "When he said that, I understood, and that's what I did," Rosemary said in 1997.[26] Five takes later, Miller had the result that he wanted. He ordered the disc to be rush released, with an immediate run of 100,000 copies. Two weeks later it was in the shops. *Billboard* praised Clooney's "electrifying" performance and Miller's "rousing, live sound"[27] and when Rosemary heard the record stores on Broadway all blaring out the disc, she knew that she had something big. The record entered *Billboard's* charts on July 7, 1951, and stayed there for 20 weeks, eight of them at #1. It transformed Rosemary's life and career. Over the remaining 50 years of her performing life she was barely able to make a live appearance without singing her Armenian folk song. *Life* magazine ran a feature on her; *Time* featured her on its cover. The one-room apartment was traded for something bigger at the more prestigious Hampshire House, and whereas she had normally squeezed in at the back of the Copa to see Sinatra, now she was ushered to a prime table. Seemingly overnight, Rosemary Clooney was rich and famous.

Miller followed up the success of "Come On-a My House" with two more harpsichord-driven releases. "You have to work out a gimmick that'll get people's attention and hold it," Miller told *Time* magazine.[28] He was true to his word. "If Teardrops Were Pennies" came from the same session as "My House" and as well as the harpsichord, featured another Miller trademark with Rosemary again multitracking her voice. The disc was a minor hit in September 1951, as was "I Wish I Wuz (Hi Ho, Fiddle De Dee)," which Rosemary recorded in August of that year, with bass, drums, guitar, and yes, harpsichord behind her. For all her unease with such trite material, Rosemary carried off her vocals with great aplomb, bouncing along with Terry Snyder's drumbeat and singing with a smile in her voice. It was a technique she learned from Maurice Chevalier, she told Larry King in 1997, and one that in turn, she passed on to Michael Feinstein.

Mitch Miller was anything but a one-trick pony, however, when it came to picking material. After "I Wish I Wuz" reached only the low 20s in *Billboard*'s charts, he changed tack and looked for a crossover song as the next vehicle for Rosemary. Just as he had done for Tony Bennett's first big hit, "Cold, Cold Heart," he found it in a Hank Williams recording. "Half as Much" reunited Rosemary with arranger Percy Faith and she delivered a vocal full of precision and relaxed confidence that reflected the belief that a major hit record can bring. The results almost matched the success of "Come On-a My House." Entering the *Billboard* charts in May 1952, the record stayed there for 27 weeks, with three weeks at #1.

A string-filled Percy Faith arrangement was again in evidence for Rosemary's next Columbia session in November 1951. With the Clooney bandwagon firmly rolling, Miller invited his lead songstress to pick a song of her own choosing for the session. Rosemary picked "Tenderly," a 1946 song from the team of Walter Gross and Jack Lawrence that was a personal favorite.[29] The song had come a long way from its origins as a three-four time waltz in the mid-'40s. By the time Rosemary had it on her song stand, there were several existing versions of it. Trumpeter Randy Brooks had been the first to make an impact with it as an instrumental piece in 1946. In 1950, the song had given the Lynn Hope Quartet their solitary chart entry with it, although among all the preceding versions, it was a 1947 recording by Sarah Vaughan that stood out. Vaughan's rendition, strongly influenced by the style of Billie Holiday, took the song away from its dance tempo origins and turned it into a haunting jazz ballad.

When Mitch Miller heard Rosemary's first take on the song, he flipped open the talkback switch in the recording booth and told his singer that he would be out to talk to her. Miller's refusal to follow the practice of other A&R men and give instructions over the open studio mike was something that Rosemary and the other Columbia artists respected. Instead, Miller would come out of the booth and speak privately to the performer. On this occasion, Miller's observation to Rosemary was that the song was intimidating her. She was too much aware of the other performances that had gone before her, he told her. "You've got to approach this as if it were the first time a recording was ever made of 'Tenderly.' I want your interpretation of it," he said.[30] Nevertheless, despite Miller's coaching, Rosemary's 1951 recording was bland—*Billboard* called it a "heartfelt warble"[31]—when compared to the expressive versions she would add later in her career. Released as a single, the results for Rosemary were modest, reaching #17 during a six-week stay in the record charts, although as years went by, it proved to be one of her most durable records. In 1956, it was voted #6 in a *Billboard* poll of all-time favorite records[32] and such by then was its association with Rosemary that she adopted it as the theme for her new weekly TV series. The song became a regular feature of Rosemary's stage act, Rosemary often introducing it as "my favorite song." When she reinvented herself in a jazz idiom in the '80s, she rerecorded a much improved version for Concord Records.

Rosemary's successes in the recording studio in 1951 catapulted her to the top step on the show business ladder. A three-week booking at the Thunderbird in Las Vegas brought a paycheck of $3,500 per week, a figure that was 150% of the *annual* income for a white family in the United States at that time. Two years previously, Rosemary had been making $150 per week. Back in New York, she appeared in the *Crusade for Freedom* telecast, the first coast-to-coast television transmission, followed by a succession of guest spots on TV and radio with such luminaries as Jack Benny, Edgar Bergen, and Milton Berle. Off-stage, though, not everything in the garden was rosy. In June 1951, her half-brother Andrew, whom Rosemary had only recently got to know, drowned in an accident in the Ohio River. Prior to that, Rosemary had been hospitalized in November 1950 with what turned out to be an ovarian cyst but which, until diagnosed, bore all the symptoms of an unwanted and career-ending pregnancy. "I wasn't pregnant but I could have been," Rosemary later wrote, a comment that reflected the liberal lifestyle of her early bachelor girl days in New York.[33] One of several suitors was Dave Garroway, the founding host of NBC's *Today* show from 1952 to 1961. The gossip columnists had the two of them walking down the aisle. "TV's Dave Garroway and the nation's top-selling girl singer Rosemary Clooney are sniffing orange blossoms," Dorothy Kilgallen cryptically noted in her syndicated newspaper column. In December 1951, another columnist, Jimmie Fidler was telling his readers that the twosome was "altar-dated for late December." Rosemary later denied that there had ever been any hint of marriage on either of their minds, although she was, she said, still seeing Garroway when he moved to New York for the *Today* show in 1952. But said Rosemary, she was seeing others too.

It wasn't just suitors who were knocking on Rosemary's door in the fall of 1951. Ever since the dawn of talking pictures in the late '20s, a natural career progression for a successful singer had been from records and radio into the movies. By the time Rosemary made her Las Vegas debut at the Thunderbird in September 1951, most of the major Hollywood studios had someone in the audience to assess her potential for the big screen. The scouts quickly saw that Rosemary, with her sharp features, pleasant personality, and quick sense of humor, had everything they wanted. Contractual offers soon followed and in October 1951, Rosemary signed a seven-year deal with Paramount Studios. Once more, it meant a change of scene for the young songbird from Kentucky, this time out west to Hollywood. Movie stardom was waiting but so too were two very unlikely consequences. One was that she would become one of the few truly close friends of the biggest name in show business. The other was that she would find the place that she called home for the rest of her life.

CHAPTER 4

"A Dame Called Rosemary Clooney"

In August 1951, three weeks before Rosemary's appearance at the Thunderbird, Bing Crosby settled into the den at his holiday home at Hayden Lake, Idaho, and dictated a letter to Paramount Pictures producer, Pat Duggan. The topic was the remake of Crosby's 1942 movie *Holiday Inn*, the film in which Crosby had introduced the song "White Christmas." Irving Berlin's song, driven by Crosby's recording of it, had become a World War II symbol of home for American GIs, and by the end of the decade, it was an indelible part of an American Christmas. Paramount had featured the song in another Berlin-based movie, *Blue Skies*, in 1946. Soon after, the idea of remaking *Holiday Inn* in full color gathered its own momentum, this time with the name of the song also becoming the title for the movie.

Crosby's association with the song meant that he was central to the casting. He was enthusiastic about the proposition but bothered by the casting of the female lead. "I think we have a good script and we can have a good picture but the delicacy of this female casting problem can't be overstated," he wrote. "How about a dame called Rosemary Clooney? Sings a good song and is purportedly personable."[1] Quite where Crosby's information—and enthusiasm for Rosemary—came from was never revealed. The two had not met at that time and with Crosby spending most of his time on the west coast, it is unlikely that he had seen any of her New York performances. His suggestion of Rosemary for the part was not much more than a hunch. But, as hunches go, it was undeniably a good one.

Bing Crosby had been the biggest name in show business for over 20 years. Starting his career in the late 1920s, Crosby had arrived on the music scene just as a wave of new technology was transforming the industry.

Electrical recording, the invention of the microphone, and the explosion of radio all opened the way for a new style of singing. Where Crosby's predecessors had, of necessity, needed the lung power to hit the back row of any theater, Crosby had been the first singer to realize that if the microphone could hear him, then so could everyone else. His intimate singing—crooning—put the emphasis on the lyric of a song rather than its dance tempo. Crosby was not the first to spot the opportunity but his baritone voice and innate sense of jazz phrasing soon made him the most popular and influential singer that the world had ever seen.

Crosby's career path took him from radio to the movies. In Hollywood, he further enhanced his reputation as a romantic lead, light comedian, and in time, a dramatic actor, winning the Academy Award in 1945 for his portrayal of a modernist Catholic priest. The Oscar marked the beginning of a spell of Hollywood dominance for Crosby and for five straight years from 1944 to 1948, he was the top box office star. Add to that the fact that he was already the biggest selling recording artist ever and the star and host of the iconic *Kraft Music Hall* on radio, and the extent of Crosby's dominance becomes clear. Clark Gable and subsequently, Elvis Presley both carried the title of "The King" but no individual star, before or since, ever straddled so many concurrent show business peaks as Bing Crosby. Much of his enduring popularity came from the character that he portrayed in his radio shows and on the screen. Affable and easygoing, the public Crosby came to typify Middle America. He was the guy-next-door who breezed through life with a smile and a song, a pipe draped from his mouth, casual and carefree, yet someone who always seemed to come out on top. His appeal was global and reached out to all ages, sexes and races. Tony Bennett said that at his peak, Crosby was "bigger than Elvis and the Beatles combined."[2] Decca Records said that Crosby's voice in 1945 had been heard by more human beings than that of anyone who had ever lived. In short, Bing Crosby was the world's first mass media star and in the late '40s, was the most famous man in the world.

Off-stage, the private Bing was a different and far more complex individual than the one he portrayed on the screen. He was one of the few entertainers to have received the benefit of a full classical education at a Jesuit college, and a quick, intelligent man, Crosby suffered no fools. Somewhat shy and withdrawn by nature, Crosby also found it difficult to deal with emotion, either in giving or receiving. He could at times be distant and appear chillingly cold and insensitive. "Perhaps," said Alistair Cooke at the time of Crosby's death, "he was one of those people who, though not at all selfish, are deeply self-centred: what they call 'a very private person.' Because he couldn't identify with other people's troubles, he was able to appear, and to be, everybody's easy-going buddy."[3] Part of Crosby's coping mechanism was a cocoon that he built around himself. Anyone who entered uninvited found himself or herself in an icebox. Few, if any, words would be spoken but the daggers in his crystal-clear blue eyes could cut a man—or woman—dead. There were other things a long way from the public image that Crosby created. He and his wife Dixie Lee had four sons, but the harmonious family life that the fan magazines portrayed concealed fissures both within the family and the marriage. Dixie had suffered from depression and alcoholism for many years while the boys discovered that when it came to balancing discipline and love, Crosby usually erred on the side of the former. "When I want to be especially flattering to one of my offspring, I say 'Nice goin'' and let it go at that," he wrote in his autobiography.[4] Taken all together, it meant that Crosby was a difficult man to get close to, a situation not helped by the reverence heaped upon him by the entertainment community. Until Elvis Presley burst upon the scene a few years later, there was not a singer on the planet who did not stand in awe of Bing Crosby. Rosemary felt it as much as anyone else. "Maybe it would be a good idea if I tried to explain the worship that other singers have for Bing," she said in a 1954 magazine feature. "Show people can talk all night about singers, Perry and Frank and the whole lot—and then there is *Bing*. The man is an institution all by himself and he has a way of spinning out a melody that no other singer can touch. He stands alone."[5] Such statements sat uneasily with Crosby. He was too intelligent not to realize the presence that he had, but too emotionally inhibited ever to deal easily with it.

Rosemary was destined to gain firsthand exposure to the complexities of Bing Crosby much sooner than she anticipated. The final casting of *White Christmas* was still over a year away when Rosemary arrived at Paramount in May 1952. As she took her first tour around the lot with publicist A. C. Lyles, she heard that Crosby was in residence, filming *Road to Bali* with his occasional screen partner, Bob Hope. Rosemary knew too that her agent, Joe Shribman, had booked her a guest spot on Crosby's radio show later in the month, but did not expect to suddenly find him cycling toward her as she strolled down one of the avenues. He stopped, dangled one leg onto the floor, and waited while Lyles made the introductions. "He said something about a radio show we were to do together and asked if I knew when it would take place," Rosemary recalled. "And I, with all the savoir-faire of the Missing Link," mumbled 'Sometime in the 20s.'"[6] Rosemary had meant sometime later in the month—the recording was set for May 26—but it had come out as the typical tongue-tied hero worship that Crosby hated. "Nothing makes Bing so uncomfortable as people who are impressed," Rosemary said later.[7] Knowing that she had laid an egg, Rosemary had the foresight—and the courage—to take matters into her own hands. Later that day, she sought out Crosby's personal villa and knocked on the door. She told him that she wanted to explain what had happened. "I'm not a numbskull," she said, "I was just terribly thrilled to meet you, that's all. I hope you understand and I hope to see you around sometime."[8] With her piece said, Rosemary turned and marched off. It was the kind of response that Crosby respected. A few days later he invited her for a drink. It was the beginning of a friendship that would endure to the end of his life.

The Paramount image creators had work to do with Rosemary long before there was any open suggestion that she might share top billing with Crosby. On her initial screen test, an internal Paramount report had described her appearance as "unprepossessing."[9] It was true. Rosemary herself said that she had turned up "looking like somebody's grandmother,"[10] ignoring advice that pointed out how unflattering a glittery white dress could be. "She looked like a star-spangled Christmas angel," one Paramount executive caustically remarked.[11] Rosemary's great asset, apart from her voice, was that she came across as wholesome—pretty without being glamorous; attractive without being sexy. Some at Paramount said that her nose was too wide and her legs too skinny, her face too long and her jaw overly prominent. But Irving Asher, who would produce Rosemary's screen debut, thought that Rosemary's essential prettiness was all that mattered. "Rosie has a wonderfully expressive face," he said. "It ought to be let alone and not glamorized to try and make her look like everyone else. Just photograph it the way it is." Asher too was struck by her naturalness. "I always call her Miss Crosby," he added, "because her manner is like Bing's. She has an offhand way. If anyone teaches her to act, they'll do her a great disservice."[12] Paramount's backroom team, which included dress designer, Edith Head, got the treatment of Rosemary just right. "She couldn't have looked prettier to Paramount tycoons if she had been fitted with Lana Turner's head," Time magazine said when her first film came out.[13]

Rosemary's initial filming commitment in Hollywood ran from May to July 1952. Before heading west, she spent the first four months of the year busy in New York. There were radio appearances on NBC's The Big Show and The Mario Lanza Show, but increasingly, it was television that was now prominent. She guested four times on Perry Como's TV show along with appearances on Royal Showcase with Bert Lahr and Joel Grey and Celebrity Time with Pat O'Brien. Her most significant pre-Hollywood commitment, however, was a Columbia recording date on April 18, 1952. After the country feel of "Half as Much" and the strings of "Tenderly," Mitch Miller was back in harpsichord-mode for another piece of novelty nonsense. "Botch-a-Me (Ba-Ba-Baciami Piccina)" dated back to 1941. It was written by Riccardo

Morbelli and Luigi Astore and first popularized, in Italian, by Alberto Rab-igliati. By the time it appeared on Rosemary's music stand, Eddie Stanley had added a set of English words, rarely surpassed in their banality. Never-theless, in keeping with Miller's philosophy, it was the sound of Rosemary's laugh-filled voice, bouncing to Freeman's harpsichord and Terry Snyder's percussion, that would sell the records. "This one has all the ingredients of a big hit. It's an appealing novelty item, with a driving beat," said *Billboard*.[14]

Miller's instincts were once again spot on. "Botch-a-Me" spent 17 weeks on the *Billboard* charts, peaking at #2 in both the best-seller and disc jockey listings. The disc's success was axiomatic of the change that Miller had brought to Columbia Records. Shortly after the recording session, *Billboard* ran a piece headed "Columbia Pop-Disk Primacy apparent in Billboard Charts." The article analyzed the strike rate of various record companies in terms of hits generated as compared to records released. Miller's Columbia in the first quarter of 1952 had a hit rate twice that of its nearest competitor: 13 hits from 108 releases, a strike rate of 12%. Next highest came Mercury with 6% (seven hits from 112 releases), with Capitol third at 3%, marginally ahead of RCA which weighed in at 2.78%.[15] Miller was riding the crest of a wave and Rosemary Clooney was one of the main reasons.

"Botch-a-Me" was not the only song slated for Rosemary's session on April 18. "On the First Warm Day," a song associated with cabaret artist, Mabel Mercer, was given the full harpsichord treatment before Rosemary was joined in the studio by the most unlikely of duet partners, screen leg-end Marlene Dietrich. Signed by Columbia in 1950, Dietrich had already begun recording with Miller and had met Rosemary on a radio show the year before. A friendship blossomed and Miller decided to capitalize on it by uniting the voice of Lili Marlene with that of his Kentucky songbird. For the "A" side of the single, Miller once again raided the country music charts. He settled on "Too Old to Cut the Mustard," written and recorded the pre-vious year by another Kentuckian, "Jumpin'" Bill Carlisle, famous as his name suggested, for taking a standing leap in mid-chorus of his songs. Clooney and Dietrich kept their feet firmly on the ground for their rendi-tion, Dietrich's "familiar Teutonic foghorn"[16] demanding a basement key, but one that suited Clooney too. As well as the main record, Miller had his pairing record a 23-second introduction to the disc. Dietrich caricatured her famous slurred drawl on the word "Hello," before Rosemary joined in, delivering a clever mimic of her partner's greeting.

The single reached #12 in the *Billboard* charts. *Time* magazine called the disc "a bit of hillbilly horseplay" and drew out the contrast between Rose-mary's wholesome image and the "glamorous Grandma Dietrich," a dis-tinction that Rosemary acknowledged. "Yeah," she admitted, "I guess it's a compliment to be called the wholesome type. With what I've got to work with, as a *femme fatale* I'm dead."[17] Despite the differences in age, appearance, and background, Rosemary and Dietrich became even firmer friends on the back of their modest chart success. When Rosemary headed for Hollywood, the German star did everything that she could to pave the way for her, writing to everyone associated with Paramount. As a result, Rosemary later recalled, she got the best of everything. Early in the shooting schedule for *The Stars Are Singing*, the foreman in charge of the scene-shifting gang approached Rosemary one day. "Everything okay?" he asked. The puzzlement was apparent on her face. "I got a letter from the Kraut," he said, "so I just wanted to make sure everything was okay."[18]

Despite Rosemary's "plain Jane" image, her off-stage love life continued to occupy the gossip columnists. As she departed for Hollywood, it was the suggestion of a liaison with the actor Joe Ferrer that attracted the most attention. The two had met on a TV show in New York while Ferrer was promoting the film *Cyrano de Bergerac*. Ferrer had made the role his own, first on Broadway in 1946 and then on film, a role that won him an Academy Award for Best Actor. The two of them were increasingly seen together around the New York party scene, prompting Walter Winchell, in his nationally syndicated column, to predict wedding bells as early as October 1952. The queen of the gossips, Louella Parsons, thought it would take longer but agreed with Winchell that "she [Clooney] will eventually marry Ferrer."[19] Parsons was right, although the path to the altar would be far from smooth.

Joe Ferrer was born into a well-to-do Puerto Rican family in 1912. His education took him to Switzerland and then to Princeton University, where he graduated in 1933. He made his Broadway debut in 1935. By the time he met Rosemary, Ferrer was much in demand, combining acting, directing, and producing on Broadway and in Hollywood and pocketing a quarter of a million dollars a year for the privilege. Fluent in several languages, Ferrer was the embodiment of a man who filled the unforgiving minute with sixty seconds' worth of distance run. "Joe announces seven projects," one Hollywood director once said of him, "and surprises the life out of you by doing six after you've just figured out mathematically that he can't possibly manage four."[20] Off-stage, Ferrer was a witty cosmopolitan, a lover of jazz, show business parties, and the good life. At one time he was taking lessons in tennis, fencing, singing, tap dancing, yoga, and judo all at the same time. He liked to paint, cook, bake a cake, and play piano. Looks were not his strong suit—one magazine said "his ears are uncompromisingly large and set at an angle unfavorable to his head. He has a nose that advances boldly in several directions, in contrast to his chins (he has two) which recede determinedly beneath a large mouth full of prominent but otherwise note-worthy teeth. He has a wide chest that outmatches his narrow shoulders, a long waist and short legs."[21] Despite his physical defects, Ferrer's impact on Rosemary was electric. "A charming man, tremendously talented—and dia-metrically opposite to any man I'd ever met," she said in 1982.[22]

Ferrer's looks certainly did not slow him down when it came to attract-ing the ladies and his reputation as a Lothario was well set by the time he met Rosemary in New York in 1951. His second show business marriage was coming to an end. The first, to actress Uta Hagen, had lasted 10 years before ending in divorce in 1948. Ferrer had immediately remarried, this time to actress and dancer, Phyllis Hill. That union would last five years, although the two had separated long before Ferrer gained the divorce he needed to marry Rosemary in 1953. Despite his charms, Ferrer was not everyone's cup of tea. "Rosemary Clooney has the best chance of becoming a top star of any newcomer to our town," Hedda Hopper wrote. "She has talent and she can put over a song, but the movie public is becoming mighty critical of the stars personal lives, and some people say she can throw it all in the ash can by becoming Mrs. José Ferrer. Many movie-goers in the land don't care for the gent."[23]

The idea that Paramount's new emblem of wholesomeness should be seen stepping out with a married man—even if he was separated—was not something that sat easily with the studio's top brass. Ferrer was filming in Paris when Rosemary finished her first outing for Paramount in the sum-mer of 1952. She planned to fly out to join him, only to be taken aside by Frank Freeman, a Paramount VP. Despite her protestations that the Fer-rers' marriage was over, Freeman handed down a stern warning. "Nobody loves a home-wrecker," he told her. "Have you read your contract?" It was a reference to the ethics clause that all studios used to protect themselves—and their stars—from the adverse publicity that could result from a scandal. And with one of their bright and bouncy female stars, Betty Hutton, having just walked out on them, Paramount did not intend to let her potential replacement press the self-destruct button.

Rosemary's rude awakening as to her moral obligations came at the end of the filming of *The Stars Are Singing*. Despite this being her debut outing, Rosemary shared top billing in a low-key movie that also starred Anna Maria Alberghetti and Lauritz Melchior. The plot concerns a young illegal immigrant, Katri Walenska (played by Alberghetti), whose singing leads to a spot on a TV talent show. She wins first prize, but her success results in her true identity being revealed, and with it, the likelihood of deportation. Rosemary took the part of Terry Brennan, a hopeful pop singer who first identifies Katri's vocal talents and who is instrumental in arranging the TV

opportunity. Despite a less than enthusiastic reception from the critics—
New York Times' Bosley Crowther called it "claptrap of the most reckless
and uninspired sort"—there was enough in Rosemary's performance to
suggest that her future in Hollywood was bright. Her acting seemed confident and assured and her appearance—with more than a hint of similarity
to June Allyson—was wholly consistent with the honest, do-gooder character she portrayed. "She's a pleasant enough young lady," Crowther added,
"a little forced and self-conscious with the charm, and, for those who like
modern balladeering done with vigor and bounce, she's right there."[24] The
score for *The Stars Are Singing* came from the partnership of Jay Livingston
and Ray Evans and included "I Do, I Do, I Do," "Haven't Got a Worry to My
Name," and "Lovely Weather for Ducks." A somewhat contrived opportunity was also created for Rosemary to sing "Come On-a My House" in a
scene where her character, Terry, is railroaded into recording a demo of a
song by an aspiring tunesmith, played on the screen by Ross Bagdasarian,
the actual writer of the song. At the end of her rendition, Terry dismisses
the song, much as Rosemary had originally questioned it with Mitch Miller.
"A peach and a pear and a pomegranate? This isn't for me. It won't sell a
record," says Terry as she walks out.

Paramount saw enough in *The Stars Are Singing* to convince them that
Rosemary could indeed fill the shoes of Betty Hutton. Producer Irving
Asher told the press that the first rushes of the shooting had shown him
that Rosemary could handle more than the bit part that had originally been
written for her. "I realized here was a girl who really comes over on the
screen," he said. "We re-wrote her part and expanded her into one of the
star roles. She can do everything Hutton can," he said, adding, sotto voce,
that she was a good deal cheaper too.[25] After newly installing her in Hutton's old dressing room, Paramount offered its newest star an improved
contract and lined her up alongside Bob Hope, Tony Martin, and Arlene
Dahl, Ferrer's Broadway co-star in *Cyrano de Bergerac*, for her next outing in
Here Come the Girls. The film was little more than the latest Paramount
vehicle for Hope's stock character of a dim, comical coward who never quite
catches on to the villainy coming his way. This time out, Hope played Stanley
Snodgrass, an over-aged chorus boy who is suddenly elevated to the lead
role in a show because the true lead (played by Tony Martin) is being hunted
down by a local mobster. Rosemary's role was that of his neglected girl-
friend, Daisy Crockett, who is also a singer and dancer in the show. Rosemary was fourth in the billing, and the film offered her little opportunity to
do anything other than sing three more Livingston and Evans songs and
moon at Hope, her supposed boyfriend who in fact was old enough to be
her father. When it saw release in time for Christmas 1953, the critics

struggled to find a good word to say. *Variety* suggested, "the laughs come from Hope's inability to do any number right and his colossal conceit in believing he can do no wrong."[26] Bosley Crowther in the *New York Times* was less kind. Saving his only half-positive comment for Rosemary ("a wistful little song-bird"), he described the picture as "a witless and labored film" and one in which Bob Hope "had seldom looked worse."[27] "The whole thing is unfortunate for Miss Clooney," said *Time*. "Every time she opens her mouth to sing, Hope shoves a gag in it."[28] Even Rosemary herself struggled to find something positive to say about it. Years later, when Hope's wife Dolores joined her for some cabaret performances in New York, her regular joke was that the film had been so bad that even Dolores refused to watch it.

Nevertheless, the two months that Rosemary spent filming *Here Come the Girls* would turn out to be two of the most significant of her life. By now, she and Joe Ferrer were living together in Hollywood, although that did nothing to inhibit her attraction to a young dancer who had a minor part in the picture. Dante DiPaolo was two years older than Rosemary and hailed from Colorado, the child of Italian immigrants who had settled there. Dante had danced almost from the day he could walk, and by the age of nine, he had won so many local dance contests that his mother decided a career in Hollywood was his destiny. At age 13, he appeared in a Bing Crosby movie, *The Star Maker*, and by the time he met Rosemary, had built a career in movies and the theater in a succession of support roles. Dante was never the star but always a more than capable member of the chorus or someone who could hold down a semi-featured role. With Dante providing some dancing lessons for Rosemary on the set of *Here Come the Girls*, the two of them, along with rehearsal pianist Ian Bernard and dance coach, Bea Allen, became a "frolicsome foursome."[29] Eventually, the foursome became a twosome and a relationship between Rosemary and Dante developed. Whether either regarded it as ever likely to be a serious one seems unlikely, but with Joe Ferrer away filming *Moulin Rouge* in Paris and seemingly dating other girls, the gossip columnists had a field day reporting the cooling of the Ferrer-Clooney liaison.[30] Nevertheless, Ferrer's hold over Rosemary was such that when he turned up in Hollywood on December 23 for the premiere of *Moulin Rouge*, it was Rosemary who was on his arm. Predictions of a 1953 marriage for the Kentucky belle were strong.

Neither Ferrer nor DiPaolo were present the following month when Rosemary had a premiere of her own to go to. Paramount arranged for *The Stars Are Singing* to open at the Russell Theater, Maysville, on January 28, 1953. With Rosemary having achieved greater fame than any previous Maysvillian, the Town Council arranged for Lower Street to be renamed

"Rosemary Clooney Street." Draped in a $7,000 Aleutian mink coat,[31] Rosemary sat atop the back seat of a red convertible, her Grandma Guilfoyle and childhood friend Blanchie Mae Chambers alongside her. An 11-car motorcade drove through the town to the naming ceremony. Along the route, most of her aunts and uncles, plus her recently divorced—again—mother and half-sister Gail watched from among the crowds. The only missing faces were sister Betty, away working in Detroit, Uncle George who was now Betty's manager, and brother Nick, now a radio announcer in Wilmington, Delaware. Arriving at the movie theater for the premiere, Rosemary was ushered on to the stage but resisted the clamor to sing "Come On-a My House." Instead, she opted for "Moonlight and Roses" in honor of her maternal grandma, and "Home on the Range," the song she had sung for "Papa" Clooney's political gatherings when she was five years old. Six weeks later on March 10, 1953, Nick and Betty joined Rosemary for the New York premiere of the film, presaging its national release the following day. A week later, she and Joe appeared together at the NBC International Theater in New York to watch the Academy Awards ceremonies from Hollywood.

Rosemary crisscrossed the country twice more during the spring of 1953 before settling down in Hollywood for her third Paramount commitment, which went into production on May 4, 1953. *Red Garters* was a spoof western that co-starred Jack Carson, Gene Barry, Guy Mitchell, and Joanne Gilbert. Rosemary took the part of saloon singer Calaveras Kate, a role originally conceived with Betty Hutton in mind. The story centered on Mitchell's character, Reb Randall, a "gallivanting cowpoke"[32] who arrives in the town of Paradise Lost, Limbo County, California, seeking the killer of his brother. From then on however, the film offered a burlesque of the traditional western shoot-out. "In *Red Garters*, the bullets are the musical numbers, the guns are songs and the rest is dancing and romance," said Paramount's advance publicity. The film was certainly ahead of its time, although Paramount was concerned that much of the satire would pass over the heads of '50s audiences, to such an extent that the film's credits opened with a text crawl explicitly stating that the movie was a spoof. Often compared to the more successful *Seven Brides for Seven Brothers*, it would be two generations before cinema critics came to understand the film's underlying surrealism.

Yet another Livingston and Evans score offered up a selection of "mighty purty" numbers. Rosemary, Guy Mitchell, and the rest of the cast worked their way through them but none registered as hit material. "The best that is to be said of them," wrote Bosley Crowther, "is that they're numerous and give the singers a chance to move." Like other contemporary reviewers,

Crowther homed in on the film's cinematic presentation. Its garish use of Technicolor, minimal sets, and artificial décor unashamedly brought the Broadway stage onto the movie set. It was, he wrote, "breezy and bouncy entertainment that seems to be strung on copper wires that are constantly being jingled and twanged like the strings of a guitar. The only trouble . . . is that it lacks a good story and first-class songs."[33] *Red Garters* marked the conclusion of Rosemary's movie-making apprenticeship. Although she had played a performer in all three films, their styles were all quite different. Rosemary had shown herself to be adaptable and confident on the big screen, with an easygoing and likable personality that transmitted well to the audiences. Her next outing would be the long awaited *White Christmas* but Rosemary had shown already that she was ready to move up to Paramount's top table. Before she did, her private life was about to take a definitive turn.

While filming *Red Garters*, Rosemary was still enjoying the company of both Ferrer and DiPaolo, but when Dante landed an archetypal part as Matt, the leader of the town boys in *Seven Brides for Seven Brothers*, the shooting plans took him off on location to Sun Valley, Idaho. His absence allowed Rosemary's love for Joe Ferrer to develop to the point that the only thing that stood in the way of marriage was the refusal by Phyllis Hill, Ferrer's estranged wife, to agree to a divorce. Finally she relented and their divorce came through in Mexico in July 1953. Ferrer was in Dallas, starring in *Kiss Me Kate* at the Dallas State Fair when he got the news. Rosemary was at home in Los Angeles with brother Nick and Dante, who was back from Idaho. Marriage plans were set, although with news of the Ferrers' divorce in the papers, the challenge for Joe and Rosemary was to find a way of getting married as quickly as possible without the event becoming a media circus. Rosemary, on her own admission, took the secrecy a step too far. Leaving for Dallas, she made no mention of her marriage plans to Nick, or more significantly, to Dante. She would not see or speak to him again for over 20 years. "Not my proudest moment," she said in later life.[34]

When Rosemary got to Dallas, she found Ferrer in the midst of a typical whirlwind existence. As well as being committed to eight appearances per week in *Kiss Me Kate*, he was also preparing an English version of the play, *The Dazzling Hour*, which he had translated from the French and was working on with playwright, Ketti Frings. With Texas state law demanding a three-day waiting period before a marriage could take place, there was no prospect of a wedding avoiding the press. Ferrer's solution was for him and Rosemary to get up early and drive 90 miles across the Oklahoma border to the town of Durant. There, on July 13, 1953, Rosemary Clooney became the third Mrs. José Ferrer, an 85-year-old county judge conducting the service. Ferrer was 41, Rosemary 25 years old. The job done, Ferrer was back in Dallas by nightfall and spent his wedding night starring in *Kiss Me Kate* before hosting a cocktail party for Olivia de Havilland. Rosemary could not have cared less. Marriage to Ferrer, she told a magazine a few weeks later, is "the most stimulating thing in the world."[35] The world it seemed was her oyster. Whereas her character, Terry, in the opening scenes to *The Stars Are Singing*, had brushed off an aspiring suitor with the words "I'd rather have my picture on the cover of *Downbeat* than marry you and have a house full of kids," Rosemary was about to discover that, in the real world, both were possible—at a price.

CHAPTER 5

A Home in the Hills

Rosemary's move to the West Coast had brought both a change of scene and a change of style to her recording work. Her first session in Los Angeles since the Pastor days teamed her with trumpet legend Harry James in the Radio Recorders Studios on Santa Monica Boulevard on May 23, 1952. With it, Rosemary clocked up a number of "firsts." It was her first solo Columbia session outside New York, her first "album" session, and the first time that her voice would be heard on a 33-rpm microgroove long-playing (LP) record. LPs were a fast-growing phenomenon in the early 1950s. Columbia had pioneered a recording revolution by introducing them in 1948. For the next two years, Columbia and its major rival, RCA, engaged in a "War of the Speeds," RCA offering a competing 7" microgroove disc that played at 45 rpm.[1] Both of the recording giants had assumed that the standard shellac 78 rpm single was an immovable object and that their 33- and 45-rpm offerings were both vying for one alternative spot alongside the 78. When it quickly became apparent that both of the new formats offered unbreakable and better sounding vinyl discs, it was the crackly 78 that was consigned to oblivion. The first LPs were 10" in diameter, the same as for the 78 so that record dealers could use the existing browsers in their stores. There were some 12" LPs, but initially, these were limited to classical music releases. The early 10" LPs held eight titles, four per side, but developments in groove technology soon extended this capacity to ten. By the mid-'50s, the disappearance of the 78—and with it the 10" browser—removed any remaining barrier to the 12" LP becoming the industry norm.

LPs also brought a new musical concept with them, that of the "album." The notion of an album of songs was not new and had first appeared just after World War II. Still working only with 78-rpm, two-sided discs, record companies had started to offer a spiral-bound "album" of four discs, thus offering an eight-title set. The first albums were basic, to say the least, with plain covers and no obvious linking theme between the songs they contained. Soon, however, singers such as Perry Como took the concept a step further, recording eight titles that were similar in style and content for release in a purpose-made album/booklet.[2] When the LP finally displaced the 78s-in-a-book, the term "album" nevertheless stuck, becoming in due course the "concept album," named to describe a collection of songs linked by a common attribute or theme.

Rosemary's California sessions with Harry James produced an 8-track 10" LP that genuinely fell within the definition of a concept album. Mitch Miller was behind the project and chose as the theme, songs that had won the Academy Award for Best Original Song. The album included the first winner, "The Continental" from 1934, and ran through to the 1951 winner, "In the Cool, Cool, Cool of the Evening." Recorded over two sessions in May, the album offered Rosemary her first real opportunity to record an extended offering of the types of songs that were close to her heart. Harry James was a fading star but the arrangements for the album gave him the opportunity to play some trademark trumpet solos that were a model for sympathetic pairing of instrument and voice. Rosemary sang the songs in an uncomplicated, almost conversational style, and while none of the renditions overtook the original Oscar-winning performances, the result was an album that further enhanced Clooney's standing as a mainstream vocalist. A single from the album, "You'll Never Know" briefly figured in the *Billboard* Disc Jockey chart while the album itself reached #3 in the magazine's fledgling album charts.

Further sessions during 1952 gave Rosemary more opportunities to diversify her recorded output. In June, she teamed up with country singer Gene Autry for two Christmas singles. Autry had developed a particular association with holiday songs through his recordings of "Frosty the Snowman" and "Rudolph the Red-Nosed Reindeer." The latter, a chart-topper at Christmas 1949, was based on a 1939 poem by Robert L. May. May's brother-in-law, Johnny Marks had set the poem to music and sought to repeat the trick with another historic poem, "'Twas the Night Before Christmas," which Autry and Rosemary used as the "A" side of their 1952 single. While not repeating the success of "Rudolph," the Autry-Clooney Christmas collaboration delivered another Top Ten hit. Rosemary followed up with another duet partner with links to the Christmas market. Jimmy Boyd was a 13-year-old boy with his heart set on a country music career when Mitch Miller rocketed him to the top of the 1952 Christmas charts with "I Saw Mommy Kissing Santa Claus." Boyd's country origins shone through in the two duet titles he recorded with Rosemary in January 1953, although neither "Dennis the Menace" or "Little Josey" repeated his success in the charts.

In between the Autry and Boyd sessions, Mitch Miller had experimented with Rosemary in a more overt country setting. In September 1952, he put her on a plane to Nashville, Tennessee, and paired her with the emergent country-crooner, George Morgan. Morgan was one of the hottest country names at the time, having taken over from Eddy Arnold at the Grand Ole Opry in 1948 and then scoring a string of country hits. Although the Morgan-Clooney duets flopped commercially, the session was, artistically at least, an eye-opener for Rosemary. When she turned up at the Castle Studios at Nashville's Tulane Hotel—the first purpose-built recording studio in the country music capital—she found the band still working out the basic arrangements for the four songs she was due to record. Only one of the five members of the band could read music. It was a world away from the high-production style that she had grown accustomed to in New York. Rosemary's voice sat easily with country music and blended well with Morgan's. The session, however, was undermined by the weakness of the four chosen songs. Two were never released, and the single that emerged, "Withered Roses," was neither crossover nor country. Released on Columbia's Country & Western series, it fell quietly between the two stools.

Rosemary's sessions with Dietrich, Autry, Boyd, and Morgan meant that she was developing a reputation as an accomplished duet singer, hardly surprising given the experience of her formative years alongside her sister, Betty. Rosemary's ease with matching her voice to that of another singer set her apart from many singers who found the setting too stifling. In Rosemary's case, however, a duet offered the opportunity to relax and take a few more risks with her vocals than was often the case in her solo offerings—never more so than in her association with her most famous duet partner that began in the summer of 1952. The recording of the radio show with Bing Crosby that had caused her to become all tongue-tied had taken place on May 26 for broadcast on June 11, 1952. The immediate rapport between Crosby and Clooney was apparent from the light-hearted banter between them before Rosemary's rendition of "Tenderly." Crosby's musical director, John Scott Trotter, offered a characteristically unobtrusive backing to Rosemary's note-perfect vocal before she joined forces with the host on "Zing a Little Zong," a song from Crosby's most recent picture for Paramount. Rosemary discovered that she and Crosby sang in the same key, a major plus factor when it came to structuring duets. There was more to their partnership, however, than a mere matching of vocal ranges. "I've recorded with almost every singer in the business," Rosemary said in 1954, "but I never get the feeling that I have when I sing with Bing. It's a strange sort of communion. With other singers, you wonder how they're going to phrase the next line, have to watch their faces for some expression that will let you know. With Bing, I stand across from him in front of the mike and I don't even have to look at the music. I know how he'll handle the next bit of the lyric and I sail right in with him. I don't know how I know. I just know."[3] Rosemary's sentiments were clearly reciprocated. Over the course of the next two radio seasons, 1952–53 and 1953–54, she made 19 guest appearances on Crosby's General Electric radio show.

Guest spots with Crosby were one thing, but 1953 came and went without Rosemary managing to add to the run of chart successes she had enjoyed in the preceding two years. Mitch Miller and the Columbia team tried just about everything to restart the hit stream with no success. There were ballads, children's songs, Christmas songs, four more duets with Dietrich, and harpsichords and French horns, but nothing scored. Miller cut a frustrated figure, spending most of his time in New York while his star songstress was 3,000 miles away. Two years on, he was in no doubt about the reason for Rosemary's drought. "You seen her films?" he told one interviewer. "They stink. Not a hit song in any of them. They don't know what to do with her out there." It wasn't just the material that angered him. "You know why there are no hit songs from her pictures? The disc jockeys cooled on her. When she was working back here, she was always in the studio of some D.J. or other, giving an interview or helping him plug. They knew what she was doing and where she was, so they mentioned her name and spun her discs. Next thing they know, she's in Vegas and she's got a Hollywood contract. Next thing you know, she's married this José Ferrer and suddenly she's with books. She's got culture and she's got him."[4]

Miller's tirade ended on a more positive note with the expectation that Rosemary's role in *White Christmas*—"that's gotta be good"—would enable her to reverse the tide. Rosemary's participation in the long-awaited movie had been written into the contract she had signed with Paramount in 1951, with Crosby's approval ("he had the final say," Rosemary said later).[5] In theory, the last word on the casting lay with producer Robert Emmett Dolan, who conducted a series of interviews for the roles. Crosby's—during a lunch break while he was filming at Paramount in 1951—was a formality. Fred Astaire, Crosby's original song-and-dance partner from *Holiday Inn*, was again the preferred choice for the second male lead. By the time shooting grew near, however, Astaire surprisingly declared himself unavailable.[6] Donald O'Connor, fresh from his knockabout success in *Singin' in the Rain*, was his replacement until a bug, caught from the mule that was his co-star in *Francis the Talking Mule*, ruled him out too. Dolan turned to Danny Kaye as his third choice. Kaye was Hollywood's "Mr. Versatile," a fair singer and dancer, but also a fast-talking, rubber-faced comedian. His presence would bring an element of slapstick to the film that Rosemary, in particular, came to enjoy.

The chopping and changing in the male support role sat uncomfortably with a nervous Irving Berlin, who was almost ever-present on the set during the filming. Berlin had tossed in his own ideas about the casting, touting Ginger Rogers and Debbie Reynolds for the female leads. Dolan finally settled on Rosemary and Vera-Ellen as the junior of the two Haynes sisters (she was actually seven years older than Rosemary). Vera-Ellen was regarded as one of Hollywood's most versatile dancers, but had one weakness for the part. She could not sing. Trudy Stevens, wife of bandleader Dick Stabile (who also had a minor part in the film), dubbed Vera-Ellen's vocals, including the standout "Sisters" duet.[7] Rosemary enjoyed her partnership with Vera-Ellen. "She was the opposite of me," she said later. "Disciplined and very patient with me. If they could have dubbed my dancing, we'd have had a perfect picture."[8]

The script for the film retained the concept of the holiday season inn from the 1942 original but moved its ownership away from Crosby's male lead character to the retired General Waverly, played by Dean Jagger, and focused it just on the Christmas holidays. Crosby and Kaye were ex-army buddies, Bob Wallace and Phil Davis, who had served under the general. Working as a postwar song and dance act, they meet up with the Haynes Sisters at a nightclub in Florida. When Davis persuades Wallace to follow the girls for a Christmas booking in New England, they discover the general running a struggling inn, bereft of seasonal snow and Christmas guests. A hastily relocated Broadway show, an army reunion, and the magical appearance of snow combined to create a feel-good Christmas movie second only to *It's a Wonderful Life* as a seasonal perennial. Despite a script that some reviewers saw as unimaginative, Paramount pulled out all the stops to guarantee the success of the movie—"short of casting John Wayne to play Santa Claus and the Marx Brothers to play the reindeer," *Life* said, "nothing else could have been done."[9] The production budget of $4 million offered the luxury of a six-week pre-shooting rehearsal and enabled Paramount to film the movie in its new high definition VistaVision, a technological development that more than doubled the usual visual intensity of the colors.

For Rosemary, the three months working on *White Christmas* was a period of seventh heaven. "I loved it. I just loved it," she said when she added a commentary to the DVD release on the movie in 2000. Irving Berlin was, she said, "just the perfect songwriter." His score offered her a major duet with Crosby as well as a sultry moment of her own with "Love, You Didn't Do Right by Me," arguably the best song in the picture; the plot required Rosemary to deliver the song as a message of reproach to Crosby's Bob Wallace character, who she wrongly thought was trying to use the old general's predicament as an "angle" to make a fast buck. Her soundtrack vocal, delivered in a nightclub setting, held just the right amount of "edge" in her voice to ensure that Berlin's message of "you done me wrong" came through to maximum effect, something she was unable to recapture when she entered the recording studio for her own album of songs from the picture. Designer Edith Head had clad Rosemary in a shimmering black gown that perfectly captured the mood for the nightclub scene, a contrast to the flowing dresses and feathered fans that Head used elsewhere in the movie to cover up Rosemary's terpsichorean limitations.

Above all, though, it was the experience of working over a prolonged period with Crosby that stood out. Their radio collaborations in the 12 months leading up to the film had cemented their friendship, and when Crosby invited her to join him and his close friends Phil Harris and Don Cherry at his Pro-Am golf clambake in January 1953, it was a sign that she was already part of his inner circle. Others could only watch and marvel at her ability to break through the ice curtain. Danny Kaye, said Rosemary, so wanted to be close to Bing and spent most of his time on the set trying to make him laugh. When he did, in a take of the Wallace and Davis send up of the "Sisters" number, the effect was such that director Michael Curtiz used the outtake in the final cut. That moment, however, was the exception. Kaye's disappointment at his inability to break through was apparent to all. "Bing wasn't close to a lot of people," Rosemary recalled. "Danny wanted to be close to Bing—but it wasn't easy."[10] But Rosemary held a magic ticket. "My fondest memory is being able to deepen and develop my friendship with Bing. That's what came out of the picture that I was left with for the rest of Bing's life. It was very important to me," she said.[11]

Commercially, the film was a massive success. Making more than $12million, it was Paramount's biggest grossing film of 1954. Its opening day take at New York's Radio City Music Hall on October 14, 1954, was $25,000—a one-day record for the theater. The critics' response was more muted. Bosley Crowther for the New York Times said, "the confection is not so tasty as one might suppose. The flavoring is largely in the line-up and not in the output of the cooks. Everyone works hard at the business of singing, dancing and cracking jokes, but stuff they work with is minor. It doesn't have the old inspiration and spark."[12] Variety singled out Rosemary's "Love, You Didn't Do Right by Me" as the "standout song presentation" adding that "Miss Clooney does quite well by the story portions and scores on her own song chores."[13] It was faint praise for a difficult role that Rosemary carried off with confidence and considerable aplomb. With Kaye and Ellen's characters both written as fly-by-nights and Crosby's imperious presence holding center stage, it was Rosemary's Betty Haynes who was called upon to provide the emotional highs and lows of the movie. "The seminal moment in her film career," was brother Nick Clooney's summation of the importance of the film to his sister.[14]

With Rosemary's filming commitment for *White Christmas* coming hard on the heels of her wedding, a honeymoon trip to Europe was postponed until January 1954. Marriage, however, did bring one significant change to Rosemary's daily routine when Joe Ferrer presented her with a new home. The actor had purchased a large, Mediterranean-style house at 1019 North Roxbury Drive from the actress Ginny Simms. It was a surprise for his new bride—Rosemary had not even seen the house before Ferrer had written Simms a cash check for $150,000. The house—and its history—would remain an indelible part of Rosemary's life, and be her main home from then until her death. Dubbed "The Street of the Stars," North Roxbury Drive sat in the heart of Beverly Hills and provided homes to at least two generations of Hollywood aristocracy. Eddie Cantor, Hedy Lamarr, and Jack Haley all lived there, and by the time the newly wed Ferrers arrived, their neighbors included Lucille Ball and Desi Arnaz, Jack Benny, and James Stewart. Subsequent generations included Diane Keaton and Peter Falk. Singer Michael Feinstein recalled the street's durability long after the tinsel had left other parts of town. "When I first visited Los Angeles before moving here, and took the obligatory movie-stars tour, I was struck by the fact that so many of the celebrities they mentioned were deceased," he said. "Except, as it turned out, on Roxbury Drive, because such a collection of celebrities still lived there."[15] Feinstein came to know the street well, and in particular the house next door to Rosemary at 1021. Lyricist Ira Gershwin—for whom Feinstein worked before launching his own career—had lived there since the 1930s. And therein lay the story of one of the ghosts who occupied Rosemary's house next door: 1019 North Roxbury Drive was built in 1928 and first owned by the actor Monte Blue. When Ira Gershwin and his brother George arrived in Hollywood in 1936, the house was available for rent. The two brothers plus Ira's wife Lee moved in. The house quickly became a meeting place for the Gershwins' ex-New York friends such as Harold Arlen and Oscar Levant (who eventually took a house farther down the same road) and their new Hollywood brotherhood that included Fred Astaire and Paulette Goddard. During their 11-month residency, the Gershwins wrote most of their film songs in the house that was to become Rosemary's home. She felt the history throughout her time there. "You know what I feel an architectural connection with?" she told a journalist in 1999, "'A Foggy Day.' I once played a tape of it that I'd done on a television show for Ira and he said he was working in the living room one night, and their piano was in the same place where mine is now, and George came bounding in from a dinner party that he'd left early, dropped his coat and said 'Ira! It can't be "a foggy day in London." It's gotta be 'a foggy day in London *town*!' And now that's with me every time I sing that song: he thought of it in the middle of a dinner party and didn't even stay to finish the dinner."[16]

Tragically, George Gershwin's time at 1019 was marked increasingly by severe headaches. He wrote his final song, "Our Love Is Here to Stay" in what became Rosemary's living room before succumbing to a brain tumor. Ira, unable to face the memories that 1019 contained, bought the house next door when it came on the market shortly after his brother's death. He lived there until his own death in 1983, although to some, the house at 1019 was forever "the Gershwin house." When Fred Astaire arrived for Ira's funeral in 1983, he unconsciously walked straight into what was now Rosemary's home.

Rosemary maintained that the house contained another ghost whose presence predated the Gershwins. Russ Columbo had come to national prominence in 1931 as America's first Italian American crooner. His emergence mirrored the solo debut of Bing Crosby and for a time a battle of the baritones developed, with some seeing Columbo as a serious long-term rival to Crosby[17]. Columbo's looks—he was far more photogenic than Crosby—made him an obvious target for Hollywood, where he moved after signing a contract with Twentieth Century Pictures in 1933. He found 1019 North Roxbury available for rental and made the house his home. Twelve months later, Columbo met his death in a freak shooting incident involving his friend, photographer Lansing Brown. The accident occurred while Columbo was visiting Brown's home at 584 N. Lillian Way,[18] but Rosemary maintained until her death that Columbo had met his end in the den at North Roxbury. The source of the confusion, said Michael Feinstein, was Crosby himself who, despite acting as pallbearer at Columbo's funeral, had transposed the location of his rival's death. Whenever he visited Rosemary's house, Crosby refused to even set foot in the den.[19]

Ghosts or not, 1019 soon became a happy home for Rosemary. As part of the sale, Joe Ferrer had also taken on Ginny Simms's butler, who headed a staff of seven servants that the Ferrers employed. Although not of the scale of some Hollywood mansions, the house boasted a swimming pool and tennis court and all the trappings of a movie star's home. A separate wing provided a home for the servants while the upper floors hosted several bedrooms, bathrooms, drawing rooms, and "a huge room, windows on three sides, that Joe planned to use as his art studio."[20] The main focal point of the house, though, was the enormous sitting room that overlooked the front of the property. Joe made the den his own although as time went by, the house increasingly came to be Rosemary's. With her husband spending much of his time in New York, a routine developed whereby he paid the bills on their New York apartment while Rosemary picked up the tabs for North Roxbury. In the mid-'50s, each partner in the marriage was earning enough for the bills to be nothing more than bookkeeping trivia, but in time, the expense of North Roxbury would be one of many challenges to confront Rosemary.

That, however, was for the future. Rosemary spent her first months in her new home living alone, with Ferrer working on four projects in New York. Her filming commitments on *White Christmas* were at the Paramount lot five miles away and she was happy to head home each afternoon. Shooting started and finished early to allow Crosby to get in a few holes of golf before heading to his Mapleton Drive mansion, less than a mile from Rosemary's. When finally both Rosemary and Joe were free of commitments, the recent-if-not-newlyweds headed to London for their honeymoon. They stopped briefly in New York to allow Ferrer to make his recording debut in two duets with his new wife. Despite limited vocal talent ("He sounds like a bull seal in heat,"[21] Mitch Miller said), Ferrer was more than enthusiastic about pairing up on disc. Johnny Desmond, the ex-band singer, had a record out called "Woman," written by Dick Gleason, who had also written a companion piece called "Man." It was perfect material for a husband and wife team, and Columbia had the disc out within two weeks of the session on December 10, 1953. Desmond's version was the bigger hit but the Ferrer/Clooney collaboration notched up a top 20 spot in January 1954.

The honeymoon lasted almost 10 weeks as the couple took in Great Britain, Ireland, France, and Spain during their time in Europe. It was Rosemary's inaugural trip, but Ferrer had first traveled to England almost 20 years earlier. That, together with his film work in Paris, meant that he was a more than able tour guide. The Ferrers spent several weeks at Claridges, one of London's top hotels. British actor John Mills loaned them a car, John Huston hosted them in Ireland, although inevitably there were some work commitments to fit in. Ferrer's movies meant that he was a well-known face in Britain, and Rosemary's record of "Half as Much" had reached #3 in the emergent British pop charts during 1952. As a country, England had been slow to recover from the ravages of World War II and still lived in a black and white world. Audiences were fascinated by the colorful glamour of American show business. Performers such as Judy Garland, Mickey

Rooney, Dean Martin and Jerry Lewis, and Danny Kaye had all been recent visitors, topping the bill at the London Palladium, which was one of the first sights that Rosemary was keen to see. She and Ferrer watched the 1952 Palladium pantomime, a Christmas tradition in England where major stars played roles in children's fairy stories. They saw comedians Frankie Howerd and Richard Hearne play in *Dick Whittington* before heading in the evening to the Victoria Palace, home of the English Marx Brothers, The Crazy Gang. Rosemary was, she said, "sick with laughter."[22]

Rosemary's work commitments included live appearances on both radio and television. Her British radio debut was in bandleader Cyril Stapleton's *Show Band Show*, where she and Ferrer performed their "Man" and "Woman" duets, repeating the performance on television on *Starlight* on January 13, 1954. Both shows were live and commercial free, the BBC still holding a monopoly on all broadcasting in Britain. Rosemary was struck by the amount of time available for rehearsal. Preparations for *Starlight* began at 1:00 P.M., more than eight hours before the 20-minute live broadcast. While she found the facilities lagging behind what she would expect in an American TV studio, the generous rehearsal time gave Rosemary the opportunity to relax, much more than she was used to before an appearance on American television. In February, Rosemary made her first British gramophone recording, although the venue for the session, Conway Hall in Red Lion Square, was a cavernous, town hall-like building rather than a purpose-built studio. Perhaps feeling the need to fill out the space, British arranger and conductor, Wally Stott gathered the largest orchestra that Rosemary had ever worked with, the string section alone numbering in excess of 50. Rosemary recorded two titles that day, "While We're Young" and "Love Is a Beautiful Stranger" although both were rejected for technical reasons. Back in California, she rerecorded identical versions, using backing tracks laid down by Stott in Conway Hall.

The Ferrers were back in New York in early March 1954 in time for Rosemary to collect the *Look* magazine award for most promising newcomer before flying back to California. Rosemary immediately renewed her radio partnership with Crosby, including a special edition of his General Electric Show to (mistakenly) mark his 50th birthday on May 2.[23] The pairing reprised the Ferrer/Clooney "Man" and "Woman" duets, with Rosemary adding a solo on "You Make Me Feel So Young." Rosemary had recorded the song in New York in December and later in 1954, it was part of Rosemary's second 10" LP concept album. This time, the theme was songs about youth and the eight titles also included its title track, "While We're Young" (using the London backings), "Younger Than Springtime," and covers of two recent *Billboard* hits, "Young at Heart" and "Too Young." "Few singers put as much feeling and warmth into a ballad as Rosemary Clooney," *Billboard* said in its review,[24] although the album would have benefited from one or two more titles taken at a higher tempo to give a change of pace.

Rosemary had put the finishing touches to the album at two May 1954 sessions in Los Angeles with the Paul Weston Orchestra before moving on to other business. One curiosity was a reprise of "Grieving for You," the song that had announced her presence as a solo vocalist five years before. Rosemary's 1954 version remained unreleased until 1960 when it appeared on a compilation album. A comparison between the 1949 and 1954 versions shows just how much ground the young singer had covered in the five years. Although Rosemary's perfections of pitch and diction shone through in both recordings, the 1954 rendition revealed a singer now able to fully exploit the emotions behind the love-lost lyric. Weston's orchestration used a saxophone quartet, and the interplay between Rosemary's vocal and the four saxes anticipates the partnership she would build with Scott Hamilton on her Concord albums in the '80s. Although Rosemary takes no liberties with the melody and offers no improvisation, Rosemary's second "Grieving for You" makes justifiable claim to be her first "jazz" vocal.

Concept albums and emergent jazz vocalizing were fine, but Mitch Miller was still on a mission to get Rosemary back into the hit parade. He achieved his goal twice over with two titles that Rosemary recorded the day after her second "Grieving for You" session. Both the hit singles came with new songs. "Hey There" was the primary ballad from the musical *The Pajama Game*, which opened on Broadway on May 13, 1954. Miller knew that the song would be a hit for someone and had already tried it out on Johnnie Ray before insisting that Rosemary record it. Miller flew into California for the sessions, accompanied by harpsichord-man Stan Freeman. Paul Weston retained the baton, but the strings and syrupy saxes gave way to two keyboards, manned by Freeman and Edwin LeMar (Buddy) Cole, who would become Rosemary's closest musical confidant until his death in 1964. Rosemary's recording of "Hey There," delivered with supreme tenderness in her vocal, was a testament of the talent of Mitch Miller. Behind her voice, Miller used both Freeman and Cole on harpsichords but played pianissimo, in contrast to the raucous way in which Miller had previously had Freeman play. Miller's penchant for over-dubbing also enabled him to replicate the original Broadway presentation of the song, placing Rosemary in conversation with her inner self, playing out the story behind the lyric to vivid effect. The disc hit top spot in the *Billboard* chart in August 1954, staying there for six weeks and spending six months in the charts. Other than "Come On-a My House," no other song attached itself to Rosemary with greater endurance.

For the "B" side, Miller had come across a new country song. Stuart Hamblen, one of radio's first singing cowboys and sometime songwriter, had been on a hunting trip and come across a deserted cabin. Inside lay the body of its last resident. Hamblen wrote "This Ole House" as a serious epitaph to the dead man's last days but the song quickly took on a novelty feel, abetted by the honky-tonk piano and harpsichord partnership that Miller orchestrated for Freeman and Cole. Add the ultra-deep voice of Thurl Ravenscroft—the voice behind Tony the Tiger, the new marketing emblem of Kellogg's Frosted Flakes—into the chorus and the result was a sparkling novelty record that surprised everyone by gaining just as many plays as "Hey There." Eventually, Columbia was forced to split market the two songs and "This Ole House" became the song that displaced "Hey There" at the top of the charts, registering a three-week stay of its own on the summit.

More duets with Ferrer and Dietrich followed during the summer of 1954, plus a nostalgic reunion with sister Betty for an authentic version of the "Sisters" number from *White Christmas*. The duet with Betty prefaced a further set of recordings of songs from the film that became Rosemary's third purpose-made album, released in the autumn of 1954 to tie in with the movie. Ordinarily, a big budget movie of the scale of *White Christmas* would sire a soundtrack album, but with Crosby and Kaye contracted to Decca, Clooney at Columbia, and Vera-Ellen providing lip-syncs only, there was no prospect of the soundtrack recordings being released. Peggy Lee and Trudy Stevens joined Crosby and Kaye on an album that did its best to claim "official" status as the record of the film, while Rosemary's eight-song offering took a similar title but bore none of the Paramount images. Rosemary may have felt ill at ease singing solo versions of songs that she had come nowhere near in the picture—Kaye and Vera-Ellen's "The Best Things Happen While You're Dancing" being the prime example—although her solo rendition of her duet with Crosby ("Count Your Blessings") made the album worthwhile.

Miller also wanted Rosemary to record a non-*White Christmas* song on the final session for the album, one that he had in mind for another assault on the charts. It required her to step out of the snow and schmaltz of the movie and dust off the phony Italian accent once more. Mitch Miller had commissioned Bob Merrill—the man behind several of Guy Mitchell's hits—to write a song that capitalized on the mambo craze that enveloped New York in 1954. "Mambo Italiano" was no closer to genuine mambo than *White Christmas*'s fake icicles were to real snow, but in Miller's hands, it mattered not. It was a tribute to Rosemary's versatility that in the course of a single afternoon she could deliver the tenderness of "Count Your Blessings," commit larceny on "The Best Things Happen While You're Dancing," and then pull off another of Miller's novelty tunes to great effect. "Mambo Italiano" became yet another Top Ten hit for Rosemary, entering the *Billboard* charts in November 1954.

As Christmas 1954 approached, Rosemary Clooney had become one of the biggest stars in American show business. She had successfully mastered the four mediums of television, radio, films, and records. The obvious pun was that everything in the garden of 1019 Roxbury Drive was rosy. Indeed, things were more than rosy; they were positively blooming, none more so than Rosemary herself. When she married Ferrer, Rosemary had been quite public in her pronouncements about wanting a family. "I want six children," she said in September 1953, "three more than Mother and three less than Grandma."[25] The Ferrers wasted little time in making her wish come true. By the time *White Christmas* hit the nation's movie screens, Rosemary was pregnant. Five babies would arrive over the next five years. Her life—and her career—would never be the same again.

CHAPTER 6

Blue Rose

Miguel José Ferrer was born in St. John's Hospital, Santa Monica, on February 7, 1955. Daughter Maria arrived in August 1956; another son, Gabriel came a year later, followed by daughter Monsita in October 1958, and finally a third son, Rafael, in March 1960. All of the children were given names for members of Joe's Puerto Rican family. A sixth pregnancy later in 1960 ended in an early miscarriage. One casualty of Rosemary's near-permanent pregnancies was her film career. "They don't write that many pregnant parts," Rosemary said later.[1] After *White Christmas*, Rosemary appeared in only one more film, a walk-on role in husband Joe's *Deep in My Heart*, a biopic of composer, Sigmund Romberg. There were other opportunities. For a time, Rosemary coveted one of the roles in *On the Waterfront*, and in 1955, she tested for the role of Sergeant Sarah Brown in the film version of *Guys and Dolls*. The role required an actress who could plausibly enact the transition from Salvation Army moralist to the love interest for the character of Sky Masterson, eventually played in the film by Marlon Brando. Frank Loesser, who composed the music for the show turned Rosemary down. "He said that I might look like a virgin, but I didn't sound like one," she said later.[2] Joe Ferrer was keen for Rosemary to do a Broadway show with him and there would be occasional TV movie roles in years to come, but despite her innate talent as an actress, Rosemary's heart was never in a nonmusical career. When asked in 1999 whether she had unfulfilled ambitions as an actress, she was unequivocal. "No," she said. "Acting's tough. I take my work under my hat. I can sing anywhere. All I have to depend on is a musician, myself and the words."[3]

After the birth of Miguel, Rosemary was quickly back to work. Radio was losing ground to television with every week that passed, but early in 1953, she had commenced a twice-weekly, 15-minute radio show for NBC. The shows resumed on February 22, 1955, on Tuesdays and Thursdays. In March, she appeared on *The Woolworth Hour* for CBS, a music and variety show with a guest list that included the George Shearing Quintet, Ann Miller, and Billy Daniels. On TV, she and Joe were the featured guests on Ed Murrow's *Person to Person* show on March 11, and at the end of the month, Rosemary sang the Oscar-nominated "The Man That Got Away" at the 27th Annual Academy Awards ceremony in Hollywood. In April, she was the mystery guest on *What's My Line?*. Rosemary's ruse for concealing her identity from the blindfolded panel was to adopt a cut-glass English accent. The charade lasted for only two questions. The first remark that provoked a laugh from Rosemary revealed the deep-throated guffaw that was so familiar to all who knew her.

Rosemary's busy post-childbirth activity meant that she needed to get back to her usual slim-line self in rapid time. A booking at the Sands Hotel in Las Vegas, at the personal invitation of its co-owner, Frank Sinatra, provided an added impetus. Working with a masseuse "with hands of iron"[4] and an ex-boxer personal trainer, Rosemary found a routine that worked so well that she repeated it after each pregnancy. That she was able to bear five children and maintain her original figure was nothing short of remarkable, especially considering her formidable appetite for food. *Time* magazine in its cover feature of February 1953 had said, "One recent evening she ate, in order of their appearance, an antipasto salad, a heavy Mozzarella cheese appetizer, a heaping plate of lasagna, a chocolate éclair, a dish of sherbet, an after-dinner drink of rum, brandy, chocolate and crème de cacao. Still feeling a little hungry, she then ordered another portion of Mozzarella."[5] Bing Crosby was a regular teaser of Rosemary's eating habits, nicknaming her the "Buffet Bandit of Bourbon County." Paramount was so concerned about her food addiction that they assigned a bodyguard to follow her around the sets and monitor her eating. "It's like being haunted," she said. "He follows me everywhere I go, watches me like a hawk when I eat."[6] But for now at least, Rosemary's coping strategy worked. She would retain her svelte appearance well into her 40s.

There was just time between Rosemary's Sands' debut and an upcoming tour of Great Britain for her to fit in three more recordings sessions for Columbia. They were her first since she had recorded an appropriately titled "Where Will the Dimple Be?" three weeks before the birth of her son. For two back-to-back sessions on June 13/14, 1955, Rosemary traveled to New York. It had been 18 months since she had last recorded in Columbia's studio on 30th Street, a period characterized by a growing estrangement from Mitch Miller. In January 1955, Miller had laid bare his frustration at Rosemary's Hollywood lifestyle in an interview for the *Saturday Evening Post*. It had done little to foster relations between them and made an enemy of Joe Ferrer. The two dates in June would be the last time that Miller would personally lead the orchestra on a Clooney session. The two primary numbers that Miller lined up for Rosemary bore all his usual trademarks. It was hard to believe that phony-accented novelty material could plummet any lower than "Botch-a-Me," but "Sailor Boys Have Talk to Me in English" reached a new depth. Rosemary's performance was spirited and bright, but the material was trite beyond belief. *Billboard* surprisingly, found it "a charming novelty" but any hint of chart success was restricted to an appearance in the Australian charts at #21. The "B" side, a song called "Go on By" by composer of "This Ole House," Stuart Hamblen, actually achieved #10 when flipped in Australia, but not even the reappearance of the harpsichord could bring American or British success.

Rosemary attributed the decline in her relationship with Miller to his loss of control over her life. With her home now in California and the distractions of a growing family, Columbia's A&R chief could no longer snap his fingers and demand that she be in the studio at 9:00 A.M. the next day. In truth, Miller's time as the most successful record producer in the business had already passed. He loathed rock'n'roll almost more than he loathed Joe Ferrer, but there was no question that the arrival of Elvis soon made Mitch Miller's presentations sound like products of a bygone age. Mitch had turned down the opportunity to buy out Presley from Sun Records and similarly rejected Buddy Holly, judgments suggesting that his ability to anticipate the record buyers' next fad had begun to wane. He had one more Guy Mitchell 1956 best seller in him, a 1956 hit with "Singing the Blues," but thereafter, Miller was forced to reinvent himself as the leader of a cozy choral group. "Sing-along with Mitch Miller and his Gang" eventually came to define Miller's popular legacy to such an extent that it was his sing-alongs rather than his groundbreaking productions that dominated his obituaries when he died in 2010.

Rosemary might have found that the gateway into the American charts was closing, but another was opening wide in England. "This Ole House" and "Mambo Italiano" had both topped the British charts in 1954, while "Where Will the Dimple Be?" hit #6 in January 1955. With husband Joe due in England in the summer to film *Cockleshell Heroes*, it made both domestic and business sense to put together a UK tour. The tour opened in Glasgow, Scotland, on July 4, 1955. The Glasgow Empire theater had a fearsome reputation on the British music hall circuit as the graveyard of

English comedians, although American visitors generally received a more sympathetic hearing. The show marked Rosemary's debut on a British stage and was well received by the British music press. Key to endearing herself to the Scots was an ability to make fun of herself. "When I started singing, everyone told me to watch my diction," she told them. "Well, I worked hard to attain the target I had set myself and then my first record came along and it had some really classic pronunciation!"[7] With that, she launched into the song that the audience had been screaming for—"Come On-a My House." The Glasgow audience was nothing if not vociferous, and Rosemary was quick to respond to their requests. It was "Botch-a-Me" and "Mambo Italiano" that they wanted, not "Tenderly."

A week later, she took to the stage of the London Palladium, arguably the most famous theater in the world and described later by Bing Crosby as the "Mecca for all strolling players."[8] As with Glasgow and all music hall theaters, the Palladium followed the "two shows a night" routine that had characterized variety in England since before the war. Shows commenced at 6:15 and 8:45 P.M., the first house aimed at the working man, who often arrived with an empty lunchbox under his arm, before playing to a more refined audience in the second house. Television had not yet killed variety in Britain, and Rosemary topped a bill that included Authors & Swinson ("masters of mime"), the Theda Sisters ("aerialists"), and comedian Leslie Randall ("A Fool among Friends"). Tickets prices ranged from half-a-crown to 14 shillings and sixpence (50 cents to $3.00).[9]

With Buddy Cole at her side, Rosemary was a smash. A xenophobic *New Musical Express* contrasted Rosemary's "tender footsteps" with the recent "invasion of America's virile beef-cake song-punchers," adding that her nurturing of the audience was "an object lesson in the art of developing polite applause into a deafening crescendo." It was a comment that could equally apply to a 1990s Clooney performance. A somewhat sour London *Times* reviewer said that Rosemary was run close by "the Scandinavian Theda Sisters who swing on the trapeze with a perilous and agile gracefulness," adding that the reviewer's own "pangs of disappointment [at Rosemary's performance] were certainly not shared by the warm-hearted audience."[10] In England, a 10" LP *Rosemary Clooney at the London Palladium* appeared, featuring live recordings from the show. (Back home, Columbia substituted unissued studio versions of songs such as "Ebb Tide" and "From This Moment On," with false applause dubbed in. The album came out as simply *Rosemary Clooney—On Stage*.)

Rosemary said that the births of her children were the happiest days of her life. Motherhood sat comfortably with her, and while the staff at 1019 expanded to include a nanny and a governess, the children became an integral part of her daily routine. In 1954, the household expanded when Rosemary's nine-year-old half-sister, Gail, arrived to live with them. After the failure of her second marriage, Rosemary's mother had announced that she planned to go on the road with Rosemary's sister Betty. She intended to put Gail into boarding school. It was Joe who suggested that Gail come and live with them. For Rosemary, it was déjà vu, a reenactment almost of the abandonment that she had suffered firsthand throughout her childhood. Worse was to follow. When Betty married bandleader Pupi Campo, her mother became persona non grata for the newlyweds. Mama doesn't have any place to go, Rosemary said to Joe, realizing almost as the words left her mouth that the statement was untrue. Frances Clooney was still in her 40s and had a family of her own back in Maysville. But Ferrer's solution was that of a man accustomed to having a large family around him. She can live with us, he said.

Rosemary had been the victim of deceit for most of her life, but with the arrival of her mother, she began to fall victim to self-deception. She later said that she had welcomed her mother into her home for a whole set of wrong reasons to do with trying to repair the wounds from her early life. There was self-deception too in her marriage. She loved Ferrer and was fascinated by the rich and varied seams that flowed through his life, but the enchantment came at a price. During their honeymoon in England, Rosemary had overheard Joe talking to a male friend and recounting the details of a recent sexual conquest. When she confronted him about it, there was neither denial nor any promise of reform. Ferrer had simply said that he would arrange for Rosemary to go home. It left Rosemary feeling that if the marriage ended there, almost before it had begun, the fault would be hers. She decided to stay and turn a blind eye, convincing herself that she could change Ferrer and denying the reality that the seeds of destruction in the marriage were already sown. The philandering continued and soon became even less concealed. "Fidelity didn't mean anything to him," she said shortly before Ferrer's death in 1992. "It wasn't important in his life, but it was so important to me."[11] Rosemary, said brother Nick, "was simply shocked to find out how Joe Ferrer expected it to be. She seemed convinced that she could change that."[12] Eventually, Rosemary was forced to acknowledge that she had never felt able to be herself in the marriage. "I don't know what Joe expected of me," she told Dinah Shore in 1989, "but I thought he expected something other than what I was, so I was never really myself with him."[13]

Nevertheless, the early years of Rosemary's marriage to Ferrer were far from unhappy. Both loved Beverly Hills and the Hollywood lifestyle—parties, nightclubs, exclusive restaurants—although for Rosemary, it was the opportunity to just be with her man that was the main thing. The Ferrers were regulars at dinner parties hosted by the Gershwins (Ira and Lee), Cole Porter, and Gary and Rocky Cooper. Bogart and Bacall became good friends, as did Bob and Dolores Hope, and George Burns and Gracie Allen. Rosemary and Joe's own parties were Monday night affairs, picked by Joe as the quietest night of the week, but as a result, one on which nobody could have a reason for saying no. Nat and Maria Cole were regular visitors, Rosemary recalling how Nat would always smoke between courses and then "tippy-toe down to the piano and just play."[14] Composer Ian Bernard recalled that the North Roxbury house seemed like a "madhouse" much of the time, with the constant parties, people coming and going, performing and singing and the whole thing lorded over by Ferrer. "He ruled the roost," said Bernard.[15]

In January 1956, Rosemary signed with NBC for a 39-show season of half-hour TV shows. Because he wanted the shows to emphasize Rosemary's singing, Joe Shribman arranged for them to be filmed using 35mm premium film stock. The technique allowed Rosemary to prerecord her vocals as she would on a Hollywood film set and then lip-sync to them during the filming. It meant that the quality of the sound recordings for the series was comparable to studio-made records.[16] Rosemary's first choice for musical director on the series had been Les Brown, but MCA, who had the contract to produce the shows for NBC, had Nelson Riddle under contract. Riddle had come to national prominence earlier in the 1950s at Capitol Records, and his work with Frank Sinatra and Nat "King" Cole meant that many in the music business regarded him as the music-for-voice arranger par excellence.

The news of Rosemary's television series came nine days after she had announced her second pregnancy. What had originally been planned as a leisurely shooting program now became a race against time. It was one thing for a sitcom star to build a pregnancy into the script, but quite another to have a singer crooning a tender ballad "looking," said one reviewer, "like an ad for maternity duds."[17] As the series progressed, the sets increasingly featured Rosemary behind a large vase of flowers, or standing behind a high fence or stable door. Even so, by the time stars such as Tennessee Ernie Ford and Guy Mitchell arrived to film their guest spots, Rosemary was beginning to cut a matronly figure. Dik Darley and the production team managed to get around 20 of the 39 shows in the can before Rosemary's pregnancy progressed to the point where it could be concealed no longer. The remaining shows were filmed during October and November 1956, after the birth of daughter, Maria.

The shows opened with a silhouette of Rosemary singing a snatch of "Tenderly," which was adopted as the show's theme. The camera then cut to the Hi-Lo's, the four-man close-harmony group who were regulars on the series. Each week, one headline guest was also featured. The list included other singers (Julie London, Buddy Greco), actors (Tony Curtis, Charles Coburn), or singer-songwriters such as Hoagy Carmichael and Johnny Mercer. The shows were basic, low-budget affairs (although the primary sponsor was Foremost Dairies, then the third largest dairy company in the world) with simple sets and minimalist scripts. The shows were syndicated to various regional stations across the country with no standard running order. Some of the shows that Rosemary had recorded after the birth of her daughter actually went out ahead of ones in which she was pregnant.

Most stations used one particular show as the opener for the series, however. In it, Rosemary joined husband Joe in a vaudeville-style song-and-dance partnership built around Sammy Cahn and Jimmy Van Heusen's "Love and Marriage." Joe, wearing a hairpiece beneath a trilby hat, was in his element, delivering what one reviewer called his "pleasant interruption."[18] Generally, the reviews of the show were good. Praise came for Rosemary's resistance to the temptation to turn herself into a comedienne or a dancer, and doing just what she did best—sing. Occasionally, the show ventured into more ambitious territory, as when Boris Karloff guested, delivering a caricature of his famous scary movie roles. In a spoof of *Little Red Riding Hood*, Rosemary sang "I Can't Escape from You" before joining the actor in a light-hearted duet. The show featured prominently in *Billboard's* "TV Program & Talent Awards" for the 1956–57 season, winning the "Best Half Hour Music Show" award in the Syndicated Film category, while Rosemary also topped the poll for "Best Musical Show Performer."[19]

The shows made no attempt to compete with the broader variety format that the top music shows on TV offered, most notably those fronted by Perry Como and Dinah Shore. Essentially, Rosemary's half-hour each week was all about music, and there was no question that what stood out most was the quality of her vocals, framed by the immaculate work of Nelson Riddle. "He was the first arranger who really looked at the words to a song and asked what they meant to me," Rosemary said to Terry Gross, host of NPR's *Fresh Air* in 1997. "He understood my feelings about what I was trying to say, or sing and he would advance that."[20] While Rosemary's "trademark" songs such as "Come On-a My House" and "Mambo Italiano" had to be accommodated in the series, the shows were best remembered for her presentation of many classic standards. "Moonlight in Vermont" was one of several featured songs that Rosemary never recorded commercially, her TV version displaying a wonderful reading built on a delightfully sympathetic Riddle arrangement. Rosemary did record most of the songs used on the shows at some time, although many had to wait until her jazz years with Concord, which would include an album dedicated to Riddle.

The relationship between Rosemary and Nelson Riddle eventually moved beyond the TV studio although precisely when is a matter of some conjecture. In both of her autobiographies, Rosemary indicates that while there was a "friendship" between the two of them for several years, their affair did not begin until her marriage to Ferrer was over, "at least, emotionally." In *This for Remembrance*, Riddle is not mentioned by name, reference only made to an anonymous "lover," but with *Girl Singer* appearing after his death, Rosemary could be more open. She stuck to the story, however, that the affair only began early in the 1960s. Riddle's biographer, Peter Levinson, offered a different account. The affair, he wrote, began as early as 1957 and lasted for six years. It was "the most intense relationship of their lives, next to their marriages."[21] Will Friedwald, in his study of Sinatra's relationship with Riddle, quotes Riddle's son, Christopher, as saying that his father "had a penchant for being swept off his feet by young lady singers," before adding that the liaison with Rosemary was the exception. It was, he said, "a full-fledged affair that lasted six or seven years."[22]

Whatever the length and depth of the relationship, there were complications that would ultimately drive it onto the rocks. Both were married to other partners and Riddle's wife Doreen was in a delicate mental state following the death of their six-month-old daughter, Lenora, in 1958. Both of their families continued to grow while the affair flourished—the Riddle's sixth child was born in 1962, around the time that Rosemary was locked into her first set of divorce proceedings with Ferrer. For Rosemary, the apparent ending of her relationship with the father of her five children brought matters to a head. When she and Riddle shared their birthday celebrations in the spring of 1962,[23] Rosemary told him that they could not carry on as they had for much longer. Her hope and expectation had been that Riddle would finally divorce Doreen, who by now knew about the affair and was on the point of a full-scale breakdown. Riddle, bothered more by the financial impact of a divorce, said nothing. He later confided in singer Sue Raney that it had taken four days sitting alone in his office before he could get over his decision to end the relationship with Rosemary. "It was the hardest thing I ever did in my whole life," he said.[24] Eventually, Riddle and his wife divorced in 1970. By then, Rosemary had become a different person.

Riddle's Capitol Records contract prevented him from openly extending his working relationship with Rosemary to the recording studio until she severed her ties with Columbia in 1958, although he nevertheless arranged six singles for her during 1956–57, working under the pseudonym of Joe Seymour.[25] When the TV series also spawned a spinoff album, Riddle also provided three more anonymous arrangements. The album's title was *Ring*

Around Rosie and was a two-thirds/one-third affair. Rosemary had four solo tracks, as did the Hi-Los, with the remaining four tracks featuring them together. With a degree of disappointment designed in for fans of one or the other, the album came up short of what a 12-track presentation of Rosemary and the Hi-Lo's might have offered. Rosemary's best solo vocal, couched in an arrangement that bore Riddle's hallmark, came on "I'm in the Mood for Love," while "How About You," sung by Rosemary in a highly seductive voice, was probably the best collaboration.

The end of Rosemary's Mitch Miller era at Columbia had been more strongly signaled by two other albums that preceded the TV spinout. The albums aligned Rosemary with two legends of jazz, Benny Goodman and Duke Ellington. The Goodman album was issued as part of Columbia's new "House Party" series of budget priced 10" LPs. These retailed at $1.98 and offered six tracks. Three of the six tracks featured vocals by Rosemary, recorded in New York in November 1955, with the remaining tracks featuring Goodman's sextet. Working with Goodman for the first time, Rosemary approached the project with a mixture of enthusiasm and trepidation. Goodman's status as a jazz icon was the draw, but his reputation as an eccentric martinet was widely known. In the end they got along fine, although their collaboration was not without its moments. The first run-through of Rosemary's songs took place at the Ferrer apartment in New York and coincided with her New York nanny's day off. Baby Miguel was in the playpen when Goodman started running up and down the scales on his clarinet, producing shrieks from the 10-month-old infant at hearing such an unfamiliar sound. When Goodman took it as criticism of his playing, Rosemary laughed at the joke and then realized that he was serious! Her three songs were all Goodman standards. "Goodbye" featured Rosemary and the Goodman sextet; "Memories of You" featured just a trio comprising Goodman, Dick Hyman on piano, and Bobby Donaldson on drums, while "It's Bad for Me" was sextet plus a vocal contribution from Goodman at the mike with Rosemary. "He couldn't sing, but he did it with great enthusiasm," Rosemary recalled.[26] Other reviewers were less diplomatic. "Goodman has a great voice for cooling soup," the *Saturday Review* said.[27] Rosemary's intimate singing—she adopted the hushed intimate style first evident in "Grieving for You"—sat easily with the music, however. All three arrangements were cast in the style of 1930s vocal refrains, each giving Goodman's clarinet an equal share of microphone time. The album was an appropriate celebration, both of Goodman's 25th anniversary of his first Columbia record in 1931 and of Rosemary's first genuine outing as a jazz singer.

Compared to the work Rosemary did with Duke Ellington three months later, the Goodman session was, however, no more than a footnote to her career. In contrast, *Blue Rose* was one of its defining moments. Examined out of context, the album might appear to be an instance of an up-and-coming singer riding the coattails of a jazz legend and in so doing, catapulting herself into a new dimension for her career. But at the time, it was Rosemary—not Ellington—who was the draw. While she was still riding the crest of her singles wave, Ellington was becalmed. His earlier recording contract with Columbia had expired in 1952, in part because Mitch Miller, who controlled the singles output, was reluctant to give precious singles slots to jazz artists. Moving to Capitol, Ellington released "Satin Doll" as a single. Its success briefly seemed to support his case, although it turned out to be his last single release of any note. By the time of his last session under his Capitol contract in January 1956, Ellington was a ship without a sail.

Back at Columbia, George Avakian, head of its Popular Music Division, had not given up on Ellington. Avakian had played a major role in bringing jazz to the label and in exposing the genre to the new technology of the LP. In particular, he had challenged the notion that the 12" long-player should be limited to classical releases, seeing the potential for jazz artists to exploit the longer-running tracks that it could accommodate. Ellington was foremost in his sights, although the route back was a surprise. When Avakian put together a series of LP reissues featuring the work of Bessie Smith from the '20s, Rosemary approached him and said she would like to do some of the repertoire in an album. "I told her that the incompatibility between the material and her image and voice was too great, whereupon she asked me if Duke would be prepared to do an album with her," Avakian said.[28] To his surprise, Ellington agreed. "I think he appreciated the purity of Rosie's voice. But he never showed an interest in such a project before. I had once proposed an LP with Sarah Vaughan, which he shrugged off politely. 'Too busy,'" Avakian said.[29] Ellington indeed had never cut an album with any singer not drawn from the ranks of his own band, although there had been individual sides with artists such as Crosby and the Mills Brothers. In the future, other than Rosemary, only Ella Fitzgerald and Frank Sinatra would have the opportunity to record a full album with him.

With the deal done, there was, it seemed, no time to waste in getting the project under way. Avakian enlisted the help of a new producer, Irving Townsend, and the two of them met with Ellington at his Café Society opening in New York on January 12, 1956.[30] They agreed that the task of arranging the album should sit with Billy Strayhorn, who had arranged many of the Ellington band's vocals since joining in 1939. "The thing about that album that got me was everything was in a hurry," Strayhorn said later. "Duke called me one Friday morning at six o'clock. Told me I had a reservation on a plane for California Monday. I didn't find out until I saw him that night that we were going to do this album with Rosemary Clooney."[31] The reason for the trip to California was Rosemary's second pregnancy. Suffering from what she later called "terminal morning sickness," she was in no condition to travel to New York, where the Ellington band was committed through the early months of the year. Years later, neither Avakian nor any of the other parties involved could recall why the project couldn't wait for Rosemary to give birth or the band to turn up on the West Coast. Instead, Avakian came up with a solution that was both novel and technically challenging. Ellington and the band would record the orchestral tracks in New York. Townsend would then take the tapes to Los Angeles where Rosemary would add her vocals. The technique of "overdubbing" had become possible with the advent of recording tape after World War II, but so far it had only been used to correct mistakes or to accommodate gimmicks such as Mitch Miller's fetish for multitrack vocals. No one before had attempted to score a complete album in that way.

To do it in a jazz setting—arguably the "livest" and most intuitive musical form and normally dependent on the mood and feel of the performers—would probably have been a step too far but for the skill of Strayhorn. Once in California, he spent 10 days with Rosemary in the house on Roxbury Drive. Initially, the two of them worked on the piano in her living room but as her sickness worsened, she spent increasing amounts of time in bed. Strayhorn would sit with her and the two talked endlessly about the album. Finally, Strayhorn had enough knowledge to enable him to return to New York, set the keys, and finalize the arrangements. He scored 13 items for the album, 12 vocals and one orchestral piece. The material he chose encompassed many Ellington standards as well as three lesser-known Ellington-Strayhorn collaborations, "Grievin" and "I'm Checkin' Out—Goombye" (both from 1939) and "If You Were in My Place" (1938). With Ellington himself at the piano, the band recorded the backing tracks in two New York sessions on January 23 and 27, 1956. Strayhorn's work was immaculate. "I didn't know what to expect, picking up one more version of 'Sophisticated Lady,'" said trumpeter, Clark Terry. "Then I played it, and I told Strayhorn, 'that chart we just played, man, that arrangement of 'Sophisticated Lady,' that is really the most fantastic chart I have heard in a long time.'"[32]

With the recordings done, Strayhorn and Townsend returned to California where Rosemary was well enough to add her vocals during two sessions on February 8 and 11. Strayhorn's role as a bridge between two shores was not yet complete, however. The only new song among the 13 was one that Ellington had written especially, which gave the album its name. "Blue Rose" was unusual in that it was a piece written for voice, but without

The young Rose Marie Clooney, Maysville, early 1930s. (Photo courtesy of the Kathy Brown Collection)

The three Clooney children: Rosemary (back) stands behind brother Nick and sister Betty. (Photo courtesy of the Kathy Brown Collection)

The Tony Pastor band in 1947. Rosemary is in the center next to Tony Pastor (dark suit). Betty Clooney is front, second right. (Photo courtesy of Henry Riggs)

The Clooney Sisters, late 1940s. (Photo courtesy Paul Barouh)

Rosemary in the recording studio, early 1950s.

An early 1950s publicity photo. (Photo courtesy of Mavis Coleman)

Guy Mitchell and Rosemary in *Red Garters*. (Photo courtesy of Greg Van Beek)

Rosemary performing "Come On-a My House" in *The Stars Are Singing*.

Rosemary and José Ferrer, late 1950s. (Photo courtesy of Greg Van Beek)

The "Count Your Blessings" scene with Bing Crosby in *White Christmas*.

With (left to right), Miguel, Gabriel, and Maria Ferrer, c. 1959. (Photo courtesy of Mavis Coleman)

A pregnant Rosemary with Buddy Cole in Las Vegas, late 1950s. (Photo courtesy of Greg Van Beek)

In her warm coat as she arrives in New York, December 20, 1956 (Photo courtesy of Paul Barouh)

Boris Karloff on Rosemary's Lux Show.

Rosemary plays baseball with a team of sea lions and porpoises in Marineland Circus, April, 1962. (Photo courtesy of Paul Barouh)

Rosemary rehearses with Perry Como for an appearance on his show in November 1960.

words, requiring Rosemary to hum and lightly scat along to Ellington's melody. Such a style was new to her. Strayhorn's direction was critical. "'Blue Rose' is not really a performance piece for you," he told her. "You are in your room and you are getting ready for a really sensational date. Duke's band is on the radio on your dressing table. As you're brushing your hair, you're singing along with it. That's the attitude I want."[33] Rosemary's humming was "superlative," jazz critic, Will Friedwald, wrote later. "Even without words, Clooney is a better storyteller than most singers who have the benefit of lyrics."[34] On "I'm Checkin' Out—Goombye," Strayhorn told her not to sing it angry. Just because you're leaving the other person, it doesn't mean you're mad," he said. "You're in charge. You might come back!"[35] Strayhorn's direction, Friedwald wrote, was the key factor in enabling Rosemary to capture the perfect mood throughout the album; defiant but not hostile on "I'm Checkin' Out"; grieving but not suicidal on "Grievin'"; jubilant but not hysterical on "Hey Baby."[36] Friedwald's fellow New York critic, Gary Giddins, said that her version of "Grievin'" was "matchless." "Sophisticated Lady," he wrote, was "one of the finest versions on record. Clooney's mastery of tempo gives her the latitude to try any kind of song, but it is through the affective gravity of her voice that she makes them her own."[37] Rosemary herself had no doubt where the credit rested for the album. "It was a work I will never forget," she said in 1997. "The relationship with Billy was the closest association I ever had with any producer."[38]

The album appeared in the shops with a cover that mirrored its production. A smoke-filled image of Ellington, in black and white, sits in the background behind a colorful image of a red-sweatered, red-lipped Rosemary. The separation inherent in the design made sure that America's mid-'50s convention of physical separation between a black man and a white woman was maintained.[39] There were suggestions too that the cover had been designed with a different album title in mind. *Intercontinental* would have emphasized the separation inherent in the way the album had been recorded, although in later years, George Avakian had no recollection of the alternative being given serious consideration.[40] The duration of the individual tracks meant that even the greater capacity of the 12" microgroove format could only accommodate 11 tracks, 10 Clooney vocals and the one Ellington instrumental. Rosemary's two missing vocals, "If You Were in My Place" and "Sittin' and A-Rockin'" appeared on a 45-rpm extended play release before the complete album finally came out on compact disc in 1999.

Mid-'50s sales of *Blue Rose* were unspectacular but its importance in the careers of both its protagonists cannot be overstated. For Ellington, it took him back to Columbia and opened the door for *Ellington at Newport '56*, which became the best-selling album of his career and launched a resurgence that sustained him until his death in 1974. For Rosemary, it convinced the girl singer from Maysville that she was more than just a chirruping hit-maker. The experience of working with Ellington, she said, "validated me as an American singer. My work would not fade with my generation. I had now moved into a very exclusive group."[41]

CHAPTER 7

Fancy Meeting You Here

After the birth of her second child in August 1956, Rosemary's first priority was to complete the remaining episodes of the TV show that her pregnancy had forced her to shelve. Shooting resumed on October 1, with Rosemary often working a full eight-hour day. "It takes a lot out of you," she told a local reporter, adding that at the end of the first week, it was dispiriting to realize that "we've still got 11 to go."[1] By mid-November however, the rest of the series was safely in the can and Rosemary was free once more to throw herself into other things.

As early as May 1956, *Billboard* had carried a speculative report that Rosemary was on the point of signing a record deal with Capitol Records. Such a move would have cleared the way for a legitimate, on-disc partnership with Nelson Riddle, but even though the breakdown in her relationship with Mitch Miller was an open secret, she continued to record for Columbia until early into 1958. Aside from the TV spinoff album with the Hi-Lo's though, it was a period lacking in shape and direction. There were no other albums, although Columbia issued another dozen or so singles featuring Rosemary during this period. These included songs from Broadway shows such as *My Fair Lady* and *West Side Story*, and a spirited "Pet Me Poppa" from the film of *Guys and Dolls* that paired her with an emergent Ray Conniff. Rosemary also returned to country vein for "Nobody's Darlin' but Mine" and another collaboration with Gene Autry on "You Are My Sunshine." There was, however, only one single that made any chart impact. That came with a song called "Mangos," from a November 1956 session, led by former Les Brown arranger Frank Comstock. The strongly Latin-flavored disc reached #10 in the *Billboard* disc jockey chart in April 1957 (#23 in the best-seller chart) but represented an unwelcome bookend in Rosemary's recording career. "Mangos" would be the last disc bearing the name of Rosemary Clooney that would appear in an American singles chart. Nevertheless, Columbia briefly had their hopes raised that her hit-making days could be recaptured and rush released a two-sider that harked back to her halcyon days. Neither of the two sides, "Sing, Little Birdie"[2] and a Calypso-style accented "Who Dot Mon, Mom" scored, and the disc effectively brought the curtain down, both on her Columbia career and her days as a hit parade singer.

By the spring of 1957, Rosemary was pregnant again and once more looking at a period of enforced absence from the stage and screen. There was just time before her pregnancy began to show to fit in a guest spot on the *Steve Allen Show* in New York, en route to England to join Ferrer who was filming *I Accuse!* Arriving in England during April, she immediately topped the bill on *Sunday Night at the London Palladium*, the hit show from the new British commercial television channel. Some radio work for the BBC followed plus a fleeting visit to Holland on April 25 for an appearance on Dutch radio in a program called *Showboat*. The appearance of a major Hollywood star was big news in Holland. Newsreel pictures of her arrival, with three year-old Miguel in her arms, appeared in cinemas all over the country and made the front page of the national papers.

Gabriel Vicente Ferrer was born two months prematurely on August 1, 1957. Initially there was concern for the infant but his condition soon stabilized and by the following month, Rosemary was back at work again. With improved timing, NBC had announced one week before Gabriel's birth that Rosemary would star in a live, half-hour television show on Thursdays from 10:00 to 10:30 P.M. The first show aired on September 26, 1957, from the NBC studios in Los Angeles. "Welcome to 'The Lux Show'" said Rosemary, in what became her standard opening line, "on behalf of Lux Soap, Lux Liquid and Rinso Blue." The shows essentially followed the format of the previous series, but the bigger name sponsor brought more money, more polish, and a higher-caliber guest list. Dik Darley continued as director, Frank de Vol picked up the orchestral baton in place of Nelson Riddle, while the ex-Glenn Miller singing group, the Modernaires, replaced the Hi-Lo's. The first show featured Tennessee Ernie Ford and Jane Wyman among the guests and was an immediate success. "Miss Clooney has come a long way, leaving a number of her fellow vocalists far behind in the personality derby," wrote Bob Bernstein in *Billboard*. "This girl can really carry a show of her own, especially with the informal air and good scripters she's been given."[3] *Time* magazine concurred. "Of all the new musicals, the best was the simplest," it said. "Whether delivering barrelhouse or blues, songstress Clooney's voice has a distinctive cello quality that makes her refreshingly different from the sound-alike mass."[4] Upcoming guests included actors William Bendix and Charles Laughton (who joined Rosemary in a medley of Al Jolson songs), plus Broadway star Carol Channing. Rosemary was indeed a natural TV host, retaining her pleasant but not over-glamorous appearance and delivering her dialogue in a relaxed manner, noticeably more slowly than the "rat-a-tat-tat" style that characterized both her live cabaret and off-stage speaking voice.

Rosemary was three weeks into the Lux run when she took time out to appear on one of the most widely promoted shows of the television season. It was for a product that would turn out to be one of the biggest all-time flops. The Ford Edsel, named after one of Henry Ford's sons, was intended to be Ford's masterstroke for 1958, an all-new car that would take America by storm. When it appeared, it did anything but. With a cumbersome looking grill and stereotyped rear fins, the product failed to live up to the pre-launch hype and proved to be one of the most spectacular flops of the 1950s. A major part of the 1957 launch, however, was a live, one-hour television show hosted by Bing Crosby with a stellar guest list that included Frank Sinatra, Louis Armstrong, and Rosemary. Crosby, Sinatra, and Armstrong had all appeared together the previous year in the hit movie *High Society* and Rosemary's inclusion on the guest list reflected not only her closeness to Crosby but also her by now established position in the upper echelons of show business.

Unlike the car that it promoted, the show was a massive hit. It gained the *Look* magazine award for "Best Musical Show, 1957" and earned an Emmy nomination for "Best Single Program of the Year." Broadcast live, the show, however, did not go without incident. On the set, Crosby was a hard taskmaster when it came to the basic disciplines of performing. Always first to arrive, and word perfect, Crosby expected any guest on one of his shows to meet the same standards. Frank Sinatra had a martinet side to him too, although that came out more in his work in the recording studio than on a live performance. On stage or television, his roguish streak made him inclined at times to just wing it. Crosby's relationship with Sinatra was cordial, publicly at least, but in private, Sinatra's lack of discipline appalled him. Rosemary later recalled how a fretting Crosby whispered to her during rehearsals that Sinatra was "gonna blow it." His prediction seemed right when Sinatra and the orchestra fell over themselves on "Blues in the Night" until Sinatra righted himself with a piece of vocal dexterity that neither Crosby nor Rosemary saw coming. "Bing and I just looked at one another," she later wrote. "The Voice could get away with anything."[5] It was a skill that the Ford Motor Company would have liked to emulate. All the cast were given Edsel cars to use during rehearsals. Only Crosby and Clooney took up the offer. Rosemary later said that the only Edsels she ever saw were the ones they gave her to drive. Coming out of the CBS building, her purple Ford awaited her, looking, she said, "like the *Normandie* in dry dock."[6] When Rosemary grabbed the door handle to get into the car, it came off in her hand. Henry Ford Jr. had followed her out of the building and was right behind. "I turned to him, holding the handle out," Rosemary said. "Mr. Ford. About your car . . ."[7] Ford's response was to make his own black Edsel available to Rosemary, but the incident was a harbinger for Ford's flagship car. By 1960, the car was history, costing the Ford Motor Company millions of dollars and making the name Edsel synonymous with failure.

Working on the show had meant a break in Rosemary's usual schedule. The routine of her own show meant rehearsals Monday to Thursday followed by the live broadcast. After the show, Rosemary would fly overnight to New York to spend the weekend with Ferrer, who was in New York most of the time preparing for his role in *Oh Captain*. She would return to the West Coast on Sundays, before starting the routine all over again the following morning. It was a physically demanding lifestyle, which compounded the emotional highs and lows of a young family and a marriage that was also becoming high maintenance. "Joe was supportive of my work, but I think he was also envious," she said many years later. "He constantly took singing lessons because he marveled at the ease with which I sang, and he wanted to be able to do the same thing. I gradually realized that one of my functions was to be a kind of once removed audience for him. . . . He was moved more by performances than by life itself. He could cry when an emotion was produced on-stage but not in actual life."[8]

Other guests on Rosemary's weekly show during the fall of 1957 included Boris Karloff, who reprised his horror spoofing that had gone down so well in Rosemary's previous series. This time, Karloff sang "You Do Something to Me," before Rosemary joined in the mood with "Bewitched, Bothered and Bewildered." The November 28 show was a family affair, with Betty, brother Nick, and kid sister Gail joining José Ferrer among the guests, the songs including the inevitable "Sisters" and "You're in Kentucky Sure as You're Born." Through Christmas and into 1958, the shows continued week in, week out. Reviews were generally favorable although by the spring of 1958, one local journalist at least was spreading rumors that Lux planned to drop the show after the current season. *The San Mateo Times* was a small paper but its staff included Bob Foster, who since 1948 had been one of the first television correspondents in the Bay Area. Foster was well connected and spent most of his days wandering around the West Coast television studios looking for gossip. Ultimately, his predictions of

Rosemary's TV demise turned out to be right but for the wrong reason. "I checked a bit further and found that the sponsor had actually decided to drop the show last January [1958]," he wrote, "but suddenly the show perked up; the ratings climbed and the response grew, so the sponsor decided to hold off and reconsider."[9] When they did review the show's status during the summer, the decision was made for them. Rosemary was pregnant again and with the baby not expected until October, she would be in no position to start a new season.

From January to June 1958, the weekly show continued to dominate Rosemary's life almost to the exclusion of any other work. In January, she completed what was to be her final recording session for Columbia before her contract expired in March. Frank de Vol conducted on three songs. Two of them came from the familiar pens of Jay Livingston and Ray Evans, "Surprise" and "You Don't Know Him." These constituted Rosemary's final single release for Columbia. A further session in February, also with de Vol, saw Rosemary record "What Is a Baby," a promotional title for Gerber Baby Foods, and "I Wonder," a track that eventually saw release on the MGM label. Indeed, MGM Records turned out to be Rosemary's next port of call as a recording artist as she moved into a two-year spell of freelancing. As well as MGM, she would also record for Coral and RCA Victor.

The first new project for MGM Records positioned Rosemary once more as the foil for her husband's vocal ambitions. Over the four days of March 14–17, 1958, the two of them recorded the full score of Oh Captain, all the songs written by the Livingston and Evans partnership. An attractive cover, showing the two of them in naval caps, concealed the increasing stress within the marriage, as indeed did their vocal performance. "The score of Broadway's Oh Captain provides a delightful romp for the noted husband-and-wife duo, and a fine debut for Miss Clooney on the MGM label," said Billboard. "Ferrer sings with charm and persuasiveness . . . and a smooth-voiced Rosie is a treat to the ears in 'Morning Music of Montmartre.'"[10] Ferrer was the guest again when the curtain finally fell on Rosemary's Lux show on June 19. The end of the grueling weekly schedule was no reason however for a spell of relaxation, despite Rosemary being in the sixth month of her pregnancy. With babies and nannies in tow, the Ferrers traveled by train, straight from the final TV broadcast, to San Francisco and then onto Reno, where Rosemary had a nine-day booking at the Riverside. From Reno, the troupe headed to Vegas where Rosemary played two shows a night for two weeks at the Sands. Variety welcomed her back to the Strip after an absence of almost three years. "She appears onstage in a tent dress, explaining that she's not doing it to follow the current styles, but simply because she's pregnant," the magazine said.[11]

Pianist and arranger Buddy Cole was central to these engagements and increasingly was becoming the preeminent musical support for Rosemary. Cole was in many ways the antithesis of Nelson Riddle, Percy Faith, and the other "big orchestra" arrangers whom Rosemary had worked with. At heart, Cole was a keyboard player—piano, celeste, and his real love, the pipe organ. He had started out playing piano in a cinema accompanying silent films, working his way up the ladder to become a cinema organist. Eventually, Cole would install a three-manual, 27-rank pipe organ in a specially constructed home studio. The demise of silent movies was career ending for cinema organists and Cole moved into the dance band arena with Frankie Trumbauer and Alvino Rey before joining the John Scott Trotter orchestra in 1947. Trotter had been Bing Crosby's musical director since the mid-'30s and it was as the pianist in Trotter's band that Cole came to know Bing, and ultimately, Rosemary. At heart, Crosby was still a jazz singer and felt most comfortable working with a small group of musicians with whom he could improvise. When Crosby moved on from his long association with Trotter, Cole was the man he turned to sustain him through his transition out of network radio and into mainstream television. And what was good enough for Bing worked for Rosemary too.

"Buddy was an interesting pianist," Rosemary told jazz critic Gary Giddins. "I don't think he was one of the best ones that worked with either one of us, but he could do the small group things and he was good about going to Bing's house to rehearse and to my house. And he was funny. Bing got along with him too. He liked him, fine, so it was just kind of a personal comfort thing."[12] Cole was at the heart of a 1957–58 season radio show for Ford (*The Ford Road Show*) that featured Rosemary and Bing, albeit on alternate days. Commencing in September 1957, the five-minute shows ran daily Monday to Saturday and twice on Sundays. Each show featured Rosemary or Bing, with announcer Ken Carpenter. All the songs—no more than one or two short renditions per show—were prerecorded, backed by Cole and a three-man rhythm section. The informality suited everyone. Cole explained in 1962 that many of the arrangements he used were undocumented. "We do maybe 4, 6, 8, 10—I've done as many as 20 songs in a day with Bing. A lot of these were head arrangements, not written." Cole also traded on the interchangeability between Bing and Rosemary. He recorded each of them doing solos on songs such as "You're in Kentucky Sure as You're Born" and Ellington's "Do Nothin' 'Till You Hear from Me," using the identical arrangement and tempo for both singers, a reflection not only of the compatibility of their voices but also the fact that they both possessed an uncanny musical ear. Like Mitch Miller, Cole was also keen on adding effects to the recording once he had the basic track captured. "We play these things back through a speaker or on a headset and then set about adding instruments and other sounds, electric guitar, organ, kettle drums, shot guns, chimes, whatever you want to add," he said.[13]

The shows ran through to August 31, 1958, by which time Cole held almost 200 Clooney vocals. Decca Records acquired 14 of these in 1959 and released a dozen on its Coral subsidiary label as a long-player called *Swing Around Rosie*. Cole was an inventive pianist but his weakness was his fetish for the pipe organ. He would frequently dub it over the piano accompaniment that he played on a recording session. Just about every track on *Swing Around Rosie* has the organ sound somewhere and its raucous sound—akin almost to Mitch Miller's harpsichord—made for a harsh listening experience. It was only when it was applied in a softer, church style, as on the standout track "Moonlight Mississippi," that it complemented rather than competed with Rosemary's voice. The organ pipes found a more natural home in June 1959 when Cole orchestrated an album of hymns for MGM. Using just a quartet of musicians that she worked with on her radio show, but with the significant addition of the Ralph Carmichael Singers, Rosemary recorded 15 hymns over three sessions. Rosemary's Catholic upbringing meant that she was unfamiliar with most of the spiritual material because it originated in Protestant churches. "I had to learn them all from scratch," Rosemary said in 2000.[14] Her vocals were suitably reverential, although she never managed to attain the same affinity with the material that similar albums by Perry Como and Gordon MacRae/Jo Stafford displayed.

Rosemary's offerings for Coral and MGM were creditable, but her most significant recording work during her freelance period was for RCA Victor. It led ultimately to her signing an exclusive deal with the label in 1960. Her RCA sessions began in the summer of 1958. Having just completed her two intensive engagements in Reno and Las Vegas, Rosemary—by now seven months pregnant—might have been expected to take a break. Instead, she embarked on a series of recordings that rivaled her work with Duke Ellington as the most significant of her pre-breakdown career. Once more, it was a collaborative event with Rosemary's partners this time being Bing Crosby and Billy May.

Rosemary's friendship with Crosby had continued to bloom since their film and radio work during 1953–54, although until 1958, their respective recording contracts had precluded any commercial sessions between them. Crosby's exclusive contract with American Decca had expired in 1955, allowing him to enter a range of experimental, freelance-based deals with labels such as Verve and Capitol. Crosby's working relationship with RCA began in 1957 with a jazz album, *Bing with a Beat*, alongside jazz trumpeter,

Bob Scobey. Many regarded it as the finest concept album of his career. RCA therefore seemed a natural choice when lyricist Sammy Cahn came up with an idea for teaming Bing and Rosemary on an album whose storyline had the dual themes of travel and rekindled love. Cahn's idea had two former lovers meeting up unexpectedly. He and his partner, Jimmy Van Heusen, wrote a new song, "Fancy Meeting You Here," which told the story of that encounter and opened the way for 10 more retrospective songs that extended around the world as the two former lovers looked back on their time together. Another new song from the same partnership, "Love Won't Let You Get Away," capped off the album as the two lovers finally accept the inevitability of their being together.

The album cast Rosemary and Crosby as lovers, but was a strictly fictional concoction. For almost all of the time that Rosemary had known Bing, he had been a single—and highly eligible—man. Crosby's first wife, Dixie Lee, had died in November 1952; after that time Crosby had been seen around Hollywood with a variety of young, female partners, a list that included Grace Kelly and Inger Stevens. Despite his availability and Rosemary's proclivity for affairs, the relationship between the two of them was never a sexual one. "Not even a one-nighter," Rosemary said in her autobiography.[15] Instead the chemistry between the two of them was more akin to the relationship Crosby had with his golfing and hunting buddies. Rosemary's elder daughter Maria said that her mother was "Bing's only female friend. They talked about anything—musicians, lyrics, boxing. When the two of them were in a room together, the rest were non-existent."[16] The ease and camaraderie inherent in their relationship was apparent throughout the three recording sessions that were scheduled during July and August 1958.

Fancy Meeting You Here was, from Sammy Cahn's perspective, a case of killing two birds with one stone. The year before, he and Van Heusen had written "Come Fly with Me" for Frank Sinatra and used that as the title song for an album of 12 round-the-world songs. Two of them, "Isle of Capri" and "Brazil" also appeared in the *Fancy Meeting You Here* listing. As well as the overlapping theme, the two albums also had in common the "falstaffian"[17] presence of Billy May as arranger and conductor. Like Nelson Riddle, May had built his reputation at Capitol Records, both with solo albums and as an arranger for Nat "King" Cole. *Come Fly with Me* was the first of many albums with Sinatra in a partnership that would run through to 1979. For Rosemary, the experience of working with May, so soon after her exposure to Riddle, could not have been more different. Where Riddle was tasteful and ornate in his arrangements, May was loud and brash. A typical May arrangement put the brass section to the fore and made regular use of two trademark devices, the trumpet mute and a saxophone glissando, widely known as his "slurping saxes." Singing to a Billy May arrangement required a totally different style from one used in working with Riddle.

Riddle and May were also opposites in their approach to their work. "Recording with Billy May is like having a bucket of cold water thrown in your face," Sinatra once said. "Riddle will come to a session with all the arrangements carefully and neatly worked out beforehand. With Billy you sometimes don't get copies of the next number until you've finished the one before."[18] Rosemary concurred. She recalled May's copyist working alongside him, frantically transcribing to the point that the musicians were working off copies with the ink still wet. May's last-minute style posed problems too for Crosby. "I knew the way Bing worked," Rosemary said. "We'd know which songs we'd have to do that day. And he would be prepared when we walked in."[19] Buddy Cole's presence on the sessions—indeed he actually conducted the first on July 28—dissipated some of Crosby's unease and what emerged was a set of lively and imaginatively scored duets. Much of the vocal work between Crosby and Clooney was complex and intricate, none more so than Frank Loesser's "You Came a Long Way from St. Louis." The two singers were called up on to handle an intertwined melody and countermelody which gave way to a counterpoint rendition from Crosby of "You Can Take the Boy Out of the Country," newly added by composer Bob Russell just for this session.

To keep a freshness in their exchanges, Crosby used a technique imported from his movie partnership with Bob Hope. Where the lyrics included some personalized interchange between him and Rosemary, Crosby would come up with a variation of his own, but which he would throw in only at the last minute. It caught Rosemary unaware and accounted for the genuinely spontaneous laughter that could be heard on some of the tracks, never more so than in her reaction to a line about breakfasting with Bardot ("you know somebody should knit her a hug-me-tight, she's gonna catch her death of cold," Crosby tossed in. "What the hell is a hug-me-tight?" Rosemary said later). When the album hit the shops—complete with a suitably travel-oriented cover photograph that used suitcases and trunks to conceal Rosemary's pregnancy—the results were well received. In England, the at times highbrow magazine *The Gramophone*, said, "it is the infectious easygoing good humor of the record which remains in the mind. That, and an occasional twist of lyric; no record can be neglected which ends a nostalgic and twang-ridden version of the "Isle of Capri" with 'I've often felt that we both might have stayed there, if it weren't for those stale mandolins.'"[20] *Time* magazine said that the album offered "infectious musical dialogue between two of the sassiest fancy talkers in the business" and that it offered "the most intriguing of musical entertainments since Noel Coward had his famous chat with Mary Martin."[21] Fifty years later, jazz critic Will Fried-wald's assessment of the album was that it is "rightfully regarded as one of the best duet vocal albums ever."[22] The acclaim given to the album was not matched by record sales, however. "It didn't sell at all," Rosemary told Johnny Green in 1961, musing that the vocal interplay between her and Bing might just have made the album too complex for the casual listener.[23]

Rosemary's fourth pregnancy ended on October 13, 1958, with the birth of her second daughter, Monsita Teresa Ferrer. The joy of the birth was briefly clouded by the New Year's Eve news of the death of Grandma Guil-foyle. By then, Rosemary had already returned to work, and rehearsal commitments for *The Perry Como Show* in New York kept her from her grandmother's funeral. When the show went out live on Saturday, January 10, 1959, Rosemary substituted Como for Crosby in one of the duets from *Fancy Meeting You Here*. The early months of 1959 saw Rosemary back to the familiar, intensive work schedule that characterized her between-pregnancy periods. She joined Crosby for the entertainment part of his annual golf clambake at Pebble Beach; guested on the George Burns and Garry Moore shows; and in March 1959, took part in a TV tribute to Manie Sachs, the man who brought her to Columbia Records and had recently passed away. March also saw her record two duets with Bob Hope, both songs from his latest picture, *Alias Jesse James*, and these in turn prompted a guest appearance on TV with the comedian in May to promote the newly issued RCA single.

The summer brought a more intensive recording schedule. Three sessions in early June were sufficient to capture the tracks for the *Hymns from the Heart* album with Buddy Cole. In July, Rosemary had two days of RCA sessions, again in part with Crosby, for a double album of songs associated with the Old West, before starting work in the label's Sunset Boulevard studios on another project, one that added yet another dimension to her repertoire. This latest project placed her alongside the mambo-king, Perez Prado, and eventually saw release as the first output under her exclusive deal with RCA, which she signed in January 1960. Prado was a Cuban legend and if not the originator of the "mambo," he was certainly its most effective exploiter and the inventor of the dance that came to characterize the music. His early '50s residency at the Park Plaza Ballroom in New York became the focal point for the craze. Rosemary herself had been caught up in the rush for mambo records at that time. Perry Como's "Papa Loves Mambo" had been the biggest commercial success and was closer to "pure mambo," but nevertheless, by title alone, "Mambo Italiano" had also given

Rosemary a seat on the bandwagon. Mambo in purest form was difficult to describe. In essence, the term meant a rhythm structure that could be played at a fast or slow tempo. Usually, the saxophones in a band set the rhythm, with the brass carrying the melody. And in Prado's hands, it was a lively sound that spawned several albums and a batch of hit singles for him and RCA during the '50s—although by the time he teamed up with Rosemary in 1959, his hit-making days were over. Rosemary approached the sessions with some trepidation. Prado and his band spoke little English, she had no Spanish, and so it was polyglot husband Joe who helped her learn the phonetic pronunciation required for some of the numbers. Despite Rosemary's characteristic sure-footedness with the vocals, the album suffered from a strangely inconsistent combination of songs that producer Dick Peirce assembled, ranging from obvious selections such as "In a Little Spanish Town" and "Magic Is the Moonlight" to less appropriate jazz titles such as "Mack the Knife" and "I Got Plenty o' Nuttin'."

The new RCA contract might have looked like a new beginning for Rosemary as a disc-maker but the truth was that by the turn of the decade, her record career had badly lost its way. The *Billboard* charts for the '50s showed Rosemary in a creditable 11th place in terms of hit singles and weeks on chart, with Patti Page and Kay Starr the only female vocalists ahead of her. Rosemary's hits, however, were already a distant memory, and whereas peers such as Ella Fitzgerald, Doris Day, and Peggy Lee were churning out album after album for their respective Verve, Columbia, and Capitol masters, Rosemary was flitting from project to project, and label to label, without any apparent sense of direction. Not that it seemed to matter. Television guest shots on *The Perry Como Show* and *The Bell Telephone Hour* brought the curtain down on her first full decade in show business, and in November 1959, she announced the news of her fifth pregnancy. Her immediate diary was full, with a busy schedule of radio, TV, and recording lined up before the next baby was due. The music scene was much changed from the one she had encountered when she went solo 10 years earlier, but despite the arrival of Presley and rock, there was little to suggest that singers such as Rosemary faced any real threat to their livelihoods. Indeed, the chain of events that would all but destroy Rosemary's career began not with a singer called Elvis but with a politician called Jack.

CHAPTER 8

Solving the Riddle

Rosemary's first two releases under her new RCA contract were the tracks recorded with Perez Prado under the title of *A Touch of Tabasco*, plus a new collection of standards to be called *Clap Hands—Here Comes Rosie*. As its title implied, *Clap Hands* was a lightly swinging album, orchestrated by Bob Thompson, with whom Rosemary had worked on *How the West Was Won* the previous year. Thompson put together a 23-piece band plus vocal chorus for three sessions in Hollywood in February 1960, with a collection of 12 songs, largely standards, which embraced most of America's great popular songwriters. Lightly swinging albums were an early 1960s vogue for many of Rosemary's peers, both male and female, and Thompson's arrangements for the album were outstanding, providing a bright and sunny set of charts that still accommodated Rosemary's vocal gifts to perfection. Songs such as "Aren't You Glad You're You" and "It Could Happen to You" were taken at a breezy tempo, yet still enabling Rosemary's unique ability to translate the lyrics into a story to come through. *Clap Hands—Here Comes Rosie* was as good as any other album that Rosemary recorded in the '50s and '60s, even though it was subsequently overshadowed by her later collaborations with Nelson Riddle. Peter Hugh Reed, for the *American Record Guide*, best captured it, saying the album was "blessed with an unusually good selection of songs" and that "Miss Clooney exudes a joy of living and healthy musicality all too rare these days."[1]

Two days after Rosemary wrapped up the final session for *Clap Hands*, CBS Radio premiered *The Crosby-Clooney Show*. In a radio career that extended back to 1931, the new 20-minute show was Bing Crosby's last hurrah. It would run, at least in some parts of the country, until the curtain finally fell on national network radio in November 1962. The *Crosby-Clooney Show* aired five days per week and featured the recordings that Bing and Rosemary had previously made for *The Ford Road Show*. In addition to their stockpiled solos, the pair also recorded a series of duets for the new show. All the songs were interspersed between specially recorded dialogue between Crosby and Clooney. The beauty of the show, from the performers' perspective, was its portability. The chat between Bing and Rosemary was recorded wherever the two happened to overlap, including Palm Springs and Las Vegas, although much of it was put together in the living room of 1019 North Roxbury, an arrangement that suited both performers. "We did the commercials first, then we would break out some scotch and ice, then do the dialogue," Rosemary told Pat Sajak later. "The only constraint was that we weren't allowed to read each other's lines."[2] Booze, it seems, was a constant part of the Crosby-Clooney radio sessions. A recording engineer on some of the earliest Palm Springs sessions remembered Rosemary as "the lady who used to drink her whisky out of a water tumbler. I admired that lady; she could really take care of it." (Rosemary's ability to hold her liquor never left her. Writer Gary Giddins, who became a close friend during the 1990s, recalled an evening out when he, some 30-plus years her junior, determined that he would match her "vodka for vodka." "I was under the table in half an hour," he said.)[3]

Murdo Mackenzie, one of Crosby's longtime radio associates, was the man behind a show that very much reflected the sexist stereotypes of its day. "We aim this at a lady audience," he said in 1961. "The tone of the conversation has to be light and we also toss in odd bits of information."[4] Looked at now, it is hard to see "light" as anything other than a euphemism for boring triviality. The discussion topics for Bing and Rosemary included such hot items as "the eccentric behavior of salmon after a still has overflowed into their stream" and "the significance of the fact that men outfaint women by three to one during Las Vegas marriages."[5] But despite the banality of the scripts, the series contained some musical gems. With Buddy Cole again orchestrating, Bing and Rosemary resisted the temptation to reprise any of the titles from *Fancy Meeting You Here* and offered instead a series of both fun and sentimental duets. Among the 27 songs they recorded for the show were "Hey Look Me Over," "Ain't We Got Fun," a beautiful rendition of the Arthur Schwartz/Howard Dietz song "Something to Remember You By," plus several medleys.

Rosemary's fifth child, Rafael Francisco Ferrer—named for his paternal grandfather—had made his appearance on March 23, 1960. Rosemary took five weeks off after the birth but was back at work for more recording sessions early in May. Although she was now full steam into her work for

RCA, she had one carryover commitment for MGM, which she completed on April 29, 1960. The four songs she recorded that day appeared with eight others in an album called *Rosemary Clooney Swings Softly*. MGM marketed the album as though it had been newly recorded as a concept album, whereas in reality it was a compilation of various titles she had recorded between 1954 and 1960. These included her remake of "Grieving for You," which MGM leased from Columbia. The album continued its somewhat confusing existence when MGM acquired the Verve jazz label from its founder Norman Granz in 1961. Subsequent issues of the album appeared under the Verve imprint, Rosemary's only appearance on that iconic jazz label.

With her commitment to MGM completed, Rosemary was free to resume work for RCA. On May 10, she recorded four titles with Nelson Riddle for release as singles, although these were mere hors d'oeuvres to two album projects that would follow. Since he had first worked with Rosemary on television, Riddle's stock in the music business as architect of vocal swing had continued to rise. An ongoing relationship with Sinatra, plus albums with Judy Garland, Dinah Shore, and Ella Fitzgerald extended his reputation, and almost every top vocalist was queuing up for his services. Indeed, while working on the first album with Rosemary, he was skipping between studios, conducting his charts for Dean Martin's *This Time I'm Swingin'* album for Capitol at the same time.

Rosie Solves the Swingin' Riddle might have been a remake of *Clap Hands—Here Comes Rosie*. Again, all 12 songs on the disc were standards, this time digging even deeper into the archive of the great American popular song with three titles dating back to pre–World War 1. The '20s were represented by the Rodgers and Hart classic "You Took Advantage of Me" whereas other titles included Hoagy Carmichael's "I Get Along without You Very Well" and two Vernon Duke songs, "April in Paris" and "Cabin in the Sky." The only remotely contemporary number was "Get Me to the Church on Time" from *My Fair Lady*, a song and an arrangement that would stay in Rosemary's repertoire well into the 1990s. Riddle put together a 31-piece band for the album sessions, featuring many of the musicians who had been part of the orchestra when it supported Rosemary on TV. The double play in the album's title was not the first time that Riddle's name had been taken to imply an unsolvable puzzle,[6] a theme that continued into the album sleeve, which showed an unfamiliar image of Rosemary, clad in red sweater and black slacks, seated on a chessboard with Riddle's head adorning the king-piece that sat alongside her. In the sleeve notes, penned under his name, Riddle included the somewhat disingenuous comment "Rosie, you are not the first to solve the Riddle. My wife and kids did it years ago."

(Maureen Riddle, his daughter, later remarked that one of the conundrums about her father was that he "could figure out a 47-piece orchestra but he couldn't figure out six kids and a wife.")[7]

Rosie Solves the Swingin' Riddle, like the *Love* album that followed it, was a project that benefited more from the subsequent revelation of the affair between its two protagonists than from its inherent musical qualities. Indeed, *Billboard*'s contemporary review was seemingly written more in hope than expectation. "The swingin' fiddles of Nelson Riddle provide just that distinctive touch that might make this a big one for Miss Clooney," it said.[8] Greater acclaim only arrived when the album reappeared in digital formats more than 30 years after its release. Riddle's biographer, Peter J. Levinson, in his 2004 sleeve notes to the CD reissue, suggested that the "familiarity" between Rosemary, Riddle, and the session players was "significant to the success of the recording." He saw the opening track, "Get Me to the Church on Time" as an example. "The exhilaration with which Clooney approaches the song is echoed by the repetitive phrases Riddle utilizes in underlining the melody. A gentle swinging feeling is established by the combination of the brass and Frank Flynn's chimes," he wrote.[9] Nevertheless, when the album first appeared in 1961, it hit the shops at a time when Rosemary's appeal as a music maker was starting to wane, and it made no impact on the album charts of the time.

Rosemary and Riddle's follow-up to the *Swingin' Riddle* album enjoyed a similar, late life renaissance. Entitled simply *Love*, this next album was recorded over three sessions in March 1961. It was a time when the personal relationship between Rosemary and Riddle was at its most intense. Rosemary discarded the swinging theme of her three previous albums in favor of an intimate collection of love songs, all chosen personally by Rosemary, and many of them little known. Friends, including film composer Bronislaw Kaper ("Invitation") and pianist Ian Bernard ("Find the Way") wrote several of the songs. This newer material sat alongside such standards as the Gershwins' "Someone to Watch over Me" and Rodgers and Hart's "Yours Sincerely." Rosemary also included "You Started Something," a song she had first recorded in 1948 with Tony Pastor. Riddle scored the piece for trombones as a private joke between him and Rosemary. "Nelson knew I'd been going with a trombone player when I first recorded it, so he wrote the new arrangement for all trombones," she said in 1995.[10]

When the album was made, Rosemary's affair with Riddle was an open secret to most people in the music business, but not everyone. Composer Ian Bernard recalled the session where Rosemary recorded "Find the Way." "She was crying at the end of the session," he said "and I thought I had written the most emotional song in the world. It was 20 years later before I found about the affair with Nelson."[11] Al Schmitt, however, the recording engineer on the session, told Riddle's biographer, "you could see the relationship between Nelson and Rosie was special—it wasn't just arranger and singer. There was a lot of touching, and whenever there were breaks, they were together talking."[12] Rosemary in her second autobiography talked of the "yearning and regret" inherent in all the songs, even though the affair was still some time away from its unfulfilled denouement. In time, one song—"How Will I Remember You," a 1951 composition by Carl Sigman and "Tenderly" composer, Walter Gross, came to be regarded as the anthem for the Clooney-Riddle affair. Sung in 1961, it was but one of several "lost love" songs on the album. When Rosemary put together an autobiographical compilation of songs for Concord in 1995, she reprised the song in tribute to Riddle.

By the 1990s, some reviewers had started to acclaim *Love* as Rosemary's greatest work, but at the time of its completion, her new employers, RCA, were so disappointed by her recent sales that they declined to release it. It was two years later before the album appeared, by which time Rosemary had moved on again, this time to Frank Sinatra's fledgling Reprise label. As part of the deal to sign Rosemary, Sinatra bought the unreleased tracks from RCA and issued *Love* as a Reprise album. Even then, it generated little interest, not even meriting a *Billboard* review. It was when Rosemary's post-breakdown renaissance was at its peak that people started to pay attention to it. When it appeared on CD in 1995, one reviewer called it "the most ravishingly beautiful album of Clooney's career,"[13] while James Gavin's notes for the reissue highlighted the simplicity and honesty of her "sweet, husky voice." In the early '60s, though, *Love* was an album that was out of step with the public image that Rosemary still enjoyed. To most record buyers, she was still the girl-next-door, now grown up and living out an idyllic Hollywood marriage but expected to be a purveyor of happy songs and glad tidings. Her audience still expected every heart-wrenching ballad to be matched by a piece of novelty material. And thoughtful and intuitive though her readings were, Rosemary's voice still had the sweetness of youth about it. Few in the early '60s would have called it "husky." The earthy raspiness that she developed in later life added a dimension to her work—particularly apparent on her rerecording of "How Will I Remember You"—but it was not there at the time she recorded *Love*. The album might now be seen as the first time that Rosemary reached inside herself to reflect her life's experience in her work, but that only became apparent when the true story of her life began to emerge. *Love* was a 1960s product that needed a 1990s Rosemary to sell it, and even now, its apparent testament to a failed love affair overstates its artistic merits.

The cover photograph for the *Love* album marked a transition in Rosemary's image, the side-parted locks giving way to the coiffured bouffant of a mature sophisticate. One West Coast reviewer described it as a "glamour photo that casts Clooney as a sultry siren of song, swathed in feathers, her eyes pointed dreamily upward, effectively capturing the mood of this richly romantic classic."[14] Rosemary's onstage image underwent a similar makeover. In Vegas, elegant black evening gowns showed off the still tightly controlled figure, while on TV, her flowing gowns were a world away from the maternity frocks that had once been standard issue. The image looked— and was—the product of an expensive lifestyle, the bills for which rested almost entirely with Rosemary. For a time, she and Joe had made New York their main home, taking a big, expensive apartment in the Dakota building. They still retained the house on Roxbury Drive and maintained a staff of servants and nannies who followed them and the children wherever they went. But with Joe finding parts harder to come by, it meant that Rosemary was finding the bills harder to pay. That the Ferrers were living beyond even their not inconsiderable means became apparent in March 1961, when the Internal Revenue Service cited Rosemary for tax arrears of $52, 522, covering the years from 1957 to 1959. A tax lien was placed on the house in Beverly Hills.

There was more stress just around the corner. Another Vegas spell at the Desert Inn in April 1961 prefaced a trip to Europe for TV and radio work in England. From there, she traveled to Paris. While sitting in the bar of the Hotel Raphael, a call came through from her mother at home in California. Daughter Maria was sick. She needed Rosemary to come home. Rosemary cancelled her bookings and caught the next plane. By the time she arrived at Roxbury Drive, the panic of Maria's fevered temperature and swollen throat (the problem was an attack of epiglottitis, inflammation of the windpipe) had passed. Rosemary's attention focused on why it had been her mother rather than her husband who had made the call. The answer quickly transpired that it was because Joe had not been home that evening. Or indeed that night. That Joe spent time with other women while Rosemary was away was not new information, but in the context of the night's events, it became the final straw. Within an hour of arriving home, she had thrown her husband out of the house he had bought for her eight years before.

On September 22, 1961, Rosemary filed for divorce, citing mental cruelty. "Joe and I have a difference of opinion as to a way of life," she told reporters, "and for the children's sake, we feel it is best to terminate the marriage." Ferrer offered only a snapped "no comment" when tracked down by reporters in Dallas. A statement from Rosemary's lawyers said that the rift between the two had begun two years before.[15] Three weeks later, both parties appeared at the Superior Court in Santa Monica and agreed that Ferrer would pay a temporary alimony of $1,500 per month pending a final settlement. Ferrer also agreed to meet mortgage payments on their New York home. Rosemary was granted custody of the children, with Ferrer having visitation rights. When asked about the prospects for a reconciliation, Ferrer said "nothing would make me happier." Rosemary's reply was that there was no prospect of such a move, "at this time."[16] A door, it seemed, was left open.

Nevertheless, the divorce hearing began on April 30, 1962. Rosemary and Ferrer spent 35 minutes in private with Judge Marvyn Aggeler but reached no agreement. In court the next day, it transpired that Rosemary had sought an $8,000 per month settlement from her husband, which Ferrer contested. "Ferrer, 49, gave a vivid account of how movie stars live beyond their means—or how easy it is to go broke on $10,000 a week," said the press reports. Ferrer's appearance in the witness box gained him little sympathy. He claimed to have been insolvent at the time of the split in August 1961, but on cross-examination, detailed income of a quarter of a million dollars between November 1961 and the date of the trial. "Even so," said press reports, "it's hard making ends meet when you're a movie star." Rosemary's turn in the witness box came the following day. "My husband engaged in affairs with other women since the beginning of our marriage" she told the court. When asked to specify the acts of mental cruelty that she had cited, Rosemary broke down, her tears soon turning to "unrestrained sobbing."[17] Recovering her composure, Rosemary defended herself against Ferrer's accusations of extravagance in the way she ran their home in Beverly Hills, denying his charge that the $6,000 per month it cost was excessive. She had found, she said, that it was costing $7,558 per month to run the house and support the children, even with two fewer servants and no husband.

Neither party emerged well from the hearing. "From what I've heard," the judge said, "both parties are as confused as the court." Newspaper reports painted a picture of extravagant mismanagement on both sides. "Both Ferrer, 49, and his wife have given graphic accounts how it is possible in Hollywood to earn millions and still be broke. Miss Clooney, for instance, testified that she grossed $305,613.43 in 1955 and wound up with a net profit for the year of $4,190.38. And that, apparently, was one of her better years because during eight years of marriage she grossed a total of $2,060,667.97— and now owes $63,632.99," one reporter wrote.[18] Settlement finally came on May 9, leaving Rosemary feeling that she had lost. The court ordered Ferrer to pay support of $300 per child per month plus $1 per year token alimony—in effect, the $1,500 per month that had been the original temporary settlement. Rosemary's legal fees were covered and she received free use of the house on Roxbury Drive until she remarried. Ownership of the house was placed in trust for the five children. She wrote later that the judge had been unduly influenced by her recent engagement in New York that had paid $20,000 per week. "The judge decided that the children and I could manage nicely on $1,500 a month from Joe," she wrote bitterly.[19]

Worse was to come. Three weeks after Rosemary had thrown Ferrer out of her home, Nelson Riddle had left his wife, Doreen, and rented an apartment in Malibu. Whether it was intended as a love nest for him and Rosemary was never clear because within weeks, he was back home. The affair continued but was reaching a point where both parties needed to decide where their futures lay. Shortly after Rosemary's divorce, she and Riddle were together at the Plaza Hotel in New York to celebrate their birthdays. As they sat on the bed, sipping celebratory champagne, Riddle's wife called to wish him happy birthday. Rosemary suddenly saw herself as the other woman. The following day, she accompanied Riddle to the airport, where he was due to board a flight to London. When she had told him that she did not think she could "keep this up," Riddle's response had been to say "I think you're right," Rosemary. "I waited for him to say the rest, but he never did," said Rosemary.[20]

Rosemary was now a single parent with five young children aged from two to seven. She was in debt and facing the need to take every booking she could to pay her way. There was also a new complication and interest in her life: politics. The passing of the '50s had meant the end of Eisenhower's America, a time in which the United States had become the land of plenty and where many had sought to brush issues of race, equality, and civil rights back under the same carpet that had concealed them for almost 100 years. There had been little in the Eisenhower landscape to distract Rosemary from her career and family commitments, but when the Democratic Party adopted a good-looking senator from Massachusetts as its candidate to replace the aged general, Rosemary took an interest. That he was descended from an Irish family and a Catholic too only added to the fascination. Jack Kennedy was a man for whom Rosemary would be happy to holler and cheer, but no one expected that his elevation to the presidency in November 1960 would spark a chain of events that would destroy her career.

"We'll sell him like soap flakes," Kennedy's father, had boasted, and they did. With JFK's sister, Pat, married to Rat-Pack member, Peter Lawford, the Kennedy campaign had a direct conduit to Hollywood. Frank Sinatra provided the campaign song and campaigned vigorously, along with fellow Rat-Pack members Dean Martin and Sammy Davis Jr. Rosemary first became involved after attending a rally organized by Janet Leigh, star of *Psycho* and married at that time to actor Tony Curtis. Lawford and his wife were also at the rally. Soon, Rosemary was helping out at fund-raising events. As the circle expanded, she moved closer to JFK and his entourage. Robert Kennedy, the candidate's brother, and his wife Ethel became good friends, entertaining Rosemary at Hickory Hill, their home in Virginia. By the time the election neared, Rosemary was actively involved. During September 1960, she played a month's engagement at the Waldorf-Astoria in New York. Such an extended stay in the East created demands for her appearance at a raft of small-scale events, before the Kennedys asked her to sing at a major rally at Madison Square Garden on October 21. There, she met the future president for the first time.

Contact continued once Kennedy took office in 1961. On the first anniversary of his inauguration in January 1962, the president invited her to sing at a party to mark the event. Later in the evening, at a dinner at the Jockey Club, she shared a table with Vice-President and Lady Bird Johnson. During the meal, the president called to thank her personally for her performance. In June, one month after the conclusion of her divorce hearing, Rosemary sang at another Democratic Party function, this time a dinner at the Mayflower Hotel in Washington, DC, for the newly appointed ambassador to Ireland. President Kennedy was there and spoke briefly with Rosemary. It was an event that seemed to have come and gone when later the same evening, Rosemary took a call from the White House, inviting her to come over and join the president for some late night drinks. Hurriedly redressing into her Edith Head gown, Rosemary dashed to the White House where she found herself joining Peter Lawford and other members of JFK's inner circle in a late night dish of scrambled eggs. She chatted at length to Kennedy as the night wore on. There was nothing in her later account of the meeting to suggest any sexual context for the meeting, although as she came to leave, she was taken aback by the president's final question. What was it, he asked, that kept her off-the-shoulder jacket from falling off? Taken aback, she paused before revealing a simple clip.

Events such as that might well have left Rosemary wondering where exactly the boundaries of reality in her life were. What had once had been simple and straightforward now seemed to be difficult and complex. She had pressures coming from all sides—the children, her mother, with whom she still never felt comfortable, plus the need to get out and earn the money that would pay off the debts. She missed Joe, but she missed Nelson Riddle more. Sleeping had been a problem for some time and Rosemary had long since turned to pills for a solution. "A lot of women took them," she said later, "my mother took them. And everybody kidded about the bennies— Benzedrine—and Miltown. I took downers—Seconal, Librium, Nembutal, Doriden. Of course, if you take too many downers, they have the reverse effect. You can't sleep at all."[21] For the time being though, Rosemary's problems remained off-stage. *Variety* reported enthusiastically about her appearances at Harrah's in Lake Tahoe and at the Copa in New York in the spring of 1962. "One of her major assets is her flawless diction," the reviewer said of her appearance in New York. "Every word she utters is understood, even onto the far reaches of the Burma Road sections of the room."[22] Through the summer of 1962, Rosemary remained busy. A visit to London in June brought a renewed liaison with Nelson Riddle that flickered and died. Then from London, she headed into mainland Europe for a tour that demanded 16 appearances over nine days in West Germany, France, and Italy.

In July, she was back in the states putting the finishing touches to what would be her final album in her brief spell at RCA. The gestation of *Rosemary Clooney Sings Country Hits from the Heart* extended back to May 1961 when Rosemary had spent two days working with Chet Atkins in RCA's Nashville studios. Six titles were recorded over those two days, including a more authentic sounding remake of Rosemary's 1951 hit "Beautiful Brown Eyes," plus a version of "Give Myself a Party," sung to an uncredited Nelson Riddle arrangement. A planned return to Nashville to finish the album never materialized, however, leaving Atkins to record a further six backing tracks on titles that included a remake of "This Ole House." Rosemary overdubbed her vocals onto the tracks in Hollywood on July 19 and 20. Despite the hiccups in its production, the album that emerged presented a seamless collection of 12 country standards that featured some of the stellar Nashville session players, including Don Gibson and Floyd Cramer plus the Anita Kerr singers and the Jordanaires. *Billboard's* comment that the album presented Rosemary in a medium "in which she seems right at home"[23] was apposite. Rosemary's 12 vocals all displayed her usual qualities of crystal-clear enunciation. She sang the songs simply and honestly and in a style that anticipated her later jazz recordings, allowing the musicians around her to create the milieu. Yet despite the quality of the albums that Rosemary recorded for RCA, sales were poor. There had been single releases too, but none had reached the charts. A solo release of "Give Myself a Party" from the country album, had "made some noise," said *Billboard*, but nothing more. Even another Riddle collaboration, "The Wonderful Season of Love," failed to chart despite being the theme song from the film, *Return to Peyton Place*, which José Ferrer had directed and which ultimately spawned the television soap opera. Her two-year tenure at RCA ended quietly in October 1962 when she signed with Reprise Records.

After concluding the overdubs for the country album, Rosemary was back across the Atlantic again. This time, she was en route to Monte Carlo to answer a call from Princess Grace to sing at a Red Cross benefit. Rosemary traveled via London. At Heathrow, the figure waiting to greet her was none other than Joe Ferrer. Rosemary played down reports of a reconciliation, saying that their get-together had purely been to discuss matters relating to the children. But said one press report, the two had "embraced ardently." What's more, when pressed, Rosemary seemed to allow more light through the already half open door. "I think it's too early to talk about it," she said.[24] One columnist at least could see the writing on the wall. "Princess Grace was beautiful and charming—but José, dancing attendance on Rosemary, almost stole thunder," Dorothy Manners wrote a few days later. "He flew in from London a few hours before she was to sing and joined John Mills's big party in Rosie's honor. Rosemary forgot a hat she used in one of her songs, and it was José who dashed back to the hotel to get it for her. Don't know whether this means a reconciliation—but he is certainly the eager beaver where she is concerned."[25]

Despite her busy crisscrossing of the Atlantic—Rosemary would be back in London again in October 1962 to star at the prestigious *Royal Variety Performance* at the London Palladium—Rosemary's loneliness had continued through the autumn of 1962. Ferrer had been a regular visitor to the house on Roxbury Drive and to the still young family, accustomed to their father being away much of the time, his absence seemed little different from his being away on a long movie shoot. And despite his philandering, Ferrer's presence brought out a side to Rosemary that no one else did. Even in later years, long after their marriage was finally over, her children would recall that Ferrer never failed to ignite a spark in her. Daughter Maria recalled that when the two of them were together, "daddy would walk in, proud as a peacock, and momma would turn into a 16-year-old giddy little girl."[26] Son Rafael also found that the "love and the bond" never went away. "He would sit in the chair in the den that he used to sit in and she would fuss over him, asking if he wanted a drink or some food. I was looking at a woman I never saw before," he said. "She didn't wait on people."[27]

Those close to Rosemary knew that she still loved Joe. Indeed, some said she never stopped loving him, and in early 1963, there was still a part of Rosemary that believed she could get him to change his ways. She convinced herself once more that the idyllic family lifestyle that she craved for was not just a pipe dream. When, early in 1963, press reports confirmed that Joe Ferrer had returned to the matrimonial home, there were eyebrows raised but no great intake of breath. Ferrer's return, with their divorce unfinalized, meant under California law that Rosemary's suit became null and void the instant that he returned to live in the marital home. It didn't matter to Rosemary. For now at least, the Ferrers were back in business.

CHAPTER 9

Road to Reno

The second time around marriage to Joe Ferrer was doomed from the day the actor moved back into 1019 North Roxbury. "Funny, talented, hard to live with," was her summary of her former husband in 1997. "But," she said, "sometimes he was so easy to live with that you got fooled—'Hey, this is gonna be a cinch.'"[1] Looking back, most of Rosemary's family members agreed with her assessment that Ferrer was a "wonderful father," but most were far less kind when it came to describing Ferrer as a husband. Indeed, it was Ferrer the father rather than Joe the husband that Rosemary truly welcomed back into the family home, but for a time, they resumed the "traveling Ferrers" modus operandi. There were even rumors of another pregnancy and hopes for a sixth child, although by the autumn of 1963, the story line had changed back to the familiar one of rows and breakup.

The marriage limped along for another two and a half years before permanent separation became a reality in April 1966. Rosemary petitioned for divorce in August of that year. The final settlement came 12 months later. When the case came before the Santa Monica Supreme Court on September 13, 1967, both parties charged the other with "extreme cruelty." "It's an unfortunate story where a man and woman fall in love, get married, and then find they could not get along," Ferrer told the press.[2] Rosemary made no public comment. The settlement was essentially the same one that had been handed down five years before. Ferrer paid a token $1 per month alimony and monthly support of $1,500 for the children. The house remained in trust for the five offspring, with Rosemary retaining the right to live there for the rest of her life.

The rapprochement with Ferrer had done nothing to stem Rosemary's increasing reliance on prescription medication. In a revealing interview in 1982, she told TV psychologist Tom Cottle that the drugs had started not long after the birth of her fifth child. By the end of 1963, it had reached the point that each performance would end with "a big bouquet of 'let's go to sleep' pills."[3] When she woke up each morning, the first thing on her mind was whether she had enough pills for the next night. The actress in her became adept at developing story lines that made sure she could get her pills without arousing suspicion. If she was touring, she told Terry Gross in 1997, her first call would be to the house physician, saying that she had forgotten her medication and could she have a couple of tablets. Usually, the apparent innocence of the request led to a large box coming her way, even on a couple of occasions, boxes of 100 pills. "It became a habit very quickly," she said. "Then it became very hard getting off."[4]

To the casual observer, there was still little sign of the turmoil that was now the behind-the-scenes story of Rosemary Clooney. When she made her first-ever professional appearance in San Francisco at the Fairmont in March 1963, one local reviewer still saw the pure and decent girl from the 1950s. The only difference was that she was now "brighter and sexier. Her act is refreshingly natural; a few quips, a lot of personality and 19 songs. When it's over, you feel like you've known the attractive blonde singer all your life."[5] A year later, *Variety* covered Rosemary's appearances in British Columbia and found her "as warm and personable as ever."[6] In later years, Rosemary was dismissive of her '60s work. "I sounded like a 1950s jukebox all the way through the next decade," she said in 1989,[7] but it was a harsh self-assessment. "Come On-a My House" and "Mambo Italiano" might still have been de rigueur, but Rosemary's repertoire also included medley tributes to Bing Crosby and Billie Holiday plus classic material from her *Blue Rose* album. Buddy Cole was still her regular accompanist, orchestrating a version for her of "Now You Has Jazz" from Crosby's 1956 movie *High Society*. Cole's premature death in November 1964 at the age of 47 was the first of several personal tragedies that Rosemary had to deal with over the coming years.

With her family now aged from four to nine, Rosemary was anxious to limit her time away from the children. It meant that she spent less time working in clubs and more time in television studios. Even when she did appear on stage, she took the children with her, after a fashion. Five more-than-life size cutouts became part of the act. Her closing number was always Disney's "M-I-C-K-E-Y Mickey Mouse," later replaced by the theme from TV's *Batman*. "The kids' favorites" she told her audiences. Stage appearances were, however, becoming fewer and fewer, and it was now through television rather than any other medium that American families gained most of their exposure to Rosemary Clooney. She was a regular guest on weekly shows with the likes of Garry Moore and Johnny Carson and a familiar face on ABC's *The Hollywood Palace* variety show. There was diversification too. In January 1963, she had played a straight role in "The Losers," an episode of *The Dick Powell Show* in which she appeared opposite Lee Marvin and Keenan Wynn. Game shows such as *Password* and *I've Got a Secret*, a comedic appearance opposite Red Skelton, and commercials for Florient air cleaner and Acrilan all created an image of Rosemary as a jack-of-all-trades celebrity, at the expense of her more customary self-branding as a "girl singer." Rosemary's willingness to take whatever work came her way reflected not only her need to make ends meet but also the apparent reality that as a singer, her best days were behind her.

The reunion with Joe only worsened Rosemary's financial position. Despite the unfavorable press coverage of the first divorce hearing, their lifestyle was still expensive. The house on Roxbury Drive was costly to run and the growing family ever more demanding. A mid-1964 court case positioned Rosemary against her former manager, Joe Shribman, each filing suits against the other. Shribman's suit claimed $20,000 in unpaid commissions while Rosemary's alleged mismanagement and waste in activities undertaken on her behalf. In December, Rosemary was again in the crosshairs of the IRS, who claimed tax arrears of $49,124 for the years 1959 and 1960. By the time Rosemary's divorce from Ferrer came through in August 1966, she was effectively bankrupt. Her annual earnings were now below the $20,000 mark and her personal debts almost three times that amount. Once again, Rosemary turned to the pill bottles for solace from her real-world troubles.

Rosemary's recording career had been the cornerstone of everything she had done since the day Mitch Miller had read her the riot act over "Come On-a My House." By 1963, however, Rosemary as a hit maker, was history. Her two-year deal with RCA had come and gone almost unnoticed. Album sales had been disappointing and her attempts to make it back on the singles charts had disappeared without trace. Rosemary's arrival at Reprise Records, newly founded by Frank Sinatra, did nothing to slow the trend. Reprise was Sinatra's attempt to finally wrest artistic control away from the faceless owners of the big labels and their record producers—the same issue that had soured his own relationship with Mitch Miller back at Columbia. When he announced the creation of Reprise Records in December 1960, Sinatra offered his signings creative freedom in what they recorded and eventually, ownership and publishing rights for their work. Cronies such as Dean Martin and Sammy Davis Jr. were among the first major names to jump ship from their existing contracts. When Sinatra himself called Rosemary late in 1962 with a request that she come to his new label, Rosemary had other things on her mind but said yes all the same. "Sure," she said, adding later that she "never knew what the deal was—still don't today."[8]

As with any new venture, Sinatra needed sales to justify the contracts that he had handed out to a mixed bag of current stars, up-and-comers, and has-beens. Rosemary was fast approaching the third category. Three Reprise singles came and went in quick succession, each offering different styles that were little more than shots in the dark in an attempt to find a hit formula. Artistically, the best song among them was "The Rose and the Butterfly." Rosemary delivered a tender vocal with characteristic purity of tone, singing largely to just guitar accompaniment. It was good listening for the Clooney fan but hardly juke box material. The rest of the sides had Rosemary battling a vocal chorus on two tracks (including an ill-conceived remake of "Mixed Emotions" from 1951) and offering a version of "A Hundred Years from Today" that musically, was a near-clone of her "Hey There" hit record from 1954.

Alongside the singles, Sinatra lined up Rosemary as one of a lengthy list of stars who made up the "Reprise Repertory Company." Taking four Broadway shows as the source of the material, Sinatra, Martin, and Davis joined forces with other new recruits such as Bing Crosby, Jo Stafford, and Dinah Shore to put together the "Reprise Repertory Theater" series. Rosemary took two solos—"How Are Things in Glocca Morra?" and "Look to the Rainbow"—on the *Finian's Rainbow* album and joined Sinatra in a duet version of "Some Enchanted Evening" for *South Pacific*. These recordings perhaps offer the first tangible evidence of the effect of Rosemary's off-stage traumas on her singing. Her rendition of "Glocca Morra" was thin-voiced and soulless. She would return to the song 30 years later for Concord Records and at the age of 66, produce a timeless reading of Yip Harburg's nostalgic Irish lyric. Her 1964 recording conveyed no message. "Look to the Rainbow" was much the same, while the duet with Sinatra continued the slightly uneasy vocal relationship that the two had encountered at Columbia. The recording was not helped by the fact that it was an artificial duet, commonplace now, but in the '60s, still unusual. Rosemary and Frank recorded their vocals separately, leaving studio engineers the job of patching them together. Years later, Rosemary was scathing about her Reprise output. "There are some things at Reprise—'Some Enchanted Evening' among 'em—that I would rather bury," she said on Merv Griffin's chat show in 1982.[9]

Rosemary reserved most of her ire, however, for the one solo album that she recorded for Reprise. *Thanks for Nothing* was intended as a concept album around the theme of lost love, a theme often used by Sinatra himself and an extension of the mood that *Love* had sought to create. The album sessions paired Rosemary with Sinatra's producer Sonny Burke and arranger Bob Thompson, responsible for the upbeat charts on *Clap Hands— Here Comes Rosie* some three years before. The song list for the album raided Tin Pan Alley for such standards as Irving Berlin's "All Alone" and Cole Porter's "Just One of Those Things." Alongside sat new songs from such writers as Felice and Boudleaux Bryant (better known for their rock-ballad offerings for singers such as the Everly Brothers) and Alan Bergman. Rosemary recorded 12 songs for the album over three sessions between September and November 1964. It would be her last solo album for almost 11 years.

The results never came close to creating the mood that the album's title implied. Bob Thompson was capable of producing arrangements that were inventive and accommodating, but this time around, they failed to generate any sustained ambience for the album. Some choices seemed almost bizarre. The opening and closing tracks for the 12-song disc were both up-tempo country songs, the Bryants' "Hello Faithless" and an old western song, "Careless Love" that Rosemary had sung on *How the West Was Won* five years before. Cover versions of "Black Coffee" and "The Man That Got Away" added nothing to the Peggy Lee and Judy Garland originals. Ultimately, *Thanks for Nothing* was a ragbag collection of songs with a title that summed up its own inadequacy. On release, it generated little interest or sales potential. It reappeared in digital format 30 years later, but unlike its predecessor, *Love*, gained nothing from the passage of time. Rosemary herself led the way. "I was doing a lot of drugs and drinking a lot. Not singing too well. I'm not proud of that record, but it reflected my life," she said in 2000.[10] There was no question that when Rosemary revisited some of the songs for Concord in later years, the resultant versions only served to make *Thanks for Nothing* even more insignificant.

Sinatra's grand plans for Reprise as an independent label were short-lived. By the time Rosemary came to complete her final session for the label in November 1964, he had sold it to Warner Brothers. Reprise's greatest success had been to reinvigorate Dean Martin's recording career and the man responsible, arranger Ernie Freeman, took charge of Rosemary's final session on November 2, 1964. That day she recorded four songs for release as singles. Three of the four featured the high-pitched vocal chorus that worked so well behind Dean Martin but not with anyone else. Sinatra, Crosby, and Vic Damone all linked up with Freeman to try to match his success with Martin but none succeeded. Rosemary was just the same. Only two of the songs recorded that day—"Stay Awake" and "A Spoonful of Sugar"—ever saw release. By 1964, Rosemary's physical and mental health problems had begun to reflect themselves in her onstage performances.

When she appeared on the *Hollywood Palace* in January 1964, the unthinkable happened. Singing "A Good Man Is Hard to Find," Rosemary struggled to stay on key. Later in the same show, she sang "Sleepy Time Gal" confidently but when she attempted to hit the song's highest note on the line "you'll love it, I know," her voice cracked embarrassingly. Reviewers who used to praise her ability to deliver a lyric were now critical. On a *Porgy and Bess* medley at a concert in San Francisco, one local reviewer wrote that despite living next door to Ira and owning the Gershwin house, "she showed absolutely no affinity for the haunting music."[11]

Rosemary's decline, however, was not totally self-inflicted. From the moment that the Beatles appeared for three consecutive Sundays on *The Ed Sullivan Show* in February 1964, the American music scene changed. The impact of '60s pop far exceeded anything that rock'n'roll had brought a decade earlier. In terms of its influence on the underlying music per se, it matched the emergence of jazz in the '20s as a musical revolution. Record buyers wanted the Beatles and everything that came in their wake. The *Billboard Hot 100* in April 1964 contained 12 Beatles records, including the top five places. Sales clustered around a handful of artists. "Instead of twenty artists selling, say, a million records each, from the Sixties on it became a matter of a single artist selling 20 million records while the other nineteen went unrecorded or got dumped into the cutout bins," wrote Will Friedwald.[12] Many of Rosemary's peers found that the familiar waters had turned icy and austere. Tony Bennett along with Johnny Mathis and others at Columbia Records now found themselves as second-string artists behind "bands called The Byrds and Paul Revere and the Raiders."[13] Rosemary's fellow '50s novelty champ, Perry Como, had his last chart entry in 1962 and quit his weekly TV show a year later. He was absent from the recording studios for two years. Only a handful of the vocalists who had ruled the world in the '50s would survive this revolution. The unlikeliest survivor of all was Rosemary Clooney.

Only one record company stayed true to the old" style singers. Capitol Records, perhaps because it had the Beatles on its roster, continued to promote singers such as Peggy Lee, Judy Garland, and Nat "King" Cole. In 1963, Bing Crosby signed a two-record deal with them, the second album planned as a follow-up with Rosemary to their *Fancy Meeting You Here* collaboration from 1958. Reprise still held Rosemary's recording contract but seemed more than happy to grant permission for her to work on the new duet project with Bing. So, the old firm of Crosby and Clooney went to work late in 1964 and over three sessions, recorded *That Travelin' Two-Beat*. The album lifted much from its predecessor from six years before. It had the same theme (travel) and the same arranger (Billy May), and where the first had been the brainchild of one songwriting partnership (Cahn and Van Heusen), *Two-Beat* relied on another pairing, that of Jay Livingston and Ray Evans. The result was a spirited and lively album but, as with many follow-ups, one that never quite matched the original. Livingston and Evans composed some new material, including the title track, as well as providing some updated lyrics for some of the older material that Bing and Rosemary chose to include. Thus, the 1883 song about a Dublin fishmonger, "Molly Malone," became an updated "Daughter of Molly Malone." A classical piece, Johann Strauss's "Tales from the Vienna Woods" became the "New Vienna Woods," while the Latin standard "Cielito Lindo" became "Adios, Senorita."

Critical response to the album was lukewarm and few reviewers thought that it matched its predecessor. Some said the Livingston and Evans reworkings were too elaborate and complicated. Others thought that May's typically bombastic arrangements, complete with bells and whistles, owed more to a marching band or circus act than it did to the purported Dixieland theme. Perhaps the greatest difference, however, was in the duet performances of Bing and Rosemary. Until the *Two-Beat* album, they had always appeared as equal partners, working in a genuinely collaborative style. *Two-Beat*, however, was Crosby's show. His voice opens virtually every track and makes almost all the running. The reason, it later emerged, was that the duets, like Rosemary's outing with Sinatra the year before, were studio creations. Crosby put down his vocals first with Rosemary filling in the gaps later. The emergence of a rehearsal recording in which Jay Livingston sang Rosemary's part ("You're very brave, Mr. Livingston," said Crosby at the end of the session) was the first indication that the duets were spliced together. At the time, union rules held that lead singers should be present in the studio at the same time as the musicians playing on the sessions. As a result, the spliced nature of the duets was concealed from public view for over 40 years.[14] Certainly when Rosemary joined Crosby on the *Hollywood Palace* early in 1966, their duet medley from the album was more spontaneous and more like the equal partnership that had characterized their previous work together. Rosemary's TV appearance with Crosby would be the last time the two would work together for nine years.

The *Two-Beat* album was to all intents and purposes the last act of Rosemary's first recording career. When her Reprise contract was not renewed, she was again forced to work on a freelance basis. It was something that Rosemary had done before, between 1958 and 1960, but times had changed; 1965 came and went without a single visit to a recording studio, and 1966 brought just one session. On August 25, she recorded four titles for United Artists with rock producer, Bill Justis. It was a session that Rosemary erased from her memory. Two of the songs were pseudo-rock creations, arguably the worst recordings that Rosemary ever made. Deborah Grace Winer, writing about them for a compilation release in 1999, described them as "distressing—the forced rawness of the voice, manic drive and sheer awfulness of the material." These might not have been the first time that Rosemary recorded kitschy material, she said, but the difference then was that Mitch Miller's commercial fodder had at least been a vehicle for an emergent talent. The United Artists session in 1966 showcased an "accomplished artiste struggling to keep her way, flailing in material that is beneath just about anybody."[15]

By 1966, Rosemary's problems, on stage and off, were becoming increasingly apparent. On the surface, her *Hollywood Palace* appearance with Crosby cast her with a modern hairstyle and canary yellow gown that glittered and gleamed. When she moved, however, her body and legs looked rakishly thin, while her eyes appeared distant and unsmiling. In June, she appeared for two weeks at the Three Rivers Inn in upstate New York. Her between-songs dialogue with the audience hinted at the problems in her life, although her remarks about "answering the unasked questions" seemed to be directed more toward herself than her public.[16] Longtime friend, Ron Shaw from Miami, was in Syracuse on business and took the opportunity to see the show and seek out Rosemary backstage. The shock was profound. When he knocked on her dressing room door, "out came this woman. Yes, physically she was Rosemary Clooney, but in every other aspect, it wasn't. This woman was so high on drugs." Gone was the familiar friendly greeting and hug. When Shaw spoke to her, her reply was like someone reading from a script. Their meeting ended with a terse "thank you very much" at which point she turned and closed the door in his face, he said.[17] Others, even closer to Rosemary, noticed it too. Nick Clooney saw his sister's sense of humor disappear. A gentle joshing from him during a phone call had usually extracted a humorous response. Now it brought silence, or worse still, outright anger. Other conversations were simply incomprehensible, Rosemary at times talking in riddles. Worse still was the frustration of trying to stem the flow of drugs going his sister's way. "I'd take away a shopping bag full of them," Nick Clooney said, "flush them, bury them, anything to get rid of them" while all the time enduring the frustration of "not knowing where the real stash was."[18]

Still the merry-go-round continued to spin. Family life continued in Beverly Hills but it was Rosemary's mother who was becoming the family rock, fueling feelings of both guilt and jealousy in her daughter. Rosemary needed money and as with all things in her life, threw herself into the task hook, line, and sinker. Concert dates took her to New York, Miami, San Francisco, and Vegas, while on TV, she filled in for a time as co-host of *The*

Mike Douglas Show. No one seemed quite sure any more as to which Rosemary would show up. Hank Fox in *Billboard* gave her top marks for the show he saw at the Americana Hotel in New York: "every song she sings, every move she makes, manifest the same conclusion—a top notch, professional entertainer";[19] yet when a *Variety* reviewer took in her show in Florida two months later, the verdict was quite different. She was, the review said, "not in particularly good voice or in the best of moods, often sounding weak and cracking on ballads and upbraiding the onstage drummer for tempo differences on one tune and publicly chastising the light man for following her off stage a few moments later."[20]

More of the same followed in1967, but with the added complication of a long-running affair with a young drummer, referred to later by Rosemary only as "Jay." An April engagement at the Waldorf-Astoria went well, although when Rosemary appeared on Joe Franklin's TV show, an argument with the host resulted in her walking off the show, live on air. Nevertheless, a four-week summer engagement at the Desert Inn in Vegas was a success, and in September, Rosemary guested on NBC's *Dean Martin Show*, one of the biggest shows on TV at that time. Musical director, Lee Hale, recalled that everyone connected with the show knew that Rosemary could be unpredictable. Producer Greg Garrison issued an instruction that everyone "should be especially nice to her."[21] The Martin show was always a chaotic affair, the host refusing to appear at rehearsals and turning up only for the actual shoot each Sunday. It meant that Martin was totally spontaneous, even if completely under-rehearsed, usually relying on cue cards for every piece of dialogue and song lyric. Nevertheless, the chaos that resulted was a hit with the viewers. Rosemary coped well, singing two solos and joining Dean in a medley of "Dean and Rosie" songs. "Dean and Rosie hugged their way through the medley, planting sincere kisses on each other at the end, and Rosie was obviously pleased," Hale wrote.[22]

When 1968 dawned, Rosemary was making plans for a world tour, but the storm clouds were soon on the horizon, both for her and her country: 1968 would prove to be one of the most disturbing years in American history, with antiwar and race issues spilling over onto the streets, and high profile assassinations of luminaries such as Martin Luther King Jr. and Bobby Kennedy. Looking back on Rosemary's life, friends and family would comment in later years that Rosemary chose to have her nervous breakdown in the year that the American nation did the same. In February, Rosemary had planned a concert tour to the Far East, returning via Europe before heading on to Canada and South America. Her affair with her drummer was still ongoing, despite a 15-year difference in their ages until her paramour delivered a bombshell. He wasn't going. Telling her that he planned to enter therapy to "get my life together,"[23] Rosemary left for Japan and Thailand alone.

Throughout the tour, Rosemary was plagued by sleeping difficulties, her behavior becaming ever more erratic and unpredictable. Her Japanese hosts did everything they could for her, but nothing was right. She was fast becoming a tightly coiled spring, just waiting for the one event that would trigger the explosion. That event came a step closer when Rosemary took time out of her tour to visit American servicemen who had been wounded in Vietnam. Her tour had coincided with the Tet Offensive launched by the Vietcong on January 31, 1968. When Rosemary arrived at Clark Field, the base in the Philippines where the military hospital was located, she saw the full horror of the war. Consistently opposed to the fighting, Rosemary found herself taking messages from wounded soldiers and faithfully relaying them to wives and girlfriends when she returned home.

On March 16, 1968, her friend from her previous involvement in politics, Senator Robert F. Kennedy, declared his candidacy for president in the election due later in the year. Kennedy's platform was essentially antiwar, a direct challenge to the incumbent Democratic president, Lyndon Johnson. It was enough to persuade Rosemary to pick up her political involvement that had lain dormant since the assassination of Kennedy's brother five years earlier, although her attraction to Kennedy wasn't purely due to his antiwar stance. Racial and economic equality and social reform were major campaign themes, essentially the same liberal Democratic ticket that Rosemary had learned from her grandfather in the '30s.

Rosemary returned home from the Far East for a brief reacquaintance with her family before resuming the European leg of her world tour. On April 4, she was in Germany when the news reached her of the murder of Martin Luther King Jr. in Memphis. The event prompted an outbreak of anti-American sentiment across Europe, which to Rosemary's fragile mental state, translated into a personal attack on her. In London a few days later, she appeared on the popular late night talk show hosted by a genial Irishman called Eamonn Andrews. The show was usually nothing more than light banter between an assortment of celebrities, but this time, the topic turned to King's assassination. When one guest, a black West Indian cricketer, launched an attack on America's treatment of racial inequality, Rosemary took it personally. She responded vigorously but eventually broke down. "That was my warning signal," she said later, "but instead of listening, I ran to Brazil and still more work."[24]

Brazil and a date in Calgary, Canada, offered little respite from the accelerating treadmill that was now Rosemary's life. By the end of May 1968, the

Kennedy bandwagon had gathered a pace that few thought possible two months before. Unnerved by a narrow victory in the New Hampshire primary that he should have won easily, President Johnson had withdrawn from the race within two weeks of Kennedy having declared his candidacy. It left the Democratic nomination as a fight between Kennedy, Vice-President Hubert Humphrey, and the overt antiwar campaigner, Eugene McCarthy, who had been the first to challenge Johnson. When Kennedy won the primaries in Indiana and Nebraska, the nomination—and the White House—seemed there for the taking. All eyes focused on the next primary in California. On May 30, Rosemary joined the senator at a rally in Oakland, California, offering a rendition of "When Irish Eyes Are Smiling." The following week, she joined him in San Diego for another rally. A newsreel film from June 3 captured a wide-eyed Rosemary alongside Kennedy and fellow singer, Andy Williams. "I can look at myself and know that I was high," Rosemary said later.[25] Indeed, anyone seeing Rosemary's behavior that night—the adoring stare into the senator's eyes, the exaggerated body language and the lame attempts at humor—would have seen a person unrecognizable from the girl who had once charmed the nation.

Rosemary, with daughter Maria in tow, flew with the Kennedy entourage back to Los Angeles the next day and drove with him in an open-top car through the city. The next evening, June 5, Rosemary, along with Maria and son Miguel, were among the crowds inside the Ambassador Hotel to hear the news of Kennedy's victory in the primary. As Rosemary waited stage left to greet the victorious candidate and offer her congratulations, the senator turned and took an alternative exit route through the hotel's kitchen area. "The shots sounded like someone breaking light bulbs," daughter Maria recalled.[26] It was only when a Kennedy aide appeared, covered in blood, that the horror became apparent. Rosemary's hold on reality lasted long enough for her to get the children away from the scene as fast as she could, using her celebrity status to get her through the security that had quickly sealed off the building. But in the days that followed, Rosemary's mind substituted the reality that everyone else saw with a world of her own. Kennedy wasn't dead. It was a conspiracy, a plan by something or someone to teach everyone a lesson. Even a telephone conversation with Kennedy's widow, Ethel, failed to persuade Rosemary that the blood she had seen in the Ambassador Hotel had been that of the murdered senator.

Three weeks after Kennedy was buried in Washington, DC, Rosemary traveled to Reno for a three-week season at Harold's Club. She was on the edge—"running, forever running, without knowing why,"[27] she said later. Her twisted and confused mind had positioned her in the middle of an enormous conspiracy. No one was safe from her bottled up angst and she saw everyone as a threat. A taxi driver who dropped her back at her hotel after one performance, innocently remarked that she was now "safely back at headquarters." The word had connotations for Rosemary that she could never later explain but it turned her, she said, into "a harridan," who berated the taxi driver with uncontrollable venom.[28] The singer who took the Reno stage every night was walking a mental tightrope. One slip was all that was needed to take her over the edge and spinning down into the abyss. On July 8, 1968, Rosemary Clooney finally lost her footing.

CHAPTER 10

"All of Us a Little Nuts"

Precisely what it was that tipped Rosemary Clooney over the edge that night in Reno will never be known. Opening night had come and gone without major incident, although Rosemary had entered the stage from the rear of the room, rather than from the side as was customary. Her premature arrival meant that the orchestra was not set up, nor were the lights and the sound ready. Once under way, she failed to find any real harmony with the club band. The drummer in particular, lagged the beat, while her singing, said *Variety*, was "faulted by obvious throat problems." It was, said the review, "disappointing to those who know Miss Clooney as the consummate performer."[1]

Disappointment was to become shock and horror when Rosemary took the stage for the first show on July 8, 1968. Charged with inexplicable anger, Rosemary stood in front of the band and ignored the cues from the musical director. As the band struck up "Come On-a My House," Rosemary eyeballed her audience. When someone from the room called out a request for her to sing, Rosemary berated them. "You can't imagine the price I've paid to sing a bunch of dumb songs for you."[2] As the band plowed on with the planned accompaniment but with no singer, Rosemary stood hands on hips before turning and marching off the stage without a thought for her audience. "They were nice people," she said later, "all on my side."[3] Fearing that she was ill—and she was—the club owner arrived in the dressing room with a doctor, whose first thoughts were that the star had had too much to drink. Rosemary had indeed been drinking but was not drunk. To her, the entire episode was part of the "plot" that had been running ever since Kennedy's assassination. Believing that the owner and the doctor were there to silence her, she ran, taking a taxi back to her motel where she trashed her room. As dawn approached, she drove her car up the Mt. Rose Highway, heading toward Lake Tahoe. Rosemary described the journey many times in later life, saying how she purposely drove on the wrong side of the road to "play chicken with God."[4] Whether the journey was quite so reckless or whether it was just one more hallucination, no one knows. But regardless of how she got there, the Rosemary Clooney who arrived in Lake Tahoe was one very sick lady.

Rosemary was now in free fall. Comedian Shecky Greene was appearing in Tahoe and had received word about the events in Reno and called another doctor. Soon an ambulance arrived to admit her to the local hospital in Tahoe. Seeing that too as part of "the plot," Rosemary threw her belongings out of the ambulance to leave a trail for the "rescuers" that she hoped would come. When tranquilizers failed to calm her mental state, her family arranged for an air ambulance to fly her to St. John's Hospital in Santa Monica, the same hospital where her children had been born. Sister Betty signed the committal papers, but Rosemary's incarceration did not last. Despite the near total loss of touch with reality, there was sufficient lucidity left in Rosemary's mind to summon her thespian skills and convince two doctors that it had all been a big mistake. Her behavior, she told them, was just the result of a mixup in the dosage of her prescription drugs. Truly, everything was just fine.

It took a medical mind, one that knew the old Rosemary intimately, to make the judgment that everything was not fine. Rosemary's cousin and childhood friend, Phyllis, the daughter of her Aunt Rose, had married a young doctor called Sherm Holvey in 1949. Phyllis was more like a sister than a cousin to Rosemary, and she and her husband remained close friends of Rosemary and her family. They were the first port of call for any medical issue. Holvey's specialty was endocrinology but his broader medical knowledge enabled him to recognize the symptoms of severe mental trauma. He also knew the doctor he wanted to treat her. Dr. Victor Monke was a psychiatrist to whom Holvey had referred patients before. He was, in Holvey's mind, perfect for Rosemary. "Calm, paternal, unflappable, an extraordinary talent," was Holvey's description of Monke's essential characteristics. "She trusted him. He walked her through the darkness into the light."[5]

On Holvey's recommendation, Rosemary committed herself to the care of Victor Monke at the Mt. Sinai Hospital, situated in the heart of Beverly Hills. It was no more than a five-minute drive from Rosemary's North Roxbury home. Monke's diagnosis confirmed Sherm Holvey's instincts. His initial report said that Rosemary had suffered a "psychotic reaction with severe depression and paranoid features. Her symptoms included hallucinations, fear, depression, violently aggressive behavior and an inability to distinguish between the real and the unreal."[6] Rosemary spent a month as an inpatient in Mt. Sinai, working in group therapy with other patients. The daily routine involved domestic tasks, such as making beds and scrubbing floors, anything that would return the 20 or so patients back to a routine of normal life. In later years, Rosemary's description of the experience became a talk-show routine. She described her fellow patients, painting watercolors of their favorite pills and watching television shows trying to spot other "crazy" people. "It was like a little commune," she told Tom Snyder in 1977, "all of us a little nuts."[7] One critical part of the experience, however, was that Rosemary learned to laugh again—at herself and at the world. When a bunch of flowers arrived from Bob Hope with a note saying, "I hope it's a boy," ("Well, that was the only reason you were ever in hospital before," he later explained), Rosemary's deep-throated laugh was the first indication to her family that recovery was under way.

After Rosemary's discharge in August 1968, the group therapy sessions would continue for another seven years, initially every day before dropping to three days per week. The recovery was slow and painful. Monke's first task had been to break Rosemary's dependence on drugs, a process that involved the same traumas of withdrawal and denial that afflict any addict. Rosemary's behavior through the immediate months was uncertain and unpredictable. The children spent lengthy spells away from her, staying with Betty and with their father. When they did return home, they found that the normal rules of family life had been suspended. "We were never sure which person was coming back," daughter Maria said. "It was a lot of years before she became a safe person to be around." Her mother, she said, slept a lot during that time, the sleep interspersed with outbursts of rage and screaming, "not at you, but about issues that became important to her."[8] Brother Nick characterized his sister's recovery as a "series of ongoing incidents and adjustments"[9] as Rosemary sought to restore the balance to her life.

Inevitably there were casualties in that process. Three years into her recovery, Rosemary felt the need to take control of her home back from her mother. Her ejection, initially to Las Vegas to live with Betty before finally returning home to Kentucky, had a destabilizing effect on the family. Many people, including Rosemary's daughters, viewed "Nana" as the one person who had brought stability to their lives. "Someone I loved and adored. A steadying force in our lives," said Monsita Botwick.[10] Her sister, Maria, echoed the same sentiment. "She was our day to day figurehead," she said. "When that is taken away, life doesn't seem very secure. My mother went away to work and came back. Our grandmother was there all the time and to a child, it was unnerving to have her leave for good."[11] Rosemary's relationship with her mother never did heal, however. Asked later if the past had been resolved before her mother's death in 1973, Rosemary's response was "not nearly enough."[12]

The world that Rosemary reentered late in 1968 was full of harsh realities. With no work and no money coming in other than Ferrer's alimony, she was broke and facing a significant hospital bill for the therapy that she needed. One of her first acts was to return to the courts and seek an increase in the payments from her former husband. Ferrer was as shocked and concerned as anyone by Rosemary's breakdown and did not oppose the request to increase his monthly payments from the token $1 to a sustainable $1,250. His monthly payment of support for the children also went up, eventually reaching $2,500. It was enough to keep the family's heads above water but not much more. Gone were the days of servants and domestic staff at North Roxbury. Instead, Rosemary found herself in a domestic routine that did not come easily. While eventually she did become a very good cook, other domestic routines remained out of reach. "Shrunk all my sweaters" was daughter Maria's recollection of her mother's talent as a laundress.

As well as losing touch with reality, Rosemary had also lost her love of singing as the '60s had progressed. Like the rest of her recovery period, it would be several more years before that returned. Nevertheless, Rosemary remained a performer at heart. She needed to work, not just to bring money in but also to satisfy her innate need to be out front, entertaining and engaging with an audience. Work, however, was no longer easy to find. The abrupt ending to her engagement in Reno had been publicly explained as an attack of influenza. Even before that, Rosemary had told her audience at the Harold's Club that the engagement would be her last and that after it was over, she would retire and become a "full-time mother."[13] That stance was soon modified with the clarification that Rosemary would continue to make records and television appearances and that her retirement would only be from live stage work. But what Rosemary or her recently appointed manager Bill Loeb said to the press mattered little against the show business jungle telegram that transmitted its own messages. Rosemary Clooney, it said, was trouble. "I couldn't get arrested," was how she later summed up her problems in finding work.[14]

The year 1969 came and went with practically nothing in Rosemary's engagement diary. In April, she returned to the nightclub scene for a two-week stay at the Blue Room at the Tropicana in Las Vegas, offering a hollow set of performances when she went through the motions of singing but with none of the flair and feeling that were her trademarks. The onstage Rosemary was also unrecognizable from the svelte blonde that audiences remembered from television appearances with Bing and Dean Martin little more than two years before. With other demons to slay, Rosemary's passion for food, and with it her weight, had become uncontrollable during the months of her recovery. She mushroomed from 120 to 200 pounds in a matter of months. "I didn't look anything like myself," she later wrote, "which pleased me because I could hide inside that fat lady. I was still hiding, not nearly ready to come out but having to work in order to live."[15] Rosemary returned to the Tropicana in July and November, with a two-week engagement at Bimbo's 365 Theater-Restaurant in San Francisco her only other major booking in between; 1970 was even worse. Fellow veteran of the Robert Kennedy campaign Andy Williams offered Rosemary a guest spot on his weekly TV show in October, but Rosemary's appearance was limited to one song—inevitably "Come On-a My House." Rosemary sang pleasantly but seemed detached from the show going on around her, lacking sufficient confidence even to join her host in the customary duet.

A more significant television appearance came on April 13, 1971. Merv Griffin had been a friend since the mid-'40s when, as a singer with the Freddy Martin band, he and Rosemary had first met. Griffin went onto to become one of America's leading talk show hosts and one who was always ready to welcome Rosemary onto his show, just to keep her in the public eye. In later years, said daughter Monsita, a call to Griffin was always the first one her mother would make if she were about to go on the road with something to promote.[16] In 1971, however, the roles were reversed. At the depths of her illness, Griffin had been one of the first people from show business to encourage Rosemary to set her sights once more on the big time, and her appearance as one of his guests was the first of several she would make over the coming years in the wilderness. The Griffin show was a start, but other than a week co-hosting the popular daytime *Mike Douglas Show* from Philadelphia, it was Rosemary's only television appearance during 1971. Indeed, a week in Las Vegas at the Fremont and a fall appearance at the Big Band Festival at Madison Square Garden were her only bookings for the year. Without a recording contract, there was no prospect of using records to plot her recovery path, and in the general absence of doors opening, Rosemary, it seemed, had only one option if she wanted to work. She must lower her sights.

No one knew quite how low they would need to go. Kemmons Wilson had founded Holiday Inns of America around the time Rosemary had been a cover piece for *Time* magazine. Since then, they had gone on to become part of the American landscape. Holiday Inn's iconic logo was a waypoint for many travelers but for Rosemary, it came to represent a place to work. In particular, it was the revolving restaurants that characterized many of the downtown Inns that she remembered—"those things that go round and round at the top."[17] In an effort to compete against more established hotels, some Inns offered a weekend cabaret and it was these that offered Rosemary her chance. "The Holiday Inn bookings told me I could make a living. It might not be the Dorothy Chandler Pavilion or the Hollywood Bowl, but at the Holiday Inn, Hawthorne, that group of people knew I could sing well. And I did," she said in 1992.[18] It wasn't just the Holiday Inns that gave Rosemary a lifeline. Her 1972 bookings included such other unlikely venues as the Kahler hotel, Rochester, Minnesota; the Ramada Inn at Portsmouth, Rhode Island; and the Blue Moon Restaurant in Chicago. Wherever she went, Rosemary found a warm, if surprised welcome. "What are *you* doing working in a place like this?" was a common question. But despite the status of some of the venues, Rosemary's professionalism in this period of her career was the thing that shone through, her performances reflecting the same effort and commitment that she would have given had the venue been a world-class concert hall. It wasn't until Rosemary traveled to Denmark in the summer of 1972, however, that her engagements became anything more than a job. Playing at Copenhagen's open-air Tivoli Gardens, Rosemary rediscovered her love of singing for the first time in years. "It was like coming outdoors after being locked in for a long, long time," she wrote.[19]

Rosemary's "Holiday Inn" period ran through 1972 and into the following year. Merv Griffin offered three more TV appearances during 1973, one of them strangely prophetic in that it placed Rosemary alongside Helen O'Connell and Kay Starr, two singers with whom Rosemary would soon share the stage in *4 Girls 4*. Meanwhile, Rosemary continued her up-and-down recovery. The therapy sessions with Dr. Monke were less frequent, but intensive nevertheless, and there were still occasional setbacks. While working at the Lookout House at Fort Wright, Kentucky, she stayed with brother Nick. He later recalled the harrowing experience of sitting up all night with an apparently comatose Rosemary. Nick held her wrist through the night to satisfy himself that there was still a pulse. When he found a bag of pills in her case, he feared the worst and confronted his sister about it. Rosemary responded in kind, insisting (legitimately) that the pills were no more than vitamins that Dr. Monke had prescribed. She left the house in tears, a temporary rift in her relationship with her brother that quickly healed.

Rosemary's weight continued to vary, although by now the size range was never less than large. Her attempts to kick her lifelong smoking habit complicated the efforts to regain her former figure. Smoking was something that had been endemic in both the Clooney and Guilfoyle families, and lung cancer or emphysema had accounted for the deaths of many of her relatives, including her mother at the age of 64. Both Nick and Rosemary had been three-packs-a-day smokers in their younger days. Nick had quit in his mid-30s, but Rosemary never did. Her smoker's cough—exactly like their mother's, said Nick—told anyone in the family when Rosemary was in the building, and from the '70s on, her smoking added a huskiness to her voice that, unexpectedly, added to its appeal. Rosemary's attempts to kick the habit eventually became a mini-soap opera within the family but she was, said daughter Monsita, "not fun to be around when she stopped. It was not pretty."[20] Eventually, those close to Rosemary realized that the public protestations at having kicked the habit merely masked a surreptitious cigarette now and then. Michael Feinstein said that the smell of tobacco was always there when he visited the downstairs cloakroom at North Roxbury. Eventually, he said, Rosemary realized that she was fooling no one. "I'm just going to the bathroom for a smoke," became a regular line. In later years, Rosemary did eventually cut down to no more than 10 cigarettes per day, fewer still after her near fatal illness in 1998.

December 1973 brought a chance encounter that would turn out to be another milestone on Rosemary's journey back to full health. Clad in a matronly headscarf and driving her open-top Corvette back home to Roxbury Drive—"naturally, from a psychiatrist's office, where else?"[21]—she stopped at a red light. A 1956 Thunderbird drew up alongside. "Rosella? Rosella," said its driver. It was Dante DiPaolo, Rosemary's dance teacher and some time beau, the same Dante she had left by the swimming pool when she departed Hollywood to marry Joe in 1953. "Nobody had called me that, before or since," Rosemary said later.[22] "Call me," she told him. As the lights changed, she shouted her number, which Dante hastily finger-lined into the accumulated dust on his dashboard. They had dinner the next night and from then on were inseparable.

The year 1974 finally brought a concerted effort by Rosemary to get her career back on track. In March, she secured a booking for a CBS-TV special called *Grammy Salutes Oscar*, a tribute to the popular songs that had won an Academy Award. Gene Kelly hosted a show that included other artists such as Jack Jones, Dionne Warwick, and silent screen star Buddy Rogers. Rosemary took the opportunity on the back of the show to go public about one of the demons she had been fighting. She told journalist Nancy Anderson that she had recently shed 60 pounds, with the help of a personal trainer and a strict diet. Publicly, the story was still that Rosemary's absence from mainstream show business was due purely to domestic priorities and that she had spent the past five years as a "homemaker and cook." Feeding a family that included three growing boys meant that there "was so much food around that I let the pounds creep up before I realized it." Now, she said, "my children are so grown-up and are doing so many things on their own that they don't need me at home all the time. I want to work—do television, record, do most anything just so I can get out of the house."[23] Nevertheless, there was realism, almost pessimism, about the extent of her ambition. "Who'd want to gamble on me now?" she said in another interview, contrasting her absence with the durability shown by other 1950s contemporaries such as Perry Como and Dinah Shore. "I've been away a long time."[24]

Nancy Anderson's assessment that Rosemary's diet had given her "a figure more like that of a beauty queen than the mother of five" was sympathetic to a fault, although her efforts had indeed been earnest. Three weeks after the *Grammy* show, Rosemary appeared with Nick and her sister Betty in a Midwest regional TV show called *A Summer Song*. During the '60s, Nick Clooney had built his own career as a TV journalist and anchorman, eventually hosting his own morning show on local stations in Cincinnati. It was Nick rather than either of his more musical sisters who was the draw for the show, which aired across five stations in the region. Filmed at the King's Island Theme Park in Mason, Ohio, the show, said Nick, was seen by Rosemary as an opportunity to put herself back in the shop window. She intended to use the tape of the show in a marketing push to get herself once more in front of promoters and publicists.

A Summer Song was filmed in the summer of 1973, and Rosemary's diet had brought some change to her appearance, but she nevertheless cast a very different image from the one most people remembered. Dressed mainly in a loose fitting, white caftan-style dress with shoulder length blonde hair, seemingly unstyled, Rosemary looked anything but a reborn star. Uncertain and lacking in confidence, Rosemary was largely overshadowed by the vibrancy that her sister Betty displayed on the screen. Her rendition of Frank Loesser's "I Believe in You" was disappointing, one of the rare occasions when she struggled with the timing of a song. It was only when she returned to familiar ground that her class became apparent. Lip-syncing "Tenderly" to a recording made for the show, her voice displayed the purity of tone that had always defined her singing.

Despite the marketing, *A Summer Song* made little difference to Rosemary's attempts to reestablish herself. July 1974 saw her back in the recording studios, this time in the very unfamiliar surroundings of Motown Records. Rosemary was now reduced to recording demos of songs for other artists to consider. It was a new low in her career. Nevertheless, there were more appearances and support from Merv Griffin, and two appearances with him, in 1974 and 1975, offered the first indication that Rosemary's career was on the way back. A chance, almost casual question in the first of them opened the way for Rosemary to reveal publicly the trauma she had gone through. "Were you in therapy?" Griffin asked, to which Rosemary replied with a simple "yes."[25] A year later, Rosemary arrived as part of a gathering of stars paying homage to Tony Bennett. "She sang 'What Are You Doing the Rest of Your Life?'" Griffin said later, "And I'll be darned, nobody moved in the theater."[26] The song, a 1969 Oscar nominee, had a lyric by Alan and Marilyn Bergman to Michel Legrand's melody. Its theme of refound love was apposite given Dante's reentry to her life. Rosemary's rendition was flawless, perhaps the first public appearance by the new Rosemary who would finally cast off the perennial associations with Mitch Miller's harpsichord. Looking slimmer (but still not slim), Rosemary sang the song with barely any movement other than in her face. Holding the microphone static and some distance away from her, it was the surest indication that Rosemary's gifts of reading a lyric and bringing it to life were undiminished.

The revival, however, was never going to come overnight. Another long-standing show business friend, Dinah Shore, also rallied to the cause and offered Rosemary several spots on her *Dinah!* talk shows, but despite the "news" of her breakdown and recovery, Rosemary still looked like a has-been. Only a wave of '50s nostalgia seemed to offer any real prospects. "I'll be singing some new songs and naturally the ones I recorded that people will expect to hear," she told local press ahead of a New Mexico appearance. "I'll be doing all of the million sellers and we're giving a couple of treatments on some of the older ones to bring them a little more up-to-date."[27] The future, it seemed, was in the past. A record deal from the budget label K-Tel in 1975 seemed to confirm that all anyone wanted to hear from Rosemary was '70s stereo versions of the hits that had made her famous. For all the misery of her late '60s recorded efforts, the five songs she recorded for K-Tel, tinny remakes of "Botch-a-Me," "Come On-a My House," "This Ole House," "Hey There," and "Half as Much" were arguably the saddest outputs of any recording studio visit.

When restoration came, it was from an unexpected source. Rosemary's affection for Bing Crosby remained undimmed although the two had seen little of each other during her difficult times. The reason in part, was a function of nothing more than geography and competing priorities. Anxious to shield his second family from the Hollywood lifestyle that had damaged his first, Crosby had moved from Beverly Hills to a San Francisco suburb during the mid-'60s. Now into his 70s, Crosby's priorities had more to do with his teenage children and his own leisure time. Although his stature was such that he could still open any door in the world of show business, he seemed content to grow old and fade away. His occasional TV appearances traded off his past glories. When Rosemary had first been admitted to the Mt. Sinai hospital, Crosby, on safari in Kenya had written a three-page letter, saying that if there was anything he could do, all she needed to do was ask. Beyond that, however, the contact had been sparse. Bing had monitored Rosemary's breakdown more closely than she realized, but emotionally, he was ill equipped to deal with it. Where Rosemary's response to a similar situation would have been to hug and shower a downtrodden friend with affection, Crosby's approach was to stand in the shadows, watching and waiting for the opportunity to help without having to confront the issue.

As Rosemary's recovery progressed, Crosby had discovered that he had problems of his own. Early in 1974, he was admitted to hospital with speculation rife that he had lung cancer. Doctors eventually diagnosed a rare fungal infection in one of his lungs, still life-threatening and necessitating the removal of part of a lung and a long period of convalescence. Most commentators thought the illness would bring down the final curtain on the career of the man who had practically invented the art of popular singing. To everyone's surprise, Crosby's illness had precisely the opposite effect. Once his recovery was complete, he traveled to England to record three new record albums and make a host of TV appearances, singing better than at any time in the past 20 years. Once back in the states, he joined the Mills Brothers on stage at Los Angeles' Dorothy Chandler Pavilion in September 1975 for a concert to mark their 50th anniversary in show business. It planted a seed in his mind about his own "demi-centennial." Crosby's career had begun when he journeyed from his native Spokane, Washington, to Los Angeles in November 1925, breaking into show business the following year. Having rediscovered the joy of singing, he was eager to mark his own golden anniversary with a major event, which he set up in Los Angeles in March 1976. It would be his first major theater appearance, incredibly, since 1939 and it would also give him the opportunity he had been waiting for to offer his friend, Rosemary, a lifeline.

Rosemary was largely unaware of Crosby's renewed interest in performing. Out of the blue, he telephoned and mentioned that he was doing "a benefit" in March and would she join him? Over dinner at their favorite Beverly Hills restaurant during December 1975, Rosemary told Betty that Bing had called. "He asked me to do a benefit with him next March. No big deal, just a St. Patrick's Day bash. It will be good to be on stage with him again. It will give me some confidence,"[28] she said. It would be some time before Rosemary realized that the "benefit" was intended to mark the beginning of a year of anniversary celebrations for Bing that would eventually take him—and her—to Broadway and London's West End. Even when that penny dropped, there was nothing to suggest that the Crosby show would open the door to a new recording contract and a chance to sing, once more, from her heart. Rosemary's second coming was just around the corner.

CHAPTER 11

Back with Der Bingle

Crosby's "little show" was set for March 17, 1976. The venue was the prestigious Dorothy Chandler Pavilion, a 3,000-seat theater that formed part of the Los Angeles Music Center. Rosemary had 10 weeks to prepare for the show, but only one other confirmed booking between Christmas and the date when she would once again join forces with her musical mentor. As the date grew nearer, Rosemary started to have doubts. The first issue in her head was what would she wear? "I couldn't wear the same tacky dress that I'd worn for the Holiday Inns, that's for sure," she said later.[1] There was also the question of what material she would use. The show was her biggest engagement for eight years but more than that, it was a landmark event for someone who meant so much to her. Something more than a couple of choruses of "Come On-a My House" was needed. True, there were other guests on the show including impressionist Rich Little and legendary jazz pianist Joe Bushkin, but other than Bing, Rosemary was the only other featured singer. The idea that she might sing a couple of songs and then slip in and out unnoticed among a parade of guest stars was a long way from the mark.

By the time Rosemary arrived for rehearsals, her nerves were truly jangling. Learning lyrics had never been something that had come easily to her, her memory needing to have the words cut out in large letters and set out around a room so that she could commit the scene into her brain. But no end of preparation could remove the fear in her mind that when her time came to walk out on stage, the words would not come with her. As Rosemary stood in the wings, nervously clutching her sheet music, she felt a hand on her shoulder. It was Bing. "I don't know this," she told him. "Then take it out there with you," said Crosby. "They're not gonna form a posse and come and get you."[2] His message that the audience was on her side was a reminder of what Rosemary had learned on her opening night for Tony Pastor. It was reassurance enough to allow her to trust her professional instincts. As Crosby strolled out into the spotlight to introduce one of his "all-time favorite leading ladies," Rosemary took a deep breath and walked out without her music and sang. She was word perfect. She joined Crosby on a reprise of "Slow Boat to China" from their *Fancy Meeting You Here* album, before blending old with new on a rendition of "Tenderly," closely followed by a lift of Paul Simon's "Fifty Ways to Leave Your Lover." *Variety* said that Rosemary "handled a short, well-done set backed by ever-helpful, excellent arrangements from [Nelson] Riddle and the orchestra."[3] Leonard Feather in the *Los Angeles Times* said that Rosemary looked "fresh and joyful."[4] A corner had been turned.

There was more to come. Rosemary had barely put the excitement of the Chandler event behind her when Bing was on the phone again. He was taking the show to London for a two-week season at the London Palladium and he wanted Rosemary alongside him. "Come and have some fun," he told her. Rosemary still had some Holiday Inn commitments to fulfill, but on June 2, 1976, she lined up with Crosby once more, this time at the Masonic Auditorium in San Francisco for what would be a dry run for the Palladium opening, scheduled for three weeks later. Adding another duet with Bing and solos on "Just One of Those Things" and Leon Russell's "A Song for You," Rosemary began to turn the clock back and anticipate the venue where she had headlined some 21 years before. With Dante and four of the kids in tow, the Clooneys joined the Crosbys on a Boeing 747 and headed for Europe. They spent over a month in the United Kingdom, a trip that daughter Maria recalled as a very happy family gathering. She and her siblings shared their mother's ease with the Crosby family, even to the point that when Rosemary was late for a final rehearsal with Bing—almost a hanging offense—Crosby pulled Maria up on stage to sing her mother's part. With son Miguel playing drums behind her in the Pete Moore Orchestra, it was unquestionably a return to the good times. Crosby was scheduled to do 13 shows at the Palladium, culminating in a July 4 special that would mark the American Bicentenary. From London, the cast traveled to Ireland for two shows in Dublin ("We did well in Ireland," Rosemary told an audience 20 years later. "Crosby & Clooney? Good") and then to Edinburgh for two more performances at the Usher Hall. The stay in London included a reception at Buckingham Palace, hosted by the Duke of Edinburgh. When Queen Elizabeth made an impromptu appearance, Rosemary and Kathryn Crosby, Bing's wife, found themselves chatting amiably with the monarch, three mothers sharing stories about their respective children.

The Crosby shows were unorthodox in that Bing eschewed the idea of top billing, preferring to open and close the show himself as both master of ceremonies and main attraction. Rosemary's contribution had by now grown to six solos, spread over two visits to the stage, plus the "Slow Boat to China" duet that they had done at the Chandler Pavilion. During the first half, she offered what one British reviewer called a "strongly felt" performance of "By Myself," the Arthur Schwartz-Howard Dietz classic from 1937.[5] Then came "Tenderly" and "Fifty Ways" before a return during the second act which included the inevitable offering of "Come On-a My House." The British press, unaware of the trauma of Rosemary's last few years, welcomed her as a returning friend. James Green, writing in the London *Evening News*, said that she was "singing better than ever,"[6] while John Gibson in the *Edinburgh Evening News* summarized her as "Miss Clooney. Delectable. Distinctive."[7] The only surprise, both to members of the press and to the fans who gathered around her, was Rosemary's appearance. She had last been seen on British television in 1968, breaking down in the aftermath of Martin Luther King's assassination. The gaunt, fading star had now become a plump figure in a flowing gown. "A large lady in red," was the *Daily Telegraph's* to the point summation of her appearance.[8] But to those who knew her, Rosemary's acceptance of her weight was now another symbol of her recovery. The diets of 1974 were a thing of the past. Rosemary, said brother Nick, was now ready to say, "This is who I am."[9] Daughter Maria saw her mother's weight as part of her "honesty," a statement on her part that she sought respect from her audience for her voice, not how she looked.[10] From now on, the long, flowing gown would be a part of the Clooney onstage persona.

Rosemary flew back to California shortly after the final concert of the Crosby tour on July 16, 1976, not realizing for a second that she was about to confront the biggest potential setback to her recovery. After appearing at Wolf Trap Farm Park, Virginia, she headed for Virginia Beach where she was due to open at the Moonraker club on August 1. Four days into the engagement, a call came from Las Vegas. Her sister Betty had collapsed in the garden of her home, two days ahead of her eldest daughter's wedding. First thoughts were that Betty's seizure had been brought on by the stress of the upcoming event, but as the hours passed, the news worsened. Betty was unconscious and in the operating room. Rosemary contemplated canceling her show and flying straight to Vegas to be at her stricken sister's side. When another call came, this time from half-sister Gail, Rosemary realized there was nothing she could do. Betty had suffered two brain aneurysms and surgery was futile. She died in the early hours of August 5 at the age of 45. Two days later, Rosemary did fly to Vegas for the funeral. When she arrived, brother Nick was already there. The realization dawned on both of them that the three siblings had drifted away from each other. It was something they could never recover with Betty, but Nick and Rosemary resolved to take a regular vacation together from then on, a commitment they maintained until Rosemary's death. Viewing her sister's body in the open casket was, said Rosemary, "the hardest thing I ever went through." She came through, suffering what she described as "normal grief" but nothing worse. The hallucinations that had followed Bobby Kennedy's death were a dragon slayed. She was back to work within days of Betty's funeral and a month later, the *Cincinnati Enquirer* reported that Rosemary was "singing again" and through her work, "learning how to cope."[11]

Meanwhile, Bing Crosby seemed to have rediscovered the joy of live performing for the first time in over 40 years, and he had plans to take the show on tour through the states. Rosemary was now an integral part of the extravaganza. First stop was a poignant return to Vegas in November 1976, less than four months after she had buried her sister there. Next, Rosemary headed to Dallas, headlining in *An Evening with Rosemary Clooney*, before meeting up with the Crosbys again in New York for a two-week season at Broadway's Uris Theater. It was Crosby's first appearance on Broadway since 1933. The show was largely a rerun of the Palladium, although Rosemary was troubled throughout by a throat ailment that she had picked up in Dallas. It meant that her reviews, while still welcoming, were less fulsome than those she had received in London. *Variety* said that she sang well, but "her remembered old excitement didn't project at the Uris."[12] Jazz critic Gary Giddins, who was later to become a close friend, thought "her high notes were strained"[13] while Douglas Watt in the *New York News* thought that "her once velvety voice [was] somewhat eroded." Her solos, he said, "had notes carefully transposed to keep them within a limited range."[14]

Into 1977, the Crosby bandwagon continued to gather pace. In February, the show played six nights at the Deauville Star Theater in Miami Beach, followed by a one-nighter at the San José Centre for the Performing Arts. Rosemary once again offered her two solo spots and now in better voice, had reviewers calling for more. "It would have been nice to hear the golden-throated Clooney perform some of the many hits she made during her long career,"[15] Sara Lane said in *Billboard*, oblivious to the fact that Rosemary hated most of that material. With the stage show doing so well, it was a natural consequence for one of the major television networks to build on it. On March 3, 1977, Rosemary lined up with Bob Hope, Pearl Bailey, the Mills Brothers, Paul Anka, and Bette Midler for *Bing—A 50th*

Anniversary Gala at the newly opened Ambassador Auditorium in Pasadena, California. The show ran for three hours, with the network planning to edit it down to a 90-minute special for transmission by CBS on March 20. Rosemary sang just one song—"Tenderly"—but was content to be part of something that offered her the biggest exposure she had enjoyed in years. As with the stage show, Crosby was at the center of everything, opening and closing the show and popping up incessantly throughout the three hours. Despite his 73 years, his energy level was high and he was clearly enjoying his return to the show business spotlight.

Rosemary and Dante had arranged to meet the Crosby family for an after-show dinner at Patsy d'Amore's restaurant in Beverly Hills and had left the theater once her own spot was taped. The three teenage Crosby children were traveling with her when they heard a newsflash on the car radio that Bing had been seriously injured in an accident at the Ambassador Theater. After returning to the front of the stage to thank the audience at the conclusion of the show, Crosby had been expected to exit stage left. A central portion of the stage, immediately behind him, had been lowered. It had been used throughout the show, enabling acts to assemble below and be lifted onto the main stage. When Crosby unexpectedly turned to retrace his steps, he stepped into the void, falling almost 20 feet and just missing the open spikes on Jake Hanna's drums. He landed on the concrete floor. As he fell, Crosby had managed to grab at some scenery that slowed the rate of descent, but for a man of his years, it was a life-threatening accident. As Rosemary turned her car around and headed back to the theater, Crosby was whisked off to hospital where x-rays revealed a ruptured disc at the base of his spine.[16] With her friend spending two weeks in hospital and even longer recuperating, the plans to take the show back to Europe and onto Australia and Japan were inevitably shelved. The hiatus disrupted Rosemary's plans, although she was already benefiting from the wave of publicity that the shows had brought. "The exposure with Crosby definitely made it easier to get more upper scale jobs," her manager at the time, Bill Loeb, said.[17] Rosemary later described the period as "a breakthrough, both personal and professional, like an apostolic blessing. Once I appeared with him, under his imprimatur, the world began to open up to me again."[18]

Rosemary already had several TV dates and live appearances planned for the spring of 1977, although the most significant—and unlikeliest—door to open was that of a recording studio. In June 1975, she had recorded her first full album since the *Travelin' Two-Beat* collaboration with Crosby in 1964. The project was the brainchild of Nashville country music producer Scotty Turner and Rosemary's manager Bill Loeb. Turner had known Rosemary from his days as musical director for Guy Mitchell, before he had moved into production with A&M Records. Now, he was in Nashville, heading up the Country Division of Liberty/Imperial/United Artists records. Established labels such as these, however, showed little interest in a Clooney project. To fund the recording of the album, Turner looked to a newly formed company, APCO Records, created by Kentucky businessman, T. P. Alexander as both a record production and artist management venture.

For the sessions at the RCA Victor studios in Nashville, Turner assembled 11 of Nashville's best session players, plus vocal backing from the Jordanaires. Rosemary had responded positively to Turner's suggestion of a "pure country album," he not realizing that this had been the music she had grown up with in Maysville. "When she came into Nashville with Bill Loeb and her then boyfriend Dante, I had a stack of songs chosen for her to go through and she seemed to love them all," Turner said later. "So we had to narrow it down to 10. The first two she chose were songs written by Waylon Jennings's wife Jessi Colter—"I'm Not Lisa" and "Storms Never Last." Another song she wanted to do was Paul Simon's "'Twas a Sunny Day" which fitted the concept perfectly."[19] Other titles included a remake of Rosemary's million-seller "Half as Much." For the instrumental break in the album's title track, "Look My Way," Turner prevailed on Dante to do a soft-shoe shuffle that the mikes captured. "It took some urging, but he finally conceded so I sprinkled some salt on the studio floor and he danced in tempo, to Rosie's delight," Turner said.

Rosemary sang well on the sessions, adopting a more overt, clipped style to her phrasing that accentuated the album's authentic country feel. Sounding good and selling records, however, were two different things. APCO was not interested in publishing the album under its name but equally was unable to sell it to another US label. For a time, it looked as though the recordings might remain unreleased until Turner brought it to the attention of Alan Warner, head of United Artists Records in the United Kingdom. Warner had recently fronted the deal in 1974 that had taken Bing Crosby back into the recording studios, an initiative that had led indirectly to Crosby's return to the live stage. With Rosemary gaining attention at Crosby's side through the summer of 1976, Warner took a chance and bought the output of the sessions. The album appeared in British record shops in time for Rosemary's appearances with Bing at the Palladium. The sleeve captured an unglamorous and unfamiliar Rosemary, sans makeup, with medium-length blonde hair tousled by a breeze. It was anything but the image of a reinvigorated star and the album came and went virtually unnoticed.

Nevertheless, with Clooney in England and enjoying a good press, Warner decided to try again. Warner's original plan was to combine Rosemary with the Ken Barnes/Pete Moore team with whom Crosby was now working, but scheduling proved impossible. United Artists therefore hired contemporary arranger/producer Del Newman to handle the project. Newman enjoyed an established reputation in the business from his work with such names as Elton John and former Beatles Paul McCartney and George Harrison. Recorded over several sessions in London during the summer of 1976, the result was *Nice to Be Around*, an album of contemporary pop songs. Rosemary handled them well, but without ever managing to come up with a definitive treatment of any of the 10 titles. Her voice lacked much of its trademark earthiness and, as with her Broadway appearance, she struggled to hold some of the endnotes. Music critic William Ruhlmann saw the album as a throwback to the half-hearted attempts that many pre-rock vocalists had made to cope with contemporary material in the 1960s. Rosemary's cover versions of songs from the likes of Paul Simon, James Taylor, and Eric Carmen were, he wrote, "misguided." "The world did not need to hear Clooney sing Simon's articulate if sour lyrics to 'My Little Town' or copy Carmen's self-pitying opus 'All By Myself.' This is not a comeback statement for her and is actually just as misbegotten in its way as the country album that preceded it."[20] Once again, there were no takers for the album in the states, but it saw release in England early in 1977, where *The Gramophone* long-windedly welcomed it as "another shining example of how talent and experience can project with maximum effect, contemporary material written by gentlemen mostly unborn when the executant artist began her career."[21] The cover this time showed Rosemary in a more elegant mode, although a strangely retouched photograph made her appear silver-haired, an image that served to only highlight her generational difference from the songs on the disc.

The two United Artists albums were little more than opportunistic ventures, their country and western and soft rock themes never likely to create a new recording platform for Rosemary. Few would have expected a small, jazz-focused label to be the answer either, and yet it was. Carl Jefferson was a businessman and civic dignitary in the northern California town of Concord. He was also a music fan, particularly of jazz, and was frustrated by the lack of outlets for the kind of music that he loved. His first step in rectifying the situation was to organize a jazz festival in Concord in the late '60s.[22] By 1976, what had started as a makeshift event built around a handful of performers was attracting crowds of over 30,000. During the 1973 gathering, guitarists Herb Ellis and Joe Pass approached Jefferson with an idea for a record album. "I was making a profit at my car dealership," he said later. "I thought, 'Hell, what can it cost?'"[23] One album led to a second and then a third and before he knew it, Jefferson had "accidentally" created a record label. By the middle of the decade, Concord's catalog had expanded to 32 albums retailing at $6.98, one dollar below the going rate for the more mainstream releases. Jefferson had growth ambitions for his fledgling label, looking to double its turnover during each three-year trading cycle, although it retained its informality and mom and pop style of operation well into the 1980s.

Jefferson's early focus was on jazz instrumentals. There was little sign in the early days that Concord Jazz might develop into a platform for jazz singing; even more unlikely was the idea that the first vocalist to sign for the label would be the seemingly washed-up star of the '50s, Rosemary Clooney. The catalyst behind both such developments was drummer Jake Hanna. A Bostonian, Hanna had a solid jazz pedigree from spells with Marian McPartland and Woody Herman before taking on a resident musician's job on *The Merv Griffin Show* in 1962. When Rosemary began appearing regularly on Griffin's show during the early years of her recovery, she and Hanna became good friends. When Hanna picked up the drumsticks in the jazz quartet that Joe Bushkin put together to support Crosby's stage show, the friendship was reinforced by the time they spent together on the road.

Hanna was also a close friend of Carl Jefferson, and in 1976 he came up with the idea of a tribute album to Duke Ellington, with proceeds going to the Ellington cancer charity.[24] Concord's limited budgets meant that Hanna was restricted to a quintet rather than a full-blown big band, although he did have a trio of stellar vocalists lined up. Tony Bennett, now freelancing after severing his career-long links with Columbia earlier in the decade, had agreed to do two songs, and when Hanna floated the project across both Rosemary and Bing Crosby during their Broadway tenure at the Uris Theater, both were enthusiastic. Crosby would cover "Don't Get Around Much Anymore," with Rosemary taking two titles, each of them songs that she had included in her *Blue Rose* album with Ellington from 1956, "I'm Checkin' Out—Goombye" and "Sophisticated Lady."

A Tribute to Duke was also the Concord debut album for tenor sax player Scott Hamilton, who along with Hanna, Nat Pierce (piano), Bill Berry (trumpet), and Monty Budwig (bass) made up the quintet that backed the three vocalists. Hamilton remembered the sessions for the album as casual, informal affairs. Because of Crosby's accident in Pasadena, the quintet was forced to record a backing track to which he would later add his vocal, but Rosemary, said Hamilton, was adamant that her titles should be done live. Hamilton had no perception of Rosemary as a jazz vocalist, nor indeed did she, but he could tell that she enjoyed the challenge of working with a jazz group. "She knew what she could do," he said.[25] Both of Rosemary's contributions to the Ellington album reflected the recording style that would become the norm for her early years with Concord. Pianist Nat Pierce would work up lead sheets for the musicians—essentially the melody and the chord structures—but no formal musical arrangement. That came from the musicians themselves when they got together in the studio. "Stimulating is one way to describe it," said trumpeter Warren Vaché, who replaced Bill Berry on Rosemary's subsequent albums. "Frightening is another."[26]

When the Ellington album appeared later in the year, reviewer Peter Reilly singled out the two Clooney tracks for particular comment. They showed, he said, "that she has aged and mellowed like some rare private-stock California brandy only a few have been lucky enough to get their hands on yet" and adding presciently that "the vibes here suggest that Clooney just may be on the verge of a second career, one even more dazzling than her first."[27] Carl Jefferson thought the same and had heard enough in Rosemary's contribution to the Ellington project to ask her if she was interested in making a solo album for his new label. Jake Hanna was once more the architect of the project, and he and Jefferson were happy to give Rosemary carte blanche to sing whatever she liked. Backed by a similar quintet to the Ellington album, Rosemary began work on her debut album for Concord Jazz in the Sunwest Recording Studios in Hollywood on July 7, 1977. Eight vocals and two instrumental pieces were laid out for the sessions, with the "arrangements" again being put together when the musicians assembled in the studio. Rosemary led on three Gershwin classics, plus other standards such as "As Time Goes By" and the Vincent Youmans/Billy Rose song, "More Than You Know." The one concession to Rosemary's former life was a lightly swinging treatment of her 1954 *Pajama Game* hit, "Hey There." While never recapturing the authority that she had shown on the two vocals for the Ellington album, there was enough in *Everything's Coming Up Rosie* to demonstrate that Rosemary had found a new home. Not seeking to scat or improvise in the manner of Ella Fitzgerald or Anita O'Day, Rosemary delivered a set of perfectly timed vocals, allowing the jazz around her to influence and dictate the overall sound of the album. It left her free to concentrate on the subtlety of her phrasing and the delivery of the lyric. *Billboard*'s review said "This excellent 1977 recording has Clooney in the comfortable role of a band vocalist as she sings live, without overdubs, in front of a dynamic jazz quintet."[28]

For Scott Hamilton and Warren Vaché, the sessions were the beginning of a relationship that would endure through the next 15 years. Looking back, Vaché said that *Everything's Coming Up Rosie* was his first real exposure to working with a "significant singer." It required some adaptation to his normal style on his solo spots, ensuring that "he waited until she stopped" before coming in and then making sure that what he played in his own spot would not confuse the singer's ears and compromise her vocal reentry. Nevertheless, Rosemary's skills meant that she was probably the easiest singer for him to cut his teeth with. "Instinctively," he said, "she was better than any singer I worked with. She had perfect pitch."[29] It was a talent that Carl Jefferson also recognized immediately. At the end of the final session, he approached Rosemary and asked if she would be interested in making an album a year for Concord. It was no mega-deal, but one that would pay good dividends to both parties.

No one anticipated that her next outing on Concord Jazz would be a eulogy to Bing Crosby. After a summer of rest and recovery, Crosby took to the stage at the newly opened Concord Pavilion on August 16. Despite his accident, he remained keen to return to the live stage, and with Bill Loeb now handling Crosby's stage bookings, the world tour plans that had been blighted by his fall began to take shape once again. First, Crosby needed to test his fitness—and his confidence—before heading for England and another two-week season at the London Palladium. Rosemary was absent from the comeback show but at Crosby's side when he arrived in Britain. The tour kicked off with two provincial outings in the north of England before opening at the Palladium on September 26, 1977. This time, the show featured less of Crosby's family and more of Clooney, a move that was well received on both counts. For their duet, Bing and Rosemary raided the *Travelin' Two-Beat* repertoire for "New Vienna Woods." Another new spot, put together for the English audiences, was a medley of Noel Coward songs, performed by Bing, his wife Kathryn, and Rosemary. Her rendition of "Mad About the Boy" was the highlight. Once more, the show played to sellout audiences throughout its two-week season, before the cast headed to Brighton on England's south coast for a final concert on Monday, October 10.

Crosby had come through the fortnight well, although the damaged disc in his back clearly inhibited his movement and left him a noticeably frailer, less certain figure than before his fall. When the Brighton performance ended, Rosemary was amazed to see Crosby, with bouquet of flowers in hand, hold out his arms to the audience and mouth the words "I love you." Such an emotional statement was a mile out of character. The spontaneous hugging that went on between members of the cast as they left the stage also surprised her. It was, she said, as though they had come to the end of a road. BBC Radio had hoped to reunite Rosemary and Bing the following day for a Christmas special that would feature much of the Palladium material, but with Rosemary booked to appear in San Antonio, Texas, as soon as the tour ended, she had recorded her input the previous week. She was due to fly back to the states the day after the show in Brighton. As she headed for her dressing room in the Brighton Center, she shared an elevator with

On the *Hollywood Palace* with Bing, February 19, 1966. (Photo courtesy of the late Ron Boalcy)

Rosemary guests on *The Dean Martin Show*, September 21, 1967.

With Jerry Colonna at the Tournament of Roses Parade in Pasadena, January 1969.

Grammy salutes Oscar—with Buddy Rogers, March 1974.

On the comeback trail June, 1977.

With Bing in his last show in Brighton, UK, October 11, 1977. (Photo courtesy of the late Ron Bosley)

4 Girls4 : (left to right) Helen O'Connell, Margaret Whiting, Rose Marie, and Rosemary Clooney. (Photo courtesy of Rose Marie)

With Sondra Locke who played Rosemary in *Rosie—The Rosemary Clooney Story* (1982).

Rosemary on stage, early 1980s. (From the collection of Pamela S. Schlereth)

With nephew George Clooney in *ER*, 1994.

Rosemary celebrates 50 years in show business, 1995.

Tony Bennett arrives at Rosemary's book signing event in 1999. (Photo courtesy of Patsy's Italian Restaurant)

With husband Dante DiPaolo at the book signing. (Photo courtesy of Patsy's Italian Restaurant)

With bandleader, Matt Catingub, 2001. (Photo courtesy Matt Catingub)

Bing. She knew that he would be heading straight for a waiting car as he always left the theater before crowds could gather at the stage door. "I guess I won't see you again," she had said to him, not knowing the import of her words. "No, you won't," Crosby replied, "I'm going to Spain for some serious golf. When I'm home, we'll go to dinner and I'll pay!" Four days later, during the afternoon of Friday, October 14, she took a call from brother Nick. The feed had just come through to the news station where he worked in Cincinnati. Bing was dead, collapsing from a massive heart attack as he left the final hole of a golf course in Madrid.

On October 18, 1977, Rosemary joined the Crosby family for a private funeral service at Culver City's Holy Cross Cemetery. Enigmatic to the end, Crosby had left clear instructions about his funeral that excluded everyone but his closest family. Kathryn Crosby had felt that it was inconceivable that her husband should be laid to rest without his closest friends in show business. Rosemary joined Bob and Dolores Hope plus Phil Harris and his wife, Alice Faye, at the dawn service. As she sat through the Mass, she allowed her mind to wander back over the 26 years that she had known Bing Crosby. She thought of their recording dates and the radio and TV shows they had done. She remembered his love and his wisdom as well as his orneriness, his refusal to reenact the final scenes of *White Christmas* for visiting royalty, and the bizarre piety that caused him to offer separate bedrooms to her and Dante whenever they visited with him. She also remembered the man who more than anyone had paved the way for a new, second career for her. As the morning sun rose and Crosby's casket was lowered to rest alongside that of his first wife, Dixie Lee, Rosemary reflected not only on the man from whom she "had learned so much about singing [and to whom] I now owed my resurrection" but also on her own future.[30] Where, she asked herself, do I go from here?

CHAPTER 12

4 Girls 4

Rosemary Clooney did not know it but she already had the answer to the "where next?" question. On September 6, 1977, she opened in *4 Girls 4* at the Beverly Doheny Plaza, an old Hollywood movie house now converted to a small theater. As the name of the act implied, the show brought together four ladies each with long solo careers behind them, but now working together, partly as a group and partly as four solo acts. Described in advance publicity as a "musical Mount Rushmore," a label that displeased Rosemary, the members of *4 Girls 4* were Rosemary, Margaret Whiting, Rose Marie, and Barbara McNair. Whiting was a 1940s vocalist, the daughter of songwriter Richard Whiting and an early protégé of Johnny Mercer. Rose Marie had been a child star in the early '30s, but was best known to contemporary audiences as Sally Rogers in TV's *The Dick Van Dyke Show*. The fourth member of the group, and the least known to most audiences, was African American TV actress and nightclub artist, Barbara McNair.

The idea for *4 Girls 4* belonged to Rosemary's manager, Bill Loeb, who managed all four girls. Each was working but, said Loeb, finding bookings was a constant struggle. "I thought I would put four old blonde [sic] broads together and make one show out of it," he said.[1] Loeb was not the first impresario in the '70s to tap into the nostalgia market, but what was unique about his idea was that it brought together four performers who each had their own personal claim to stardom. That in turn brought its own challenges. The four girls might have had lots in common—age, longevity, and a catalog of marriages and divorces—but each also had her own ego and star status. "We fought at least once a day," Rosemary said in 1983, "but we got along."[2] For Rosemary, sharing the spotlight with three others also provided a degree of shelter. She was, on her own admission, still tentative onstage, and much as the Crosby show had done, 4 Girls 4 provided some refuge, allowing more time for her stagecraft to rebuild.

Loeb's idea might have been simple in concept but he soon discovered that making it work in practice required attention to detail. "Who's on first?" was a hackneyed showbiz phrase but still potentially the reason for a major fallout. All agreed that they should open the show together with an ensemble number. The girls also knew that they had to close together, perhaps with some special material. The big question however was how to arrange the meat in the sandwich. Loeb's idea was that each girl should do a 25-minute solo spot, but in what order? Nobody wanted to be the first at bat. The first compromise idea was to rotate the order across shows, but the resultant chopping and changing was a recipe for disaster. A coin toss left too much to chance—Rosemary and Margaret Whiting were similar in style and needed space between them. Finally, Whiting broke the deadlock and offered to open. From there, the order fell naturally into place. Barbara McNair would follow Whiting and play through to the interval, with Rose Marie's raucous humor then providing a lively restart. That left Rosemary coming on last and de facto, top of the bill.

When opening night came, the show was still a work in progress. McNair, caught in the midst of some domestic problems, arrived only at the last minute. Missing most of the rehearsal, she was never able to gain command of the orchestrations that Frankie Ortega had put together and some friction with the musicians spilled over into the act. The closing number utilized some special lyrics to the old song, "Side by Side," although none of the four could remember them without the help of cue cards. Ultimately, the detail did not matter. Richard Houdek in the Los Angeles Times said that the show was "fun primarily because the participants were having a good time. Their hastily devised finale, a chaotic, sometimes harmonious rendition of "Side by Side" might be embarrassing to anyone but four real pros who have no problems with themselves or each other." Rosemary's larger than expected size was clearly a surprise to Houdek, who described her dress as like "one of those bird outfits in 'The Magic Flute,'" although his later comment that she was "so gentle and disarming that she could wear a paper sack and hold an audience" offered a degree of mitigation.[3]

Audience reaction went beyond anyone's expectations. "At the end, the entire crowd rushed down to the stage," Whiting wrote later. "I could see arms outstretched and hands reaching for us. It had never happened to me before. In fact, I had never seen that kind of overwhelming approval."[4] Tickets for the rest of the week sold out immediately, and when they closed, an offer came in for three weeks at the Huntington Hartford Theater in Hollywood. Three of the girls said yes, but McNair decided that the show wasn't for her. At 43, she was the youngest of the group by six years from Clooney (and 10 and 11 years, respectively, from Whiting and Rose Marie). "I didn't really fit in with the other ladies because they were from a different era," she said later.[5]

The three remaining members talked to a number of possible replacements, including Connie Haines, Jo Stafford, and Kay Starr, before settling on former Jimmy Dorsey vocalist, Helen O'Connell. Despite being the oldest of the revised foursome, O'Connell brought glamour to the act. "She was gorgeous!" Rose Marie said. "In her sixties, she looked like she was twenty!"[6] Looks were one thing, but the girls quickly realized that O'Connell brought something else too; a giant ego and a desire to take control. "She's gone now, but Helen O'Connell was a pain in the ass," Rose Marie recalled. "Helen caused all kinds of trouble by saying things and doing things and then coming around and saying, 'I'm sorry. Forgive me.' There were times when we never talked to her."[7] Even the settled batting order had to change, with O'Connell demanding that she and Rosemary should alternate in the second and fourth spots.

The revamped *4 Girls 4* opened on November 22, 1977, at the Huntington Theater to a celebrity audience. Lucille Ball, Bob Hope, Milton Berle, and Danny Thomas were there to witness a show that pushed all the right buttons. "We caught the public's imagination," Margaret Whiting wrote later. "There was a whole audience out there, wondering what had happened to their lives, wondering indeed what had happened to ours."[8] The show was a smash and soon Bill Loeb was fielding offers from top venues across the country. Four sets of schedules, however, meant that it was May 1978 before the foursome could take to the stage again. When they did, they broke house records at the Fairmont Hotel in New Orleans, before taking the show to Savannah, San Diego, Anaheim, and San Francisco. *Variety's* reviewer said that the Fairmont show in San Francisco was a success because "all know how to work a house and glean the most from their mature pipes. They're immensely solid pros."[9] For the next 18 months, *4 Girls 4* could do no wrong, and as Rosemary's fifth decade in show business dawned, the momentum showed no sign of abating. No matter what tensions might arise between O'Connell and the rest of them, the four girls had been around too long to allow any backstage fallouts to impair their onstage professionalism. When they hit Dallas in March 1979, the review from the local press sounded a familiar tone. "It all comes together so naturally and so beautifully, it's hard to believe the act is only a year and a half old," wrote Diane Werts.[10]

By 1980, the $20,000 a week that 4 Girls 4 had commanded when they started out, had jumped to $60,000. It was big money, and welcomed especially by Rosemary, whose finances had still not recovered from the nonearning years that followed her breakdown. The return to a busy touring schedule also sat well with her. Son Gabriel said, "Performing was the yin and the yang of her existence." If his mother was not on the road for a spell, he added, she would "get twitchy. She needed to have spells in her life where she was in a hotel room, where the most important issue of the day was 'What time is Showtime?'"[11] There was further proof that she was now firmly back in the public eye when tissue manufacturer, Georgia-Pacific, polled audiences and found that Rosemary topped a list of 15 celebrities, about whom they had asked the question "Who do you trust most?" It led to a lucrative contract for a series of TV commercials for Coronet towels.

Out on the road, the girls had the company of Dante DiPaolo. Dante was Rosemary's man but got on well with the three other girls, cooking for them, pressing their gowns, and even running midnight errands when one of them needed some medication. For a spell, DiPaolo was the nearest thing the girls had to a road manager. By the end of 1979, however, the touring schedule had grown to the point that Rose Marie thought they needed someone in that role full time. The other three, all with an eye on the bottom line, took some persuading before hiring Allen Sviridoff in time for their opening at Lake Tahoe in February 1980. Sviridoff was a generation younger than the four girls, a baby boomer but one raised on the Broadway musical rather than rock. Starting out as a lighting engineer, he had moved into production management with Mitzi Gaynor and then Ginger Rogers, with whom he was working in Buenos Aires when a mutual friend told him about the 4 Girls 4 opportunity. There was no question that there was a big job to do. The girls were now appearing 40 weeks out of 52 and traversing the country like never before. Sviridoff soon made an impact. Rosemary later described it as like moving from amateur to professional status. "Everything was seen to," she remembered. "It was something like the way of life, and the way of working, I'd been accustomed to; it was well worth the added expense."[12]

Sviridoff's role soon grew and within a year, he had taken over as the production manager for 4 Girls 4 and eventually as manager for Clooney on an individual basis. When they played the Westbury Music Fair on Long Island in May 1981, a chance remark from a promoter revealed that the underpinning contracts for the show were not as the girls had understood them. The issue was around payments to a booking agent. The girls claimed to have made it clear to Bill Loeb that if he needed to pay an agent to help with bookings, it should come from his share of the take, not theirs. The

Westbury experience, however, suggested that there were some double contracts in place—one that the four girls saw but a different one for the venue. Loeb consistently denied any wrongdoing, referring only to the dispute as "mix-up over contractual arrangements."[13] "There was no double-contracting at all," he said. "There were contracts made, and all of the girls saw what they were. The agent at the time was getting his regular commission, and the money that was left over after his commission was split up."[14] Eventually, lawyers were called in and a settlement reached, but confidence in Loeb had been broken. For Rosemary, it marked the end of the road with him. She asked Sviridoff to take charge of her affairs, a role that he performed for the rest of her career.

Sviridoff's approach to taking charge of Rosemary's career brought with it a change of emphasis. Seeing himself as more of a business partner than a manager, Sviridoff took the role on with nothing more than a handshake and a commitment to an open, honest relationship. One of his first tasks was to put more into Rosemary's individual career outside of 4 Girls 4. She had continued to take individual bookings alongside the 4 Girls 4 bandwagon, but when Sviridoff took charge, there was, he said, only one confirmed solo booking in her diary.[15] More to the point, Rosemary's solo offering had not moved on from the spot she had put together for the Crosby shows some four years before. 4 Girls 4 was essentially a nostalgia show, as was her solo act. It went down well with critics and audiences alike, but with Rosemary still in her early 50s—and now the youngest of the reconstituted 4 Girls 4—Sviridoff thought that she was being undersold. His sights were set on building a second career for her that would sustain through the next two decades.

One critical piece in the jigsaw was her relationship with Concord Records. Since she had cut her debut album in 1977, there had been four more outings on Concord. During 1978, she recorded two tribute albums. First was the inevitable homage to Crosby on Rosie Sings Bing and then Here's to My Lady, a tribute to Billie Holiday. Rosemary had met the enigmatic "Lady Day" in the middle '50s, forming a friendship that led to Holiday becoming godmother to Rosemary's daughter, Maria. The two tribute albums were followed by the first in a series of records dedicated to individual songwriters. Rosemary's longtime neighbor, Ira Gershwin, was the first subject in a collection of 10 songs that picked up not only his work with his brother George, but also collaborations with Harold Arlen and Jerome Kern. Ira, Rosemary said later, had always been her favorite lyric writer. "He had a way of putting words in your mouth," she said, making his songs easy to sing.[16] Ira was prevailed upon to contribute a sleeve note for Rosemary's album, although it took some persuasion from Michael

Feinstein, then working as an archivist for him, to make something happen. Ira, said Feinstein, was reluctant because he thought that the idea of writing a note on a collection of his own songs would be "self-serving and egotistical."[17] Feinstein persevered and eventually persuaded the elderly lyricist to put his name to a two-line letter that included a four-word postscript. "I loved every word," it read.

Rosemary's next Concord outing brought a change of material. *With Love*, recorded in November 1980, had its origins at the Gershwin session the year before when Rosemary expressed a wish to Carl Jefferson that she might do an album of contemporary tunes, but with the same group of jazz musicians. *With Love* was the result. Scheduling necessitated some changes of personnel, but with Hamilton, Vaché, Cal Collins, and Nat Pierce forming the core and Jake Hanna returning with the drumsticks, continuity was preserved. Similarly, the final list of songs for the new album contained only five that could be described as contemporary, with standards "Hello Young Lovers," "Just In Time," and "Tenderly" also there. New or old, it mattered not as each song was given a lengthy treatment, Rosemary's top drawer vocals nestling into a vibrant setting that retained enough individuality to allow each of the seven musicians to place their own signatures on the songs. Rosemary reserved her best vocal for the Oscar-winning "The Way We Were," which proved to be especially popular in Japan and paved the way for several live appearances there. Its popularity masked an uncharacteristic error by Rosemary in the opening lyric, however. Where Alan and Marilyn Bergman had written "scattered pictures," Rosemary sang "shattered." "I guess that's how I feel about romance," Rosemary told Michael Feinstein when he pointed out the mistake.[18]

The only difficulty that any reviewer had on *With Love* was deciding which of the nine tracks shone brightest. Warren Vaché's cornet piece on the remake of "Tenderly" gained as many plaudits as the vocal itself, as did Cal Collins's guitar extemporization on "Hello Young Lovers." It was the new Rosemary Clooney, however, who gained most of the attention. In an interview with *Stereo Review*, she offered some insight into the way in which recent events in her life had influenced her approach to singing. "I think that today I have a better approach to everything, that I can deal with the feelings I have now instead of any of the residual feelings from back then. All that garbage has been cleaned out. When I find a piece of material that's new to me now, such as Billy Joel's *Just the Way You Are*, or Paul Anka's [sic][19] *Alone at Last* on the new album, I can meet it and sing it on its own terms. There's no more of that wistfulness I used to have no matter what song I was doing, which came from my wondering, 'God, am I ever going to get out from underneath all this?' There's no feeling any more that I have to fit the song to that 'thing,' that performer named Rosemary Clooney, which I had created and which wasn't me at all."[20]

Despite the critical acclaim and decent sales, not everything in the Concord garden was rosy. The contractual relationship with the label was informal and relied heavily on the personal relationship between Rosemary and Carl Jefferson. The two got on well—mostly. Jefferson, said Concord Executive Vice-President John Burk, was "a gruff ol' guy" who was "tremendously proud of having played a role in establishing the second part of Rosemary's career."[21] The relationship between them, however, could be unpredictable. Allen Sviridoff concurred, describing it as a "love-hate" relationship that could easily go off course. Rosemary, he said, enjoyed poking fun at the expense of Jefferson's alter ego in her description of him as a "used car salesman." Clooney had been important in establishing the fledgling record label as a force in mainstream music, but, said Sviridoff, "without Jefferson, she might never have had the musical resurgence that she had."[22] Despite the inherent symbiosis, however, the Concord partnership was not guaranteed. One of Sviridoff's first priorities was to put the commercial arrangement onto a firmer footing, one free from the vagaries of the personal relationship.

Allen Sviridoff still had a role in *4 Girls 4* although it was becoming increasingly apparent to him that Rosemary was the key performer in the group. "From a promoter's standpoint, she was the most salable. I don't want to take away from the fact that five years of promotion of *4 Girls 4* certainly helped her. But you have to remember that Rosemary Clooney was, for want of a better comparison, the Madonna of the early 1950s," he said later.[23] Sviridoff was much taken by the way one of Rosemary's contemporaries, Tony Bennett, had been reinvented and reinvigorated by a new management approach and he saw the same potential in Rosemary. He knew that it was a long-term game—"it might take ten years"—but there was time. Rosemary was 53 years old, two years younger than Bennett, and still had a long career ahead of her if she wanted it.

Loeb's departure meant that Rosemary had lost her booking agency as well as her manager. As a replacement, Sviridoff targeted David Hanson at International Creative Management (ICM), the agency that handled some of the promotion for *4 Girls 4*. Sviridoff persuaded him that Rosemary's potential matched that of Bennett and together, they developed a strategy that was designed to put her in front of the same audience groups. The best and most obvious means of doing that was by placing her alongside Tony Bennett himself. It meant, said Sviridoff, accepting second billing and less money, but in the long term, it was a price worth paying.[24] With Bennett and Clooney fellow survivors of the Mitch Miller era at Columbia, it was an easy combination to make. The first manifestation of Sviridoff's plan came in November 1982, when Rosemary played a week at the Valley Forge Music Fair in Pennsylvania, alongside Bennett and the Count Basie Orchestra. One week later, the same three stars played the Westbury Music Fair on Long Island. More dates with Bennett followed in 1983, and by the time the pair hit Harrah's in Reno in July, it was Rosemary who was winning the hearts of the reviewers. *Variety* said that Clooney came off the better of the two, "not because her songs or arrangements or voice is better, but simply because Rosemary Clooney is feeling her music and lyrics and communicating them." Her treatment of "The Way We Were," the reviewer said, "gave every ounce of feeling to a series of memory slides, not just of Clooney's career but of American history."[25] Her medley of Ira Gershwin's lyrics was, it said, "stunning." Sviridoff's tactics meant that Rosemary came to the attention of Bennett's agents and promoters as well as his audience. Roger Vorce was one of the founding partners of the Agency for the Performing Arts (APA). He was, said Sviridoff, "a genius in the agency business."[26] After much chasing and cajoling, Vorce agreed not only to handle Rosemary, but also to recruit Hanson as a West Coast representative. This created the infrastructure that oversaw Rosemary's career for the rest of her life.

Sviridoff's long-term plan for Rosemary was one thing but his priority in 1981 was keeping the *4 Girls 4* show on the road. Even before the dispute with Bill Loeb, some of the tensions inherent in the group were beginning to spill over. When the four appeared on the Mike Douglas Show in 1979, Rose Marie's contempt for Helen O'Connell was clear for all to see. "Oh, why don't you go and get your hair combed," she snapped at one point. Things finally came to a head at Caesar's in Atlantic City in June 1981. When Rose Marie overran her slot one night, significantly cutting into Clooney's spot, Rosemary's Irish temper blew. Margaret Whiting recalled the incident as the last straw for Rose Marie. "She retreated to her room, got one of her migraines, and couldn't do the second show; it was the only time I remember that she couldn't perform. That's when she made her decision to leave."[27] Rose Marie herself attributed the breakup as being solely due to Helen O'Connell. "Helen seemed to think that *4 Girls 4* belonged to her," she wrote in her autobiography.[28] "I was almost having a nervous breakdown because of her," she said later. "She was a very hard person to live with and to work with."[29] Margaret Whiting quickly followed Rose Marie in leaving the group. Whiting had always been the one with the greatest sense of ambition for *4 Girls 4*. She had tried to persuade the others to set their sights on Broadway, or even a *Golden Girls* style TV sitcom, although she denied that frustration had been a factor in her decision to quit. "I had already announced some time before that I thought five years with *4 Girls 4* was enough'" she later wrote.[30]

Whiting's departure marked the end of the original foursome. Helen O'Connell moved quickly to try to ensure that legal ownership of the act now resided with herself and Rosemary. Veteran comedienne Martha Raye was recruited to fill the gap left by Rose Marie, while Kay Starr came in to take Whiting's place. By the time *New 4 Girls 4* took to the stage for the first time in St. Louis on December 2, 1981, the act was starting to resemble a game of musical chairs. It had been further complicated by Rosemary and Margaret Whiting's decision to launch their own spinoff act. Opening on November 17, 1981, the duo played two weeks in New York at the New Ballroom on West 28th Street. In *Fancy Meeting You Here*, the two singers presented a cut down version of the original *4 Girls 4*, the highlight of which was a 55-song medley, "Daddy and the Boy Next Door." Daddy, of course, was composer Richard Whiting, while the boy next door was Rosemary's long-time neighbor, Ira Gershwin. Whiting had flown out to Hollywood to rehearse the show at Clooney's home when Michael Feinstein arrived with a message that Ira wanted to see the two ladies right away. "So we went," Rosemary told the *New York Times*. "Me in my terrycloth slippers and robe, Margaret dressed to the nines, as usual. We sang our medley for him. I had never sung for him before and I felt as though I was 10 years old."[31]

New 4 Girls 4 dominated Rosemary's life through most of 1982 with a series of one-nighters, plus longer stays at venues such as the Royal Poinciana Playhouse in Palm Beach and the Bayfront Center Theater in St. Petersburg, Florida. Kay Starr and Martha Raye brought energy and unpredictability to the act, while Rosemary and Helen O'Connell now blended their hits with more contemporary material for their individual slots, O'Connell winning particular plaudits for "Don't Cry Out Loud." Bill Loeb was by now long gone from the scene, but there was no question that his formula for "four blonde broads" had proved to be highly commercial. In March, Rosemary starred in a TV special built around her *With Love* album and filmed in Los Angeles the previous summer. A trip to England for some TV and radio work also offered a respite from the *New 4 Girls 4* schedule as well as reminding the public that Rosemary was more than just part of a girl group.

Rosemary's most significant exposure of 1982, however, came in a film where she was heard but not seen. In 1977, she had written *This for Remembrance*, an autobiography ghosted for her by author Raymond Strait. The book's origins came from her disclosure to Merv Griffin that she had undergone therapy. Rosemary's willingness to discuss it led to an approach from

Ladies Home Journal for a feature that appeared in March 1976. Rosemary's story caught the eye of the book publishing market and a contract soon followed. Strait taped hours of interviews with Rosemary to come up with the book, which took its title from *Hamlet*. It majored on Rosemary's breakdown, the details of which occupied its first 80 pages. Written in a candid and open style, the book was almost a self-penned exposé, laying bare the wreckage of Rosemary's life since the mid-'60s. When it appeared, Rosemary worked hard to promote it, becoming a TV talk show regular. There, she offered the same openness that she had displayed in the tapes for Strait. When Tom Snyder asked her why she had been so open about such personal issues, her reply was characteristically blunt. "Because that's the reason the publisher gave me an advance to do it," she said.[32] When Snyder developed the theme, asking Rosemary and Helen O'Connell why they worked so hard at this stage of their lives, Rosemary was first in with the answer. "Money," she said, raising no more than an eyebrow to Snyder's follow-up suggestion that everyone assumed "they were loaded."

Over the next few years, Rosemary's account of her breakdown—the story of the white-knuckle ride up the old mountain road in Reno, the cocktails of pills and the insider's account of life in a psychiatric ward—made good television, to the point that it almost became an act in itself. It was as if the old Rosemary, bursting with guilt, frustration, and betrayal locked up inside her, had now turned full circle. In its place, sat the ultimate earth mother, scarily uninhibited and seemingly prepared to engage with anyone's agenda on whatever terms. "I'm freer because I don't give a damn," Rosemary said later. "I can say almost anything I please. It has freed up a lot of feelings."[33] The release that Rosemary felt also freed up another side of her. Those who knew her offstage loved her raucous, laugh-out-loud sense of humor, but it was a side to her character that stayed essentially private until the post-breakdown Rosemary emerged. "I've never seen your sense of humor the way I am seeing it today," Snyder said to her during the interview in November 1977. "You're funny. You're really funny."[34]

One talk show appearance stood out against all others. however. During 1982, Rosemary was the featured guest of TV psychiatrist, Tom Cottle in his *Up Close* series. In an hour's interrogation, shown over two consecutive days, Rosemary faced her demons, up close and personal. It was riveting, if harrowing, television. Twice she was forced to stop as tears overcame her. She talked openly about her early life, her unresolved issues with her mother, and the death of Betty. The starkest moments of the interview came however when she discussed the events of 1968. "I knew I was losing it," she said when she talked about the wounded servicemen she had seen in the Philippines and the way she had reacted.

Bobby Kennedy, she said, had offered a personal as well as a political life-line. "You pinned your psychological well-being on him?" Cottle asked. "Yes," was the answer. "I couldn't accept that he had been shot," she said. "I really think I broke then. I just couldn't believe it."[35]

Cottle's final question was about how Rosemary had become so able to answer such probing questions with such detachment and honesty. Her answer was simple. "Because I'm proud of myself," she said. Writer and close personal friend, Deborah Grace Winer thought that the openness Rosemary displayed was the inevitable consequence of what she had been through. Rosemary, she recalled, had told her that her entire life had been spent trying to please others, to make everything okay for those around her. It was a tiring, exhausting way of life and post-breakdown, something that Rosemary no longer had the energy or the patience to maintain. "She threw it out the window," said Winer. All that remained was total honesty. That freedom—to be herself, to say what she thought and to pour love and affection all over those people she liked and cared about—was what made her comfortable with her own skin. This, said Winer, was the bracingly candid Rosemary who emerged on talk shows in the '70s and '80s.[36] Not everyone found Rosemary's outspokenness quite so reassuring. New York critic, Stephen Holden, witnessed most of Rosemary's appearances in the city over her final two decades as well as her TV appearances. For him, Rosemary played the "mother confessor" just a little too enthusiastically for her own good. "For all her warmth, love and the maternal thing, the same demons that were inside her when she had her breakdown were still there," he said.[37]

Rosemary's autobiography had always been potential film material and in 1982, it formed the basis for *The Rosemary Clooney Story*, which aired on CBS-TV on December 8. Sondra Locke, who played the part of Rosemary, had won great acclaim and an Academy Award nomination for her role in *The Heart Is a Lonely Hunter* in 1968. Merv Griffin played a critical role in getting Locke to take the part and had been the one who introduced her to Rosemary. The chemistry between Rosemary and Locke was good, even to the point that the actress became acquainted with Dr. Monke, Rosemary's therapist. "I trusted Sondra so I knew it would be all right," Rosemary said in an appearance on Griffin's show.[38] During the filming, Rosemary made only one 40-minute visit to the set, recounting the strangeness of seeing someone else wearing the costume that she had worn in *Red Garters* almost 30 years before. Rosemary also provided all the vocals for the movie, to which Locke lip-synced, an experience that both found challenging. For scenes featuring the early days of the Clooney Sisters, Rosemary needed to record vocals for both her own and Betty's voice, with a harmony between the "two" voices. Michael Feinstein recalled being at the session when Rosemary needed to duet with herself on "Hawaiian War Chant." It was something, he said, that took much lengthier preparation than a normal Clooney vocal performance. The ghost of Betty, the more natural harmony singer, was still there.

Allen Sviridoff had been enthusiastic about the exposure that the film would bring to his new charge, as was Rosemary. "At the time, she was thrilled to have an income and the attention from it," he said. Artistically, though, the film did little more than prove the old adage that any publicity is good publicity. "Poor script, poor cast, mediocre director," was Sviridoff's summation of the production, although Rosemary's singing, he said, was "perfection—as usual."[39] John O'Connor in the *New York Times* agreed. "An irritating example of the kind of television biography that seems to be revealing a lot but is really carefully vague," he wrote. "The film portrays many of the basic facts about Miss Clooney's life but it shies away from making crucial connections or exploring sensitive motivations. Too much of the time Miss Locke is left looking like a mildly confused zombie. Miss Clooney is far more interesting than that. She's a seasoned and classy woman who has paid her dues, on all fronts."[40]

Spurred on by the publicity around the film, however, Rosemary pursued a busy schedule through the winter of 1982, her *New 4 Girls 4* commitments mixed in with solo spots and another return to London for some TV and radio appearances. In terms of impact, *New 4 Girls 4* had picked up where its predecessor had left off. When the girls played several dates in Florida in the spring of 1982, *Variety* said the show was "striking for its musicality."[41] Clooney's reviews were consistently good, her rendition of "Come in from the Rain" from the *With Love* album stopping the show, although it was the newcomer Martha Raye who was now winning the biggest ovation. While Starr, O'Connell, and Clooney were all at pains to retain a contemporary feel to their material, Raye felt no such need. "The old routines still work," said *Variety*.[42] The new act played its way through 1982 but by the end of the year, Martha Raye had left. Audiences had loved her outrageous brand of humor, but before long, she too found one member of the foursome hard to bear. "How the hell could you stand that Helen O'Connell?" Raye said to Rose Marie when their paths crossed some time later. Comedienne and singer, Kaye Ballard became her regular replacement.

Meanwhile, Sviridoff's strategy for promoting Rosemary Clooney in her own right was beginning to pay dividends. May 6 had seen her in Cincinnati, celebrating "Rosemary Clooney Day" with a 50-minute concert for an audience of over 5,000 at the Serpentine Wall. A solo spot at Charley's in Washington, DC, was followed by an East Coast tour with Tony Bennett. More and more of Rosemary's bookings now had an overt jazz context about them. In June 1983, she teamed up uncomfortably with Mel Tormé for *A Salute to the Swing Era* at the Kool Jazz Festival in New York. When she declined Tormé's suggestion that the two of them should combine for a medley he had written ("Mel's medleys are only about Mel," she told Sviridoff), it put her manager in the firing line for a stream of abuse from Tormé, whose self-centered performance dominated John S. Wilson's review in the *New York Times*. He reserved his positives, however, for Rosemary. "In the ease and flow of her performance," he said "she showed how successfully she has made the transition from the pop world to a subtle jazz interpretation."[43]

August found her playing the Hollywood Bowl with Lionel Hampton and Les Brown and his Band of Renown, followed three days later by an appearance at the Concord Jazz Festival with the Woody Herman Band. When Jack Hawn of the *Los Angeles Times* tracked her down ahead of the Bowl appearance, she outlined her autumn schedule. First was another album for Concord, then it was off to Japan for three concerts, then Toronto, San Francisco, and England in November, followed by Louisville and San José for the New Year. It was an ambitious schedule for a 55-year-old grandmother, Hawn noted, and one perhaps that contained a hint of danger? Her rebuttal of the risk was firm. "This might be the favorite period of my life," she told him. "It seems as if all my life experiences have come together for the better. It is very fulfilling."[44] Rosemary's second career was now in full flow and with it, she was building an artistic reputation that would far exceed anything that she had achieved before. Her part in *New 4 Girls 4* was, however, becoming a distraction. The group had served its purpose, replenishing her coffers and allowing time and space to rebuild her stage presence. Her last appearance came in Philadelphia at the end of July 1983. In a strange twist, Margaret Whiting returned to replace Rosemary. In time, there were more changes of personnel, the act even becoming *3 Girls 3* for a time, and it continued in various forms until the end of the decade. But for Rosemary, it was 1949 all over again. It was time to go solo.

CHAPTER 13

All That Jazz

After varying her Concord theme for the *With Love* album, Rosemary resumed her songbook series by shifting the focus to two more songwriters. The subjects were Cole Porter and Harold Arlen, both of whom she had known personally. Her songbook series began to draw comparisons with Ella Fitzgerald's Verve songbooks from the late 1950s, although the two sets were different, both in concept and execution. Ella's work had been about cataloging the output of the great songsmiths. Recorded mainly as double albums, they had been extensive, offering 30 or more titles from each writer's portfolio, relying on the then-new microgroove technology to squeeze them onto two vinyl discs. Although known best for her jazz improvisation and scat singing, Ella had sung the songs just as they had been written. The albums were, said critic Gary Giddins, more about establishing the reputations of the songwriters than showcasing Ella's interpretation of them.[1] In contrast, Rosemary's songbook offerings were personal snapshots. Until CDs replaced vinyl discs in the 1990s, none of the albums exceeded 10 songs, all of them selected because of some meaning or personal significance that they held. *Rosemary Clooney Sings the Music of Cole Porter* was recorded in January 1982. Porter had been Rosemary's father's favorite songwriter. She and Porter had met during the '50s when their paths had crossed on the movie party circuit. "Very bright, very elegant, a nice man," was her summation of him in a 1991 interview,[2] despite her recollection of having been admonished by him for switching seating plans to suit her preferences at one such party. She was less kind about his songs. "He must not have liked singers," she told Charles Grodin in 1995 "because he gives you nowhere to breathe."[3] On another occasion, she echoed an oft-quoted Ella Fitzgerald remark that Porter's penchant for catalog songs was like "singing a laundry list."[4] Reviewing the album, John S. Wilson in the *New York Times*, was more enthusiastic about the musicians' performances than Rosemary's vocals but nevertheless ranked the album highly. "She may be a little shaky in the upper register but it's the spirit and the phrasing and the sensitivity to her surroundings that make this record an appealing example of unselfconscious jazz singing," he wrote.[5]

Not everyone regarded the reborn Rosemary as a jazz singer. It was a debate that would extend through and beyond the remaining 20 years of her life. *Downbeat* had been one of the first journals to raise the issue in its review of two of her early Concord albums in 1979. The idea of pop singers working with jazz bands was not new, said the magazine, but it was "risky." Rosemary, it said, had been best known as "a vendor of trifling ditties," and

> the major part of her one time following was not likely to be keyed in on the activities of a small independent jazz label, and especially one with limited advertising. However, jazz purists, despite their common disdain for show biz successes, have usually encouraged the defection of re-born artists from the enemy camp, providing those artists are able to demonstrate sufficient sincerity, talent, and adaptability. There is no doubt that Rosie possesses all of these characteristics. What is more, by simply being herself she neatly avoids the pitfalls awaiting so many other aspiring jazz singers, particularly those hopefuls who seek acceptance through the emulation of their betters. Rosie sings the only way she knows how, and if that fresh, all-American charm that was once so winning has now taken on an additional maturity, it makes her jazz singing that much more of a treat.[6]

Others, however, were less prepared to admit Rosemary to the jazz singers' emporium. Singer Anita O'Day was a self-appointed gatekeeper to the tent and her definition of the jazz strike zone was much smaller than *Downbeat's*. "I'd say she was the best ballad singer ever," she said. "She's so precise and understandable and she sings a good melody. I do just the opposite—I fight the melody. That's called jazz, that's called improvising on the chord so it's a different style. But she stays on the melody. I can't stand singers who sing the melody, but I can stand Rosemary Clooney."[7] Carmen McRae was another for whom jazz singing began and ended with the ability to improvise. "You know they call Rosemary Clooney a jazz singer," she told *Downbeat* in 1991. "This woman never improvised in her life. She sings a song exactly the way it's written."[8] O'Day's and McRae's assessments were close to Rosemary's own positioning of her style. "I don't do anything that's absolutely inventive," she said in an interview with the *New York Times*.

"I don't do the kinds of things that Ella Fitzgerald does, or Carmen McRae, or Sarah Vaughan, the kinds of people that take a melodic line and absolutely change it within the chord structure to a different thing. I don't have those kinds of talents. I have good interpretive sense. I sing in tune and I have good time and I enjoy singing with good musicians. Probably that's as close to jazz as I'll ever get."[9] In a radio interview a few months later, she added an important rider. "I feel as though I'm the only one with the words, so I should be tending to that," she said.[10] Rosemary's positioning never varied. Recording a duet with her for his *Pure Imagination* album in 1989, Michael Feinstein attempted to move her onto a different plane. The session, he said, was not going well, in part because Rosemary herself seemed out of sorts. To try and create a spark of effervescence, Feinstein suggested a scat routine over one of the instrumental breaks. Rosemary refused point blank. "Momma don't scat," she barked. When the producer finally settled on a take, it was Feinstein who did the scatting. Rosemary sang a lyrical counterpoint that deviated not an inch from the composer's melody.[11]

Jazz critic Leonard Feather dismissed the debate about Rosemary's jazz credentials as an irrelevance. "Whether or not Rosemary is a jazz singer seems to me entirely unimportant," he wrote in his sleeve note to her *Cole Porter* album. "What does matter is that given a jazz setting, she seems completely at ease and her performance is substantially enhanced."[12] Guitarist Bucky Pizzarelli shared Feather's view. "She was a master at singing the melody," he said, but was also capable of mixing things up to "play the room" where she was working. "The label doesn't mean anything."[13] Cornetist Warren Vaché was similarly dismissive. "The kind of thing old men debate," he said when asked if he considered Rosemary a jazz singer. "Just because she had the brains and the ability to do 'Mambo Italiano' doesn't make her any less of a jazz singer. Everybody has to eat."[14]

Regardless of whether Rosemary had become a bona fide jazz singer, by the early '80s there were undeniable changes in both the sound and the style of her singing. Some were to do with nothing more than the passage of time. In her youth, she had been blessed with a crystal-clear, bell-like tone to her voice. When set alongside her impeccable diction, it gave an almost clinically sharp edge to her vocals, her voice cutting through the lyrics of a song like a knife through softened butter. But, like any other part of the body, the vocal cords are not immune from the aging process. All singers experience a thickening of the voice as they move into their 50s, usually accompanied by some loss of range in the upper register which to a degree, can be compensated by greater depth at the lower end of the scale. Add to that the effects of a lifetime's smoking and the consequence was that Rosemary developed a gritty raspiness to her voice. It was by no means unattractive and in many ways, more suited to the autobiographical style of singing that she was moving toward. Nevertheless, the pure sound of a voice that had once mimicked the birds in the trees had gone for good.

If Rosemary had chosen to stick with the style of singing that had made her famous, it would have been no great surprise. Many of her contemporaries from the '50s earned good money on the nostalgia circuit trotting out 30-year old hits in a 30-year old style. Indeed, *4 Girls 4* owed much of its success to that. What separated Rosemary Clooney from the pack was that as she moved into her fifth decade of performing, she was still capable of developing and growing her art. It was a quality that reviewer Peter Reilly drew out when assessing her *Cole Porter* album. "Rosemary Clooney's greatest accomplishment here has been to take her voice, which for the last few decades has been one of the most distinctive and recognizable sounds in American popular music, and put it to the service of a hard-won new musical sensibility and style," he wrote. "It's one of those signs of growth that appear all too rarely in any kind of music, particularly pop. That she's carried it off with the same laid-back good humor and easy warmth that helped make her a star in the first place is just another indication of the depth of her talent."[15]

The transformation in Rosemary's singing was an evolutionary process, but by the mid-1980s, Rosemary had developed into jazz and popular music's supreme storyteller. Where once she had offered a glacier-like expression of a lyricist's art, now she brought their subjects to life, inhabiting and interpreting the songs in a way that no one else could. The journey had no Damascene moment although there were several notable milestones along the way. Her stunning rendition of "What Are You Doing the Rest of Your Life" had stopped Merv Griffin's TV audience in its tracks in 1975. A 1978 appearance on the *Jim Nabors Show* saw Rosemary sing "Tea for Two" as a tender love song rather than the knockabout treatment that it usually received, while her 1979 Gershwin album produced a version of "But Not for Me" that was delivered like an intricate jigsaw, attention focused on each word in Ira's lyric while still painting an overall picture of self-pity and indulgence. Rosemary's ability to grow, vocally, owed much to her rediscovered love of singing, something she commented on in several interviews in the early '80s and which was never more apparent than in a series of virtuoso performances in Holland in 1981 at the North Sea Jazz Festival. Rosemary now looked for a personal meaning or message in every song she sang. "I need to be able to take something that's happened to me that I can put into the dramatic situation so I can take that point of view," she said toward the end of her life. "For instance, 'Come in from the Rain' is a love song about a man and a woman. Not to me. 'Come in from the Rain' is about my children and that's what I think of."[16] New York music critic Stephen Holden expressed it more starkly. "Material solidity replaced the dreamy romanticism," he said.[17]

As Rosemary's rebirth continued, she often returned to songs that she had performed or recorded earlier in her career. Drawing a timeline through two or three versions of the same song offers a graphic illustration of the development of her art. On *Blue Rose* in 1956, she had sung Duke Ellington's "Sophisticated Lady." Originally written as an instrumental piece, the song's fame came from Mitchell Parish's lyric, added later. It was a song about illusion and disillusion. In 1956, Rosemary delivered a word-perfect vocal with the care and precision of a ballerina tiptoeing through a minefield. What captivates in that recording is the enunciation of each syllable. The listener focuses on each word much as a stereophile might listen to the detail of individual instruments on a new set of speakers, the musical equivalent of failing to see the wood for the trees. Rosemary's 1956 brushstrokes do create a picture of the "dining, dancing" sophisticate who is the song's heroine, but it is a picture painted remotely and without empathy. Fast-forward 20 years to Rosemary's part in the Ellington tribute on Concord. Rosemary's vocal on the same song is now more relaxed, engaging, and closer to the subject. Where 20 years ago, Rosemary was looking in through the window of the ballroom where the song's scene takes place, now she is inside and on the edge of the dance floor. Still, however, she watches and observes. Flip ahead again to 1995 and Rosemary's third recording of the song for her *Demi-Centennial* album. What emerges then is almost unrecognizable compared to her *Blue Rose* offering. By then, the song had become the regular closer for her jazz club act. Now, she lives out the loss and longing of Mitchell Parish's heroine, never more so than when she answers the rhetorical "is that all you really want?" with a half chuckled "No." It was a been-there, done-that, got-the-scars moment in song.

Harold Arlen was Rosemary's next Concord subject after Cole Porter. The album was short, nine songs with a running time of not much over 30 minutes, and was hastily compiled. Allen Sviridoff recalled that he and Rosemary had picked the songs during the flight to Toronto for the recording session in January 1983. Rosemary was kinder in her assessment of Arlen than she had been about Porter. "He seemed to write in a southern-kind of way," she said fondly.[18] Arlen returned the compliment, sending Rosemary a dozen white roses and a note that said, "You're exquisite."[19] The album would be the last one that would be done just with head arrangements. Allen Sviridoff's plans for building Rosemary's second career meant that the Concord albums needed to provide the basis for her live engagements. That meant they had to replicate easily on stage, creating an album/tour package that could be renewed and repeated each year. The free-spirited gigs such as the North Sea Jazz Festival of 1981 had been great fun for all concerned but essentially had relied upon the musicians remembering the treatment of the songs from the records. Something different was needed now and arrived in the form of a young musician called John Oddo. After graduating from the Eastman School of Music in 1978—ironically, the same musical alma mater as Mitch Miller—Oddo had joined the Woody Herman band as a keyboard player and arranger. Herman was a dinosaur from the halcyon days of the big swing bands in the '30s. Fronting several generations of "Thundering Herds," his latest incarnation had signed with Concord Jazz and by 1983, there were five Herman albums available on the label. When Rosemary expressed a desire do a big band album, Carl Jefferson suggested a pairing with Herman.

The sessions were arranged for August 1983. An album of big band swing was a departure from the informality of Rosemary's small group sessions. Herman worked with a 16-piece orchestra, and a full set of charts was necessary for each of the eight songs that Rosemary, Herman, and Jefferson had selected. Ordinarily, the job of preparing the orchestrations for Herman fell to John Oddo, although Rosemary too had her own arranger. Frankie Ortega had handled all of the arrangements for 4 Girls 4 plus much of Rosemary's solo work on stage but had been absent from her Concord albums. Jefferson's proposal had Oddo doing four arrangements and Ortega doing the rest. The idea was an unusual compromise for the hard-nosed owner of the label and probably always doomed to failure, even had Ortega not fallen ill in the run up to the sessions. When the dates came around, his ailment meant he was too ill to be present. His charts were unfamiliar to the Herman musicians and it was soon apparent that for the first session, the only usable arrangements were the four prepared by Oddo. Overnight, the young Eastman graduate came up with three more arrangements for the next day's recording. It left "The Glory of Love" as the odd man out on the album, Michael Patterson providing the emergency cover for that track.

The arrangements were arguably the album's best feature. Herman's musicians could swing with gusto and Rosemary was happy to stand toe to toe with them. The disc, however, never recovered from the weaknesses in its song list. Most titles were contemporary items, similar to Rosemary's With Love selection but ill-suited to a swing band. The two strongest songs were both old standards. "I'm Beginning to See the Light," an Ellington composition, benefited from an all-too-rare clarinet solo from Herman, while the album's title track, "My Buddy," gave Rosemary an opportunity to apply her interpretive skills to the venerable Kahn-Donaldson song.

Down the years, the album was far more significant for having provided the genesis of Rosemary's musical partnership with John Oddo. The two had first met the year before in New York. The Herman band was playing at the *Fat Tuesday* club and Rosemary came in one evening during her appearance with Tony Bennett and the Count Basie band at the Westbury Music Fair. At the time, neither knew much about the other but by the time *My Buddy* was complete, Rosemary had Oddo in her sights. Stories that she had poached him from Herman were untrue, however. "I had done three years with Woody and had already given him my notice," Oddo said.[20] Herman had asked him to stay until the album with Rosemary was done and Rosemary called him soon after. It was the beginning of a relationship that would endure for the remainder of Rosemary's life and career.

It is hard to overstate the importance of John Oddo to Rosemary Clooney's career. He was an "impeccable" choice, said brother Nick, "the exact, right person. He did not need to be the star."[21] Impresario John Schreiber said that Oddo "knew what would enable her to shine."[22] Bass player Jay Leonhart said that Oddo was "the consummate musician" who took charge of everything and on whom Rosemary placed total reliance, especially as she got older.[23] "I admire him more than anybody," Rosemary said in 1995. "I love the fact that he breathes with me on stage."[24] When Rosemary resumed her songbook series of albums for Concord in June 1984, the impact of Oddo was immediately apparent. *Rosemary Clooney Sings the Music of Irving Berlin* was the first small-group album to have the parts for each musician sketched out in advance. Oddo's work fell short of full arrangements, said Scott Hamilton, but it was enough to "change the nature of what we were doing in a very positive way."[25]

The Berlin album was perhaps the most obvious songbook for Rosemary given her association with the composer that dated back to *White Christmas* in 1954. The set featured 10 tracks, the best two being the pair of songs that Rosemary sang just to the accompaniment of Ed Bickert's guitar. "Be Careful, It's My Heart" came from the 1942 movie, *Holiday Inn*, starring Bing Crosby. Ahead of the picture's release, song pluggers had the song down to be the film's big hit, until Berlin unveiled the specially written "White Christmas." The other song with Bickert, "What I'll Do," was one of Berlin's most tender songs, written in 1923 and a perfectly wistful vehicle for the new Rosemary. Despite Oddo's influence, the album still contained the lengthy instrumental solos that had been a characteristic of the earlier Concord discs. They were a feature that not everyone liked, including Irving Berlin. Approaching his 96th birthday, the legendary songwriter was still sufficiently tuned in to raise the issue with Rosemary. "Why do you wait so long between choruses? Why don't you sing right away?" he asked. "It's a jazz album and I have to let the musicians play," said Rosemary. Berlin was not for turning. "I don't know, I think it's a long time for those instruments," he said.[26] Nevertheless, *Downbeat*'s assessment was that the instrumental solos were "beautifully crafted" and that "Clooney and company have come up with another small-scale gem."[27]

After teaming up with John Oddo for the Herman album, Rosemary had embarked upon the ambitious touring schedule that she had mapped out to Jack Hawn in Los Angeles. First stop was Japan for three nights at the Aurex Jazz Festival, with appearances in Tokyo, Osaka, and Yokohama. Bandleader Harry James had been due to make the trip with Rosemary, the first professional reunion for the two of them since their Columbia recordings in 1952. Earlier in the year, however, James had been diagnosed with cancer. He had continued to work but died on July 5. His passing meant that the support orchestral role went to Les Brown and his Band of Renown. Rosemary was back in the states by the time her daughter-in-law, singer Debby Boone, gave birth to twins on September 17, 1983. The babies were Rosemary's second and third grandchildren, a figure that would eventually rise to 10. The role of grandmother fitted Rosemary like a glove and she took to it with all her usual gusto and enthusiasm. "The most incredible grandmother—ever," said Boone.[28]

By the time Rosemary flew off to London in November 1983, John Oddo was part of the touring ensemble. Rosemary would give few performances without him for the rest of her career. "I would fly 3,000 miles for a three-minute song on a TV show," he said.[29] The London trip included a performance at the Barbican Center alongside Vic Damone, Buddy Greco, and Kay Starr. It was the first significant appearance in Britain for the restyled Clooney. The London *Times* found her to be "something of a revelation. While it would be stretching a point to describe what she does as jazz, there was no doubt that her performance in London on Thursday night represented interpretative popular singing of a very high order. She showed herself to be the possessor of a sunny, slightly throaty contralto and a firm, straight forward line of phrasing." The reviewer, Richard Williams, was less kind, however, when it came to describing Rosemary's appearance. "A motherly figure whose voice emerged from the top of something resembling a red and purple brocade tent," he wrote.[30]

Back home for Christmas, Rosemary renewed acquaintances with Danny Kaye on a *Merv Griffin Show* in December. She took some time off through the winter months, returning to the road in April 1984 with a 10-night spell at the Sands in Las Vegas. Another UK trip, this time to guest on *The Val Doonican Show*, followed. Doonican was an Irish crooner and a disciple of Crosby. The two had golfed together not long before Bing died. Crosby had encouraged him to try to get Rosemary on his TV show, telling him that she was "the best duet singer around."[31] Back in Hollywood, she headlined at the Hollywood Bowl in a tribute concert to Harry James, before embarking upon a zigzag tour of the country. Within the space of a few days during July and August, she appeared in Cincinnati, and then Concord, New Hampshire, with Tony Bennett, plus dates in Long Beach, Boston, Syracuse, and Detroit. Despite the exposure, reviewers were still rediscovering her. Welcoming her to *Charlie's* in the nation's capital, the *Washington Post* said that her appearance would come as "a delightful surprise to those who only remember the wistful pop hits she made in the 50s."[32]

The resurgence of interest notwithstanding, the harsh reality was that Rosemary Clooney needed to work for the money as much as for the enjoyment she got from her singing. Her finances had never recovered from her years of decline in the '60s and '70s. Michael Feinstein recalled that when he first became a regular visitor to Rosemary's home on North Roxbury in the late '70s, it was though time had stood still. She was, he said, still using "ancient audio equipment," seemingly unchanged from the '50s, surrounded by stacks of old 78-rpm records. The kitchen, the route by which everyone entered the house, was old and in poor condition, and there was no air conditioning. When the money started to roll in again through the success of *4 Girls 4*, Rosemary started to spend freely again, but little of it went on the house. When she died, the cost of modernizing it would have been greater than that of building a replacement, said Feinstein. The financial problems that Rosemary suffered did nothing to change her approach to money. "She usually just spent what she earned because money seemed to have little importance to her," said Allen Sviridoff. Once again, she found the taxman at her door with a demand for tax arrears of $600,000. When Rosemary played a three-week stint at *Michael's Pub* in New York in the spring of 1986, she found her earnings sequestrated by the city authorities. "They took every penny from those three weeks," said Sviridoff.[33]

Rosemary's personal financial problems were at odds with the person who was generally regarded as quite savvy when it came to money and sponsorship. It was an attribute seen most obviously when Rosemary took up a particular cause. In 1984, Sandi, the daughter of her cousin, Phyllis Holvey, had suffered a brain injury in a boating accident. Phyllis's husband, Sherm, was the doctor who had orchestrated Rosemary's own care and treatment after her breakdown. As well as wanting to help the Holveys, the injury resonated with Rosemary's sensitivity to brain illness that had been triggered by Betty's death. It sparked off an idea to do something that would benefit those in the Holveys' position and also create a lasting memorial to her sister. With Sherm Holvey as chairman, the Betty Clooney Foundation for the Brain Injured held its first event at the Dorothy Chandler Pavilion in Los Angeles on April 7, 1986. *The Singers' Salute to the Songwriters* became an annual event, with artists giving their time freely to present a show that each year paid tribute to five or six composers and lyricists. Rosemary's old friend, Ron Shaw, who had become CEO of Pilot Pens, arranged for his company to be one of the sponsors. The first event had Bob and Dolores Hope, Tony Bennett, Debby Boone, Diahann Carroll, and José Ferrer, among others, honoring a songwriting lineup that included Alan and Marilyn Bergman, Sammy Cahn, Cy Coleman, Barry Manilow, and Jule Styne. Rosemary herself acted as emcee and lead performer. Each event raised between $350,000 and $500,000. On April 12, 1988, Betty's birthday, the Betty Clooney Center opened its doors in Long Beach, California, providing a day care facility for patients. *The Singers' Salute* ran for a further eight years, raising over $3 million for the charitable cause and becoming in itself a major show business event, with over 200 stellar names joining Rosemary at the annual benefit shows.

Meanwhile, Rosemary's 1985 Concord album, her 10th, had deviated slightly from the individual songwriter theme. *Rosemary Clooney Sings Ballads* was an Allen Sviridoff suggestion—"because she was such a good ballad singer"—and featured 10 songs, all with solid pedigrees in American music. The collection anticipated the three further songbook albums that she would record with the inclusion of songs by Johnny Mercer, Johnny Burke/James Van Heusen, and Rodgers and Hart. Rosemary returned to her individual songwriter theme the following year with an album devoted solely to the music of Van Heusen. As a composer, Van Heusen enjoyed two enduring partnerships, first with lyricist Johnny Burke, followed by an equally successful teaming with Sammy Cahn. These alliances gave Van Heusen the unique standing of having been the songwriter-of-choice for America's two most significant vocalists, Bing Crosby and Frank Sinatra. Cahn and Van Heusen had also been behind Rosemary's 1958 collaboration with Crosby on *Fancy Meeting You Here*. Rosemary chose to reprise one of the songs specially written for that album, "Love Won't Let You Get Away," recording two vocal tracks that enabled her to sing both her own and Crosby's original parts. The Van Heusen collection also featured a repeat by Rosemary of two songs that she had recorded during her RCA years in the early '60s. "It Could Happen To You" appeared on the *Clap Hands! Here Comes Rosie* album in 1960 while "Imagination" had been one of the tracks on the much-vaunted *Love* album a year later. Both offered interesting comparisons with Rosemary's new Concord versions. Neither song was taken at a significantly different tempo in the rerecording, but Rosemary's original vocals had been couched in big band arrangements. They had been good but to a degree were straitjacketed by the highly prescriptive orchestrations. Now in the setting of a jazz sextet, Rosemary's freedom to balance her voice against each of the instruments is striking. While her singing on these songs would not pass the O'Day/McRae improvisation test, it clearly demonstrates an ability to treat the voice like an instrument itself, varying the tone and texture of her delivery to match her surroundings and complement her fellow musicians.

Rosemary's touring schedule during 1986 brought her close to home with a 10-night engagement at the Vine St. Bar and Grill in Los Angeles. While there was no question that cavernous venues such as the Hollywood Bowl offered bigger bucks, Rosemary's management realized that smaller, intimate settings were ideally suited to her emerging musical persona. Vine St. was one such, with a capacity of 100 and top ticket price of $20. It had been almost 40 years since Rosemary had played a Hollywood nightclub. That had been in the Tony Pastor days when she and Betty had appeared at the Hollywood Palladium, just a couple of blocks away. Rosemary offered two different shows each night. The first, at 9:00 P.M., was built around her *Blue Rose* album. Later in the evening, her second appearance showcased songs from her Irving Berlin Concord album. Philip Elwood found her to be "a remarkably free musical soul; she takes chances with songs and interpretation. And, years ago, she learned how to bounce vocally off of instrumentalists, to make them part of her act."[34] Gerald Nachman, writing in the *San Francisco Chronicle* said, "Clooney just keeps on getting better. [She] is so much more interesting, and real, today than during her 'prime.' She was only famous then. Vocally, this is the prime of her life."[35]

Nightclubs on the West Coast were one thing, but Rosemary's team had a bigger priority. They needed to find the right venue for her in New York. "Everything happens in New York City," was Rosemary's maxim, said Allen Sviridoff. Audiences there were different, more sophisticated and more demanding, and the reviewers carried more weight. The income from the booking was almost irrelevant. Good reviews and good profile would offer massive paybacks in terms of the business they would generate for the rest of the year. Sviridoff's first try-out venue in New York had been at Park Ten, on Park Avenue and 34th Street, in May 1985. Her appearance there brought a set of top-class reviews. Influential critic, John S. Wilson in the *New York Times*, anticipated the autobiographical theme that would soon come to dominate her performances. Noting that her first career was still represented in her act (there was a chorus still of "Come On-a My House"), Wilson observed that "now, three decades later, with a rougher and more colorful voice, she can sing songs that have character and she can mix pop, jazz and comedy to create a rounded performance that depends, in some measure, on the years of living she has experienced since she first came in view."[36]

Rosemary's next settling point in New York was the tax-afflicted booking at *Michael's Pub* before moving onto the *Blue Note* club at 131 West Third Street in Greenwich Village. Since opening in 1981, the club had quickly established a reputation as one of the leading jazz venues in New York. Rosemary's presence there "validated the jazz aspects of her style," Sviridoff said.[37] A five-night stint in March 1987 was sufficient to generate two separate reviews in the *New York Times* and she was back again in January 1988 for a second visit. The music of Irving Berlin, with his 100th birthday approaching, dominated that show. Johnny Mercer was also featured, having been the subject of Rosemary's latest Concord venture, recorded during the summer of 1987. *The Blue Note* was fine but Sviridoff was still looking for a venue that could provide Rosemary with a regular place in New York. She had another Carnegie Hall date lined up for May, and though the famous venue would figure prominently in Rosemary's career through the following decade, it could never be the solution that Sviridoff was seeking. Finally, it came his way. Rosemary's New York venue was to be found on the 65th floor of the Rockefeller Center. She was about to reach for the stars.

CHAPTER 14

Rainbow and Stars

As Rosemary Clooney headed toward her 60th birthday, she was arguably at the zenith of her second career. It was also the happiest and most contented period of her life. Onstage, she still cut a glamorous figure. The attempts to lose weight might be a thing of the past, but there would be no significant addition to the number she registered on the scales, at least for a few more years. And she carried her weight well. Always clad in immaculately cut gowns that disguised much of the excess, her facial features remained sharp and attractive, the chiseled profile that reflected her Irish descent still undeniably a strong and handsome attribute. Her hair was well styled, mainly blonde in color, and her demeanor was generally one of high energy and enthusiasm. The image that Rosemary presented onstage reflected the contentment she felt off it. Her children were now all mature adults, and while her seven grandchildren were a source of fun and amusement, she also enjoyed the absence of parental responsibility. "I can just turn the key in the lock and go," she said in 1991.[1]

A major reason for Rosemary's contentment was the presence of Dante DiPaolo. Since their reunification in 1973, the two had been constantly together. It was a relationship built on deep mutual affection and companionship. And it was quirky. On the surface, the two appeared to bicker endlessly—"like watching Burns and Allen," said one friend.[2] Almost always, Dante was the loser. Rosemary's wit had always been razor sharp and when combined with her directness and lack of patience, it made her a formidable adversary. Dante was the exact opposite. It had always been his feet rather than his head that did the talking. To many he was delightfully vague, a dreamer of a man. One favorite musing was what it would be like to open a nightclub on Mars. "What the Hell does that mean?" would be Rosemary's impatient response to Dante's occasional ruminations. At times, some thought that she overstepped the mark, using words such as "brutal" to describe Rosemary's treatment of her partner. The upfront turbulence of the "Rosemary and Dante Show," however, disguised a deeply symbiotic relationship that was light years away from the destructive passion of her marriage to José Ferrer. "The difference was that Dante was damned good to her," said one friend.[3] "Whenever he was on the road with her, she was happy," said another.[4] "Dante was a nurturer," said Deborah Grace Winer, "a provider of comfort, someone who took worries away. Home was wherever he was."[5] There was no question too that Dante offered Rosemary the support that she needed, and when she needed it most. Allen Sviridoff was very clear that Dante's presence impacted both Rosemary's public and personal life. "There might not have been a second career without him," he said.[6] And brutal or not, Rosemary always paid Dante a salary for the support he gave to her career.

Rosemary celebrated her 60th birthday on May 23, 1988. She marked the occasion with an appearance close to home at the Convention Center in Cincinnati in a concert that celebrated both the 125th anniversary of the Red Cross and the bicentenary of the City of Cincinnati. Unknown to her, the concert organizers also tagged on a special celebration in honor of her own birthday. Turning 60 did nothing to slow Rosemary down, and for the next five years, she was constantly on tour. During those years, her schedule included over 350 concert appearances, five more Concord albums, charity events, TV specials, chat shows, interviews, fairs, summer balls, and presidential dinners. She worked both ends of the generational spectrum. Her quasi-mother/son relationship with Michael Feinstein developed into a regular concert pairing, as did her friendship with rock singer Linda Ronstadt. One of the last projects that Nelson Riddle had worked on before his death in 1985 had been a set of crossover albums with Ronstadt. The bond with Riddle that both artists felt they shared led to an unexpected and unlikely pairing. At the other end of the scale, Rosemary renewed her friendship with Bob Hope, now nearing 90 years of age but still active. Their work included a USO tour to the newly unified Berlin, a throwback to Hope's legendary forces' shows that had extended from World War II through to Korea and Vietnam. When Hope finally gave up live appearances in the mid-90s, his wife Dolores, barely a few years younger, picked up the microphone and revived her own career as a singer that had petered out in the '30s, even sharing a two-week billing with Rosemary in New York in 1997.

Life on the road was no easier than it had been back in the touring days of the Pastor band, but Rosemary still found it irresistible. "I like the road," she had told Larry King in 1987,[7] even if the "road" usually involved air travel, which Rosemary hated. She was a nervous flyer in much the same way that she appeared to be a nervous performer, at least in the few minutes before she was to go on stage. Her pre-show routine had never involved anything resembling the vocal warmup that a trained singer might regard as a necessity. "The extent of Rosemary's vocal warmup," said daughter-in-law, Debby Boone "was to hum the first few bars of 'The Best Is Yet to Come,' take one good cough and she was good to go."[8] Preparing her throat involved nothing more than sucking on a cough drop, as she paced about. "I hate this." . . . "I can't keep doing this." When the moment came to walk out on stage though, "mama would spit out her cough drop, cough twice, and step out of the shadows," said daughter Monsita.[9] Whatever nerves there had been disappeared as soon as Rosemary reached for the microphone and started to sing.

The onstage Rosemary had always cut a confident and commanding figure. Her customary singing position was to stand close to the piano, barely a yard from the ever-present figure of John Oddo at the keyboard. Her body movement was minimal—"I gave up high kicks long ago," she once said. Like her mentor, Bing, one foot tapped regimentally to the beat. One hand—it could be left or right—gripped firmly on the microphone while the other finger-snapped to the tempo. Some singers of Rosemary's vintage developed a technique of moving the mike closer for deeper notes and further away for anything when a vocal crack might become apparent. Not Rosemary. Her control of her voice remained impeccable. Whatever variation in sound she needed to produce came purely from her use of her vocal cords. The microphone remained an instrument to hear and transmit, not compensate and conceal. It never became a crutch.

Many of the musicians who worked with Rosemary stood in awe of her instinctive musicianship. That Rosemary didn't read music was an irrelevance. "She learned a song quickly," said pianist and composer Ian Bernard. "Second time through, she knew it. Betty was the same. They both had an innate musicality that you can't teach."[10] Others working with Rosemary for the first time quickly learned how formidable a presence she could be. "You had to bring your A-game," said guitarist John Pizzarelli. "She knew everything that went on, on the bandstand. She'd been there and seen the tricks."[11] It was not that Rosemary was difficult or overdemanding, but equally, she did not suffer fools. Michael Feinstein said that Rosemary was easy to get along with—mostly. "If she was not in a good mood, or if something had rubbed her up the wrong way, she could be very tough," he said. Sooner or later, everyone, it seemed, felt the force of Rosemary's tongue. When Feinstein himself inadvertently crossed her on what seemed a triviality, Rosemary delivered a broadside. "So what?"

Rosemary's daughter, Maria, told him when he sought solace. "You've been dodging a bullet for years."[12]

Even the audience was not totally immune from the force of Rosemary's wit and occasional short temper. Dealing with the occasional drunk or heckler went with the territory in the nightspots of New York and Chicago, and Rosemary's usual technique for handling them relied on turning the reprobate into the butt of one of her jokes. "Excuse me, sir, but I work alone," was usually her first response, followed if necessary by "You have no lines here, sir." Occasionally, something more forthright was necessary. "There's a bus leaving in ten minutes; be under it," she once told a transgressor. Only once was Rosemary drawn into a situation where she overstepped the mark. During one of her sojourns at Rainbow and Stars in New York, Rosemary found herself confronted by a persistent heckler who resisted all the usual hints. Deborah Grace Winer witnessed the encounter. "The first time he interrupts on this round, she makes a quick zinger (and everybody laughs); the next time, and the next, she wisecracks, and then finally she stops the show cold, and says plainly, 'Listen—are you going to shut up, or what?' She goes on to tell him that he's got to be quiet. 'Because you see,' she tells him, 'when you keep doing that, what you're doing is you're throwing off my concentration. And then I can't do a good show. And all these people came out in this weather, and paid their money, and I really want to do a good show for them. So you've just got to shut up.' The room is stunned into silence. 'And if you don't want to shut up,' she goes on, 'well, then, I'll be happy to pick up your check. OK?' She says it all pleasantly and matter-of-factly, and the guy has been sitting there, wordless for the first time all night, looking up at her with a smirk of embarrassment."[13] The battle was won but the price was Rosemary's rapport with the audience. That night's bubble was broken beyond repair. "It was like, 'Whoa, the teacher yelled at us,'" said Winer.[14] It was Rosemary herself who was the loser. When that show was over, there was none of the usual conviviality with friends backstage. She was distraught, said Winer.

Rosemary's preparations for her recording sessions were not much different from the way she approached a live show. To her, a session was just another live appearance, something that surprised some of the newer arrivals to the record business. John Burk joined Concord Records in the late '80s as vice-president and was immediately struck by Rosemary's insistence on working live with the musicians. She used a recording booth in order to get maximum separation of her voice track but at a time when most singers had moved to recording with just prerecorded backing tracks, Rosemary insisted on being in there with the band. More surprising to Burk was her preparedness to sing a song through from start to finish.

When Rosemary had first begun recording in 1946, the industry knew no other way of making a record, but by 1989, a disc had become an amalgam of mixes and edits. It made Rosemary's completist approach look delightfully old-fashioned. More surprising still was the number of occasions when Rosemary would nail the recording on the first take. John Pizzarelli made a guest appearance on one track for a 1993 date for Concord. When he expressed surprise that their first take of "It's Only a Paper Moon" had prompted a call of "next number," Rosemary's response to his puzzlement was simple. "Well, we were good," she said.[15] On the same session, Rosemary toiled through a dozen or more takes on Dave Frishberg's "Do You Miss New York?" only to conclude that her first attempt had been the best.

Rosemary's ongoing relationship with Concord had progressed from the on-the-hoof spontaneity of 10 years before, with John Oddo's talents now ensuring that each album was easily replicable on stage. The routine of one album per year felt comfortable, both to Rosemary and Concord, and was carefully planned. "There was a reason behind every album and every song on every album," said Allen Sviridoff.[16] Each new Concord offering meant that Rosemary was able to offer a new repertoire each year for the concert halls to which she made annual pilgrimages. The style and nature of her recordings, however, was about to change, but not before Rosemary had delivered two more albums built around the catalogs of the great songwriters. In the autumn of 1988, she put together a collection of songs ostensibly drawn from Broadway shows. The 12 titles gave Rosemary license to select from the work of such composers as Burton Lane, Frank Loesser, and Noel Coward although it was a new song that stood out from the rest. Strictly, "Where Do You Start?" had no locus in a *Show Tunes* album in that it did not come from a show. Rosemary liked the song as soon as she heard Michael Feinstein sing it and was determined to find a way of including it in her next album. Having heard Feinstein sing it on Broadway seemed reason enough. The song's theme of picking up the pieces of a failed relationship resonated with Rosemary. It soon became a regular part of her stage act and anticipated the shift toward an autobiographical focus that would dominate her work through the next decade.

There was one final songwriter tribute to discharge before the change of direction. *Rosemary Clooney Sings Rodgers, Hart & Hammerstein* was an obvious, if unusual, theme that Richard Rodgers's publishing arm had suggested. Singers normally treated Rodgers and Hart and Rodgers and Hammerstein as separate entities, but Rosemary's album offered 12 titles, six with lyrics by Lorenz Hart and five by Oscar Hammerstein II. The remaining song— "The Sweetest Sounds"—was a comparatively rare example of words and music by Rodgers himself. Rosemary worked with the usual six-piece band on the session but with some changes of personnel. Jack Sheldon took on the trumpet/cornet spot normally filled by Warren Vaché, and to good effect, adding his vocal to Rosemary's for what *Downbeat* called "a typically wacky mile-wide-smile duet on 'People Will Say We're in Love.'"[17] Another new feature was the appearance on five of the tracks by the L.A Jazz Choir, a vocal ensemble put together by choral specialist Gerald Eskelin in 1980. The group acted like a string section on songs such as "Little Girl Blue" and "My Romance" in a style not dissimilar to that of the Hi-Lo's on Rosemary's 1950s television series. It was not a move that found much favor with supporters of Rosemary's new style. "A bit hokey," said *Downbeat*.[18] Other reviewers were fulsome with their praise of Scott Hamilton's saxophone and Chauncey Welsch's trombone ("a revelation") while offering little more than a footnoted acknowledgment that there had been a choir present too. As with previous songbooks, Rosemary was able to add a personal touch from her firsthand knowledge of the composers. "You have to do Rodgers," she told one interviewer, "although I didn't particularly like him as a man. He was very rude to me the first time I met him."[19]

Rude or not, there was no question that Richard Rodgers and Lorenz Hart had given one part of New York the song that served as its anthem. They wrote "Manhattan" in 1925 for the show *The Garrick Gaieties*. Rosemary had included it in her *Show Tunes* album and when Allen Sviridoff finally came up with the venue he had been looking for in New York, the song was a shoo-in for her February 1989 opening. The venue that Sviridoff found was of similar vintage to Rodgers's classic song. The Rockefeller Center, a complex of 19 commercial buildings sitting between 48th and 51st streets, had risen from the ashes of the Great Depression in 1932, the largest privately funded building project the world had seen. Although built primarily for commercial use, entertainment had always been part of the building's raison d'être. It provided a home to the Radio City Music Hall and to the entertainment giant, RCA. The music hall was located on the ground floor of the complex. Higher up, on the 65th floor, John D. Rockefeller had also created an entertainment facility—the Rainbow Room—which quickly established itself as one of New York's hottest nightspots during the '30s. Noel Coward, Beatrice Lillie, and Duke Ellington were among those who played there to great acclaim. Fifty years on, David Rockefeller, grandson of John D., invested $25 million in a facelift that now offered a smaller venue alongside the Rainbow Room. During daytime, it was known as the Evergreen Club, but when night fell, it became Rainbow and Stars. With seating for little more than 100, fine dining, and unparalleled views of the New York skyline, it was destined to take on the mantle of its famous predecessor of the '30s. When it opened for business in the New Year of 1989, the priority was to find a big New York name to establish the room. Tony Bennett was the obvious candidate, with Rosemary next in line. It was the beginning of a nine-year association with the venue that came to mean as much to her as any other she had ever played. Deborah Grace Winer thought that the venue "embodied everything about what she had arrived at and who she wanted to be. She valued it above everything else that she did. It literally represented the tippy-top of New York," she said.[20]

While never lucrative in their own right, Rosemary's annual visits brought attention and profile. Her ability to attract and woo the city's most influential critics, none more so than New York Times columnist Stephen Holden, was key to her success, although that particular relationship was not easy. "She was scared to death of him," Allen Sviridoff recalled.[21] Just why was never clear. Rosemary had always been savvy in the way she built and sustained relationships with the critics, but it was perhaps the professional distance that Holden liked to keep that put him out of reach. Her fears were unfounded because Holden was almost always on her side, never more so than on her first night. "Rosemary Clooney exudes comfort, coziness and serenity, just as her friend and champion, Bing Crosby, once did. If her delivery is not as soft as that of a crooner, she also never really raises her voice. The tone she adopts for both ballads and up-tempo songs is warm but matter-of-fact. Like Crosby's, her technical proficiency is such that her singing seems nearly effortless, though of course it isn't," he wrote.[22] Variety was similarly enthusiastic, describing her phrasing as "miraculous as ever" and her voice as having the "consistency of coconut milk."[23] Other critics picked out Rosemary's rendition of Hart's lyric to "Manhattan," including her comment that it was a song she had sung "a thousand times but never in such a perfect setting."[24] Ever the traditionalist, Rosemary's rendition was faithful to Hart's original 1925 lyric, including its reference to the '20s musical, Abie's Irish Rose, which, by the modern era, was usually replaced by a reference to My Fair Lady.

Over the next nine years, Rosemary would devote a winter month each year to Rainbow and Stars. The stints were hard work, two shows a night from Tuesday to Saturday, often in the depths of the New York winter. Each year, the show built its own momentum, seats selling steadily in advance and picking up apace once the run opened. By the second week, Rosemary was into her stride. By the third, she was beginning to tire and by the fourth, she couldn't wait for the run to end. But still she came back. During her early visits, she sang a chorus of "Come On-a My House"—"Now you know I'm going to get round to that one. Just hang in there with me," she told the audience. Eventually, she decided that it was so far out of step with the rest of her repertoire that she found the courage to drop it.

Rainbow and Stars was not Rosemary's only New York venue. She was also a regular at events at Carnegie Hall. In June 1989, she appeared as part of the JVC Jazz Festival alongside Dave Brubeck and jazz pianist Marian McPartland. Two years later, she returned, for the first time as the headline attraction. In a show called *Rosemary Clooney and the Arrangers*, much space was given over to her work with Nelson Riddle, whose son Christopher conducted some of his father's arrangements. New York jazz critic Gary Giddins saw the show as a seminal moment in changing perceptions of Rosemary. "Two emphatic highlights of the evening were her interpretations of 'Bewitched, Bothered and Bewildered,'" he wrote, "as arranged by Matz, and 'The Shadow of Your Smile,' as arranged by its composer, Mandel. In both instances, she sang the little known verse, using it to build tension before embarking on the well-known chorus. The first performance was a lesson in reading a lyric. I don't think I'd ever found myself really hearing the words before. Choosing her high notes with deliberation and hitting them like chimes, and phrasing cagily so that her chest tones were as full at the ends of her phrases as at the beginnings, she opened up the song, dramatized it, made it new. Similarly, with the help of a dilatory tempo that understated the usual Latin rhythm, she reclaimed "The Shadow of Your Smile" from the countless readings that made the song a cliché in the '60s."[25]

Rosemary's change of tack at Concord Records manifested itself in an album of World War II songs called *For the Duration*. Rosemary recorded the album in October 1990, three months after the death of her Uncle George, whose picture in wartime uniform adorned the cover. Brother Nick penned the sleeve note, detailing the songs that Rosemary had first encountered "as a bobby-soxer" during the war years. Giddins again was enthusiastic about the collection, saying it was "perhaps the finest overall achievement since her comeback and one of the four or five best albums she has made in the past 40 years." Rosemary's voice, he wrote, "with its decisive disposition, heady vibrato, and unmistakable humor, reclaims these songs not as nostalgia for a bygone age but as a shared musical past that can be revisited without sorrow or recrimination."[26] The titles included two songs, "No Love, No Nothin'" and "They're Either Too Young or Too Old" that expressed the loneliness of the girls left at home, from which another reviewer said Rosemary extracted "every ounce of fun."[27] At the other end of the scale "(There'll Be Bluebirds Over) The White Cliffs of Dover" represented the war's most optimistic song, notwithstanding that fact that its American composers, writing about the war zone on the south coast of England, ignored the fact that there are no bluebirds in Britain. It mattered not. Rosemary's rendition, sung just to Oddo's piano, brought new life to the song that had been a wartime anthem across the Atlantic.

As Rosemary moved on and through the '90s, her annual outings on Concord, plus her regular visits to Rainbow and Stars, began to act as a barometer of the inevitable physical and vocal decline that began to set in. Although Rosemary's artistry was never questioned—*Variety*'s 1990 comment that the show offered "a post-graduate seminar in how to perform in a night club," could have stood for each year of the decade at the Rockefeller venue[28]—she was undeniably aging. Her features that had retained a youthful sharpness in 1988 soon began to take on a jowly appearance. The glasses that had once been seen only in private were now ever present. More ominously, Rosemary's weight once more began to increase, all adding to the matronly appearance that she was now beginning to display.

Rosemary had never been one to cling onto a fading youth, but her weight gain concerned those who were close to her. Sherm Holvey was one. "I tried everything I could," he said, "but there was no way to change her behavioral patterns."[29] Dante DiPaolo discovered the same thing. "She was stubborn when it came to things like that," he said. "If she wanted to do something, you weren't going to stop her. Forget about it."[30] Other friends, such as Michael Feinstein and Ron Shaw, each broached the subject of her weight to no avail. For one fleeting moment, Shaw was surprised to hear Rosemary raise the subject with him as she tucked into a plentiful dinner, the irony behind the timing of her comments strangely passing her by, he said. There was interest too from a major diet and weight-loss organization, seemingly prepared to offer a very hefty payment-by-results sponsorship, but Rosemary refused to commit.

Rosemary's vocal powers were similarly atrophied by the passage of time. The decline was less obvious and more easily managed, but both her weight and long history of smoking contributed to a diminution in her vocal range and an increasing breathlessness in her singing. The change was more apparent to Rosemary than to anyone else. Although critic Gary Giddins was enthusiastic about *For the Duration*, Rosemary told him that she thought it was the first album where the flaws in her voice were apparent. Stephen Holden noticed the change too on her mid-'90s dates in New York, but thought her "innate musicality" concealed it to such an extent that few in the audience would have picked it up. Rosemary handled it, he said, by changing her phrasing to fit an increasing number of short breaths. Ken Peplowski, who played clarinet on some of the Rainbow dates, concurred, saying that at times, she could "barely squeeze out the notes, but still managed to make the most of what she had. Still honest," he said.[31] As ever, Rosemary was willing to confront the issue head on. In an appearance with Larry King later in the decade, she claimed that since stopping smoking (publicly, at least), she had noticed an improvement. "But there's always a way to overcome it," she said. "People don't talk with long, long breaths."[32]

Rosemary's remarkable ability to seemingly do more with less carried her through three more Concord albums between 1991 and 1993. First came *Girl Singer*, her first big band album since the Woody Herman collaboration. Using her favored description of herself as the title, the album paid tribute to the great swing bands and their female vocalists. *Do You Miss New York*, recorded in 1992, was for many people the closest representation on disc of Rosemary's Rainbow and Stars performances. Despite the use of Dave Frishberg's memoir to the city as the title song, the album was more a set of personal reminiscences than a New York–themed set, including tributes to Lena Horne and Nat "King" Cole and the inclusion of an Ellington song, "I Ain't Got Nothin' but the Blues" that had originally been intended for the *Blue Rose* album. Not for the first time, however, it was Nelson Riddle who stole the show, Rosemary reusing, to great effect, his arrangement of "I Get Along without You Very Well" ("that used to be our song, kind of," she said)[33] that had first appeared on *Rosie Solves the Swinging Riddle*. In 1993, Rosemary returned to the travel theme for *Still on the Road*. Vocal arranger Earl Brown was now a significant member of the Clooney team, writing many of her vocal arrangements and guiding her through new and unfamiliar material. For the new album, Brown co-wrote the title song, a melancholic reminiscence of the less glamorous side of the life of an itinerant singer. The cover illustration for the album offered an image of the 1950s Rosemary ("40 years younger and 80 pounds lighter," she said), waiting for a train at the Maysville station. There were many echoes of Crosby in the album, recorded in the year of his 90th birthday, a milestone that Rosemary had celebrated with a Carnegie Hall concert in his honor. "Ol' Man River" recreated the arrangement that he had used to close their shows together in the '70s, while on "Road to Morocco" Rosemary recreated the fun of the Hope and Crosby duets, in tandem once again with trumpeter Jack Sheldon. Rosemary also chose to revisit the perennial lament of Irish homesickness, "How Are Things in Glocca Morra," a song she had included on the *Show Tunes* album just six years before. This time, Rosemary added more intimacy to her reading but the loss of depth and range to her voice over that period was apparent. Despite the obvious vocal decline, however, it was once again a simple voice and piano offering that stole the show. "(Back Home Again in) Indiana" was a 1917 song, recorded by the Original Dixieland Jazz Band and seemingly forever locked into a breezy ragtime tempo. In the hands of Clooney and Oddo, it became a melancholic tale of early days, growing up in the Midwest. Rosemary's interpretation put the song alongside "Glocca Morra" as a plaintive recollection of a long-lost home.

February 1994 saw a nervous Rosemary open another month's season at Rainbow and Stars. Ten days before she arrived in New York, an earthquake had hit her home in Beverly Hills, bringing down a chimneystack. "I went through the Los Angeles earthquake, so truly, I'm very glad to be here," she told an audience in Hamden, Connecticut, en route to New York. By the time she and Dante made it to their New York apartment for the run, Rosemary was fighting a head cold. A badly planned one-nighter in Toronto on January 29, just ahead of her New York opening, did little to soothe her mood. With weather forecasters full of doom and New York reeling from five big snowstorms, a flight to Toronto was the last thing she wanted. Much of the material for her Rainbow and Stars show was still unfamiliar and all that Rosemary wanted to do was settle into the run. "I wish you could start on the second night," she told her first night crowd.[34] As ever, her fears were groundless. Although the material, drawn mainly from *Still on the Road* did not please everyone, the critics once again lined up to sing her praises. "The album grows on you," wrote Gene Seymour in *Newsday*, "even when the material isn't always worthy of her. But nothing beats seeing her live. Don't deny yourself the pleasure."[35]

Rosemary's cold was a minor ailment but there were increasing signs of more significant health problems along the way. She knew that she needed a knee replacement, a consequence of a fall on some ice in the '70s and an injury inevitably aggravated over time by her excessive weight. In September 1994, she was hospitalized for the removal of a kidney stone—"five children in five years but nothing was more excruciating than the pain of a kidney stone," she said[36]—while in November of the same year an attack of bronchial pneumonia caused her to miss her White Christmas Party shows that had become an annual mini-tour. The lost dates included a sell-out booking at the Lincoln Center in New York, but despite the setbacks, the Clooney bandwagon continued to roll. She took time out from her singing to appear in two episodes of the medical drama *ER*, playing the part of an Alzheimer's sufferer who wandered around the hospital, spontaneously breaking into song. It earned Rosemary an Emmy nomination and was her only experience of working with the next rising star of the Clooney clan, nephew George. The son of her brother, Nick, he had boarded with Rosemary in Los Angeles when, as an aspiring young actor, he had trailed his way around the studios looking for his first break. He had also taken a turn chauffeuring Rosemary and the other *4 Girls 4* to various gigs. "There was nothing sweet and subtle about driving those broads around," he said later. "In the backseat, Martha Raye would shout, 'Georgie, pull the car over, I have to take a leak.' Then she'd hang a leg out the window and do her stuff while I kept looking forward. Meanwhile, my Aunt Rosemary would say, 'Honey, don't turn around. You'll learn too much about the aging process.'"[37]

Rosemary ended 1994 looking forward. The next year would see her 50th anniversary in show business, the same anniversary that she had helped Bing Crosby celebrate in 1976, fueling her own comeback. Crosby's celebration had come in the year of the American Bicentennial, prompting him to come up with the term "Demi-Centennial" to describe his own milestone. It was a phrase that Rosemary was eager to adopt for her own golden anniversary. During October and November 1994 she entered the Group IV recording studios in Hollywood to put together her most personal album yet for Concord. Titled simply *Demi-Centennial*, it assembled 16 songs, each with its own particular significance for her. Her opening choice was "Danny Boy." the selection that had puzzled brother Nick when he came to write the sleeve notes. Later, when the album provided the basis for a series of concerts, the same song also provided an amusing moment for bass player Jay Leonhart. Rosemary used "Danny Boy" regularly as an opener. One night, he recalled, she got to the high note that climaxes the line "I'll be *there* in sunshine or in shadow." As ever, her warmup had been virtually nonexistent and when she went for the note, first time through, nothing came out. "John Oddo went into the break and she whispered across to me 'sing that high note for me,'" he said. Second chorus, he did just that. "No one overheard Rose tell me to sing it," he said, "so both the audience and the rest of the band were slightly astounded that I would jump in and sing. But Rose requested it, and who was I to say no?"[38]

Beyond "Danny Boy," the *Demi-Centennial* album included a duet with Rosemary's niece, Betty's daughter Cathy Campo, on "The Coffee Song," plus other titles for Tony Pastor, Nelson Riddle, and Dante. When she sang "Falling in Love Again" in tribute to her friend Marlene Dietrich, Rosemary eschewed the boasting that was inherent in Dietrich's rendition in favor of a treatment that brought out the helpless vulnerability of the femme fatale, unable to resist the attractions of a new lover to the extent that the final line—"can't help it"—became almost a cry of despair. "That's what I heard when Marlene sang it," Rosemary said.[39] There were inherent messages in the album for her children and grandchildren plus memoirs of friends such as Tony Bennett, Bob Hope, and of course, Bing. The album also formed the basis for Rosemary's first music video, filmed at a specially recorded concert at Disneyworld later in 1995. It gave Rosemary the opportunity to poke fun at her association with novelty songs. She was, she said, constantly asked to sing, "How Much Is That Doggie in the Window?"—Patti

Page's chart topping hit from 1953. "I recorded so many bad songs that they figure that if it's a crap song, then I must have done it," she said. "I can only hope that Patti Page is working somewhere tonight and that someone is asking her to sing 'Come On-a My House.' It would be fair."[40] There seemed little doubt then that Rosemary's 50th anniversary was just another staging post in a career that was now becoming legendary. There was no hint that Rosemary had any thoughts about retirement. "I don't know what I'd do," she told Larry King. Spending more time with the kids and grandkids would be good she said, but not enough. "I have to sing."[41] With the 50th anniversary duly chalked off, Rosemary moved smoothly into the 51st year of her professional career without breaking stride. Her bookings were plentiful and her ambitions high. But she also had a surprise in store. Wedding bells were about to peal.

CHAPTER 15

Get Me to the Church on Time

A s soon as Rosemary's demi-centennial visit to Rainbow and Stars was over on March 4, 1995, she finally got around to the knee replacement that was by now long overdue. It was eight weeks before she was mobile enough to resume performing—"they never told me how tough this was going to be," she told one journalist—but once done, it gave her a new line of patter on stage. "The whole joint is now made out of steel," she said. "You know what's funny? Every time I go through airports I send bells gonging like crazy."[1] The surgery disrupted her usual summer scheduling to such an extent that she made only a handful of live appearances before arriving in Florida in August to record her demi-centennial video concert. It was a happy anniversary event although there were other dates now appearing increasingly in Rosemary's diary that bore stark reminders of the passing years. In 1994, she had sung at the funeral of her friend Dinah Shore and in December 1995, she found herself singing Dean Martin's theme song, "Everybody Loves Somebody" at his wake in Los Angeles. It was Martin himself who had once said to her that he had reached the point where he had more friends "on the other side" than here, a thought that was in her mind as she performed.

Rosemary's knee problems might have interrupted her live schedule but the disruption was more than compensated by an upsurge in recording work. It coincided with a change of ownership at Concord Records. Late in 1994, a dying Carl Jefferson had sold the label to the recently established media distribution group, Alliance Entertainment. Jefferson's last act before the sale had been to secure the succession, appointing Glen Barros to lead the company. Alliance's acquisition of Concord, along with its simultaneous purchase of the British label, Castle Communications, was its first step on an ambitious diversification and growth plan. For a time, the deal gave Concord more muscle than ever before, and despite her affection for Jefferson, Rosemary saw it as a step forward. "I've found that the new owners of Concord Records (Alliance Entertainment Corporation of New York) really do care about their artists, and promote our new CDs," she said in a 1996 interview that sounded more like a corporate press release. "You know, Jeff (Carl Jefferson, founder of Concord Jazz) was just wonderful to me. He encouraged me to make records again and appear at his jazz festivals; he was a close friend. But he had trouble distributing and promoting his records."[2]

Rosemary's first album under the new regime continued her series of personal retrospectives. *Dedicated to Nelson* took Rosemary's television relationship with Nelson Riddle from the mid-'50s as its theme. It was arguably the most challenging assignment she would ever give to her musical Man Friday, John Oddo. Although tapes of Rosemary singing the songs from her TV shows survived, none of Riddle's written scores were to be found. Oddo had the job of transcribing them by ear. There were other complications too. Riddle's pieces were invariably short. With no orchestral break built into the TV versions, they ran to little over two minutes, too short for an album track. Oddo had to extend them into full versions, second-guessing the way Riddle might have broken up the song. Oddo also had to deal with the fact that Rosemary's vocal range had changed in the 40-odd years since Riddle had created his originals. He found that he needed to take all of the keys down, most by a fourth and some by a minor third. The workload was so great that Oddo had to call in other arrangers to help with a handful of the tracks, although the album was undeniably Oddo's magnum opus. It seemed only fitting that a chance remark of his should provide the album title. "About this album that's dedicated to Nelson . . ." he said one day in a phone call to Allen Sviridoff.[3] From that moment, the album had its title.

Oddo's epic was completed in time for Rosemary to record the 16 chosen titles over four days at the end of September 1995. The result, said Gary Giddins in his sleeve note, was "miraculous—a 1996 [*sic*] album by Rosie and Nelson!" Backed by a full orchestra a la Riddle, the songs, by definition, were all a minimum of 40-plus years old. Indeed, "You're in Kentucky," written by fellow Kentuckian Haven Gillespie, dated back to 1923. Walter Donaldson's "At Sundown" dated from 1927, but the best track once again came from close to home for Rosemary. "A Foggy Day" was the Gershwins' masterpiece that had been finalized in the living room of 1019 North Roxbury. Rosemary had recorded the song twice before, in London (appropriately) in 1957 and again 20 years later on her debut album for Concord, as well as singing the song countless times on stage. It had always been Rosemary's practice to add a slight pause in the line "as I walked through the foggy streets . . . alone," a clear statement that the song is about loneliness, not London. Her new rendition had her delivering the verse just to Oddo's piano accompaniment, and when she came to the critical line, the pause now became a chasm. There are few, if any, examples of a singer generating more emotion from a five-letter word than Rosemary does on her delivery of the word "alone."

Dedicated to Nelson was Rosemary's biggest seller for Concord to date, reaching #8 in the *Billboard* Top Jazz Albums chart. By now, Concord's portfolio of jazz-styled vocalists had extended to include Mel Tormé, Susannah McCorkle, and Keely Smith, but it was Rosemary who had developed into the label's most successful artist, with 12 chart entries between 1985 and 2002. During the same period, Concord registered 65 album hits, with Rosemary accounting for almost one in five. *Dedicated to Nelson* also brought a Grammy nomination, although as with similar accolades in 1992, 1993, and 1994, Rosemary wound up as runner-up to Tony Bennett. When she shared a guest spot with him on *The Rosie O'Donnell Show*, Rosemary was characteristically direct. "I'm mad at you," she told him. "If I'm nominated in the same category, I can't win. One year, don't make an album . . ."[4] Rosemary used the *Nelson* album as the basis for her Rainbow and Stars month in February 1996, and for the first time saw the tangible benefit of the new muscle behind Concord Records. To repeat the Riddle orchestrations required the same 14-piece band that Rosemary had used on the disc, but the club owners were reluctant to finance the changes that would be needed to accommodate a big band. The new Concord came to the rescue, paying for the adaptations and setting up a sellout three-week run. "We sold a lot of CDs, too," said Rosemary.

They sold even more of Rosemary's next Concord product. New CEO Glen Barros was usually happy to leave the ideas for her albums to Rosemary and her management team, but a chance discussion in the winter of 1995 proved to be the exception to the rule. Artistically, her association with the Christmas season was now stronger than ever, and with Danny Kaye's passing in 1987, Rosemary was the last surviving member of the quartet that had starred in the 1954 movie. All of which prompted Glen Barros to ask the question "When did you last do a Christmas album?" "Never," came the reply.[5] Barros was amazed. "Are you kidding me?" he asked. "No," said Rosemary, characteristically turning the question around and putting Barros on the spot. "Are you suggesting one?" she asked. He was, and in April 1996, Rosemary arrived at the Capitol Studios in Hollywood for four days of recording that produced *Rosemary Clooney—White*

Christmas.[6] The CD, complete with a simulated snow dome cover ("a disastrous idea—they leaked all over the place," said Allen Sviridoff)[7] was in the shops for the 1996 Christmas season. By then, Rosemary's December scheduling was dominated by *Rosemary Clooney's White Christmas Party*, a seasonal concert offering that had grown both in scale and popularity since she had first tested the water with it in the late 1980s. Often joined by daughter-in-law Debby Boone and assorted grandchildren, it was family entertainment at its best and remained an indelible part of Rosemary's annual schedule until the end of her life. Locations varied, the Westbury and Valley Forge Music Fairs being regular stop-offs, but over the years, Rosemary and her supporting cast took the show to all parts of the country. "If Clooney's performance had to be crystallized," wrote one local reviewer in 2000, "it would all come down to two utterly transcendent numbers. One was Irving Berlin's "Count Your Blessings," Crosby's favorite song from the picture and one that Clooney also obviously adores. It was sung with a nearly heavenly reverence, with Clooney allowing its starkly simple message of hope to shine. And to no one's surprise, she closed the show with "White Christmas" itself, a flawless performance of the ultimate holiday song by a woman who is just as much of a classic herself."[8] It wasn't just Rosemary's public who shared in the Christmas celebrations. Allen Sviridoff had come up with the idea for a musical Christmas card, a cassette tape on which Rosemary would sing a Christmas favorite, interspersed with a personal spoken message to the recipient. The idea was inspired when Rosemary told Sviridoff about the little keepsakes that Bing Crosby used to send to friends and business associates every year. What started as a handful of musical cards had grown by the late '90s to over 600, a mammoth task but one that Rosemary maintained to the end of her life.

The *White Christmas* CD turned out to be Rosemary's best seller for Concord, even outstripping *Dedicated to Nelson* by reaching top spot in the *Billboard* jazz charts early in 1997. Musically, it was less satisfying. Reviewing the album, *New York Times* jazz critic Peter Watrous said, "If there's a line between sentiment and sentimental, Rosemary Clooney, accompanied by a big orchestra and strings, along with the Earl Brown Singers, lands on the side of sentimentality. In many ways, the album is a throwback to big-budget pre-rock projects, where irony and wit don't apply."[9] Rosemary's brush with sentimentality extended into her next Concord project. *Mothers & Daughters*, recorded in October 1996, became her third album in less than a year, an indication of the greater commercial ambition of Concord's new owners, albeit at the potential expense of Rosemary's newly established jazz credentials. *Mothers & Daughters* was targeted at the 1997 Mother's Day market, each song on the album dedicated to a woman in

Rosemary's life—chiefly her sisters, daughters, and granddaughters. Without understanding the special significance that each song held only for her, however, the distant listener heard only an assortment of songs with little that obviously bound them together. It was a disappointing album, one that for a time threatened to end her Concord tenure on an unsatisfactory note as the label found itself heading for the rocks. By the end of 1997, the rosy picture of life under Alliance Entertainment had gone sour. The parent company, overstretched and suffering a drop in distribution revenue, filed for Chapter 11 bankruptcy protection in November 1997. Concord was but a small part of the ailing empire, but technically, it meant that the record label was bankrupt too. The uncertainty lasted over 12 months. When Alliance finally emerged from shelter, Concord resided in the ownership of its secured creditors. It wasn't until June 1999 that a new owner was found, this time with Glen Barros and the management also having a stake in the business. Through the uncertainty, Rosemary stood by the label that had offered her a second chance in the record business. "I never thought we would lose her," said Barros, attributing Concord's survival to the "trust and loyalty that Jefferson had created" with Rosemary and her fellow performers.[10]

By the time the Alliance group hit the skids, Rosemary's mind was elsewhere. During the summer of 1997, Rosemary had surprised everyone by announcing that she and Dante were to be married in the fall. The news came not long after they, together with a group of family and friends, had visited Rome. Rosemary's friend, Dolores Hope, used some of the goodwill she had built up from supporting the Catholic Church over the years to arrange an audience for Rosemary and her party with Pope John Paul. The event gave rise to one unforgettable exchange. As Rosemary and her party waited in line to receive their blessing, she and her group were struck by the appearance of the woman immediately in front of them. "She was dressed to the nines," said Nick Clooney, "very stylish and very sexy. She had armloads of stuff to give to the Pope, flowers, presents, everything." "Gee, I thought he had everything he needed," Rosemary whispered to her brother. When the pollen in the flowers induced a sneeze from the pontiff, Rosemary instinctively said, "God bless you!" The remark brought a twinkle to the eyes of the frail-looking Pope. "No, no Miss Clooney, I bless you," he said.[11]

There were unfounded suggestions that an adverse papal comment had brought about Rosemary and Dante's wedding; however, any clerical pressure there was came from closer to home. "It was the Cardinal in Los Angeles," explained brother Nick. "Every time they did something for the Church, he would always ask if they were married yet. 'He's never asked me,' was Rosemary's standard response."[12] Publicly, Rosemary's explanation for the marriage was that her grandchildren were forever asking when she and Dante had got married. They weren't, she said, but by the time the grandchildren had become teenagers, the reply was prompting other questions. Rosemary's standard reply to the "so how come you share a room?" question was that she and Dante were roommates. It no longer held water, she said. Whatever the motivation, the decision made for an expansive and joyous celebration, one that also attracted significant publicity nationwide. The wedding service took place in Maysville in St. Patrick Church where Rosemary had been baptized. Despite the encouragement that she and Dante had received from the priesthood, there was no relaxation of the due diligence required for a full-blown Catholic wedding. Dante had to go some lengths to produce the requisite nullification certificate from his previous marriage to a Las Vegas showgirl, while Rosemary, despite her divorce(s) from José Ferrer, was asked to show his death certificate. Not having one, she produced a copy of his obituary from the *New York Times* instead.[13] When the day came, over 800 people filled the church, including Bob and Dolores Hope in one of their last public appearances together. An even bigger crowd turned up for the reception, hosted by Nick and Nina after Rosemary inadvertently issued an open invitation on local television days before. The service was an emotional event. Both Rosemary and Dante seemed close to tears when they exchanged vows and Rosemary cried again when a children's chorus sang Mozart's "Agnus Dei" to the couple. "It's my gift to you," the priest who celebrated the Mass, told them. "I know it takes a lot of nerve to sing in front of Rosemary Clooney, but we have plenty of nerve here," he said.[14]

The newlywed Rosemary moved into 1998 with a new spring in her step, literally. Her knee had now healed sufficiently for her to resume her normal summer touring routine and she had again—she said—quit smoking. Not everyone believed it, but there was no question that at least the partial elimination of tobacco helped her voice. Philip Elwood, in a long distance telephone interview in the summer of 1996, observed, "I've never heard her voice so clear—no wheeze, not a cough in a half hour's conversation."[15] A year later, she could be heard telling Larry King that the decision had helped her breath control, though with typical Clooney honesty, she admitted that she still retained the longing for cigarettes. "If I see someone smoking in the street," she said, "I slipstream in behind them."[16]

Nevertheless, there were those who remained concerned about Rosemary's health. By now she was suffering from emphysema and asthma, all of which added to her breathing problems. Some too still worried that her weight was out of control. New York critic Stephen Holden led on it in his review of her final appearance at Rainbow and Stars in May 1998. Privately, Holden's view was that Rosemary had become "morbidly obese" to the point that she was "scary looking."[17] He moderated his tone somewhat for his written piece, but still hoped that his "dangerously overweight" comment might shock Rosemary into "reality." Instead, his comment was perceived as a hostile review and brought only a cold shoulder from her. It wasn't, said those close to Rosemary, that she refused to recognize the issue; it was more a case that she had now lived it with it for so long that it had become part and parcel of her. The lady was not for turning.

Rosemary's breathing problems increasingly drew comment from reviewers. Her weight and the fact that she was about to enter her 70s also had an impact on her gait and steadiness. Things were not helped when her knee problems returned. Now when she took the stage, she did so on Dante's arm. Carefully positioning her by the piano ("which she would more or less cling to for the rest of the evening," one unkind reviewer said),[18] Dante would discreetly exit, returning at the end of show to escort her away. One night at the Hollywood Bowl, however, Dante stepped out of character and tossed in a dance step as he left the stage. It brought a burst of ire down on him from his new wife. "What the Hell do you think you are doing?" she yelled at him later. "This is *my* show."[19]

The biggest threat to Rosemary's health, however, came neither from her lungs nor from her weight. In February 1998, she was in Florida for a series of concerts as part of the Pilot Pen Song Festival when she began to suffer headaches and a fever. The decision was made to return to New York by road, a 24-hour trip in a limo during which time, her condition steadily deteriorated. By the time she arrived, her temperature had reached 101 and she was both unsteady on her feet and incoherent. She was admitted to Lenox Hill hospital on February 13. Within a day, her temperature had reached 107 and she had slipped into a coma where she would remain for three days. Doctors initially diagnosed viral meningitis but struggled to identify the precise strain of the disease. Eventually, they concluded that Rosemary had encephalitis—inflammation of the brain itself rather than the surrounding membranes—probably caused by a mosquito bite in Florida. She was placed on a ventilator and put under an ice blanket but beyond that, doctors said they could do nothing but let nature take its course. They told her immediate family that her chances were 50-50 at best. After a tense few days during which the family imposed a news blackout on Rosemary's condition, she gradually began to recover. Nick Clooney recalled the moment that his sister emerged from her period of unconsciousness. She was awake but "starry eyed and tubed up," he said. "This is the greatest moment of my life," he told her. "I can say any damn thing I want and you can't say a single word." Rosemary, he said, laughed so hard that she spat the breathing tube out of her mouth. "That was when I knew she was going to be okay," he said.

Rosemary later recalled the vivid and bizarre dreams she had when she had been unconscious, and by the time she returned to the stage in May 1998 for what would be her last appearance at Rainbow and Stars (it closed later that year), her near-death experience had given her a new topic to add to her onstage repartee. "If you're going to go, try going into a coma first," she told the audience, going on to outline some of the wacky dreams she had experienced. Moving on from Rainbows to Carnegie Hall for a booking she had been due to fulfill the day she fell ill, Rosemary kept the same theme. "I am 108 days late" she told that audience. Her appearance at her favorite New York venues coincided with another celebration. On May 23, 1998, Rosemary celebrated her 70th birthday, a milestone that she embraced unwillingly. While never one to conceal her age, she had little enthusiasm for getting old. Reflecting with Jonathan Schwartz in a radio interview about how she had forgotten the words to "Our Love Is Here to Stay" at Carnegie Hall the previous year, she eschewed any idea that age might be an excuse. "Senior moment? Dumb moment more like. I hate it," she said.[20] Concord Records released a celebratory CD that comprised mainly reissues from earlier recordings, although Rosemary recorded two new tracks. These included James Taylor's "Secret O' Life" which became one of her favorite numbers. Allen Sviridoff had been quick to exploit Concord's enthusiasm for Rosemary's birthday because it brought Rosemary a healthy advance check on sales and required her to work for only one day to record the new tracks. His idea for a cover with "70" in big numbers—plus handouts for the concerts too— scored less well with his client. "The CD had the biggest damn '70' you've ever seen in your life," Rosemary said. "It could have been anybody recording it. If you can find 'Rosemary Clooney' on there, good luck. I thought the 70 would be a little discreet thing in the corner."[21]

As well as the birthday album, Rosemary also had another new CD to promote during the summer of 1998. *At Long Last* united her with the Count Basie Band, a project that Allen Sviridoff had been seeking to bring about almost for as long as he had represented Rosemary. Indeed he had first discussed the idea with Basie himself, not long before the pianist's death in 1984. When it finally came to fruition, it remained a troubled project. Scheduling problems meant that while the band was preparing for the session in California, Rosemary was working in Cincinnati. She had to listen to and approve the tempos over a telephone line. "Not ideal," admitted Sviridoff. Because of Rosemary's illness, the final edits to her vocals could not be completed until she had recovered in June 1998. The result was an adequate album, but with Rosemary's voice sounding thinner than on any other session to date, it served only to highlight the seemingly irreversible vocal decline. The process continued into her next album. *Brazil* saw Rosemary combine with guitarist John Pizzarelli on a set of Latin rhythms, authentically styled and benefiting from some outstanding vocal arrangements by Earl Brown. Nevertheless, her vocals fell a long way short of the standards she had set earlier in the decade.

Back to full health, Rosemary appeared at the Hollywood Bowl in July 1998 along with the Basie Band for an evening that Don Heckman in the *Los Angeles Times* called "timeless music-making." One track from the album, "In the Wee Small Hours of the Morning" took on an unintended meaning with the passing of Frank Sinatra a few weeks before. Rosemary used it to end the concert in a note of homage to a singer who had influenced so much of her phrasing and lyrical interpretation. Three months later, Rosemary herself was the recipient of lavish tributes at a gala evening at the Beverly Hilton Hotel when she received the prestigious Ella Lifetime Achievement Award from the Society of Singers. Nephew George presented the award. "My aunt has had a pretty amazing year," he said. "She celebrated 50 years in show business this year [sic] and she scared the hell out of us with a bout of meningitis. She married a guy she had been dating for 25 years. I sent her a note and said, 'What's the hurry? You should check him out.' She sent me a note, joking 'I'm pregnant.' My aunt's a class act and the most talented singer I've ever seen."[22]

Anniversaries continued to dominate Rosemary's schedule during the summer of 1998 with the centenary of the birth of George Gershwin. Her friendship with Ira and her more recent association with Gershwin disciple Michael Feinstein meant that Rosemary was the most obvious choice for any promoter looking to cash in on the anniversary. She teamed with Feinstein for a show at Harrah's in Vegas in August and then headlined herself in "Fascinating Rhythm: 100 Years of George Gershwin" at the Masonic Auditorium in San Francisco in November. A possibly over-loyal critic Philip Elwood said that her performance was "marvelous, a delightful dozen-song set of mostly Gershwin, sensibly structured, with Clooney's inimitable, informal commentary linking the selections together. Her voice is strong and melodic; she's sustaining notes as in younger days, having kicked her smoking habit in recent years, and her timing is impeccable."[23]

The winter of 1998–99 found Rosemary busy recording her *Brazil* album, guesting on *Sesame Street*, and singing with the Colorado Symphony Orchestra in Boettcher Hall, Denver. One thing was missing, however. With the expiration of its lease, Rainbow and Stars had closed its doors for the last time in December 1998. Making money from vintage pop was a difficult challenge, as confirmed by the almost simultaneous demise of middle-of-the-road New York radio station WQEW. Rosemary had regularly appeared on it with Jonathan Schwartz, but now its spot on the dial went to a Disney-sponsored children's station. The closure of Rainbow and Stars left Rosemary distraught. Venues such as Carnegie Hall were always open to her but there was nowhere else that Allen Sviridoff could see that would offer the intimacy of the room at the top of the Rock. A solution arrived via Rosemary's close friend, Michael Feinstein, who by this time, was also managed by Sviridoff. Feinstein and Sviridoff had discussed the idea of creating a nightclub that would bear Feinstein's name, and after considering several different locations, Sviridoff came up with the Loews Regency Hotel as a potential venue. He took the idea to Sherrie Laveroni, a Loews Executive, and the new club—"Feinstein's at the Regency"—opened for business on October 5, 1999, with Rosemary as the main attraction. "I was thrilled for Rosemary to open the room," Feinstein recalled.[24] Stephen Holden was there to witness her first night. "Blunt, jolly and loquacious, she projects the warmth of a den mother opening her arms to her flock," he wrote. "When she sings, with perfect enunciation, a casually swinging authority and a sound that still conveys a flavor of spring flowers, you're less aware of technique and interpretation than of a life poured directly into song."[25] Rosemary would headline at the new club on three more occasions during the next two years, and while she never lost her affection for Rainbow and Stars, Feinstein's became her final New York home.

Rosemary moved on from the new club to begin the promotion of her second autobiography. *Girl Singer*, co-written with author Joan Barthel, inevitably covered much of the same ground as *This for Remembrance* but offered a more balanced and less sensationalist account of Rosemary's life. Barthel's writing skillfully recreated the open, no-holds-barred style of Rosemary on stage and television. Concord issued a double CD, again largely comprised of previously issued tracks, using the same title and cover illustration as the book. Rosemary worked hard at publicizing the book on TV and at book signings, but though the reviews were generally favorable, sales were disappointing, barely justifying the significant advance that she had received from the publisher. Allen Sviridoff attributed the poor sales to inadequate marketing but others were less surprised. Stephen Holden said that the book had "nothing new in it,"[26] while Michael Feinstein's view was that the book was, like its predecessor, too subjective. "It's as she remembered it; not necessarily the truth," he said.[27]

Rosemary celebrated the new Millennium with a concert in Tucson, in tandem with Feinstein, on New Year's Eve, 1999. As she moved into a new century, the self-styled "old broad" seemed to be like Jerome Kern's "Ol' Man River"—she just kept rolling along. Inevitably, there were more concessions to age. She had taken now to sitting down for some of her performances, borrowing a line in justification from cabaret icon, Mabel Mercer. "I'll stand as long as I can," she told audiences, "and when I can't stand, I'll sit." She also now openly took a lyric sheet on stage with her, and eventually, a lectern to hold it. "Do you forget many lyrics?" Terry Gross had asked her some years before. "I'm 68, darling," had been Rosemary's wry reply.[28] Her onstage patter also expanded, offering more time for recovery between songs but also drawing on an ever-increasing repertoire of stories about her grandchildren. During a concert performance in Chicago in March 2000, she told a story about her grandson Harry, son of her daughter, Monsita. Driven to distraction by the constant fighting between her sons, Monsita had admonished them, saying that she "couldn't stand the raging hormones anymore." "Does Grammy have raging hormones?" Harry had asked. Trying to conceal her laughter, Monsita said she didn't think so, but why did he ask. "Cause that's how she yells at Papa [Dante] all the time!!" said Harry.

Other concert dates during 2000 included familiar venues such as Davies Symphony Hall in San Francisco and the Hollywood Bowl in the midst of another busy year of touring. She also returned to Maysville, for the Second Annual Rosemary Clooney Music Festival, seeking to raise funds for the restoration of the Russell Theater that had hosted her first movie premiere in 1953. May and December saw her back at Feinstein's in New York, the latter for *Rosemary Clooney's White Christmas Party* which she also took to Salt Lake City that year. Christmas Day saw her singing on the *Today* program, offering two songs, "White Christmas" and "Have Yourself a Merry Little Christmas" as her family gathered for their traditionally expansive holiday celebration at North Roxbury. There was, it seemed, much to look forward to in the coming year. Another album was planned, with a new band that offered yet another change of direction, and there was talk too of performances in England and her ancestral home, Ireland. It would be the first time she had been back there since performing with Bing in Dublin in 1976. What nobody realized was that, as the Christmas bells rang out on North Roxbury, dark clouds were forming over the horizon. Christmas 2000 would be the last one that would be merry and bright.

CHAPTER 16

When October Goes

Rosemary Clooney died peacefully at her home on North Roxbury Drive on June 29, 2002, with her family around her. Her passing came after a six-month battle with lung cancer that had been first diagnosed during December 2001.

The shocking news of Rosemary's illness had come at the end of a typically busy year that had taken her on a travelogue around many of her favorite venues. She had kicked off with an appearance close to home at the Louisville Palace on March 3, 2001. The concert marked the final show in the Bank One Louisville Pops concert series. Brother Nick acted as MC and Rosemary performed an hour's worth of songs. Her list included "We're in the Money," which she dedicated to nephew George, and a rendition of "Thanks for the Memory," just with piano, bass, and drums. One local reviewer said it was "riveting in its sweetness."[1] From Kentucky, she flew to Florida for three separate dates before returning to New York and her third spell in less than a year at Feinstein's. During her two-week stay at the new club, she took time out to receive a Lifetime Achievement Award from the Manhattan Association of Cabarets and Clubs (MAC).

Rosemary's show at Feinstein's positioned her alongside a new set of musicians in the form of the Big Kahuna and Copa Cat Band, a 12-piece swing band from Honolulu. The Hawaiian musician, Matt Catingub, had formed the band two years earlier, earning plaudits with two debut albums on Concord. Catingub and Rosemary had first met in 1995 when both appeared at Carnegie Hall in a Frank Sinatra tribute concert. The son of jazz vocalist, Mavis Rivers, Catingub was a musical jack-of-all trades who had cut his teeth early in the music business. Still shy of his 40th birthday,

Catingub had been working with singers and bands since his teens. Will Friedwald's assessment was that "he knows practically everything there is to know about accompanying a vocalist."[2] After their Carnegie meeting in 1995, Catingub had conducted at several concerts for Rosemary, working alongside the ever-present John Oddo. When the idea came forward to put the Big Kahuna Band behind her on an album, Rosemary was immediately enthusiastic. Catingub's musicians were young, several of them aged between 18 and 20, but the age gap posed no problems for her: "72 looking at 27" was how she described herself on one TV appearance with the young band.[3] "She loved working with the band because she saw it as a throwback to her early days, touring with the Tony Pastor band," Catingub said.[4]

Like many musicians before him, Catingub could not help but be impressed by the strength of Rosemary's stage presence. She might have needed help onto the stage, "but once there, wow, look out," he said. Their show together at Feinstein's was built around the *Sentimental Journey* CD that Rosemary had put together with Catingub's entourage, partly from a studio session at Skywalker Sound and partly with material recorded at the Rosemary Clooney Music Festival in Maysville. Catingub had been struck by Rosemary's approach to the recording. With no warmup—"she just walked in," he said—Rosemary had rattled through the songs very quickly, Catingub having provided her with the arrangement demos on CDs ahead of the recording sessions. With a young band, the occasional mistake was inevitable, but Rosemary had taken it all in her stride. The new band—the album's subtitle was "The Girl Singer and Her New Big Band"—gave a freshness to the CD that set it apart from her more recent Concord outings. Its content owed much to the big band swing recordings that she had done for the label almost 10 years earlier, and the songs were once again selected for their meaning to Rosemary and her life and times. The two obviously autobiographical choices were "I'm the Big Band Singer," written by Rosemary's old friend and ex-big band vocalist Merv Griffin, and "The Singer," a tribute to Sinatra written by two of his musical acolytes, Vinnie Falcone and Joe Cocuzzo. "Rockin' Chair" was a memory of Mildred Bailey. "My favorite singer," Rosemary had said in 1998,[5] ("she was Bing's favorite too," she told Jonathan Schwartz), and there were three songs with links to Bob Hope. They included "Ya Got Class," a Hope-Clooney duet from the 1953 film *Here Come the Girls*, with Catingub himself becoming the latest, and last, addition to Rosemary's long line of duet partners. The album had more fizz than anything Rosemary had recorded since her Concord tribute to Nelson Riddle in 1995 and the same sense of pep and vigor accompanied her to Feinstein's. Writing what would be his final review of a Clooney performance, *New York Times* critic, Stephen

Holden, said that the band's "big, brawling sound brings out the swinger in Ms. Clooney," and "visibly stirred new energy into the singer."[6]

With the album finished, Rosemary made plans for a nostalgic return to London in June 2001, in tandem with Michael Feinstein. As a dry run, the twosome appeared at the Cerritos Center for the Performing Arts in Los Angeles during April. In May, she was back in Vegas, again with Catingub's band, before joining Feinstein on a plane to London. They had two shows planned, at the Royal Festival Hall on London's South Bank on June 18 followed two days later by a repeat performance at the National Concert Hall in Dublin. By now, she and Feinstein had developed a double act to complement their individual performances. Duets on "Our Love Is Here to Stay" and "Isn't It a Pity" were standard items, as was a piece of repartee about the latter song. "I don't know if you know this, Rosemary," Feinstein would say, "but 'Isn't It a Pity' is Barbra Streisand's favorite Gershwin number." "Can I tell you how little I care?" was Rosemary's response, spontaneous and unrehearsed when Feinstein first tossed in the line but one that went so well that it became a regular part of the act. Despite their rehearsed jokes, Feinstein by now knew Rosemary well enough to also expect the unexpected. Another frequent duet for them was Irving Berlin's "You're Just in Love." "You introduce this song," Rosemary once said to Feinstein onstage, adding as an aside to the audience "he knows everything." Feinstein went through a brief history of *Call Me Madam* and Ethel Merman, only for Rosemary to interject one night—"Aha! I gotcha! Perry Como and I sang the song on radio before the show opened. So *I* introduced this song, see."[7]

After returning from Europe, Rosemary took the summer off to recharge her batteries. On September 10, 2011, she was booked to perform at the Southern Governors' Conference in Lexington, Kentucky, with brother Nick as master of ceremonies. Vice-President Cheney was guest of honor. Cheney flew back to Washington that evening, while Rosemary headed to her home in Augusta, prior to her next concert date, due four days later at the recently redeveloped Evansville Auditorium and Convention Center in Indiana. She awoke to witness the 9/11 terrorist attacks unfolding on television before her eyes. "Like everyone else," she told a local journalist, "I couldn't stay away from the TV the last few days." She had, she said, considered canceling the show but decided to go ahead. "I needed to sing," she said, "that's what I do."[8] In recent years, Rosemary had often taken to closing her shows with Irving Berlin's "alternative national anthem," "God Bless America," but when she sang it in Evansville, it took on an altogether different significance. "Arguably the best moment of the entire evening came when she sang and led the now-standing crowd in 'God Bless America,'" said the reviewer. "Tears were openly shed. And not just because of the lyrics and their current significance, but also because Clooney truly makes a lyric come to life."[9]

In October, Rosemary headed for the Westbury Music Fair with the Big Kahuna Band before making her final national television appearance on ABC-TV. Hosted by Barbara Walters, *The View* represented one of fate's uncanny coincidences: 24 years earlier, Walters had also been the host when Bing Crosby had made what became his last national TV appearance. Rosemary was there to plug her new CD but sang "Count Your Blessings" as a special request to try to capture the upside of life post-9/11. Back home in California, her next appearance came at the Davies Hall in San Francisco before Rosemary and Dante, along with other family and friends, flew to Hawaii for a holiday. Hawaii was a favorite retreat for her, but on this trip, she agreed to add in a couple of concerts at the end of the vacation. The decision presented an opportunity for her to work with the Honolulu Symphony Pops orchestra, under Matt Catingub's direction. At the time, the orchestra was pitching for a recording contract with Concord, which decided to record the concert with Rosemary as an audition for the band. It was a fortuitous decision. A few months after Rosemary's death in 2002, the concert recordings were released under the title *Rosemary Clooney—The Last Concert*. The disc captured Rosemary in fine form and excellent voice, clearly reveling in the company of the young musicians around her.

Despite the title of the CD, Rosemary's actual last concert appearance came almost a month after she returned from Hawaii. On December 14, 2001, she appeared at the Orchestra Hall, Minneapolis, in a Christmas show before flying to Red Bank, New Jersey, where she repeated the show the following night at the Count Basie Theater. By then, the storm clouds that Rosemary had sung about in Berlin's "God Bless America" lyric, were gathering in her own life. Some abnormalities detected during a routine physical led to her undergoing a chest x-ray at the Mayo Clinic in Rochester, Minnesota. It showed a shadow on Rosemary's left lung. Further tests were planned for the New Year. Rosemary spent what would be her final Christmas at home with her family before returning to Mayo in January. It would be five months before she saw her home again. On January 9, 2002, the news broke that Rosemary had lung cancer. Two days later, she underwent surgery for the removal of the upper lobe of her left lung. Recovery was slow. Hopes that she might be well enough to attend the Grammy Awards in New York in February soon disappeared, and it was son Miguel who collected a Lifetime Achievement Award on her behalf. It was not until May that she was well enough to leave the clinic and return to California in time to celebrate Mother's Day and then her 74th birthday with her family. For a brief time, there was hope for a recovery and resumption of touring. Allen

Sviridoff visited her at North Roxbury and found her sitting up and asking about where they were working next. There was talk of the next Rosemary Clooney Music Festival in September and of a 75th birthday concert at Carnegie Hall in May 2003. It was not to be. On June 26, 2002, Reuters ran a press release from the family saying that Rosemary was undergoing treatment at home for a recurrence of the disease. Its tone was despondent. "She's comfortable and she's surrounded by her family," it said. Michael Feinstein, appearing in Cincinnati at the time of Rosemary's death, told the *Cincinnati Enquirer* that Rosemary had been "frightened and surprised" by the recurrence, which came only three weeks before her death, "but she immediately made peace with the fact that she was going to die," he said.[10] Nick Clooney spoke to his sister on the telephone on June 28 and found her spirit strong. "What hurts?" he asked. "Nothing" came the reply. When he asked how her throat was and if she could still sing, Rosemary sang "When October Goes" down the phone line. The song was a posthumous collaboration between lyricist Johnny Mercer and Barry Manilow, after Mercer's death. His hitherto unpublished verse with its poignant theme of times passing away had been a favorite of Rosemary's ever since it first appeared. Mercer's lyric had never been more appropriate. "She sang it strong," said Nick.[11] It was Rosemary Clooney's last song. Her condition rapidly deteriorated to the extent that Nick and his wife Nina were still en route to California when the news came that around 6:00 P.M. on June 29, 2002, Rosemary Clooney had passed peacefully away.

The funeral Mass took place at Good Shepherd Catholic Church on July 3, 2002. Her body was then transported to Maysville where a second service was held on July 5 in St. Patrick Church. It was where Rosemary had been baptized and recently married. She was laid to rest in St. Patrick Cemetery under a simple white marble headstone that bore just her name and the dates of her birth and death. Her home on North Roxbury Drive survived her, but not by much. Despite local conservationists' efforts, the house fell victim to the wrecker's ball in the summer of 2005.

Tributes filled the pages of the world's press. All of them told the remarkable rise, fall, and rise again story of Rosemary's life, and most took the line that Rosemary had defied time and gotten better as she got older. "Clooney's singing was a perfect marriage of warmth and wit, with a tone that could be both sultry and nurturing and a sense of rhythmic intuition admired by jazz and pop connoisseurs alike," Elysa Gardner wrote in a piece that was representative of obituaries from around the world.[12] Even those for whom the birdlike qualities of the young Clooney voice resonated most strongly acknowledged the completeness of the vocalist that she became. In a summation piece for the *New York Times*, Terry Teachout said that he viewed her 1960s albums with Nelson Riddle as her legacy. "But," he added, "I'll remember Clooney the Elder, the unglamorous, utterly self-confident performer who treated the stage of Carnegie Hall as if she had just bought it at a garage sale. By then, she looked like a double-chinned grandmother who favored caftans and sensible shoes, but she sang like a worldly, pain-toughened woman who knew everything about life and love. We should all have such a last act."[13]

Friends and family remembered other characteristics of the woman they loved. The bear hugs, the inimitable laugh, the cough, the acerbic wit, the Irish temper, the honesty, the fun, and the love for her children and grand-children. Mother confessor, earth mother, the world's grandmother were all labels that sat easily with Rosemary Clooney but none as much as "Girl Singer," the one she prized most. "I was a singer when I was a three-year-old child," she had said in 1999 "and I was a singer at 70. I have been a mother, a wife and all those things but first and foremost, I am a singer. It's what I really love to do and it's what I will be. Always."[14]

Rosemary Clooney on Record

This discography shows all of the commercial recordings made by Rosemary Clooney from 1946 to 2001, including live concerts that were recorded for commercial release.

Discographical information was obtained from many sources including the compact disc sets released by Bear Family, a German company, which include all of Rosemary's recordings from 1946 to 1968, the select discography prepared by Michael Feinstein and included in the book *Girl Singer*, Allmusic.com, Tyrone Settlemier's Online Discographical Project (available at http://www.78discography.com/), and Peter Muldavin (see www.kiddierekordking.com/). We are also grateful to Paul Barouh, Mark Sendroff, Rogier Rubens, and www.Rosemaryclooney.com for album details and for information that filled other gaps.

TONY PASTOR AND HIS ORCHESTRA—COSMO RECORDS

1946

Sep Everybody Has a Laughing Place (*The Clooney Sisters with Tony Pastor, Tommy Lynn, and chorus*) / How Do You Do (*The Clooney Sisters with Tony Pastor, Tommy Lynn, and chorus*) / Zip-A-Dee-Doo-Dah (*The Clooney Sisters with Tony Pastor*) / Uncle Remus Said (*The Clooney Sisters with Tony Pastor, Tommy Lynn, and chorus*) / Sooner or Later (*with Tony Pastor*)
(The Bear Family set gives the date of May 1946 for this session but Rosemary had not joined the band at that time.)

TONY PASTOR AND HIS ORCHESTRA—COLUMBIA RECORDS 1947–1949

1947

Jun 5 Tira Lira Li (The Song of the Gondolier) (*The Clooney Sisters with Tony Pastor*) / I'm Sorry I Didn't Say I'm Sorry (When I Made You Cry Last Night) (*with Tony Pastor*) / Bread and Butter Woman (*The Clooney Sisters with Tony Pastor*) / My O'Darlin' My O'Lovely My O'Brien (*The Clooney Sisters with Tony Pastor*)

Sep 29 Grieving for You / Gonna Get a Girl (*The Clooney Sisters with Tony Pastor*)

Oct 30 The Chowder Social (*The Clooney Sisters with Tony Pastor*) / The Click Song (*The Clooney Sisters with Tony Pastor*) / It's Like Taking Candy from a Baby (*with Tony Pastor*) / At a Sidewalk Penny Arcade

Dec 22 I'm My Own Grandpaw (*The Clooney Sisters with Tony Pastor*) / The Secretary Song (Bibidi Boo Bot) (*The Clooney Sisters with Tony Pastor*) / A Boy from Texas, a Girl from Tennessee (*The Clooney Sisters with Tony Pastor*) / Saturday Night Mood (*The Clooney Sisters with Tony Pastor*)

Dec 23 Who Killed 'Er (Who Killed the Black Widder?) (*The Clooney Sisters with Tony Pastor*) / There's a Man at the Door (*The Clooney Sisters with Tony Pastor*) / You Started Something

1949

Mar 3 When You're in Love / It's a Cruel, Cruel World (*The Clooney Sisters with Tony Pastor*) / Busy Line (*The Clooney Sisters with Tony Pastor*) / "A" You're Adorable (The Alphabet Song) (*The Clooney Sisters with Tony Pastor*) / San (*The Clooney Sisters with Tony Pastor*)

Mar ?? If I Had a Million Dollars (*The Clooney Sisters with Tony Pastor*) / Cabaret / Bargain Day
(The Bear Family set gives a date of March 28 but the band was on tour in Pennsylvania at that time.)

ROSEMARY CLOONEY ON COLUMBIA RECORDS 1949–1958

1949

With orchestra conducted by Norman Leyden
Jun 16 Lover's Gold / The Four Winds and the Seven Seas

With orchestra conducted by Hugo Winterhalter

Sep 14 Don't Cry Joe (Let Her Go, Let Her Go, Let Her Go) / There's a Broken Heart for Every Light on Broadway / Oh, You Beautiful Doll / The Kid's a Dreamer (The Kid from Fool's Paradise) / Chicago

Dec 1 Why Don't You Haul Off and Love Me

1950

With the Percy Faith Orchestra

Mar 9 The Canasta Song / I Only Saw Him Once / A Good Time Was Had by All / I Found My Mamma / Me and My Teddy Bear

Mar 29 On an Ordinary Morning (*with Johnny Thompson*) / Crying Myself to Sleep

With orchestra conducted by George Siravo

Apr 8 Peachtree Street (*with Frank Sinatra*)

With the Percy Faith Orchestra

Apr 18 Little Johnny Chickadee / Peterkin Pillowby / Who'll Tie the Bell (on the Old Cat's Tail) / Little Sally One Show

May 23 Crying Myself to Sleep (*overdub of recording from March 29, 1950*)

Jun 21 Why Fight the Feeling?

Aug 23 Where Do I Go from You

With orchestra conducted by Tony Mottola

Aug 24 Punky Punkin (The Happy Pumpkin) / The Wobblin' Goblin Fuzzy Wuzzy (Wuz a Bear) (*with male chorus*) / My Choc'late Rabbit

With orchestra and male quartet conducted by Norman Leyden

Aug 28 C-H-R-I-S-T-M-A-S / (Remember Me) I'm the One Who Loves You / I Whisper Your Name / Bless This House

Oct 21 Marrying for Love / You're Just in Love / The Place Where I Worship (Is the Wide Open Places) / The House of Singing Bamboo (*all with Guy Mitchell*)

With orchestra conducted by Axel Stordahl

Dec 11 Love Means Love / Cherry Pies Ought to Be You (*both with Frank Sinatra*)

With Tony Pastor and His Orchestra

Dec 30 Sentimental Music (*with Tony Pastor*)

1951

With the Percy Faith Orchestra
Jan 2   I Still Feel the Same about You / I Still Feel the Same about You
         (*with Betty Clooney*) / When Apples Grow on Cherry Trees
Jan   The Land of Hatchy Milatchy

With orchestra conducted by Mitch Miller
Jan 27   Beautiful Brown Eyes / Shot Gun Boogie

With the Percy Faith Orchestra
Feb 22   Mixed Emotions

With Art Ryerson Quartet
Mar 26   Kentucky Waltz / The Syncopated Clock

With the Percy Faith Orchestra
Apr 27   Songs from the film *Alice in Wonderland* (Alice in Wonderland /
         The Unbirthday Song / All in the Golden Afternoon / I'm
         Late)

With orchestra conducted by Tony Mottola
May 31   Suzy Snowflake / Little Red Riding Hood's Christmas Tree / Dan-
         dy, Handy and Candy / Willie, the Whistling Giraffe

With trio led by Mitch Miller
Jun 5   The Lady Is a Tramp / I'll Be Around

*With Quartet comprising Mundell Lowe, Frank Carroll, Jimmy Crawford, and
Stan Freeman*
Jun 6   Come On-a My House / Rose of the Mountain / If Teardrops Were
         Pennies

*With Quartet comprising Mundell Lowe, Frank Carroll, Terry Snyder, and Stan
Freeman*
Aug 8   Find Me / I'm Waiting Just for You / I'm from Texas / Stick with
         Me / I Wish I Wuz (Hi, Ho, Fiddle-dee-dee)

With the Percy Faith Orchestra
Aug 23   Half as Much

With the Percy Faith Orchestra
Nov 21   Be My Life's Companion / Did Anyone Call? / Tenderly / Why
         Don't You Love Me

1952

Jan 4   Eggbert, the Easter Egg / Bunny on the Rainbow / On the Good Ship Lollipop / Poor Whip-Poor-Will (Move over, Move over)

With small jazz group comprising Joe Loyacano, Monk Hazel, Armand Hug, Sid Davilla, Lester Boughton, Jack Delaney, and George Girard
Mar 14   I'm Going Home / Bourbon Street Parade / A Good Man Is Hard to Find / You Cooked Your Goose with Me (*unissued until included in Bear Family set "Memories of You"*)

With small group comprising Mundell Lowe, San Salvador, Frank Carroll, Terry Snyder, and Stan Freeman
Apr 18   Botch-a-Me (Ba-Ba-Baciami Piccina) / On the First Warm Day / Too Old to Cut the Mustard (*with Marlene Dietrich*)

With the Percy Faith Orchestra
Apr 25   Who Kissed Me Last Night / Blues in the Night

With orchestra conducted by Jimmy Carroll
May 19   Good for Nothin' (*with Marlene Dietrich*)

With Harry James and His Orchestra—the tracks form Rosemary's first 10" LP "Hollywood's Best"
May 23   Sweet Leilani / You'll Never Know / When You Wish upon a Star / Over the Rainbow
May 26   On the Atchison, Topeka and the Santa Fe / The Continental / In the Cool, Cool, Cool of the Evening / It Might as Well Be Spring

With orchestra conducted by Carl Cotner
Jun 20   The Night before Christmas Song / Look Out the Window (The Winter Song) (*both with Gene Autry*)

With the Percy Faith Orchestra
Sep 10   If I Had a Penny / I Laughed Until I Cried / You're After My Own Heart / Lonely Am I

With orchestra conducted by Marvin H. Hughes
Sep 12   You're the Only One for Me / Withered Roses / You Love Me Just Enough to Hurt Me / Grapevine Swing (*all with George Morgan*)

With Paul Weston and His Orchestra
Dec 9   Haven't Got a Worry / I Do, I Do, I Do / What Would You Do (If You Were in My Place) / Lovely Weather for Ducks

1953

With orchestra conducted by Norman Luboff
Jan 13   Little Josey / Dennis the Menace (*both with Jimmy Boyd*)

With the Percy Faith Orchestra
Feb 3   All the Pretty Little Horses / Close Your Eyes (Brahms' Lullaby) /
It Just Happened to Happen to Me / When I See You

With orchestra conducted by Jimmy Carroll
Feb 17   Cheegah Choonem (I Haven't Got It) / Dot's Nice, Donna Fight
(*with Marlene Dietrich*) / It's the Same (*with Marlene Dietrich*) /
Besides (He's a Man) (*with Marlene Dietrich*)

With the Tony Mottola Orchestra
Mar 13   The Teddy Bears' Picnic / Little Red Monkey / Little Tink-a-Toy
Man / Little Joe Worm (Son of Glow Worm)

With orchestra conducted by Jimmy Carroll
Mar 17   My Baby Rocks Me

With Paramount Studio Orchestra conducted by Joseph J. Lilley
May 1/2   Red Garters* / Man and Woman* (*with Guy Mitchell*)
Jun 1   Bad News*
(* issued as part of the 10" album "Red Garters")

With Paul Weston and His Orchestra
Jun 23   The Kitty Kats' Party / (Ting-a-Ling- Ling) Here Comes the Ice
Cream Man / Betsy, My Paper Doll / Winter Wonderland

With orchestra conducted by Norman Luboff
Jun 28   Shoo, Turkey, Shoo / Peachy Peachy / C-H-R-I-S-T-M-A-S

With Paul Weston and His Orchestra
Sep 17   Happy Christmas (Little Friend) / We'll Be Together Again
Nov 8   When You Love Someone

With orchestra conducted by Norman Leyden
Dec 10   You Make Me Feel So Young / Woman (Uh Huh) (*with José Ferrer*) /
Man (Uh Huh) (*with José Ferrer*)

With the Percy Faith Orchestra
Dec 15   Good Intentions* / What Is There to Say / Brave Man* / Tomorrow I'll Dream and Remember
(* issued as part of the 10" album "Red Garters")

1954

With the Wally Stott Orchestra

Jan   While We're Young / Love Is a Beautiful Stranger

With Paul Weston and His Orchestra

Apr 30   Marry the Man / Ay Ay (Who's the Guy) / A Bunch of Bananas
         (The Heming Way) (*all with José Ferrer*)

*Overdubs of tracks prepared by the Wally Stott Orchestra and by the Percy Faith
Orchestra*

May 3   Younger Than Springtime / Hello Young Lovers / While We're
         Young / Love Is a Beautiful Stranger / Crying Myself to Sleep

With Paul Weston and His Orchestra

May 21   Too Young / Grieving for You / Love You Didn't Do Right by
         Me / Young at Heart (*overdub of track prepared by the Wally Stott
         Orchestra*)

May 22   Hey There / This Ole House / Besides (He's a Man) (*with Marlene
         Dietrich*)

May 27   Land, Sea and Air (*with Marlene Dietrich*)

With MGM Studio Orchestra conducted by Adolph Deutsch

Jun 11   Mr. and Mrs. (*with José Ferrer*)

With Paul Weston and His Orchestra

Jun 23   Blame It on My Youth / Young Man, Young Man / Sisters (*with
         Betty Clooney*) / A Touch of the Blues

Jul 2   Mr. and Mrs. (*with José Ferrer*) / My Baby Sends Me

With orchestra conducted by Sid Feller—with the Quartones

Jul 9   Shaun, Shaun, the Leprechaun / The Little Shoemaker / (Let's
         Give) A Christmas Present to Santa Claus

With the Percy Faith Orchestra

Sep 22   Snow / White Christmas / Gee, I Wish I Was Back in the Army /
         Mandy
(*The tracks recorded on September 22 were for a 10" LP called "Irving Berlin's
White Christmas"*)

With Paul Weston and His Orchestra

Sep 23   Count Your Blessings Instead of Sheep* / The Best Things Happen
         While You're Dancing* (**Also part of the album "Irving Berlin's
         White Christmas"*) / Mambo Italiano (with The Mellomen)

With the Buddy Cole Quartet
Dec 23   Open up Your Heart (And Let the Sunshine In) / The Lord Is
          Counting on You (The Sunday School Song) (both with Gail
          Stone)

1955

With the Buddy Cole Orchestra and The Mellomen
Jan 13   Where Will the Dimple Be? (with Thurl Ravenscroft) / Love
          among the Young
Jan 20   Peter Cottontail / Easter Parade

With Buddy Cole Group
Jun 10   Ebb Tide / Learning the Blues

With orchestra led by Jimmy Carroll and Mitch Miller
Jun 13   Wake Me / A Little Girl at Heart / From This Moment On
Jun 14   Sailor Boys Have Talk to Me in English / Go on By / The Key to
          My Heart

With the SKYROCKETS Orchestra, with Buddy Cole on piano
Jul
19–Aug 1 From This Moment On / Tenderly / It's De-Lovely / Love, You
          Didn't Do Right by Me / This Ole House / You Make Me Feel So
          Young / Danny Boy / Medley: (Come On-a My House / Botch-a-
          Me (Ba-Ba-Baciami Piccina) / Mambo Italiano) / Where Will
          the Dimple Be? / Close Your Eyes (Brahms' Lullaby))
*(Issued on 10" LP "Live at the London Palladium" on the Philips label in
the UK)*

With Ray Conniff and His Orchestra
Sep 19   Pet Me, Poppa

With Benny Goodman Sextet
Nov 14   It's Bad for Me / Good Bye / Memories of You (*With Benny
          Goodman Trio*)

With unknown backing
Dec 8   Mommy, Can I Keep the Kitten? (*with Gail Stone*)

With Paul Weston and His Orchestra
Dec 29   Snow White and the Seven Dwarfs (Parts 1 & 2) / Little Red
          Riding Hood / Goldilocks and the Three Bears

1956

With Duke Ellington and His Orchestra (vocal overdubs) for the album "Blue Rose"

Feb 8   I'm Checkin' Out—Goombye / Sophisticated Lady / I Let a Song Go out of My Heart / It Don't Mean a Thing (If It Ain't Got That Swing) / Just a Sittin' and a-Rockin' * / I Got It Bad

Feb 11   Grievin' / Me and You / Blue Rose / Mood Indigo / If You Were in My Place (What Would You Do?) * / Hey Baby

(*omitted from the original 12" LP)

With The Tunesmiths

Feb 27   You Are My Sunshine *(with Gene Autry, Carl Smith, Don Cherry, and the Collins Kids)*

With Paul Weston and His Orchestra

Mar 3   I've Grown Accustomed to Your Face / I Could Have Danced All Night

With orchestra led by Johnny Bond

Apr 23   No Letter Today / Nobody's Darlin' but Mine

With Paul Weston and His Orchestra

May 14   I Could Have Danced All Night

With Frank Comstock and His Orchestra

Jun 29   Come Rain or Come Shine / For You

Sep 24   Always Together / (Don't That Take the) Rag Offen the Bush / That's How It Is / It's a Nuisance Having You Around

Nov 24   Love Is a Feeling / Mangos / Independent (On My Own) / He'll Be Comin' Down the Chimney *(with Gail Stone)*

1957

With Frank Comstock and His Orchestra

Feb 14   I'm Glad It's You / Love Letters / Everything Happens to Me / I'm in the Mood for Love

Feb 16   Doncha Go 'Way Mad / Together / What Is There to Say / How About You *(all with The Hi-Los)*

(The tracks recorded on February 14 and 16 were for the album "Ring Around Rosie")

With orchestra conducted by Jimmy Carroll
Apr 2   Sing, Little Birdie, Sing / Who Dot Mon, Mom?

With Frank De Vol Orchestra
Date
unknown   (You Can't Lose the Blues with) Colors (2 versions)

With the Wally Stott Orchestra
Sep 13   Love and Learn / A Foggy Day / I'm Glad It's You / I Can't Stop Crying

With Frank De Vol Orchestra
Oct 18   Tonight / Love and Affection

1958

Jan 7   You Don't Know Him / Surprise / You Ol' Sun of a Gun
Feb 8   I Wonder / What Is a Baby

ROSEMARY CLOONEY—FREELANCE 1958–1960

With orchestra under the direction of Phil Moore—Tracks recorded for the "Oh, Captain!" album on the MGM label
Mar 14   A Very Proper Town / Give It All You Got (*both with José Ferrer*)
Mar 15   Hey Madame / We're Not Children (*both with José Ferrer*)
Mar 16   Morning Music of Montmartre / Keep It Simple (2 versions) / Life Does Man a Favor (*with José Ferrer*)
Mar 17   Captain Henry St. James / You're So Right for Me (*both with José Ferrer*)
Apr   Morning Music of Montmartre / Give It All You Got / Hey Madame / You're So Right for Me (*last three with José Ferrer*)
Jun 15   The Story of Celeste (*narration by Rosemary for 12" album issued by MGM*)

With the Billy May Orchestra—all tracks recorded for the "Fancy Meeting You Here" RCA album with Bing Crosby
Jul 28   Brazil / How About You / Love Won't Let You Get Away / On a Slow Boat to China
Aug 7   It Happened in Monterey / Hindustan / Fancy Meeting You Here / Calcutta
Aug 11   Isle of Capri / Say "Si-Si" / You Came a Long Way from St. Louis / I Can't Get Started / Love Won't Let You Get Away (reprise)

With orchestra led by Buddy Cole
Aug 14   It's a Boy / The Loudenboomer Bird (Early Ev'ry Morning) (*both for MGM label*)
Nov 21   Love, Look Away / Diga Me (Deega May—Tell Me) (*both for Coral label*)

With orchestra under the direction of Sy Oliver—tracks issued on the MGM label
Dec 1   I Love Him, That's Why (*with José Ferrer*) / Flattery (*with José Ferrer*) / Love Eyes / Sorry for Myself / What I Mean to Say

With Buddy Cole Trio—date transcriptions purchased for the "Swing Around Rosie" album issued by Coral.
Dec 26   'Deed I Do / You Took Advantage of Me / Blue Moon / Sing, You Sinners / A Touch of the Blues / Goody Goody / Too Close for Comfort / Do Nothin' Till You Hear from Me / Moonlight Mississippi / I Wish I Were in Love Again / Sunday in Savannah / This Can't Be Love / I'm Beginning to See the Light / I Gotta Right to Sing the Blues (*the last two tracks were not included in the album*)

1959

With Gus Levene Orchestra. Single issued on the RCA label.
Mar 25   Ain't A-Hankerin' / Protection (*both with Bob Hope*)

With the Buddy Cole Group and the Ralph Carmichael Singers for the MGM album "Hymns from the Heart"
Jun 4   The Little Brown Church in the Vale / The Old Rugged Cross / What a Friend We Have in Jesus / Onward Christian Soldiers / Living for Jesus;
Jun 5   In the Garden / It Is No Secret / Jesus Loves Me / Softly and Tenderly / Sweet Hour of Prayer
Jun 6   Abide with Me / Rock of Ages / Nearer, My God, to Thee / The Ninety and Nine

With orchestra led by Bob Thompson for the RCA album "How the West Was Won"
Jul 23   Crossing the Plains / Buffalo Gals / Green Grow the Lilacs / Skip to My Lou / Jennie Jenkins (*all with Bing Crosby*)
Jul 24   Bound for the Promised Land (*with Bing Crosby*) / Sweet Betsy from Pike / California Ball / A Railroader's Bride I'll Be / Careless Love

ROSEMARY CLOONEY WITH RCA-VICTOR 1959–1962

With Perez Prado Orchestra for an album called "A Touch of Tabasco"

Jul 31   In a Little Spanish Town / I Only Have Eyes for You / I Got Plenty o' Nuttin' / Bali Ha'i

Aug 15   Magic Is the Moonlight / Adios / Sway / You Do Something to Me

Aug 29   Cu-Cu-Rru-Cu-Cu Paloma / Corazon de Melon (Watermelon Heart) / Like a Woman / Mack the Knife

1960

Feb 15   Summertime Love / Amor (*the last two tracks were not included on "A Touch of Tabasco"*)

With orchestra and chorus led by Bob Thompson for the "Clap Hands, Here Comes Rosie" album

Feb 18   Hooray for Love / Aren't You Glad You're You / Oh! What a Beautiful Mornin' / Everything's Coming up Roses

Feb 23   Mean to Me / Something's Gotta Give / Makin' Whoopee / You Got

Feb 27   Clap Hands, Here Comes Rosie / Give Me the Simple Life / Too Marvelous for Words / Bye, Bye Blackbird / It Could Happen to You

With orchestra led by Ian Bernard—tracks issued by MGM on a compilation album called "Rosemary Clooney Swings Softly"

Apr 29   Always Be in Love / With the Night / Looking for a Boy / With You and Me

With orchestra led by Dick Reynolds

May 10   Swing Me / Danke Schon / Many a Wonderful Moment / Vaya, Vaya (Go My Darling, Go)

Overdub session

May 16   Danke Schon / Vaya, Vaya (Go My Darling, Go)

With orchestra led by Nelson Riddle for the album "Rosie Solves the Swingin' Riddle"

May 25   I Ain't Got Nobody (And Nobody Cares for Me) / Shine on Harvest Moon / Some of These Days / You Took Advantage of Me

May 27   Angry / How Am I to Know? / April in Paris / Limehouse Blues

Jun 2   Get Me to the Church on Time / By Myself / Cabin in the Sky / I Get Along Without You Very Well

Overdub session

Aug 30   Swing Me

With orchestra led by Jimmy Haskell
Nov 7   What Takes My Fancy? / Hey, Look Me Over

1961

With orchestra led by Nelson Riddle for the album "Love"
Mar 6   How Will I Remember You / I Wish It So / It Never Entered My Mind
Mar 21   Yours Sincerely / Someone to Watch over Me / More Than You Know / If I Forget You / Invitation
Mar 24   You Started Something / Why Shouldn't I? / Imagination / Find the Way

With orchestra led by Nelson Riddle
Apr 18   The Wonderful Season of Love / Without Love

With group led by Floyd Cramer for the album "Rosemary Clooney Sings Country Hits from The Heart"
May 8   I'm So Lonesome I Could Cry / Beautiful Brown Eyes / Give Myself a Party
May 9   If I Can Stay Away Long Enough / Love Has Come My Way / Kiss Him for Me

1962

Jul 19   Half As Much (*unissued*) / Any Time / I Really Don't Want to Know / This Ole House
Jul 20   How's The World Treating You / Please Help Me I'm Falling / Just Because

ROSEMARY CLOONEY WITH REPRISE RECORDS 1963–1964

1963

With orchestra led by Chuck Sagle
Jan 22   The Rose and the Butterfly / Mixed Emotions / I Will Follow You (*separate mono and stereo versions*)
Mar 4   A Hundred Years from Today / The Prisoner's Song

With orchestra led by Morris Stoloff
Jul 25   Some Enchanted Evening (*with Frank Sinatra*)
         How Are Things in Glocca Morra? / Look to the Rainbow / It Came upon the Midnight Clear

With orchestra led by Bob Thompson for the "Thanks for Nothing" album

Sep 16   All Alone / Miss Otis Regrets / Hello Faithless / Baby the Ball Is Over

Oct 10   Thanks for Nothing (At All) / Black Coffee / Just One of Those Things / The Man That Got Away

Nov 8   A Good Man Is Hard to Find / I Gotta Right to Sing the Blues / Careless Love / The Rules of the Road

1964

With orchestra led by Billy May for an album called "That Travelin' Two-Beat" for Capitol Records

Aug 15   That Travelin' Two-Beat / The Poor People of Paris / Adios Senorita / Roamin' in the Gloamin' (*all with Bing Crosby*)

With orchestra led by Ernie Freeman

Nov 2   Stay Awake / A Spoonful of Sugar / Into Each Life Some Rain Must Fall / To Each His Own

With orchestra led by Billy May for an album called "That Travelin' Two-Beat" for Capitol Records

Dec 2   Come to the Mardi Gras / Ciao, Ciao, Bambina / The Daughter of Molly Malone / I Get Ideas (*all with Bing Crosby*)

Dec 3   Hear That Band / New Vienna Woods / Knees up, Mother Brown / That Travelin' Two-Beat (*all with Bing Crosby*)

ROSEMARY CLOONEY—FREELANCE 1966–1976

1966

With orchestra led by Bill Justis for United Artists Records

Aug 25   I Need a Broken Heart (Like a Hole in the Head) / Round and Round / The Girl in the Mirror / The Belle of Old Baghdad

1968

With orchestra led by Shorty Rogers for Dot Records

Mar
12/26   Let Me Down Easy / One Less Bell to Answer / Too Little Time

1974

Recordings for Motown Records as demonstration recordings for other artists
Jul 14   We're Always Saying Goodbye / Tell Me What She Got / Just Before
        I Say Goodbye

1975

Date unknown but thought to be 1975. Recorded for K-Tel Records.
        Hey There / Come On-a My House / Half as Much / This Ole House /
        Botch-a-Me (Ba-Ba-Baciami Piccina)

*Produced by Scott Turner for APCO Records in Nashville, Tennessee. The album
is called "Look My Way."*
Jun   Half as Much / Roses in the Garden / When Will I Be Loved? / Storms
        Never Last / Look My Way / 'Twas a Sunny Day / There I've Said It /
        I'm Not Lisa / Don't the Good Times (Make It All Worth While) / Sing-
        ing the Blues / When You Got Love / The Very Thought of Losing You

1976

*With orchestra led by Pete Moore. Recorded live at the London Palladium and
issued on a K-Tel album "Bing Crosby—Live at the London Palladium*
Jun
24/25   On a Slow Boat to China (*with Bing Crosby*) / By Myself / Tenderly /
        Fifty Ways to Leave Your Lover / Just One of Those Things / A
        Song for You

*With orchestra led by Alan Warner for an album called "Nice to Be Around."
Produced by Del Newman for United Artists Records in the UK*
Jun   You / Fifty Ways to Leave Your Lover / Send in the Clowns / Music /
        Thank You Baby / All by Myself / My Little Town / The Hungry
        Years / I Won't Last a Day Without You / Nice to Be Around

ROSEMARY CLOONEY—FOR CONCORD JAZZ/OTHER LABELS

1977

*With a small combo comprising Nat Pierce, Jake Hanna, Scott Hamilton, Bill
Berry, and Monty Budwig for the Concord Jazz label LP "A Tribute to Duke"*
        I'm Checkin' Out—Goombye / Sophisticated Lady

With a small combo comprising Nat Pierce, Jake Hanna, Scott Hamilton, Bill Berry, and Monty Budwig for the album "Everything's Coming up Rosie." Her first solo album for the Concord Jazz label.

Jul 7   I Cried for You / More Than You Know / I Can't Get Started / A Foggy Day / I've Got a Crush on You / Hey There / As Time Goes By / Do You Know What It Means to Miss New Orleans

Probable date of recordings in Japan for Kitty Records

Close Your Eyes (Brahms' Lullaby) / Faded Love

1978

With a small combo comprising Nat Pierce, Jake Hanna, Scott Hamilton, Cal Collins, and Monty Budwig for the Concord Jazz label album "Rosie Sings Bing"

Jan 6   But Beautiful / Pennies from Heaven / Blue Skies / I Surrender, Dear / Where the Blue of the Night / It's Easy to Remember / Swinging on a Star / Just One More Chance / I Wished on the Moon / Too-Ra-Loo-Ra-Loo-Ral

Probable date for the recording of the "Christmas with Rosemary Clooney" album for Mistletoe Records

Rudolph, the Red-Nosed Reindeer / The Christmas Song / Little Drummer Boy / Silent Night / White Christmas / Jingle Bells / It Came upon the Midnight Clear / Count Your Blessings Instead of Sheep / Suzy Snowflake / Have Yourself a Merry Little Christmas

With a small combo comprising Nat Pierce, Jake Hanna, Scott Hamilton, Warren Vaché, Cal Collins, and Monty Budwig for the Concord Jazz label album "Here's To My Lady—Tribute to Billie Holiday"

Sep   I Cover the Waterfront / Good Morning, Heartache / Mean to Me / Lover Man (Oh Where Can You Be?) / Don't Explain / Comes Love / He's Funny That Way / God Bless the Child / Them There Eyes / Everything Happens to Me

1979

With a small combo comprising Nat Pierce, Jeff Hamilton, Scott Hamilton, Warren Vaché, Roger Glenn, Chris Amberger, and Cal Collins for the Concord Jazz label album "Rosemary Clooney Sings the Lyrics of Ira Gershwin"

Oct   But Not for Me / Nice Work If You Can Get It / How Long Has This Been Going On / Fascinating Rhythm / Love Is Here to Stay / Strike up the Band / Long Ago and Far Away / They All Laughed / The Man That Got Away / They Can't Take That Away from Me

1980

With a small combo comprising Cal Tjader, Scott Hamilton, Warren Vaché, Cal Collins, Nat Pierce, Bob Maize, and Jake Hanna for the Concord Jazz label album "With Love"

Nov   Just the Way You Are / The Way We Were / Alone at Last / Come in from the Rain / Meditation / Hello Young Lovers / Just in Time / Tenderly / Will You Still Be Mine

1982

With a small combo comprising Scott Hamilton, Warren Vaché, David Ladd, Cal Tjader, Nat Pierce, Cal Collins, Bob Maize, and Jake Hanna for the Concord Jazz label album "Rosemary Clooney Sings the Music of Cole Porter"

Jan   In the Still of the Night / My Heart Belongs to Daddy / I Get a Kick Out of You / Get Out of Town / I Concentrate on You / Just One of Those Things / I've Got You under My Skin / It's De-lovely / You're the Top / Anything Goes

1983

With a small combo comprising Ed Bickert, Scott Hamilton, Jake Hanna, Warren Vaché, Dave McKenna, and Steve Wallace for the Concord Jazz label album "Rosemary Clooney Sings the Music of Harold Arlen"

Jan   Hooray for Love / Happiness Is a Thing Called Joe / One for My Baby / Get Happy / Ding Dong the Witch Is Dead / Out of This World / My Shining Hour / Let's Take the Long Way Home / Stormy Weather

With Woody Herman and His orchestra for the Concord Jazz label album "My Buddy"

Aug   I Believe in Love / Summer Knows / The Glory of Love / You're Gonna Hear from Me / Don't Let Me Be Lonely / I'm Beginning to See the Light / My Buddy / You've Made Me So Very Happy

Live at the Aurex Jazz Festival with Les Brown and His Band of Renown in Tokyo, Japan. Album issued on the Aurex label (Japan)

Sep   Come On-a My House / Tenderly / April in Paris / But Not for Me / I Can't Get Started / You'll Never Know / I Cried for You / Who's Sorry Now / Goody Goody / Hey There / The Way We Were

1984

With a small combo comprising Scott Hamilton, Warren Vaché, John Oddo, Ed Bickert, Chris Flory, Phil Flanigan, and Gus Johnson for the Concord Jazz label album "Rosemary Clooney Sings the Music of Irving Berlin"

Jun   It's a Lovely Day Today / Be Careful, It's My Heart / Cheek to Cheek / How About Me / The Best Thing for You Would Be Me / I Got Lost in His Arms / There's No Business Like Show Business / Better Luck Next Time / What'll I Do / Let's Face the Music and Dance

1985

With a small combo comprising Scott Hamilton, Warren Vaché, John Oddo, Ed Bickert, Chuck Israels, and Jake Hanna for the Concord Jazz label album "Rosemary Clooney Sings Ballads"

Apr   Thanks for the Memory / Here's That Rainy Day / The Shadow of Your Smile / A Nightingale Sang in Berkeley Square / Bewitched, Bothered and Bewildered / The Days of Wine and Roses / Easy Living / Spring Is Here / Why Shouldn't I / It Never Entered My Mind

With Michael Feinstein for the album "Pure Gershwin" issued on the Elektra label

Apr 16   Isn't It a Pity? (*Note: There were two versions of the song—a short version issued only on the LP and cassette, and a long version issued on the CD. They came from two different takes.*)

1986

With Wild Man Fischer, issued on the Rhino label

Mar 15   It's a Hard Business

With a small combo comprising Ed Bickert, Emily Remler, Scott Hamilton, Warren Vaché, John Oddo, and Joe Cocuzzo for the Concord Jazz label album "Rosemary Clooney Sings the Music of Jimmy Van Heusen"

Aug   Love Won't Let You Get Away / I Thought About You / My Heart Is a Hobo / The Second Time Around / It Could Happen to You / Imagination / Like Someone in Love / Call Me Irresponsible / Walking Happy / The Last Dance

With Michael Feinstein (piano) for the album "Mostly Mercer" issued on the Harbinger label

Aug 29   Ask Me Again

With a quartet led by John Oddo for the album "Mostly Mercer" issued on the Harbinger label
Aug 29   I'm Old Fashioned

1987

With a small combo comprising Scott Hamilton, Warren Vaché, Dan Barrett, John Oddo, Ed Bickert, Michael Moore, and Joe Cocuzzo for the Concord Jazz label album "Rosemary Clooney Sings the Lyrics of Johnny Mercer"
Aug   Something's Gotta Give / Laura / Any Place I Hang My Hat Is Home /
             Talk to Me Baby / I Remember You / When October Goes / Dream
             Medley: Dream; Hit the Road to Dreamland / G.I. Jive / Skylark /
             Hooray for Hollywood / P.S. I Love You / Goody Goody

1988

With a small combo comprising Scott Hamilton, Warren Vache, John Oddo, John Clayton, and Jeff Hamilton for the Concord Jazz label album "Show Tunes"
Aug/
Nov   I Wish I Were in Love Again / Manhattan / I Stayed Too Long at
             the Fair / Everything I've Got / How Are Things in Glocca Morra? /
             Come Back to Me / Where Do You Start / Taking a Chance on Love /
             I'll See You Again / All the Things You Are / My Ship / Guys and
             Dolls

With Lance Ong and The Bird 'N' Butterfly Chorale for the Painted Smiles Records album "The Time Has Come! The Songs of Marshall Barer"
Date
unknown   Christmas Is an Island

1989

With Erich Kunzel and the Cincinnati Pops Orchestra for the album "Christmas with the Pops" released on the Telarc label
             Have Yourself a Merry Little Christmas / White Christmas

With Michael Feinstein and an orchestra led by Eddie Karam for the album "Pure Imagination" released on the Elektra label
Aug   Ten Feet off the Ground

With a small combo comprising Jack Sheldon, Scott Hamilton, Chauncey Welsch, John Oddo, John Clayton Jr., Joe LaBarbera, and the L.A. Jazz Choir for the Concord Jazz label album "Rosemary Clooney Sings Rodgers, Hart & Hammerstein"

Oct   Oh, What a Beautiful Morning / People Will Say We're in Love (*with Jack Sheldon*) / Love, Look Away / The Gentleman Is a Dope / It Might as Well Be Spring / The Sweetest Sounds / I Could Write a Book / You Took Advantage of Me / The Lady Is a Tramp / Little Girl Blue / My Romance / Yours Sincerely

Probable date for recording the Debby Boone "Home for Christmas" album for Benson Records.

           White Christmas (with Debby Boone)

1990

With a small combo comprising Scott Hamilton, Warren Vaché, John Oddo, Chuck Berghofer, Jim Hughart, and Jake Hanna for the Concord Jazz label album "For the Duration"

Oct 15–17   No Love, No Nothin' / Don't Fence Me In / I Don't Want to Walk without You Baby / Ev'ry Time We Say Goodbye / You'd Be So Nice to Come Home To / Sentimental Journey / For All We Know / September Song / These Foolish Things / They're Either Too Young or Too Old / The More I See You / (There'll Be Blue Birds over) The White Cliffs of Dover / Saturday Night Is the Loneliest Night of the Week / I'll Be Seeing You

1991

With a big band led by John Oddo and Peter Matz for the Concord Jazz label album "Girl Singer"

Nov / Dec   Nice 'n' Easy / Sweet Kentucky Ham / Autumn in New York / Miss Otis Regrets / Let There Be Love / Lovers after All / From This Moment On / More Than You Know / Wave / We Fell in Love Anyway / Ellington Medley [It Don't Mean a Thing (If It Ain't Got That Swing) / I'm Checking Out (Goombye)] / Of Course It's Crazy / Straighten Up and Fly Right / The Best Is Yet to Come

Dec 5   Christmas Time Is Here (for "A Concord Jazz Christmas" album)

1992

With a small combo comprising John Pizzarelli, Scott Hamilton, Warren Vaché, John Oddo, Bucky Pizzarelli, David Finck, and Joe Cocuzzo for the Concord Jazz label album "Do You Miss New York?"

Sep 14–17   Do You Miss New York? / Gee Baby, Ain't I Good to You / As Long As I Live / May I Come In / (Get Your Kicks on) Route 66 / A Beautiful Friendship / It's Only a Paper Moon (*with John Pizzarelli*) / I Ain't Got Nothin' but the Blues / I Wish You Love / I Get Along without You Very Well / We'll Be Together Again

1993

With a big band led by John Oddo for the Concord Jazz label album "Still on the Road"

Nov 22–23   On the Road Again / Rules of the Road / Corcovado (Quiet Nights of Quiet Stars) / How Are Things in Glocca Morra? / Let's Get Away from It All / Moonlight Mississippi / Back Home in Indiana / Ol' Man River / Take Me Back to Manhattan / How Deep Is the Ocean / Road to Morocco (*with Jack Sheldon*) / Still on the Road / Till We Meet Again (*with Earl Brown*) / Let's Eat Home / Still Crazy After All These Years

1994

May 25   That Old Feeling (*for the soundtrack of Radioland Murders*)

With Barry Manilow and the Jimmy Dorsey Orchestra. Issued on the album "Singin' with the Big Bands" on the Arista label.

Jul   Green Eyes

With a big band led by John Oddo for the Concord Jazz label album "Rosemary Clooney—Demi-Centennial"

Oct 10–13 /
Nov 11   Danny Boy / The Coffee Song (*with Cathi Campo*) / I'm Confessin' (That I Love You) / I Left My Heart in San Francisco / Old Friends / White Christmas / There Will Never Be Another You / Falling in Love Again / Sophisticated Lady / How Will I Remember You / Mambo Italiano / The Promise (I'll Never Say Goodbye) / Heart's Desire / We'll Meet Again / Time Flies / Dear Departed Past

1995

With a big band led by John Oddo for the Concord Jazz label album "Dedicated to Nelson"

Sep 27–30   A Foggy Day / We're in the Money / It's So Peaceful in the Country / Limehouse Blues / Do You Know What It Means to Miss New Orleans? / I Got It Bad and That Ain't Good / The Continental / Mean to Me / You're in Kentucky / As Time Goes By / Haven't Got a Worry / Mangos / At Sundown / A Woman Likes to Be Told / What Is This Thing Called Love / Come Rain or Come Shine

1996

With a big band led by John Oddo and the Earl Brown Singers for the Concord Jazz label album "White Christmas"

Apr 1–4   The Christmas Song / Let It Snow! Let It Snow! Let It Snow! / I'll Be Home for Christmas / It's the Most Wonderful Time of the Year / Have Yourself a Merry Little Christmas / Christmas Love Song / Winter Wonderland / Christmas Time Is Here / Christmas Mem'ries / Spirit of Christmas / Santa Claus Is Comin' to Town—Hey Kris Kringle (*with Michael Feinstein*) / Count Your Blessings Instead of Sheep / The Christmas Waltz / White Christmas / Sleep Well, Little Children / Don't Wait Till the Night before Christmas (*with Nick Clooney*)

1997

With a big band led by John Oddo for the Concord Jazz label album "Mothers and Daughters"

Jun 23/
Oct 23–24   Thank Heaven for Little Girls / Always / That Face / Baby Mine / The Best Gift / Maria / God Bless the Child / Look to the Rainbow / Turn Around (*with Keith Carradine*) / Hello Young Lovers / Wrap Your Troubles in Dreams / And I'll Be There / Pick Yourself Up / Look for the Silver Lining / Funny Face / A Child Is Only a Moment / Sisters

With Matt Catingub and his band for a Concord Jazz album called "George Gershwin 100"

Sep   I've Got a Crush on You

| Sep 28 | Fools Rush In (Where Angels Fear to Tread) (for the sound-track of *Midnight in the Garden of Good and Evil*) |

Records two tracks to be added to a Concord Jazz label compilation album called "70—A Seventieth Birthday Celebration"

| Oct 3 | Secret o' Life / Love Is Here to Stay (*with Linda Ronstadt and k. d. Lang*) |

With the Count Basie Orchestra for the Concord Jazz label album "At Long Last"

| Nov | Just in Time / Like Someone in Love / Willow Weep for Me / Lullaby of Broadway / Old Devil Moon / Everything Happens to Me / I Want to Be a Sideman / In the Wee Small Hours of the Morning / How About You (*with Barry Manilow*) / The Man That Got Away / Seems Like Old Times / Guess I'll Hang My Tears Out to Dry / It Just Happened to Happen to Me / I Got Rhythm / Gypsy in My Soul / If Swing Goes I Go Too |

1999

With an orchestra led by John Oddo for the Concord Jazz label album "Brazil"

| Mar 15–18,
Mar 25 /
Jan 24, 2000 | Brazil / Corcovado (Quiet Nights of Quiet Stars) / The Boy From Ipanema (*with Diana Krall*) / Once I Loved / Desafinado (Slightly Out of Tune) (*with John Pizzarelli*) / I Concentrate on You / Samba De Uma Nota So (One Note Samba) (*with John Pizzarelli*) / Insensatez (How Insensitive) / Let Go (*with John Pizzarelli*) / Aquas De Marco (Waters of March) (*with John Pizzarelli*) / I Will Wait For You / A Day in the Life of A Fool / Brazil (*with John Pizzarelli*) |

For the Sony Music album "A Rosie Christmas"; all proceeds benefited the All Kids Foundation.

| Nov | Santa Claus Is Comin' to Town (*with Rosie O'Donnell*) |

2000

For the Linda Ronstadt album "A Merry Little Christmas" issued on the Elektra label.

| | White Christmas (*with Linda Ronstadt*) |

With the Big Kahuna and Copa Cat Pack led by Matt Catingub for the Concord Jazz label album "Sentimental Journey: The Girl Singer and Her New Big Band"
> That Old Black Magic / I'm Glad There Is You / I've Got My Love to Keep Me Warm / You Go to My Head / And the Angels Sing / Happiness Is a Thing Called Joe / I'm The Big Band Singer / You Belong to Me / I'll Be Around / I Gotta Right to Sing the Blues / Ya Got Class / Rockin' Chair / The Singer (this track recorded Feb. 24, 2001) / They Can't Take That Away from Me / Sentimental Journey / Medley: (I Cried for You / Who's Sorry Now? / Goody Goody) (the last two tracks recorded live at the Rosemary Clooney Music Festival, Maysville, Kentucky—Sep. 30, 2000)

With Big Kahuna and the Copa Cat Pack and the Honolulu Symphony Orchestra— taken from a live concert and issued on the Concord Jazz album Rosemary Clooney: THE LAST CONCERT
Nov 16 Medley (Tenderly / White Christmas / Half as Much / Sisters / This Ole House) / Sentimental Journey / I'm Confessin' That I Love You / Just in Time / Happiness Is a Thing Called Joe / You Go to My Head / Rockin' Chair / Ol' Man River / The Singer / They Can't Take That Away from Me / God Bless America

ISSUED RECORDINGS BY CATALOG NUMBER

COSMO RECORDS 1946

Label No.	Title
721	Uncle Remus Said / Sooner or Later
722	Everybody Has a Laughing Place / How Do You Do?
723	Zip-A-Dee-Doo-Dah

COLUMBIA RECORDS 1947–1958

Columbia had several different series for their single releases. For the bulk of their releases Columbia 78s used 5-digit numbers in the 35000s. The series had reached 38600 around 1950 and continued into the 1950s, passing the number 40000 in the middle of the decade.

There were separate numerical groups for "race" (30000–30243) and country and western. (20000–21571). Children's records were also placed in a different run on nonbreakable records. In addition, Columbia issued selected songs on their cheaper Harmony label.

In January 1949, Columbia introduced 7" 33 1/3-rpm singles, which were numbered in their own series, with a prefix 1- before a low number, not exceeding 3 digits. A number of these records featuring Rosemary Clooney are held by the Library of Congress and can be viewed in the Sonic section of the Library's website.

Columbia originally resisted issuing 45-rpm singles, as that was a speed originated by its competitor RCA Victor Records. However, in late 1950 Columbia began to issue 45s with numbers identical to the corresponding 7"33 1/3 singles, only using the prefix 6- instead of the prefix 1-.

Early in the 1950s, the system was changed to give singles at all speeds the same numbers except that the 33 1/3-rpm records had a prefix, now 3-, and the 45-rpm records also a prefix, now 4-, added to the number of the 78. In due course the only speed issued was 45 rpm, and the 4- prefix was dropped.

Columbia Records issued the following Rosemary Clooney singles and long playing albums (excluding reissues and compilations) in the United States.

Columbia Singles (main listing—microphone label)

Label #	Title
37562	I'm Sorry I Didn't Say I'm Sorry (When I Made You Cry Last Night)
37839	Tira Lira Li (The Song of the Gondolier) / My O'Darlin' My O'Lovely My O'Brien
37973	Gonna Get a Girl
38068	I'm My Own Grandpaw / The Secretary Song (Bibidi Boo Bot)
38142	At a Sidewalk Penny Arcade / Who Killed 'Er (Who Killed the Black Widder?)
38178	There's a Man at the Door
38207	A Boy from Texas, a Girl from Tennessee
38297	You Started Something / The Click Song
38355	The Chowder Social / It's Like Taking Candy from a Baby
38383	Saturday Night Mood / Grieving for You
38449	It's a Cruel, Cruel World / "A" You're Adorable (The Alphabet Song)
38454	When You're in Love / San
38501	Cabaret / Bargain Day
38577	If I Had a Million Dollars

38678	The Kid's a Dreamer (The Kid from Fool's Paradise) / Why Don't You Haul Off and Love Me
38741	Busy Line
38766	I Found My Mamma / Me and My Teddy Bear
38767	The Canasta Song / A Good Time Was Had by All
38804	I Only Saw Him Once / On an Ordinary Morning
38851	Little Johnny Chickadee / Peterkin Pillowby
38853	Peachtree Street
38900	Crying Myself to Sleep / Why Fight the Feeling?
38962	Bread and Butter Woman
38972	Punky Punkin (The Happy Pumpkin) / The Wobblin' Goblin
38983	Where Do I Go from You / (Remember Me) I'm the One Who Loves You
38988	C-H-R-I-S-T-M-A-S / Bless This House
39052	Marrying for Love / You're Just in Love
39054	The Place Where I Worship / The House of Singing Bamboo
39141	Love Means Love / Cherry Pies Ought to Be You
39158	Sentimental Music
39185	When Apples Grow on Cherry Trees / I Still Feel the Same about You
39212	Beautiful Brown Eyes / Shot Gun Boogie
39333	Mixed Emotions / Kentucky Waltz
39467	Come On-a My House / Rose of the Mountain
39535	If Teardrops Were Pennies / I'm Waiting Just for You
39536	Mixed Emotions / I Wish I Wuz (Hi, Ho, Fiddle-dee-dee)
39591	I Only Saw Him Once / Find Me
39612	Suzy Snowflake / Little Red Riding Hood's Christmas Tree
39631	Be My Life's Companion / Why Don't You Love Me
39648	Did Anyone Call? / Tenderly
39710	Half as Much / Poor Whip-Poor-Will (Move over, Move over)
39730	Tenderly
39767	Botch-a-Me (Ba-Ba-Baciami Piccina) / On the First Warm Day
39812	Too Old to Cut the Mustard / Good for Nothin'
39813	Who Kissed Me Last Night? / Blues in the Night
39852	You'll Never Know / In the Cool, Cool, Cool of the Evening
39853	When You Wish upon a Star / On the Atchison, Topeka and the Santa Fe
39854	The Continental / It Might as Well Be Spring
39855	Sweet Leilani / Over the Rainbow
39876	The Night before Christmas Song / Look out the Window (The Winter Song)

39892	If I Had a Penny / You're After My Own Heart
39905	You'll Never Know / The Continental
39931	I Laughed until I Cried / What Would You Do (If You Were in My Place)
39943	Haven't Got a Worry / Lovely Weather for Ducks
39980	Dot's Nice, Donna Fight / It's the Same
39988	Little Josey / Dennis the Menace
40003	It Just Happened to Happen to Me / When I See You
40024	Stick with Me / Cheegah Choonem (I Haven't Got It)
40031	Tenderly / Blues in the Night
40056	Shoo, Turkey, Shoo / Lonely Am I
40102	C-H-R-I-S-T-M-A-S / Happy Christmas (Little Friend)
40142	When You Love Someone / My Baby Rocks Me
40144	Woman (Uh-Huh) / Man (Uh-Huh)
40158	Red Garters / Man and Woman
40159	Bad News
40160	Brave Man
40161	Good Intentions
40187	Brave Man / Tomorrow I'll Dream and Remember
40233	Ay Ay (Who's the Guy) / A Bunch of Bananas (The Heming Way)
40266	Hey There / This Ole House
40305	Love, You Didn't Do Right by Me / Sisters
40317	(Let's Give) A Christmas Present to Santa Claus
40355	White Christmas / Count Your Blessings Instead of Sheep
40356	The Best Things Happen While You're Dancing / Mandy
40357	Snow / Sisters
40358	Gee, I Wish I Was Back in the Army / Love, You Didn't Do Right by Me
40361	We'll Be Together Again / Mambo Italiano
40370	White Christmas / Count Your Blessings Instead of Sheep
40407	Marry the Man / Mr. & Mrs.
40422	Open up Your Heart (And Let the Sunshine In) / The Lord Is Counting on You (The Sunday School Song)
40434	Close Your Eyes (Brahms' Lullaby) / Where Will the Dimple Be?
40496	When You Wish upon a Star / It Might as Well Be Spring
40498	Love Among the Young / A Touch of the Blues
40534	Sailor Boys Have Talk to Me in English / Go on By
40579	Wake Me / Pet Me, Poppa
40616	It's Bad for Me / Memories of You
40619	A Little Girl at Heart / The Key to My Heart

40625	Good Bye
40676	I've Grown Accustomed to Your Face / I Could Have Danced All Night
40701	Grievin' / Sophisticated Lady
40723	Peachy Peachy / Hello Young Lovers
40760	Nobody's Darlin' but Mine / You Are My Sunshine
40774	Come Rain or Come Shine / It's a Nuisance Having You Around
40808	Mommy, Can I Keep the Kitten? / He'll Be Comin' Down the Chimney
40812	(Don't That Take the) Rag Offen the Bush / Love Is a Feeling
40835	Mangos / Independent (On My Own)
40917	Sing, Little Birdie, Sing / Who Dot Mon, Mom?
40981	That's How It Is / (You Can't Lose the Blues with) Colors
41053	Tonight / Love and Affection
41107	You Don't Know Him / Surprise
41547	Dennis the Menace
49954	Happy Christmas Little Friend
50007	Blues in the Night/ Come On-a My House
50037	Tenderly / Half As Much

Country & Western Series

21071	Withered Roses / You Love Me Just Enough to Hurt Me
21423	Go on By / I Whisper Your Name

Harmony

1050	Lover's Gold / The Four Winds and the Seven Seas
1071	Don't Cry Joe (Let Her Go, Let Her Go, Let Her Go) / Oh, You Beautiful Doll
1074	There's a Broken Heart for Every Light on Broadway / Chicago

Nonbreakable Children's Records

MJV70	Me and My Teddy Bear / I Found My Mamma
MJV73	Little Johnny Chickadee / Peterkin Pillowby
MJV86	Punky Punkin (The Happy Pumpkin) / The Wobblin' Goblin

MJV95   Fuzzy Wuzzy (Wuz a Bear) / My Choc'late Rabbit
MJV98   Little Sally One Shoe / The Land of Hatchy Milatchy
MJV109   Who'll Tie the Bell (on the Old Cat's Tail) / The Syncopated Clock
MJV112   Alice in Wonderland—The Unbirthday Song / All in a Golden Afternoon—I'm Late
MJV117   Dandy, Handy and Candy / Willie, the Whistling Giraffe
MJV123   Suzy Snowflake / Little Red Riding Hood's Christmas Tree
MJV131   Eggbert, the Easter Egg / Bunny on the Rainbow
MJV138   On the Good Ship Lollipop / The Land of Hatchy Milatchy
MJV149   The Night Before Christmas Song / Look Out the Window (The Winter Song)
MJV164   Little Red Monkey / Little Joe Worm (Son of Glow Worm)
MJV168   The Teddy Bears' Picnic / The Kitty Kats' Party
MJV174   Betsy, My Paper Doll / Little Sally One Shoe
MJV175   Winter Wonderland / C-H-R-I-S-T-M-A-S
MJV182   Dennis the Menace / Little Josey
MJV189   Little Tink-a-Toy Man / (Ting-a-Ling-Ling) Here Comes the Ice Cream Man
MJV191   All the Pretty Little Horses / Close Your Eyes (Brahms' Lullaby)
MJV213   Shaun, Shaun, The Leprechaun / The Little Shoemaker
MJV220   (Let's Give) A Christmas Present to Santa Claus
MJV232   Open up Your Heart (and Let the Sunshine in) / The Lord Is Counting on You (The Sunday School Song)
MJV234   Peter Cottontail / Easter Parade
CO-8501 Snow White & the Seven Dwarfs, Part 1 / Snow White & the Seven Dwarfs, Part 2
CO-8502 Little Red Riding Hood / Goldilocks and the Three Bears

VARIOUS LABELS 1958–1983

Single Releases on 45 rpm for the M-G-M Label

K12654   Morning Music of Montmartre / Give It All You Got
K12655   Hey Madame / You're So Right for Me
K12705   It's a Boy / The Loudenboomer Bird (Early Ev'ry Morning)
K12760   Flattery / Love Eyes
K12823   I Wonder / For You
K13349   Love and Learn / I'm Glad It's You

Single Releases on 45 rpm for the Coral Label

62064	Love, Look Away / Diga Me (Deega May—Tell Me)
62137	A Touch of the Blues / I Wish I Were in Love Again

Single Releases on 45 rpm for the RCA Label

47-7517	Ain't A-Hankerin' / Protection
47-7707	Corazon de Melon (Watermelon Heart) / Summertime Love
47-7754	Many a Wonderful Moment / Vaya, Vaya (Go My Darling, Go)
47-7806	Danke Schon / Swing Me
47-7819	What Takes My Fancy / Hey, Look Me Over
47-7887	Theme from "Return to Peyton Place" (The Wonderful Season of Love) / Without Love
47-7948	Give Myself a Party / If I Can Stay Away Long Enough

Single Releases on 45 rpm for the Reprise Label

R20145	The Rose And The Butterfly / I Will Follow You
R20173	Mixed Emotions / The Prisoner's Song
R20222	A Hundred Years from Today / Hello Faithless
R20285	Some Enchanted Evening
R20327	Stay Awake / A Spoonful of Sugar

Single Release on 45 rpm for the Dot Label

45-17100	Let Me Down Easy / One Less Bell to Answer

Single Release on 45 rpm for Apco Records

AP-4775	When You Got Love / The Very Thought of Losing You

Single Releases on 45 rpm for the United Artists Label

UA 50076	I Need a Broken Heart (Like a Hole in the Head) / Round and Round
UA 97724	Half as Much / When You Got Love

Single Release on 45 rpm for Kitty Records, Japan

DKQ 1045   Close Your Eyes (Brahms' Lullaby) / Faded Love

Long-Playing Records—Columbia

This listing shows the entire main catalog LPs issued by Columbia Records in the United States. Albums marked with * were compilations rather than specially recorded albums, but are included because they were issued in Columbia's main catalog of Clooney releases.

10"

Catalog #	Title
CL 6224	Hollywood's Best
CL 6282	Red Garters
CL 6297	While We're Young
CL 6338	Irving Berlin's White Christmas
CL 2525*	Tenderly
CL 2569*	Children's Favorites
CL 2572	A Date with the King
CL 2581	Rosemary Clooney on Stage

12"

CL 585*	Hollywood's Best
CL 872	Blue Rose
CL 969*	Clooney Tunes
CL 1006	Ring around Rosie
CL 1230*	Rosie's Greatest Hits
CL 2581	Rosemary Clooney on Stage

Long-Playing Record for the Phillips Label (England)

10"

BBR 8073   Rosemary Clooney Live at the London Palladium

Long-Playing Records (all 12" from now on) for the M-G-M Label

E/SE 3687   The Ferrers: Rosemary Clooney and Jose Ferrer Sing selections from the Broadway Musical "Oh, Captain!"

E/SE 3709   The Story of Celeste
E/SE 3782   Hymns from the Heart
E/SE 3834*   Rosemary Clooney Swings Softly

Long-Playing Records for the RCA Label

LSP 1854   Fancy Meeting You Here
LOP 6070   How the West Was Won
LSP 2133   A Touch of Tabasco
LSP 2212   Clap Hands! Here Comes Rosie
LSP 2265   Rosie Solves the Swingin' Riddle
LSP 2565   Rosemary Clooney Sings Country Hits from the Heart

Long-Playing Record for the Coral Label

7-57266 12 Swing Around Rosie

Long-Playing Record for the Capitol Label

ST2300   That Travelin' Two-Beat

Long-Playing Records for the Reprise Label

RS6088   Love
RS6108   Thanks for Nothing
FS2015   Finian's Rainbow (two tracks only)
FS2018   South Pacific (one track only)
R50001   Frank Sinatra and His Friends Want You to Have Yourself a
            Merry Little Christmas (one track only)

Long-Playing Records for the United Artists Label

UAS29918   Look My Way
UAS30008   Nice to Be Around

Long-Playing Record for the K-Tel Label

KTEL
NE951   Bing Crosby—Live at the London Palladium

Long-Playing Record for the Mistletoe Records Label

MLP-1234   Christmas with Rosemary Clooney

Long-Playing Record for the Aurex Label (Japan)

EWJ-80268   Rosemary Clooney with Les Brown and His Band of Renown

CONCORD JAZZ 1977–2002

Early albums originally issued as LPs and then later as Compact Discs

CJ-47	Everything's Coming up Rosie
CJ-50	A Tribute to Duke
CJ-60	Rosie Sings Bing
CJ-81	Here's to My Lady—Tribute to Billie Holiday
CJ-112	Rosemary Clooney Sings the Lyrics of Ira Gershwin
CJ-144	With Love
CJ-185	Rosemary Clooney Sings the Music of Cole Porter
CJ-210	Rosemary Clooney Sings the Music of Harold Arlen
CJ-226	My Buddy
CJ-255	Rosemary Clooney Sings the Music of Irving Berlin
CJ-282	Rosemary Clooney Sings Ballads
CJ-308	Rosemary Clooney Sings the Music of Jimmy Van Heusen
CJ-333	Rosemary Clooney Sings the Lyrics of Johnny Mercer
CJ-364	Show Tunes
CJ-405	Rosemary Clooney Sings Rodgers, Hart & Hammerstein
CJ-444	For the Duration
CJ-496	Girl Singer
CCD-4537	Do You Miss New York?
CCD-4590	Still on the Road
CCD-4633	Rosemary Clooney—Demi-Centennial
CCD-4685	Dedicated to Nelson
CCD-4719	White Christmas
CCD-4754-2	Mothers & Daughters
CCD-4795-2	At Long Last
CCD-4804-2	Rosemary Clooney 70: A Seventieth Birthday Celebration
CCD-4884-2	Brazil
CCD-4952-2	Sentimental Journey
CCD-2166-2	The Last Concert

Rosemary Clooney on Television

REGULAR SERIES

Songs for Sale (CBS-TV)

Air date July 7, 14, 21, & 28, 1950
Air date August 4, 11, 18, & 25, 1950
Air date September 1, 8, 15, 22, & 29, 1950
Air date October 6, 13, 20, & 27 1950
Air date November 3, 10, & 17, 1950
Air date December 22 & 29, 1950
Air date January 5, 12, 19, & 26, 1951
Air date February 2, 9, 16, & 23, 1951
Air date March 2, 9, 16, 23, & 30, 1951
Air date April 6 & 13, 1951
Air date May 25, 1951
Air date August 25, 1951

Robert Q's Matinee (CBS-TV)

Air date October 16, 1950
Air date November 9, 17, & 20, 1950
Air date December 18, 21, & 28, 1950
Air date January 2 & 9, 1951

The Rosemary Clooney Show (syndicated program)

Air dates of this syndicated series commenced on May 15, 1956. The show was seen in a different order on different dates at many TV stations.

Because of this, the quoting of dates would be confusing and the shows are listed therefore in the order that they were filmed.

1. Guest: José Ferrer. Rosemary sings "Secret Love," "Love and Marriage" (with José Ferrer) "Come On-a My House" and "Mambo Italiano."
2. Guest: Janet Leigh. Rosemary sings "Haven't Got a Worry," "While We're Young," "This Ole House" (with The Hi-Lo's), "A Man, Oh a Man" (with Janet Leigh), "Blues in the Night" (with The Hi-Lo's) and "Close Your Eyes."
3. Guest: Tony Curtis. Rosemary sings "Taking a Chance on Love," "Hey There," "The Continental," "A Little Girl at Heart" and "You Make Me Feel So Young."
4. Guest: Robert Clary. Rosemary sings "It's a Most Unusual Day," "Cela M'est Egal," "C'est Si Bon" (with The Hi-Lo's), "Don'cha Go 'Way Mad" (with The Hi-Lo's), "On the Sunny Side of the Street."
5. Guest: Gene Nelson. Rosemary sings "Give Me the Simple Life," "I Guess I'll Have to Change My Plan," "Why Don't You Do Right," "I've Got the World on a String" (with Gene Nelson) and "Goodnight Sweetheart."
6. Guest: The Mary Kaye Trio. Rosemary sings "Chicago," "The Kid's a Dreamer," "Ya Got Class" (with Clark Burroughs) and "Ebb Tide."
7. Guest: Gail Stone. Rosemary sings "Sisters" (with Gail Stone).
8. Guest: Judy Canova. Rosemary sings "It's a Lovely Day Today," "You're in Kentucky Sure as You're Born," "A Little Red Barn on a Farm Down Indiana Way" (with Judy Canova and The Hi-Lo's) and "Manhattan."
9. Guests: Julie London and Lee Scott. Rosemary sings "Just You, Just Me," "If I Forget You," "Let's Call the Whole Thing Off" (with Gene Puerling) and "Come Rain or Come Shine."
10. Guest: Buddy Greco. Rosemary sings "Let It Snow! Let It Snow! Let It Snow!" "Spring Is Here," and "It's Bad for Me."
11. Guests: Mona Freeman and Pete Hanley. Rosemary sings "It's All Right with Me," "Do You Know What It Means to Miss New Orleans," "Louisiana Purchase Medley" (with Pete Hanley and The Hi-Lo's), and "Count Your Blessings Instead of Sheep."
12. Guests: Charles Coburn and Renee Godfrey. Rosemary sings "Great Day," "The Nearness of You," "Happiness Is a Thing Called Joe," "Will You Still Be Mine" (with The Hi-Lo's), and "I'll Be Seeing You."
13. Guest: Johnny Mercer. Rosemary sings "Too Marvelous for Words," "I Remember You," "Let's Take the Long Way Home," and "What Makes the Whatchamacallit Go" (with Johnny Mercer).
14. Guest: Beatrice Kay. Rosemary sings "You Were Meant for Me," "I'm Old Fashioned," "Stanley Steamer Song" (with The Hi-Lo's), and "As Time Goes By."

15. Guest: Joanne Gilbert. Rosemary sings "Thou Swell," Limehouse Blues," "On a Slow Boat to China" (with Joanne Gilbert and The Hi-Lo's), and "You're Just in Love" (with Joanne Gilbert).

16. Guests: Dani Crayne and Joe Bushkin. Rosemary sings "Please Don't Talk about Me When I'm Gone," "Blame It on My Youth," "I've Got a Crush on You" (with Joe Bushkin), "Oh! Look at Me Now" (with Joe Bushkin and The Hi-Lo's). (As part of a Rocket Launching Skit, Rosemary also sings snatches of "Please Don't Talk about Me When I'm Gone," "When First We Kissed," "I've Got a Crush on You," and "Oh! Look at Me Now" [parody]).

17. Guest: Dick Contino. Rosemary sings "Getting to Know You," "On the Atchison, Topeka and the Santa Fe," "You Do Something to Me" (with Dick Contino), "There Will Never Be Another You," and "All I Do Is Dream of You."

18. Guests: Jeri Southern and Pete Candoli. Rosemary sings "Grievin'" and "I'll See You Again."

19. Guests: Bobby Troup and Dorothy Malone. Rosemary sings "When the Red, Red Robin Comes Bob, Bob, Bobbin' Along," "They Can't Take That Away from Me," and "(Get Your Kicks On) Route 66" (with Bobby Troup and Dorothy Malone).

20. Guests: Olga San Juan and the guitar virtuoso Vincente Gomez. Rosemary sings "Hooray for Hollywood," "Tangerine" (with The Hi-Lo's), "Frenesi," and "For You."

21. Guest: Rex Allen. Rosemary sings "Three Little Words," "Buttons and Bows" (with Rex Allen), "Half as Much," and "Get Happy."

22. Guest: Guy Mitchell. Rosemary sings "We're in the Money," "A Foggy Day," "Keep It Gay," "Marrying for Love" (with Guy Mitchell), and "I'm Checkin' Out—Goombye."

23. Guest: Jerry Colonna. Rosemary sings "I Know That You Know," "The Land of Hatchy Milatchy," "Them There Eyes," and "Going My Way."

24. Guest: Gail Stone and Buster Keaton. Rosemary sings "Swinging on a Star," "Mean to Me," and "The Lord Is Counting on You (The Sunday School Song)" (with Gail Stone).

25. Guest: Tennessee Ernie Ford. Rosemary sings "My Blue Heaven," "Lazy River," "Play a Simple Melody" (with Tennessee Ernie Ford), and "At Sundown."

26. Guest: José Ferrer. Rosemary sings "Who Cares," "Autumn Leaves," and "There's No Business Like Show Business" (with José Ferrer).

27. Guest: Dorothy Shay. Rosemary sings "Lullaby of Broadway," "New York's My Home" (with Dorothy Shay and the Hi-Lo's), and "Undecided."

28. Guest: Dorothy Kirsten. Rosemary sings "Life upon the Wicked Stage" (with Dorothy Kirsten).
29. Guest: Carol Channing. Rosemary sings "New Sun in the Sky," "Everything Happens to Me" (with Carol Channing), "How About You" (with The Hi-Lo's), and "Moonlight in Vermont."
30. Guest: Elena Verdugo. Rosemary sings "It's a Big, Wide, Wonderful World," "Weekend of a Private Secretary," "Danny Boy" (with The Hi-Lo's), and "I Can't Believe That You're in Love with Me."
31. Guest: Marguerite Piazza. Rosemary sings "Love," "I Got It Bad (And That Ain't Good)," "A Good Man Is Hard to Find" (with Marguerite Piazza), and "As Long as I Live."
32. Guests: Hildegarde and José Ferrer. Rosemary sings "What Is There to Say," "All the Pretty Little Horses," and "Where Is Your Heart" (with Hildegarde).
33. Guests: Frances Bergen and Matt Dennis. Rosemary sings "Seems Like Old Times," "That's How It Is," "Let's Get Away from It All" (with Frances Bergen and Matt Dennis), and "Nighty Night."
34. Guest: Mel Tormé. Rosemary sings "I've Got My Love to Keep Me Warm," "It's So Peaceful in the Country," and "The Christmas Song."
35. Guest: Vincent Price. Rosemary sings "Just One of Those Things," "Why Fight the Feeling," "Happy Ending" (with Vincent Price), "You Came a Long Way from St. Louis," and "Goodnight (Wherever You Are)."
36. Guest: Hoagy Carmichael. Rosemary sings "You Are My Lucky Star," "Mangos," "A Woman Likes to Be Told" (with Hoagy Carmichael), "Music, Always, Music" (with Hoagy Carmichael and The Hi-Lo's), "The Best Things in Life Are Free" (with The Hi-Lo's), and "After You've Gone."
37. Guest: Zsa Zsa Gabor. Rosemary sings "Sunday in Savannah," "Dixie" (with The Hi-Lo's), "Love Is a Feeling," and "Dream (When You're Feeling Blue)" (with The Hi-Lo's).
38. Guest: Cesar Romero. Rosemary sings "Don't Take Your Love from Me," "Cleopatterer," "Looking for a Boy," "I'm Learnin' My Latin" (with Cesar Romero), "Bess You Is My Woman/Porgy, You Is My Man" (with Bob Morse of The Hi-Lo's), and "Bless This House."
39. Guest: Boris Karloff. Rosemary sings "The World Is Waiting for the Sunrise," "I Can't Escape from You," "You'd Be Surprised" (with Boris Karloff), and "After the Ball."

The Lux Show with Rosemary Clooney (NBC-TV)

Air date September 26, 1957. Guests: Jane Wyman, Paula Kelly, and Tennessee Ernie Ford. Rosemary sings "That's How It Is,"

"Side by Side" (with Tennessee Ernie Ford), "Hooray for Hollywood" (with The Modernaires), and "Blow, Gabriel, Blow" (with The Modernaires).

Air date October 3, 1957. Guests include William Bendix and Walter Brennan. Rosemary sings "April in Paris," "Chances Are," "Goody Goody," "Love Is a Feeling," and "Recognize the Tune" (with William Bendix).

Air date October 10, 1957. Guests include Edward Everett Horton and Paula Kelly. Rosemary sings "It's a Most Unusual Day," "My Heart Reminds Me," "For You," "Hush-a-Bye," "I Won't Dance" (with Edward Everett Horton), and "Life upon the Wicked Stage" (with Paula Kelly).

Air date October 24, 1957. Guests include Ken Murray and Paula Kelly. Rosemary sings "Come On-a My House," "Do You Know What It Means to Miss New Orleans," "Early Autumn," "Too-Ra-Loo-Ra-Loo-Ral," and "Brush up Your Shakespeare" (with Ken Murray).

Air date October 31, 1957. Guests include Boris Karloff and Paula Kelly. Rosemary sings "Bewitched, Bothered and Bewildered," "Don'cha Go 'Way Mad" "Sleep, Sleep, Sleep," and "You Do Something to Me" (with Boris Karloff).

Air date November 7, 1957. Guests include Carol Channing and Paula Kelly. Rosemary sings "I'm Beginning to See the Light," "Jailhouse Rock," "I'm Checkin' Out—Goombye" "Rock-a-Bye Baby," and "Independent" (with Carol Channing).

Air date November 14, 1957. Guests include Wally Cox, The Modernaires, and Paula Kelly. Rosemary sings "It's a Good Day," "Ca, C'est L'amour," "Show It," "All Shook Up" (with Wally Cox), and "On the Sunny Side of the Street."

Air date November 28, 1957. Guests include Betty Clooney, Nick Clooney, Gail Stone, José Ferrer, The Modernaires, and Paula Kelly. Rosemary sings "Tonight," "Haven't Got a Worry," "Sisters" (with Betty Clooney, Nick Clooney and Gail Stone), "You're in Kentucky as Sure As You're Born" (with Betty Clooney, Nick Clooney and Gail Stone), "Love and Affection," and "May the Good Lord Bless and Keep You."

Air date December 5, 1957. Guests include Marie Wilson, Paula Kelly, and The Modernaires. Rosemary sings "Hooray for Love," "All the Way," "The Lady Is a Tramp," and "Tenderly."

Air date December 12, 1957. Guests include Charles Laughton. Rosemary sings "Keep Your Sunny Side Up," "April Love," "Lover, Come Back to Me," Medley with Charles Laughton ("Moonlight Bay," "Waiting for the Robert E. Lee," "De Camptown Races," "Oh, Susanna"), and "Hey There."

Air date December 19, 1957. Guests include Patty McCormack and Tim Hovey.

Air date December 26, 1957. Guests include Spring Byington.

Air date January 2, 1958. Guests include John Forsythe.

Air date January 9, 1958. Guests include Lauritz Melchior.

Air date January 16, 1958. Guests include Alan Young. Rosemary sings "Love Is Sweeping the Country" and "Catch a Falling Star."

Air date January 30, 1958. Guests include Paul Lynde and Ferlin Husky.

Air date February 6, 1958. Guests include Peter Leeds, Wayne & Shuster.

Air date February 13, 1958. Guests include Rex Allen. Rosemary sings "Who Cares," "Wait Till the Sun Shines, Nellie" (with Rex Allen), Kansas City Medley (with Rex Allen), and "Open up Your Heart."

Air date February 20, 1958. Guests include Robert Clary and Don Adams. Rosemary sings "The Best Things in Life are Free" and a *South Pacific* medley (with Robert Clary).

Air date February 27, 1958. Guests include Andy Devine, The Hi-Lo's, Marvin Kaplan and Ben Lessy.

Air date March 6, 1958. Guests include José Ferrer. Rosemary sings "Beyond the Blue Horizon," "A Kiss to Build a Dream On," "Sunday Morning in Montmartre" (with José Ferrer and The Modernaires), and "You're So Right for Me" (with José Ferrer).

Air date March 13, 1958. Guests include Nelson Eddy and comedian Ben Lessy. Rosemary sings "Shall We Dance?" (with Nelson Eddy).

Air date March 20, 1958. Guests include Mel Tormé.

Air date March 27, 1958. Guests include opera star Salvatore Baccaloni and Don Adams.

Air date April 3, 1958. Guests include John Raitt and Bob Williams. Rosemary sings "Surprise," "Eggbert the Easter Egg," and with John Raitt she duets "Hey There," "Easter Parade," and "Whispering Hope."

Air date April 10, 1958. Guests include Robert Horton, Don Knotts, and Shelley Berman. Rosemary sings "The World Is Waiting for the Sunrise."

Air date April 17, 1958. Guests include Spring Byington.

Air date April 24, 1958. Guests include Don Cherry.

Air date May 1, 1958. Guests include George Gobel.

Air date May 8, 1958. Guests include Guy Mitchell, Arnold Stang, and Shelley Berman.

Air date May 15, 1958. Guests include Wally Cox.

Air date May 22, 1958. Guests include Stan Freberg.

Air date May 29, 1958. Guests include Bobby Troup and Lou Costello.

Air date June 5, 1958. Guests include John Raitt and Bob Williams and his dog.

Air date June 12, 1958. Guests include Earl Holliman and Shelley Berman.

Air date June 19, 1958. Guests include José Ferrer. Rosemary sings "Luck Be a Lady," "For You," "I Remember It Well" (with José Ferrer), "Nursery Rhyme Love Song," and "Love Is Here to Stay" (with José Ferrer).

GUEST APPEARANCES

This listing mainly contains shows that aired nationally although there are some exceptions. Rosemary made many local TV appearances and we do not have details of all of these. If known, the songs performed by Rosemary Clooney on each show are shown in *italics*.

Eddie Condon's Floor Show (NBC-TV)—Air date March 5, 1949
Way Down Yonder in New Orleans / Do You Know What It Means to Miss New Orleans

Eddie Condon's Floor Show (NBC-TV)—Air date March 12, 1949
There'll Be Some Changes Made

Eddie Condon's Floor Show (NBC-TV)—Air date September 17, 1949
Do You Know What It Means to Miss New Orleans / Chicago

Toast of the Town (CBS-TV)—Air date December 25, 1949
A Dreamer's Holiday / Why Don't You Haul Off and Love Me

The Morey Amsterdam Show (DuMont TV)—Air dates February 2 and May 11, 1950

Eddie Condon's Floor Show (CBS-TV)—Air date May 13, 1950

Eddie Condon's Floor Show (CBS-TV)—Air date June 24, 1950
You Started Something / Oh, Look at Me Now (with Joe Bushkin)

Eddie Condon's Floor Show (CBS-TV)—Air date June 6, 1950

Broadway Open House (NBC-TV)—Air date summer, 1950

The Morey Amsterdam Show (DuMont TV)—Air date July 20, 1950

Van Camp's Little Show (NBC-TV)—Air dates August 31, September 12, October 31, and November 14, 1950

Toast of the Town (CBS-TV)—Air date December 24, 1950

Cavalcade of the Bands (DuMont TV)—Air date January 9, 1951

The Johnny Johnston Show (CBS-TV)—Air date January 22, 1951

The Perry Como Show (CBS-TV)—Air dates February 7 and March 28, 1951

Cavalcade of the Bands (DuMont TV)—Air date April 17, 1951

Kreisler Bandstand (ABC-TV)—Air date May 16, 1951

Robbins' Nest (DuMont TV)—Air date July 5, 1951

Cavalcade of Stars (DuMont TV)—Air date August 10, 1951

Crusade for Freedom (all networks)—Air date September 23, 1951

Texaco Star Theater (NBC-TV)—Air date October 16, 1951

Ford Festival presents The James Melton Show (NBC-TV)—Air date November 1, 1951

Ken Murray Show (CBS-TV)—Air date December 1, 1951

Ford Festival presents The James Melton Show (NBC-TV)—Air date December 13, 1951

The Paul Whiteman Revue (ABC-TV)—Air date December 16, 1951

Ford Festival presents The James Melton Show (NBC-TV)—Air date January 3, 1952

Faye Emerson's Wonderful Town (CBS-TV)—Air date January 5, 1952

Royal Showcase (NBC-TV)—Air date January 13, 1952
Be My Life's Companion / Come On-a My House / New York's My Home

The Perry Como Show (CBS-TV)—Air date January 18, 1952

This is Show Business (CBS-TV)—Air date February 17, 1952
Looking for a Boy

Dude Ranch (WDTV, Pittsburgh)—Air date March 26, 1952

Royal Showcase (NBC-TV)—Air date March 30, 1952
New York's My Home

The Perry Como Show (CBS-TV)—Air dates March 31 and April 7, 1952

Royal Showcase (NBC-TV)—Air date April 13, 1952

Ken Murray Show (CBS-TV)—Air date April 26, 1952

The Perry Como Show (CBS-TV)—Air date April 30, 1952

The Ralph Edwards Show (NBC-TV)—Air date May 14, 1952

Peter Potter's Party (CBS-TV)—Air date May 19, 1952

The Gene Norman Show (KHJ)—Air date May 22, 1952

Colgate Comedy Hour (NBC-TV)—Air date September 21, 1952
Half as Much / Botch-a-me

Colgate Comedy Hour (NBC-TV)—Air date November 9, 1952
It's a Most Unusual Day / Oh, What a Beautiful Mornin' / Two Sleepy People (with Bob Hope)

Colgate Comedy Hour (NBC-TV)—Air date March 29, 1953
Haven't Got a Worry to My Name / Getting to Know You (with Bob Hope)

The Orchid Award (ABC-TV)—Air date May 24, 1953
Come On-a My House

Colgate Comedy Hour (NBC-TV)—Air date June 14, 1953

Honey / It's De-Lovely (with Bob Hope) / Home Town Medley (with Bob Hope and Frankie Laine—Rosemary sings a couple of lines of "You're in Kentucky Sure as You're Born" and joins Hope and Laine in a parody of "Carolina in the Morning")

Toast of the Town (CBS-TV)—Air date July 26, 1953

Boy Wanted / Stick with Me

Merry Christmas with the Stars (NBC-TV)—Air date December 25, 1953

Happy Christmas, Little Friend

Toast of the Town (CBS-TV)—Air date December 27, 1953

Winter Wonderland / Sisters (with Betty Clooney)

Starlight (BBC-TV)—Air date January 13, 1954

General Foods 25th Anniversary Show (CBS-TV & NBC-TV)—Air date March 28, 1954

No Other Love (with Tony Martin)

The Bob Hope Show (NBC-TV)—Air date April 13, 1954

What Is This Thing Called Love?

Toast of the Town (CBS-TV)—Air date July 11, 1954

Sisters (with Betty Clooney)

The Red Skelton Show (CBS-TV)—Air date August 4, 1954

Person to Person (CBS-TV)—Air date March 11, 1955

27th Annual Academy Awards (NBC-TV)—Air date March 30, 1955

The Man That Got Away

Toast of the Town (CBS-TV)—Air date April 10, 1955

Mambo Italiano

What's My Line? (CBS-TV) — Air date April 24, 1955

The Perry Como Show (NBC-TV)—Air date September 17, 1955

Too Marvelous for Words (with Perry Como)

Show Biz (NBC-TV)—Air date October 9, 1955

Don't Sit under the Apple Tree (with Anyone Else but Me)—You'd Be So Nice to Come Home To

The Ed Sullivan Show (CBS-TV)—Air date October 16, 1955

Sailor Boys Have Talk to Me in English / Wake Me / Pet Me, Poppa

The Perry Como Show (NBC-TV)—Air date November 19, 1955

Pet Me, Poppa

The Ed Sullivan Show (CBS-TV)—Air date May 13, 1956

The Ed Sullivan Show (CBS-TV)—Air date December 2, 1956

April in Paris

The Perry Como Show (NBC-TV)—Air date December 22, 1956

I've Got My Love to Keep Me Warm / He'll Be Coming down the Chimney When He Comes (with Gail Stone)

The Ford Show starring Tennessee Ernie Ford (NBC-TV)—Air date January 17, 1957

Love Is a Feelin' / Hog Tied over You (with Tennessee Ernie Ford)

The Chrysler Festival (CBC-TV)—Air date February 20, 1957

Independent / April in Paris / Botch-a-Me / Mambo Italiano / Come On-a My House

The Bob Hope Show (NBC-TV)—Air date March 3, 1957

Mangos / Wringle Wrangle (with Bob Hope)

The Steve Allen Show—Salute to the All-American Basketball Teams (NBC-TV)—Air date April 7, 1957

Mangos / Don't Take Your Love from Me / Manhattan (with Steve Allen)

Sunday Night at the London Palladium (ATV in the UK)—Air date April 14, 1957

April in Paris / Tenderly / Mangos / Don't Take Your Love from Me

Saturday Spectacular – The Rosemary Clooney Show (ATV)—Air date April 20, 1957

From This Moment On / Hey There / Mangos / Come On-a My House / New Sun in the Sky / That's How It Is / Close Your Eyes

The Edsel Show (CBS-TV)—Air date October 13, 1957

I Guess I'll Have to Change My Plan / Medley with Bing Crosby and Frank Sinatra, Rosemary contributes a few lines of: Love Is the Sweetest Thing—I Want to Be Happy—Love Thy Neighbor—Somebody Loves Me—I'll Walk Alone—Why Don't We Do This More Often?—I've Got a Feelin' You're Foolin'—I Get a Kick out of You—June Night—Just One of Those Things—'S Wonderful—No Other Love—Tea for Two (parody)—My Blue Heaven (parody—with Bing Crosby and Frank Sinatra)—Three Little Fishes (with Bing Crosby and Frank Sinatra)—On the Atchison, Topeka and the Santa Fe—Columbia, the Gem of the Ocean (with Bing Crosby and Frank Sinatra)—Side by Side (with Bing Crosby and Frank Sinatra)—On the Sunny Side of the Street (with Bing Crosby, Frank Sinatra, and Louis Armstrong)

The Ford Show starring Tennessee Ernie Ford (NBC-TV)—Air date November 21, 1957

Medley with Tennessee Ernie Ford (Would You Like to Take a Walk—Let Me Put My Arms around You (Ernie only)—You're an Old Smoothie (Rosemary only)—Gimme a Little Kiss (Will Ya, Huh?) (Ernie only)—Ma, He's Makin' Eyes at Me (Rosemary only)—Ain't We Got Fun / Would You Like

to Take a Walk (parody)) / Western medley with Tennessee Ernie Ford
(San Antonio Rose—Tumbling Tumbleweeds—Ragtime Cowboy Joe) /
Give Me a Straw Hat and a Cane (with Tennessee Ernie Ford) / Bill Bailey,
Won't You Please Come Home (with Tennessee Ernie Ford)

The Steve Allen Show (NBC-TV)—Air date December 8, 1957

A Foggy Day / Tonight / Dixieland (with Sal Mineo, Peter Lawford, and Steve
Allen backed up by Guy Lombardo and His Orchestra)

The George Gobel Show (NBC-TV)—Air date April 8, 1958

The Steve Allen Show (NBC-TV)—Air date May 11, 1958

Who's Sorry Now? / I Guess I'll Have to Change My Plan

The Perry Como Show (NBC-TV)—Air date January 10, 1959

Love, Look Away / On a Slow Boat to China (with Perry Como) / Sunshine
Cake (with Perry Como and Jane Wyman)

The George Burns Show (NBC-TV)—Air date January 27, 1959

The Voice of Firestone (ABC-TV)—Air date February 9, 1959

Some of Manie's Friends (NBC-TV)—Air date March 3, 1959

You Started Something

The Garry Moore Show (CBS-TV)—March 17, 1959

The Bell Telephone Hour (NBC-TV)—Air date April 9, 1959

Medley from "Gigi" (The Night They Invented Champagne [with José Ferrer] /
Say a Prayer for Me Tonight / Waltz at Maxim's [She Is Not Thinking of Me]
[with José Ferrer] / The Parisians / I Remember It Well [with José Ferrer])

The Bob Hope Show (NBC-TV)—Air date May 15, 1959

I Can't Get Started / Showmanship / Ain't A-Hankerin' (with Bob Hope)

Summer on Ice! Ice Capades! (NBC-TV)—Air date June 1, 1959

It's a Big, Wide, Wonderful World / I've Got My Love to Keep Me Warm (with
Tab Hunter and Tony Randall)

**The Ford Show starring Tennessee Ernie Ford (NBC-TV)—Air
date June 11, 1959**

Lazy Afternoon / Medley with Tennessee Ernie Ford (Catfish Take a Look at
That Worm / Row, Row, Row Your Boat / Paddlin' Madeline Home)

The Ed Sullivan Show (CBS-TV)—Air date September 20, 1959

I Wish I Were in Love Again / For You

**Perry Como's Kraft Music Hall (NBC-TV)—Air date October 21,
1959**

I Got Plenty O' Nuttin' / Medley with Perry Como (Rosemary contributes The
Glory of Love—Blue Room—Blue Moon—I Let a Song Go out of My
Heart—Just One of Those Things—I Get a Kick out of You—You're Just
in Love) / Ac-Cent-Tchu-Ate the Positive—Life Is Just a Bowl of Cherries
(both with Perry Como and Nat "King" Cole) / Campfire medley (Rosemary
contributes Red River Valley (with Perry Como)—I'm an Old Cowhand)

(with Perry Como)—*Tumbling Tumbleweeds (with Perry Como, Nat "King" Cole, and Gail Davis) —Git Along Little Dogies (with Perry Como, Nat "King" Cole, and Gail Davis))*

The Bell Telephone Hour (NBC-TV)—Air date December 18, 1959

Jingle Bells / The Christmas Song / Santa Claus Is Comin' to Town / Have Yourself a Merry Little Christmas

The Ed Sullivan Show (CBS-TV)—Air date January 17, 1960

The Lawrence Welk Show (ABC-TV)—Air date April 9, 1960

The Ed Sullivan Show (CBS-TV)—Air date July 3, 1960

For You / Bali Ha'i / You Do Something to Me

The Bing Crosby Show for Oldsmobile (ABC-TV)—Air date October 5, 1960

Let's Take an Old-Fashioned Walk (with Bing Crosby) / Song Writers Medley Rosemary contributes: I Want to Be Happy (with Bing Crosby)—Great Day!—Over the Rainbow—Feudin' and Fightin' (with Bing Crosby)— Long Ago (And Far Away)—A Foggy Day (with Johnny Mercer)—I Want to Be Happy (with Bing Crosby, Johnny Mercer, and Carol Lawrence)) / There Will Never Be Another You / Medley with Bing Crosby (Rosemary contributes fragments of If I Had My Druthers—You Are My Lucky Star (parody)—The March of the Gladiators (parody)—The Man on the Flying Trapeze (parody)—Love Is Sweeping the Country (parody)—How About You?—Tea for Two (parody–with Bing Crosby)—I Get a Kick out of You (parody–with Bing Crosby)—You Gotta Be a Football Hero (To Get Along with the Beautiful Girls) (with Bing Crosby)—Aren't You Glad You're You? (with Bing Crosby)—I Like the Likes of You—Aren't You Glad You're You? (Reprise–with Bing Crosby)—There Will Never Be Another You (with Bing Crosby))

Perry Como's Kraft Music Hall (NBC-TV)—Air date November 2, 1960

Bye, Bye, Blackbird / Lullaby Medley (Lullaby of Broadway—Love and Marriage (a capella)—Rock-a-Bye Your Baby (with Perry Como)—Old Folks at Home (snatch) (with Perry Como))

No Place Like Home (NBC-TV)—Air date November 24, 1960

I'm Old-Fashioned / Cabin in the Sky / Our House (with José Ferrer) / Home medley (with José Ferrer, Carol Burnett, and Dick Van Dyke—details not known)

The Bell Telephone Hour (NBC-TV)—Air date January 20, 1961

Rosemary sings a number of Irving Berlin songs—details not known

Marineland Circus (NBC-TV)—Air date April 2, 1961

The Ed Sullivan Show (CBS-TV)—Air date May 7, 1961

Get Me to the Church on Time / I Ain't Got Nobody

The Jo Stafford Show (ATV in the UK)—recorded in the United Kingdom on July 21, 1961, and shown there in the fall. Later syndicated in the United States

June Is Bustin' Out All Over / County Fair (with Jo Stafford) / 'Tis Autumn

The Rosemary Clooney Show (ATV in the UK)—Air date August 5, 1961

Fancy Meeting You Here (with Bing Crosby)—other songs not known

Parade – The Swingin' Sound of Nelson Riddle (CBC-TV)—Air date October 8, 1961

Get Me to the Church on Time / Baa Baa Black Sheep / Cabin in the Sky / Why Shouldn't I / Medley (Down by the Riverside—I Hear Music—Lucky Day—Alexander's Ragtime Band—Down by the Riverside [reprise–with Nelson Riddle])

New March of Dimes: The Scene Stealers (various stations)—Air dates throughout January 1962

Why Shouldn't I?

The Ed Sullivan Show (CBS-TV)—Air date January 7, 1962

Everything's Coming up Roses / Bye, Bye, Blackbird / Show Me

The Ed Sullivan Show (CBS-TV)—Air date March 11, 1962

Cabin in the Sky / Give Me the Simple Life / It's a Great Day for the Irish (with Maureen O'Hara)

Marineland Circus (CBS-TV)—Air date April 22, 1962

The Tonight Show (NBC-TV)—Air date April 26, 1962

What's My Line? (CBS-TV)—Air date June 10, 1962

Juke Box Jury (BBC-TV)—Air date July 7, 1962

The Tonight Show (NBC-TV)—Air date October 15, 1962

Royal Variety Performance (BBC-TV)—Air date November 4, 1962

Some People / Tenderly / Sleepy Time Gal

The Ed Sullivan Show (CBS-TV)—Air date November 25, 1962

Limehouse Blues / Sleepy Time Gal / How About You (with Tony Bennett)

The Red Skelton Comedy Hour (CBS-TV)—Air date December 11, 1962

Tenderly / I Won't Dance

Password (CBS-TV)—Air date January 6, 1963

The Dick Powell Show—"The Losers" (NBC-TV)—Air date January 15, 1963

He Told Me So (with Adam La Zarre)

March of Dimes Telethon—Air date February 9 10, 1963

Why Shouldn't I?

The Garry Moore Show (CBS-TV)—Air date March 5, 1963

The Rose and the Butterfly / Salute to Fred Astaire and Irving Berlin (songs not known)

I've Got a Secret (CBS-TV)—Air date March 11, 1963

Password (CBS-TV)—Air dates March 12 and April 29, 1963

The Garry Moore Show (CBS-TV)—Air date April 30, 1963

The Prisoner's Song / Dancing in the Dark

The Tonight Show (NBC-TV)—Air dates May 14 and May 31, 1963

Parade (CBC-TV)—Air date June 26, 1963

Hello, Hello There / What's New? / Ol' MacDonald / Make Someone Happy / Try a Little Tenderness (parody) / Cabin in the Sky

The Tonight Show (NBC-TV)—Air date June 27, 1963

The Steve Allen Show (NBC-TV)—Air date August 8, 1963

The Jimmy Dean Show (ABC-TV)—Air date September 26, 1963

The Red Skelton Comedy Hour (CBS-TV)—Air date October 15, 1963

Married I Can Always Get / Why Shouldn't I?

Password (CBS-TV)—Air dates November 6 and November 21, 1963

The Hollywood Palace (ABC-TV)—Air date January 11, 1964

A Good Man Is Hard to Find / Sleepy Time Gal

I've Got A Secret (CBS-TV)—Air date January 20, 1964

The Bing Crosby Show (CBS-TV)—Air date February 15, 1964

Something to Do (with Bing Crosby, Kathryn Crosby, and Peter Gennaro) / Medley with Bing Crosby (Don't Fence Me In—I'm an Old Cowhand (From the Rio Grande)—She'll Be Comin' Round the Mountain—The Crawdad Song—San Antonio Rose—Down in the Valley—On Top of Old Smokey—You Are My Sunshine) / Imagination / Love Makes the World Go Round (with Bing Crosby) / A Scarf, a Stool, a Song and Imagination (with Bing Crosby, Kathryn Crosby, and Peter Gennaro)

Password (CBS-TV)—Air date March 12, 1964

The Garry Moore Show (CBS-TV)—Air date March 17, 1964

All Alone / Moon River

The Garry Moore Show (CBS-TV)—Air date May 26, 1964

Miss Otis Regrets / Baby, the Ball Is Over

Password (CBS-TV)—Air date November 12, 1964

The Entertainers (CBS-TV)—Air date December 18, 1964

Songs from Mary Poppins (details not known)—Tea for Two (with Ed Wynn)

The Entertainers (CBS-TV)—Air date January 23, 1965

The Hollywood Palace (ABC-TV)—Air date March 13, 1965

Cabin in the Sky / Come On-a My House / Botch-a-Me / Hey There / Tenderly / Style (with Victor Borge)

The Tonight Show (NBC-TV)—Air date April 30, 1965

Password (CBS-TV)—Air date May 6, 1965

The Mike Douglas Show (syndicated)—Air date July 8, 1965

The Tonight Show (NBC-TV)—Air date September 13, 1965

The Ed Sullivan Show (CBS-TV)—Air date February 6, 1966

Baby, the Ball Is Over / All Alone

The Hollywood Palace (ABC-TV)—Air date February 19, 1966

I Gotta Right to Sing the Blues / You Don't Know about Misery / Mood Indigo / Medley with Bing Crosby (Hear That Band—The Daughter of Molly Malone—Poor People of Paris—New Vienna Woods—Hear That Band [Reprise])

The Tonight Show (NBC-TV)—Air date April 2, 1966

An Evening with Rosemary Clooney (syndicated)—Air date May 14, 1966

The John Gary Show (CBS-TV)—Air date August 10, 1966

The Best Thing for You / Big Spender / I'm Gonna Live Till I Die

The Tonight Show (NBC-TV)—Air date September 13, 1966

The Mike Douglas Show (syndicated)—Air dates October 3 & 4, 1966

The Pat Boone Show (syndicated)—Air date January 25, 1967

Tenderly

The Pat Boone Show (syndicated)—Air date January 26, 1967

Sunny Disposition (with Pat Boone)

The Merv Griffin Show (syndicated)—Air date April 3, 1967

You Don't Say (NBC-TV)—Air date May 22, 1967

The Mike Douglas Show (syndicated)—Air dates May 29–31, June 1–2 and June 28, 1967

The Dean Martin Show (NBC-TV)—Air date September 21, 1967

I Cried for You / Who's Sorry Now? / Goody, Goody / Medley with Dean Martin (Mary (parody)—Ma Blushin' Rosie (parody)—Oh, Johnny (parody)— Whatever Lola Wants (parody)—If You Knew Susie (parody)—Wait, Till the Sun Shines, Nellie (parody)—Mame (parody)—Good Evening Friends) / Cook's Tour (with Dean Martin, Minnie Pearl, and Buddy Hackett)

The Joey Bishop Show (ABC-TV)—Air date December 8, 1967

The Pat Boone Show (syndicated)—Air date January 15, 1968

Today (ITV-UK)—Air date April 1968

Rowan & Martin's Laugh-In (NBC-TV)—Air date October 14, 1968

The Donald O'Connor Show (syndicated)—Air date October 31, 1968

The Steve Allen Show (NBC-TV)—Air date November 3, 1968

Rowan & Martin's Laugh-In (NBC-TV)—Air date November 18, 1968

Win with the Stars (syndicated)—Air date January 29, 1969

The Nick Clooney Show (WCPO)—Air date June 2, 1969

In a Little Red Barn (on a Farm down in Indiana) (with Nick Clooney and Betty Clooney)—Tenderly

The Nick Clooney Show (WCPO)—Air date June 3, 1969

The Andy Williams Show (NBC-TV)—Air date October 24, 1970

Come On-a My House

The Merv Griffin Show (CBS-TV)—Air date April 13, 1971

The Phil Donahue Show (syndicated)—Air date March 2, 1973

The Merv Griffin Show (syndicated)—Air dates March 15, July 12, December 12, 1973

Grammy salutes Oscar (CBS-TV)—Air date March 30, 1974

The Merv Griffin Show (syndicated)—Air date April 17, 1974

A Summer Song (WCPO-TV, Cincinnati)—Air date April 18, 1974

Tenderly / I Believe in You / Those Lazy, Hazy, Crazy Days of Summer (with Betty Clooney, Nick Clooney, and Dave McCoy)

Celebrity Bowling (syndicated)—Air dates May 18, June 22, 1974

The Merv Griffin Show (syndicated)—Air date July 12, 1974

Name That Tune (syndicated)—Air dates July 29 & 30, 1974

The Merv Griffin Show (syndicated)—Air date August 15, 1974

The Merv Griffin Show (syndicated)—Air date September 17, 1974

The Tommy Banks Show (CBC-TV)—Air date October 14, 1974

Dinah! (syndicated)—Air date February 18, 1975

The Merv Griffin Show (syndicated)—Air date March 17, 1975

What Are You Doing the Rest of Your Life?

Dinah! (syndicated)—Air date July 7, 1975

The Merv Griffin Show (syndicated)—Air date May 19, 1976

Stars on Sunday (Yorkshire Television, UK)—First Air date September 5, 1976, and three other occasions after this. One song was used in each program

This Ole House / Bless This House / Danny Boy / I Believe

The Mike Douglas Show (syndicated)—Air date October 1, 1976

The Merv Griffin Show (syndicated)—Air date October 14, 1976

Looks Familiar (ITV, UK)—Air date November 9, 1976

Dinah! (syndicated)—Air dates December 8 and 22, 1976

Bing–A 50th Anniversary Gala (CBS-TV)—Air date March 20, 1976

Tenderly

The Merv Griffin Show (syndicated)—Air date March 8, 1977

Dinah! (syndicated)—Air dates May 6 and July 5, 1977

The Merv Griffin Show (syndicated)—Air date August 31, 1977

Stars on Ice (CTV)—Air date October 4, 1977

Tenderly

Today (NBC-TV)—Air date November 3, 1977

The Merv Griffin Show (syndicated)—Air date November 7, 1977

Tomorrow in Los Angeles (NBC-TV)—Air date November 23, 1977

Dinah! (syndicated)—Air date January 12, 1978

The Jim Nabors Show (syndicated)—Air date February 6, 1978

Tea for Two / Fifty Ways to Leave Your Lover (with Jim Nabors)

Tomorrow (NBC-TV)—Air date February 7, 1978

The Mike Douglas Show (syndicated)—Air date March 2, 1978

The Jim Nabors Show (syndicated)—Air date April 24, 1978

Over Easy (PBS-TV)—Air date May 2, 1978

NBC Reports: Escape from Madness (NBC-TV)—Air date June 28, 1978

The Merv Griffin Show (syndicated)—Air date August 28, 1978

The Mike Douglas Show (syndicated)—Air date September 13, 1978

Dinah! (syndicated)—Air date October 4, 1978

Tomorrow (NBC-TV)—Air date January 2, 1979

The Merv Griffin Show (syndicated)—Air date February 20, 1979

A Song for You / Together, Wherever We Go (with Margaret Whiting, Helen O'Connell, and Rose Marie)

The Mike Douglas Show (syndicated)—Air date May 1979

But Beautiful

Dinah! (syndicated)—Air date June 18, 1979

Comeback: Rosemary Clooney—Air date 1979

The Pat Boone Family Christmas Special (ABC-TV)—Air date December 8, 1979

Over Easy (PBS-TV)—Air date January 17, 1980

The Merv Griffin Show (syndicated)—Air date May 6, 1980

The Tonight Show (NBC-TV)—Air date July 24, 1980

Hello Young Lovers / The Promise (I'll Never Say Goodbye)

The Merv Griffin Show (syndicated)—Air date August 20, 1980

The Mike Douglas Show (syndicated)—Air date September 5, 1980

The Merv Griffin Show (syndicated)—Air date November 13, 1980

A Tribute to the National Juke Box Awards (NBC-TV)—Air date November 19, 1980

The Mike Douglas Show (syndicated)—Air date November 26, 1980

Sketches in Jazz (PBS-TV)—Air date November 29, 1980
The Wind of May / Did You / Blackberry Winter

4 Girls 4 (syndicated)—Aired on various dates in 1981
4 Girls 4 (all 4 girls) / Together, Wherever We Go (all 4 girls) / Tenderly / Hey There / Come On-a My House / A Song for You / 4 Girls 4 (all 4 girls)

The Mitch Miller Show—A Sing Along Sampler (NBC-TV)—Air date January 10, 1981
Tenderly / Come On-a My House

Bob Hope's 30th Anniversary Show (NBC-TV)—Air date January 18, 1981

Toni Tennille Variety Talk Show (syndicated)—Air date January 27, 1981

The 50's—Moments to Remember (PBS-TV)—Air date March 21, 1981
Hey There / Tenderly / This Ole House / But Not for Me / Come On-a My House

The Merv Griffin Show (syndicated)—Air dates April 6, April 28, and October 21, 1981

The Dick Cavett Show (PBS-TV)—Air date December 9, 1981
I Can't Get Started / Medley with Margaret Whiting (Rosemary sings: Loneliness—I Stayed Too Long at the Fair)

Tomorrow (NBC-TV)—Air date January 6, 1982

The John Davidson Show (syndicated)—Air date January 19, 1982

Twilight Theatre (NBC-TV)—Air date February 13, 1982
Come On-a My House

Rosemary Clooney with Love (syndicated)—Air date March 12, 1982
Tenderly / Hey There / Meditation / Just the Way You Are / Love Is Here to Stay / Strike up the Band / But Beautiful / He's Funny That Way / I Can't Get Started / As Time Goes By / I'm Checkin' Out—Goombye / The Way We Were

Swinging Rosie (AVRO-TV, Holland)—Air date March 20, 1982
Hey There / I Cried for You / But Beautiful / Love Is Here to Stay / I Can't Get Started / Will You Still Be Mine / Just the Way You Are

Night Music (BBC-TV)—Air date June 5, 1982

I'm Back / But Not for Me / Hey There / This Ole House / Come In from the Rain / Medley: I Cried for You—Who's Sorry Now—Goody Goody—Tenderly—Come On-a My House

The Val Doonican Show (BBC-TV)—Air date June 12, 1982

Come In from the Rain / Medley with Val: Half as Much— Hey There— Come On-a My House—Tenderly—This Ole House (all duets with Val except "Tenderly," which Rosie sings alone)

Up Close with Tom Cottle (two episodes) (syndicated)—Air date 1982

The Merv Griffin Show (syndicated)—Air date December 1982

It's Easy to Remember

Rosie: The Rosemary Clooney Story (CBS-TV)—Air date December 8, 1982

Rosemary Clooney specially recorded new versions of the songs featured in this TV drama, which were lip synced by the girls playing Rosie and Betty (Sondra Locke and Penelope Milford). Rosemary sang both parts for the Clooney Sisters duets.

The newly recorded songs were as follows—all Rosemary solos except those marked (CS) which were the double-tracked recordings used by the Clooney Sisters actresses. Come On-a My House; Hawaiian War Chant (CS); Sentimental Journey (CS); How Deep Is the Ocean (CS); I'm in the Mood for Love (CS); Will You Still Be Mine (CS); Someone to Watch over Me; Everything Happens to Me; It's Easy to Remember; I'm Checkin' Out—Goombye; Everything's Coming up Roses; Tenderly; Hey There.

The film ends with the real Rosemary on stage in 1978 at the Royal Festival Hall in London singing "Goody Goody."

Entertainment Tonight (syndicated)—Air date December 15, 1982

Bob Hope's Road to Hollywood (NBC-TV)—Air date March 2, 1983

Eubie Blake: A Century of Music (PBS-TV)—Air date May 7, 1983

Memories of You

Today (NBC-TV)—Air date June 28, 1983

Aurex Jazz Festival (Japanese TV)—Air date, possibly September 1983

Come On-a My House / Tenderly / April in Paris / But Not for Me / I Can't Get Started / You'll Never Know / I Cried for You—Who's Sorry Now—Goody Goody / Hey There / The Way We Were

The Jonathan Schwartz Show (Madison Square Garden Network)—Air date October 1983

My Shining Hour / It's De-Lovely / Everything Happens to Me / Will You Still Be Mine / Ask Me Again / Love Is Here to Stay (with Jonathan Schwartz)

The Bob Monkhouse Show (BBC-TV)—Air date October 24, 1983

You're Gonna Hear from Me / Fancy Meeting You Here (duet with Bob Monkhouse) / Tenderly

The Merv Griffin Show (syndicated)—Air date December 22, 1983

White Christmas / We Wish You a Merry Christmas (with Danny Kaye and Merv Griffin) / O Holy Night (with Merv Griffin)

Unforgettable Swingtime (Channel 4, UK)—Air date December 31 1983

This Ole House / Hey There / White Christmas

Late Night America (PBS-TV)—Air date February 2, 1984

The Val Doonican Show (BBC-TV)—Air date thought to be May 1984

On a Slow Boat to China (with Val Doonican) / April in Paris

Steve Allen's Music Room (Disney Channel)—Air date August 7, 1984

You're Gonna Hear from Me / Hey There / You Started Something / But Beautiful / Revenge Medley (with Lou Rawls—Rosemary sings Who's Sorry Now—Goody Goody [with Lou Rawls])

Forty Years of Fine Tuning (WNEW-TV)—Air date September 2, 1984

The Tonight Show (NBC-TV)—Air date October 11, 1984

You're Gonna Hear from Me / What'll I Do

CBS Morning News (CBS-TV)—Air date March 1, 1985

I Got Lost in His Arms / Cheek to Cheek / Let's Face the Music and Dance / There's No Business Like Show Business

The Merv Griffin Show (syndicated)—Air date March 27, 1985

The Sally Jessy Raphael Show (syndicated)—Air date May, 1985

What'll I Do / Tenderly

James Brady Show (CBS-TV)—Air date May 8, 1985

Thanksgiving Day Parade (NBC-TV)—Air date November 28, 1985

White Christmas

Hardcastle and McCormick (ABC-TV)—Air date January 6, 1986

Benny Goodman – Let's Dance show (PBS-TV)—Air date March 15, 1986

Somebody Else Is Taking My Place / You Turned the Tables on Me / And the Angels Sing / There's No Business Like Show Business

Hour magazine (syndicated)—Air date April, 1986
Lifestyles of the Rich & Famous (syndicated)—Air date May 17, 1986
The Tonight Show (NBC-TV)—Air date October 22, 1986
When October Goes
Sister Margaret and the Saturday Night Ladies (CBS-TV)—Air date January 17, 1987
Today Show (NBC-TV)—Air date April 2, 1987
The Larry King Show (CNN)—Air date April 20, 1987
The Tonight Show (NBC-TV)—Air date May 19, 1987
In the Still of the Night / It Never Entered My Mind
Royal Variety Performance (LWT)—Air date November 29, 1987
Tenderly
Celebrating Gershwin—'S Wonderful (PBS-TV)—Air date December 4, 1987
A Foggy Day
Kennedy Center Honors (CBS-TV)—Air date December 30, 1987
10 O'clock News (WNYW)—Air date January 21, 1988
Rosemary's appearance at the Blue Note is featured with excerpts shown from her singing: Hey There / Let's Face the Music and Dance / What'll I Do
Omnibus (ABC-TV)—Air date May 26, 1988
They Can't Take That Away from Me / Isn't It a Pity? (with Michael Feinstein)
Irving Berlin at 100 (CBS-TV)—Air date May 27, 1988
Count Your Blessings Instead of Sheep / White Christmas
Ford's Theatre Gala (PBS-TV)—Air date July, 1988
I Remember You / Something's Gotta Give / Come Rain or Come Shine
The Tonight Show (NBC-TV)—Air date July 27, 1988
G. I. Jive / Pieces of Dreams (aka "Little Boy Lost")
Live with Regis & Kathie Lee (syndicated)—Air date November 29, 1988
I'll Be Home for Christmas (single chorus with Regis Philbin and Kathie Lee) / White Christmas / Winter Wonderland (with Regis Philbin and Kathie Lee—snatch only over closing credits)
Eyewitness News (ABC-TV)—Air date November 29, 1988
Brief interview—short extract from "Live with Regis & Kathie Lee" shown featuring Rosemary singing "White Christmas"
Happy New Year, USA! (PBS-TV)—Air date December 31, 1988
Something's Gotta Give / Come Rain or Come Shine / When October Goes / In the Still of the Night / Auld Lang Syne (with cast and audience)

Live with Regis & Kathie Lee (syndicated)—Air date February 6, 1989

The Pat Sajak Show (CBS-TV)—Air date April 18, 1989

I Wish I Were in Love Again / Where Do You Start?

Live with Regis & Kathie Lee (syndicated)—Air date June 14, 1989

How Are Things in Glocca Morra / Guys and Dolls (with Regis Philbin and Kathie Lee Gifford)

The Tonight Show (NBC-TV)—Air date August 10, 1989

Guys and Dolls / It Never Entered My Mind / Where Do You Start?

A Conversation with Dinah (TNN)—Air date September 1, 1989

The Bob Hope Christmas Special from Hawaii (NBC-TV)—Air date December 16, 1989

Silver Bells (with Bob Hope)

Today (NBC-TV)—Air date February 2, 1990

Live with Regis & Kathie Lee (syndicated)—Air date February 12, 1990

Bob Hope's USO Road to the Berlin Wall and Moscow (NBC-TV)—Air date May 19, 1990

Memory / Old Friends medley (with Bob Hope)

The National Memorial Day Concert (PBS-TV)—Air date May 27, 1990

God Bless America / America the Beautiful (with U.S. Rep. Robert Michel of Illinois)

Live with Regis & Kathie Lee (syndicated)—Air date December 25, 1990

Christmas Love Song / Me and My Teddy Bear (with Tessa Ferrer)

Live with Regis & Kathie Lee (syndicated)—Air date February 4, 1991

A Gift of Music (WSJK-TV)—Air date June 8, 1991

I'll Be Seeing You / Isn't It a Pity? (with Michael Feinstein)

Michael Feinstein & Friends (PBS-TV)—Air date October 11, 1991

Love, You Didn't Do Right by Me (with Michael Feinstein) / You're Just in Love (with Michael Feinstein) / I Got It Bad (and That Ain't Good) / It Don't Mean a Thing (If It Ain't Got That Swing) / I'm Checkin' Out—Goombye / Sophisticated Lady

The Early Show (CBS-TV)—Air date October 15, 1991

Primetime Live (ABC)—Air date January 1992

Live with Regis & Kathie Lee (syndicated)—Air dates January 31 and February 12, 1992

Today (NBC-TV)—Air date February 17, 1992

The Magic of Bing Crosby (PBS-TV)—Air date March 20, 1992
One on One with John Tesh (NBC-TV)—Air date April 28, 1992
Live with Regis & Kathie Lee (syndicated)—Air date January 26, 1993
This Morning (CBS-TV)—Air date February 2, 1993
Tom Snyder (CNBC-TV)—Air date April 14, 1993
Bob Hope: The First 90 Years (NBC-TV)—Air date May 14, 1993
I'll Be Seeing You
An Evening at Pops (PBS-TV)—Air date August 1993
Get Me to the Church on Time / More Than You Know / By Myself / But Not for Me (with Linda Ronstadt) / Time Flies (with Linda Ronstadt) / They Can't Take That Away from Me (with Linda Ronstadt)
A Salute to the Newport Jazz Festival (PBS-TV)—Air date September 12, 1993
Sweet Kentucky Ham
Jacksonville Jazz Festival XIV (WJCT)—Air date 1994
Hey There / Straighten Up and Fly Right / Don't Fence Me In / How Are Things in Glocca Morra / Come On-a My House
Live with Regis & Kathie Lee (syndicated)—Air date January 28, 1994
Quiet Nights of Quiet Stars
ER (NBC-TV)—Air date September 29, 1994 – Episode title "Going Home"
Nice and Easy / (Get Your Kicks on) Route 66 / Time Flies
ER (NBC-TV)—Air date December 15, 1994 – Episode title "The Gift"
By Myself (snatch only) / We Three Kings of Orient Are (snatch only while helping another man to sing it) / Have Yourself a Merry Little Christmas
Live with Regis & Kathie Lee (syndicated)—Air date February 1, 1995
I'm Confessin' (That I Love You)
The Charles Grodin Show (CNBC-TV)—Air date February 2, 1995
I'm Confessin' (That I Love You) / Love Is Here to Stay
This Morning (CBS-TV)—Air date November 3, 1995
The Rosemary Clooney Golden Anniversary Celebration (A&E)—Air date November 11, 1995
Danny Boy / Straighten Up and Fly Right / I'm Confessin' (That I Love You) / The Coffee Song (with Cathi Campo) / I Left My Heart in San Francisco / There Will Never Be Another You / I'll Be Seeing You* / They Can't Take That Away from Me (with Michael Feinstein) / When October Goes / Old Friends / You've Got a Friend (with Lily Tomlin) / Mambo Italiano* / Hey There / White Christmas / We'll Meet Again [*in home video version only]

Frank Sinatra: 80 Years My Way (ABC-TV)—Air date December 12, 1995

That's Life

The Late Late Show with Tom Snyder (CBS-TV)—Air date December 18, 1995

George & Alana (syndicated)—Air date December 21, 1995

White Christmas / White Christmas (reprise with Debby Boone)

Pat Boone Family Christmas—Air date December 21, 1995

Live with Regis & Kathie Lee (syndicated)—Air date January 31, 1996

A Foggy Day

This Morning (CBS-TV)—Air date February 14, 1996

The Rosie O'Donnell Show (syndicated)—Air date September 17, 1996

Do You Know What It Means to Miss New Orleans?

Danny Kaye—A Tribute to an American Master Clown (PBS-TV)—Air date December 11, 1996

Ira Gershwin at 100: A Celebration at Carnegie Hall (PBS-TV)—Air date March 12, 1997

A Foggy Day / Love Is Here to Stay / Of Thee We Sing (with entire cast)

The Rosie O'Donnell Show (syndicated)—Air date May 9, 1997

God Bless the Child

The Larry King Show (CNN)—Air date May 10, 1997

Hello Young Lovers / Always / Thank Heaven for Little Girls / God Bless the Child / Funny Face / A Child Is Only a Moment / Love Is Here to Stay (with Michael Feinstein)

The Late Late Show with Tom Snyder (CBS-TV)—Air date July 15, 1997

Live with Regis & Kathie Lee (syndicated)—Air date October 9, 1997

Holiday at Pops! (A&E)—Air date December 18, 1997

Have Yourself a Merry Little Christmas / White Christmas

The Rosie O'Donnell Show (syndicated)—Air date May 25, 1998

The Late Late Show with Tom Snyder (CBS-TV)—Air date July 20, 1998

The Late Late Show with Tom Snyder (CBS-TV)—Air date February 16, 1999

Love Is Here to Stay

Sesame Street (PBS-TV)—Air date February 22, 1999

Sunny Day

LateLine (NBC-TV)—Air date March 16, 1999

The Rosie O'Donnell Show (syndicated)—Air date November 5, 1999

Good Morning America (ABC-TV)—Air date November 8, 1999

Love Is Here to Stay

Sunday Morning (CBS-TV)—Air date November 28, 1999

Brief excerpts of Rosemary singing Thanks for the Memory / What'll I Do / A Foggy Day / Will You Still Be Mine are shown

Christmas in Rockefeller Center (ABC-TV)—Air date December 1, 1999

White Christmas

Swing It! (PBS-TV)—Air date November 28, 1999

If Swing Goes, I Go Too / Love Is Here to Stay / Hey There / In the Wee Small Hours of the Morning / Just in Time / It Don't Mean a Thing (If It Ain't Got That Swing) (with Dee Dee Bridgewater)

A Rosie Christmas (ABC-TV)—Air date December 5, 1999

Santa Claus Is Comin' to Town (with Rosie O'Donnell)

The Cincinnati Pops Orchestra Live (PBS-TV)—Air date July 4, 2000

God Bless America

This Morning (CBS-TV)—Air date summer 2000

The Boy from Ipanema (with Diana Krall)

Today (NBC-TV)—Air date December 25, 2000

White Christmas / Have Yourself a Merry Little Christmas

The Rosie O'Donnell Show (syndicated)—Air date March 28, 2001

Ol' Man River

The View (ABC-TV)—Air date October, 2001

Count Your Blessings Instead of Sheep

Rosemary Clooney: A Selective Chronology

FAMILY BACKGROUND

Nicholas Clooney (born in Ireland about 1830) married Bridget Byron (born 1836 in Ireland) on May 24, 1862, in Mason County, Kentucky. Their son Andrew B. Clooney (1874–1947) married Crescentia (aka Cynthia) Koch (1876–1939) and became a jeweler and a mayor of Maysville, Kentucky. Their son Andrew Joseph Clooney (1902–1974) married Marie Frances Guilfoyle (1909–1973) on August 15, 1928.

Marie Frances Guilfoyle (1909–1973) was the daughter of Michael J. Guilfoyle (1876–1928) who had married Martha Adelia (Ada) Farrow (1884–1958) in 1905. The grandfather of Marie Frances Guilfoyle was Cornelius Guilfoyle (born in Ireland in 1845). He married Rosanna Sweeney (1854–1934) on August 26, 1869 in Mayslick, Mason County, Kentucky.

1928

May 23, Wednesday. Rose Marie Clooney is born in Maysville, Kentucky.

1930

April. The US Census shows Rose Marie living with her parents at the Maysville home of her grandfather, Andrew B. Clooney, who is described as a jewelry merchant. Rose's father is said to be a jewelry salesman and her mother does not have an occupation indicated. Olivette, a daughter of

Andrew B. Clooney (born 1900 and shown as "Alwette"), is also living there and is listed as a musician with an orchestra.

The population of Maysville at that time was 6,557, of whom 59 were indelicately described in the Census as being "Negro."

1931

April 12. Elizabeth (Betty) Anne Clooney (Rosemary's sister) is born in Lewisburg, Kentucky.

Rosemary Clooney makes her first public appearance at the age of three, at the Russell Theater in Maysville, singing "When Your Hair Has Turned to Silver."

1932

> Rosemary Clooney, attractive young daughter of Mr. & Mrs. Andrew Clooney Jr., was painfully injured last night when she fell from a moving street car at the East End loop.
>
> (*Public Ledger*, August 10, 1932)

1933

August 18. Rosemary sings at the Central Hotel, Maysville.

> Maysville, Ky. Lieut-Gov. A. B. Chandler spoke last night at the centennial dinner at the Central hotel, which was well attended. . . . At the conclusion of the address, little Rosemary Clooney, daughter of Mr. and Mrs. Andrew Clooney Jr of Market Street, sang three songs.
>
> (*Middlesboro Daily News*, August 19, 1933)

1934

January 13. Nicholas Joseph Clooney (Rosemary's brother) is born in Maysville.

1939

January 20. Crescentia Clooney (Rosemary's grandmother) dies in Maysville. Rosemary, Betty and Nick move to live with their Grandmother Guilfoyle.

1940

April. The US Census shows Rosemary, Betty, and Nicholas living with their grandmother, Ada Guilfoyle, and their uncle George (aged 18) and aunt Christine (15) at 331 West Third Street in Maysville. The property is rented for $25 per month.

Rosemary graduates from St. Patrick's Grade School, Maysville. The Guilfoyle family moves to Ironton, Ohio, where Rosemary's uncles George and Chick open up a service station.

October 13. Rosemary's Aunt Ann dies at the age of 25.

1942

Uncles George and Chick go out of business in Ironton. The Guilfoyle family moves to Fairfax Avenue in Cincinnati, Ohio. Rosemary attends Withrow High School. Uncle George gets a job with the Baldwin Piano Company in their loading dock.

The Guilfoyle family moves to an old farmhouse on Indian Hill Road, Cincinnati.

Rosemary's mother divorces her father, comes home, and moves her children to an apartment building on Clinton Springs Avenue, Cincinnati. She then marries William Miller Stone of Lexington.

1943

Rosemary's mother leaves for California to be with Mr. Stone, who is stationed at Treasure Island in San Francisco, taking Nick Clooney with her. Rosemary's father returns and moves Rosemary and Betty in with him to an apartment on Elberon Avenue, Cincinnati.

1944

The Clooney Sisters appear before the Maysville Rotarians to sing "The Old Covered Bridge," "Home on the Range," and "God Bless America."

1945

February 9. Rosemary's mother gives birth to a daughter named Gail Anne. Mr. and Mrs. Stone return to Kentucky bringing Nick with them.

Rosemary and Betty attend one of the open auditions held by radio station WLW every Thursday. They are offered a basic $20 a week each, which is increased to an extra $7 per show if they do more than three half-hour programs. They sing on radio after school and during the summer vacation. Their first appearance is on the *Moon River* program and they sing "Walkin' by the River." They move in with their Auntie Jeanne in Greenhills, Cincinnati.

Summer. The Clooney Sisters sing on the "Crossroads Café" (a 15-minute show at 5:15 P.M.) and "Moon River" (a late Sunday night show) on WLW. They also sing at high school dances with a band led by Billy Petering.

> They are the babies of the WLW vocal staff both in age and experience but that fact hasn't prevented the Clooney Sisters from winning listeners on their first assignments at the Crosley station. At present, they reside at 6 Burnham Avenue, Greenhills and attend Mercy High School on Freeman Avenue.
>
> (*Public Ledger*, September 17, 1945)

Fall. Rosemary is a senior at Our Lady of Mercy High School in Cincinnati. The Clooney Sisters join the Barney Rapp band.

1946

June 12. Tony Pastor and His Orchestra appear at Moonlite Gardens, Coney Island, near Cincinnati.

Summer The Clooney Sisters sign up to join the Tony Pastor band and are to be paid $125 each per week. Their Uncle George (age 24) is to accompany them as a chaperone.

July 10. The Clooney Sisters make their debut with Tony Pastor in the Marine Ballroom on the Steel Pier in Atlantic City. Rosemary and Betty tour with the band for the rest of the year.

August 16. Tony Pastor and his troupe begin a week's engagement at Moonlite Gardens on Coney Island, near Cincinnati.

> **Clooney Sisters get ovation as they open at Coney Island.**
>
> Maysville born Rosemary and Betty Clooney, featured vocalists with Tony Pastor and his Orchestra, received a memorable ovation at Coney Island last night when the band opened a week's engagement in Moonlite Gardens. They had been living in Indian Hill with their maternal grandmother, Mrs. W. J. Guilfoyle, and they attended Our Lady of Mercy High School in the Queen city. The Clooney Sisters have been singing since, as mere tots, their aunt, Mrs. Stafford Rolph, (Olivette Clooney), one of Maysville's most accomplished pianists,

took them in hand for a bit of musical training. They had an unusual record with station WLW where they were engaged on their very first audition in itself an extraordinary experience. They were heard on Crossroads Café, Fashions in Melody, Shelf of Melody, Accent on Music and Circle Arrow programs. Two of these—Fashions of Melody and Circle Arrow—were fed to the NBC network.

(Public Ledger, August 17, 1946)

September. In New York City, The Clooney Sisters make their first recordings with Tony Pastor for Cosmo Records.

November 30. The Clooney Sisters and their duly appointed guardian, George Guilfoyle, sign an agreement with Barney Rapp and Charles Trotta. This appoints Rapp and Trotta as exclusive business managers for the Clooney Sisters for a five-year period on 10% commission from all earnings.

December 18, 1946-January 10, 1947. The Pastor band is part of an hour-long variety show at the Paramount in New York with the Andrews Sisters and the Les Paul Trio.

1947

The Clooney Sisters continue to tour with the Pastor Band.

February 24–March 6. Tony Pastor and His Orchestra perform at the Click Theater restaurant in Philadelphia and on March 6, they are featured in *One Night Stand*, a 30-minute radio program from the restaurant.

April 29–June 9. The Tony Pastor Band has an extended stay at the Hollywood Palladium.

Sharing vocal stint with Pastor are Clooney Sisters, who pass eye-and-ear test with plenty to spare. Gals offer a pleasant, harmonic blend of voices, as well as taking solo rides and teaming with Pastor on novelties.

(Alan Fischter, Billboard, May 31, 1947)

April 29 / May 13. The Clooney Sisters take part in further *One Night Stand* programs on CBS with Tony Pastor. While in Hollywood, Pastor and his group appear in one of Universal's "Name Band" shorts in which the Clooney Sisters sing "Hawaiian War Chant" and Rosemary sings "Movie Tonight" with Pastor.

October 26. The Tony Pastor Orchestra plays the Ritz Ballroom, Bridgeport, Connecticut.

Tony Pastor had his birthday surprise Sunday night at the Ritz instead of on WNAB's "1450 Club" show in the afternoon. The Clooney Sisters, Tony's grand little vocalists, appeared on the WNAB show in place of their boss who was delayed in reaching town. And the girls plotted with the bandsmen to spring the surprise on Tony when he called for an intermission break at the ballroom. Instead of taking the break, the bandsmen swung into "Happy Birthday," the gals ran over and kissed Tony while Ray Colonari ran in with a birthday cake.

Incidentally, the Clooney girls have been with Tony about a year, even though they have no contract with the band. Their affairs are managed by their uncle, a young chap not much older than the girls themselves.

(*Bridgeport Post*, October 28, 1947)

November 1. Andrew B. Clooney (Rosemary's grandfather) dies in Maysville.
November 18–20. Pastor and his team move on to the Paramount Theater in Waterloo, Iowa.

Aided and abetted by the two pulchritudinous Clooney sisters, Tony and his boys proved they have really Pastor-ized music by practically rewriting "The Hawaiian War Chant." Incidentally, those two eye-filling gals were both solid, but it would be interesting to know which of them hushed the audience with a feverish, half-breath rendition of "I Wish I Didn't Love You So." Tony didn't bother to tell the audience which was which, but one has blond hair, the other has jet black, both have fine voices and curves which meet all standard requirements

(Robert M. L. O. Johnson, *Waterloo Daily Courier*, November 19, 1947)

1948

Rosemary and Betty Clooney continue to tour with Tony Pastor's Orchestra.
January 1. A strike by the American Federation of Musicians commences and prevents recording studio work for most of the year.
February 16. Rosemary ties for first place on *Arthur Godfrey's Talent Scouts* on CBS radio. Tony Bennett, then known as Joe Bari, comes third. The show is broadcast from the CBS Studio Building on 52nd Street, New York.

Miss Clooney Ties for Top Honors

Miss Rosemary Clooney, elder member of the singing Clooney Sisters, natives of Maysville, tied for top honors in the audition contest on "Arthur Godfrey's Talent Scouts" broadcast last night over the Columbia Broadcasting System. Singing the popular ballad "Golden Earrings," Miss Clooney finished in a tie with Richard Broderick, impersonator. Several other performers competed.

As a result of her gaining a tie for top honors, Miss Clooney will be given three appearances on Godfrey's morning show and will be given an opportunity to perform before New York's leading night club, movie and Theater managers. Each competitor on the show received $100 for appearing. Miss Clooney, niece of Mrs. Stafford Rolph, of the Germanstown Road, was presented by her maternal uncle, George Guilfoyle, of Cincinnati, also a former Maysvillian.

(*Public Ledger*, February 17, 1948)

October 13. Tony Pastor and His Orchestra are at the New York Paramount with Vic Damone in a cine-variety show.

The band did some nice work with a couple of standards, with the Clooney Sisters warbling in the key spots. The girls, a blonde and brunette, did some pleasant tho highly stylized things, with *Paper Moon* and *Hallelujah*, assisted by glee club effects from sidemen. . . . His [Pastor's] teaming up with the Clooney gals in the *Man at the Door* number got equally pleasant results.

(*Billboard*, October 23, 1948)

1949

Rosemary and Betty Clooney remain with the Pastor band until May 1949.

March 5. Rosemary appears on *Eddie Condon's Floor Show* on NBC-TV.

May 23. Rosemary turns 21 and goes solo. Joe Shribman becomes her manager, replacing her Uncle George. Betty Clooney returns to Cincinnati. Rosemary is offered a contract by Manie Sachs, head of A&R at Columbia Records, and signs this on May 24, 1949.

June 16. Makes solo recordings in New York City. The recordings are issued by Harmony Records, a cheaper 49 cent label in the Columbia stable.

August 27. Guests on the *Sing It Again* show on CBS radio.

September 2–5. The Clooney Sisters reunite to sing with Clyde Trask's Orchestra at Moonlite Gardens, Coney Island, Ohio.

October 22, Saturday. *Billboard* magazine's Third Annual Disk Jockey Poll has Rosemary in top place in the female band singer category.

November 12. Guests on Vaughn Monroe's *Camel Caravan* radio show on CBS and makes a further appearance on December 24.

December 12. Opens a week's engagement at the Seventh Avenue Hotel, Pittsburgh.

December 25. Makes her nationwide TV debut on Ed Sullivan's *Toast of the Town* on CBS-TV.

Best of the acts was songstress Rosemary Clooney, blonde looker with a bewitching personality. . . . Miss Clooney demonstrated a voice to match her looks and, backed by the show's regular line, did a neat selling job on a ballad and a pleasant novelty tune titled,"Haul Off and Love Me."

(*Variety*, December 28, 1949)

1950

Manie Sacks (Manager of Popular Repertoire) leaves Columbia for RCA-Victor.

February. Mitch Miller joins Columbia Records as head of its Pop Singles Division.

February 4. Rosemary appears on Vaughn Monroe's *Camel Caravan* radio show on CBS. Rosemary makes further appearances on the show during the year.

April 8. Records "Peachtree Street" with Frank Sinatra in New York.

June 30. Appears on the first "Songs for Sale" show on CBS radio and becomes a regular for the rest of the year.

July 3. Commences a five nights a week 15-minute radio show with Tony Bennett called "Stepping Out" which continues until August 25.

September 7–9. Appears at the Meadowbrook Club, Cedar Grove, New Jersey with Woody Herman and his Orchestra.

September 24. NBC radio puts on a preview of the new musical *Call Me Madam* with Perry Como and Rosemary singing the songs.

October. The annual disc jockey poll in *Billboard* magazine has Rosemary in second place as most promising new female vocalist. Mindy Carson is first.

October 16. Guests on the first *Robert Q's Matinee* hosted by Robert Q. Lewis. Rosemary becomes a regular on the daytime TV show.

December 24. Guests on Ed Sullivan's *Toast of the Town* on CBS-TV.

1951

Continues to make regular appearances on the *Songs for Sale* shows, on Vaughn Monroe's *Camel Caravan* radio shows, and on *Robert Q's Matinee* on CBS-TV

January 27. Records "Beautiful Brown Eyes." The song enters the Billboard charts on March 3 and reaches #11 during a 14-week stay in the lists

April. Performs at the Hippodrome, Baltimore in an 18-minute set.

With a background of name-brand stints and video appearances, this good looking chirp has what it takes to hold her own in Theater and nitery dates. Nicely gowned and giving out with an aura of wholesome charm she punches out a good mixture of pops with ample voice and a good feel for the right phrasing. Smartly contrasted routine includes "From This Moment," "Be My Own," an elaborate "Lullaby of Broadway," "One More Time," and for the enthusiastic response, encores with her current disclicks, "Beautiful Brown Eyes" and "Shot Gun Boogie."

(Variety, April 25, 1951)

April 29. Guests on *The Big Show* on NBC radio hosted by Tallulah Bankhead.

June 6. Records "Come On-a My House" and it becomes a huge hit. It enters the charts on July 7 and spends eight weeks at No. 1 during a 20-week stay.

June 16. Opens at the Olympia Theater, Miami.

July 15. Rosemary guests on the "Quiz Kids" radio program on NBC.

July. Appears at the Chicago Theater in Chicago with Frankie Laine.

August 3. Entertains at Shibe Park, Philadelphia, in front of a crowd numbering 25,000.

August 11–12. Appears at the Illinois State Fair with Jack Benny.

August 23. Records "Half As Much." This enters the charts on May 3, 1952, and soon reaches #1. It spends 27 weeks in the charts in all. The song reaches the #3 position in the United Kingdom and tops the charts in Australia.

August 31–September 16. Appears at the Thunderbird in Las Vegas, receiving $3,500 a week. The publicity attracts Hollywood interest.

September 30. Guests on the Jack Benny radio show on CBS.

October 7. Rosemary guests on *The Charlie McCarthy Show* on CBS radio with Edgar Bergen.

October 19. Opens at the Capitol Theater in Washington, DC, with Tony Bennett.

October 20. Rosemary is signed to a term contract by Paramount Pictures.

October 29. Opens at the New York Paramount.

1952

March 23. Rosemary guests on *The Big Show* on NBC radio hosted by Tallulah Bankhead. Others appearing include Marlene Dietrich, and Rosemary gets to know her well. Rosemary is paid $750 for her appearance.

April 2. Takes part in "Two Girls On Broadway" with Joan Blondell as part of the *MGM Musical Comedy Theater of the Air* series.

April 4. Guests on *The Mario Lanza Show* on NBC radio.

April 18. Records "Botch-a-Me." The song enters the charts on June 28 and during a 17-week stay reaches the #2 spot.

April 30. Rosemary and Eddie Fisher front *The Perry Como Show* on CBS-TV in the absence of Perry who is entertaining in North Carolina.

May–July. Films *The Stars Are Singing* at Paramount studios in Hollywood. Meets Bing Crosby for the first time.

May 18. Guests on *The Charlie McCarthy Show* with Edgar Bergen on CBS radio.

May 26. Records *The Bing Crosby Show* which airs on CBS radio on June 11. Rosemary receives a fee of $1,000. This is her first appearance with Bing.

August 13. Opens in Reno, Nevada, for two weeks giving three shows nightly.

> Standing room only has been the status in the Terrace Room of the New Golden Hotel-Bank Club Casino since the arrival of Rosemary Clooney. A skillful blending of talent and experience combined with her vital and youthful personality has made Miss Clooney one of the best received big-time personalities to appear in Reno. Appreciative of the applauding crowds in the Terrace Room, Miss Clooney favors with a rounded program including her "signature" song, "Come On-a My House," Gershwin's "Tenderly" [sic] and amusing ditties which Miss Clooney classes as self-descriptive numbers.
>
> (*Reno Evening Gazette*, August 22, 1952)

September 16. Guests on *The Martin and Lewis Show* on NBC radio.

November–December. Films *Here Come the Girls* with Bob Hope.

November 6. Rosemary and Gordon MacRae star on *The Bing Crosby Show* on CBS radio. James Stewart is the emcee in the absence of Bing whose wife, Dixie, has just died.

December. Rosemary places third in the *Downbeat* poll behind Sarah Vaughan and Ella Fitzgerald.

1953

January 9–11. Rosemary is at the Bing Crosby Pro-Am at Pebble Beach and entertains at the clambake dinner on January 11 with Bing, Phil Harris, and Don Cherry.

January 10. Tapes a Bing Crosby Show at Fort Ord. The other guest is Bob Hope and the show is broadcast on January 15.

January 28. Rosemary returns to Maysville for the world premiere of her film *The Stars Are Singing*. The film is shown at 8:00 P.M. and at 10:15 P.M. and Rosemary appears on stage on both occasions. Rosemary arrives in a motorcade from Cincinnati at 2:30 P.M. and at 3 P.M. she joins a parade through the town. At 4 P.M. there is a ceremony when Lower Street is renamed Rosemary Clooney Street and dedicated with a bottle of Kentucky limestone water as Rosemary unveils the street marker.

February 7. Appears on the *Grand Ole Opry* radio show from Nashville, Tennessee. She sings "Come On-a My House."

February 23. Rosemary is pictured on the cover of *Time* magazine. She also appears on the *Suspense* program on CBS radio in an episode titled "St. James Infirmary Blues."

March 19–21. Rosemary performs at the Fox Theater, Detroit.

April 3. Opens at the Chicago Theater, Chicago, for a week.

May 4–June. Films *Red Garters* with Gene Barry and Guy Mitchell.

May 5. Commences a 15-minute twice-weekly radio show for NBC. Bob Hope guests on the first show.

May 24. Guests on the premiere of a musical show called *The Orchid Award* on ABC-TV. Ronald Reagan is the emcee and Mitch Miller also appears.

July 13. Rosemary (age 25) marries José Ferrer (age 41) in Durant, Oklahoma.

September 7–November 25. Films *White Christmas* with Bing Crosby, Danny Kaye, and Vera-Ellen. Rosemary is paid $5,000 a week.

October 22. The *Here Come the Girls* film is released.

December 27. Hosts *The Toast of the Town* TV show in the absence of Ed Sullivan.

It is no secret that Rosemary Clooney is a very pretty girl with a special rich warmth. It is also no secret that Rosie is a thoroughly nice girl with a charm as natural as the wag of a puppy dog's tail. However, Miss Clooney handed me a surprise the other Sunday when she subbed for the vacationing Ed Sullivan. She had all the poise of a young queen, and at the same time her own special quality came through the TV screen like a handshake from an old friend.

It was a happy thought for Rosemary to have her sister Betty on the show with her and the girls sang a song together, like in the old days in Maysville, Kentucky. I guess that's what makes Rosie so nice. She is still just a good gal from a little town, and her friendliness shines right through her talent.

(Faye Emerson, syndicated column, January 1, 1954)

1954

January. Flies to London. Appears on the *Cyril Stapleton Show Band* radio show and sings "Man and Woman" with José Ferrer.

January 13. Rosemary appears in BBC-TV's *Starlight* show.

February 3. Rosemary's film *Red Garters* has its world premiere at the Majestic Theater in San Antonio, Texas.

February. Visits England, France, and Spain with José Ferrer

March 7. Rosemary wins the *Look* magazine award for most promising newcomer.

May 22. Records "Hey There" and "This Ole House." Both songs reach #1 in the Billboard charts. "This Ole House" also reaches #1 in the United Kingdom.

July 12. Rosemary announces that she is pregnant.

July. Films her contribution to the film *Deep in My Heart*.

September 16. Guests on the *Amos 'N' Andy Music Hall* radio show.

September 23. Records "Mambo Italiano" and it reaches the #10 slot in the Billboard charts. In the United Kingdom it goes to the #1 position.

October 12. Starts a new radio series on CBS called *Rosemary Clooney Sings*. It is taped in advance and she is accompanied by Buddy Cole and His Trio.

October 14. The film *White Christmas* is released and it becomes the top film of 1954 in the United States at the box office, taking $12 million in rental income in its initial release period.

December 24. The film *Deep in My Heart* is released. Rosemary has a cameo role in which she sings "Mr. & Mrs." with José Ferrer.

1955

January 13. Records "Where Will the Dimple Be." It is intended to be released simultaneously with the arrival of her next child. The song reaches #6 in the British charts.

February 7. Miguel José Ferrer is born in St. John's Hospital, Santa Monica, California. He weighs seven pounds, nine ounces.

March 11. The *Person to Person* TV show features Edward R. Murrow interviewing José Ferrer and Rosemary at their home.

March 30. Performs at the Annual Academy Awards Show, singing "The Man That Got Away."

May. Appears at The Sands in Las Vegas.

> Smartly gowned in blue lace, covered with iridescent sequins, the star is a poise-
> ful warbler and shows unmistakably the great distance she has travelled since

the heyday of the Clooney Sisters with the Tony Pastor Orch. "We're In the Money" and Cole Porter's "Delightful, De-Lovely" get the show on the road swiftly for the girl with the infectious grin. "Hey There!" "This Old House" "Make Me Feel So Young" and "Tenderly" are also boffo. Alone with the piano, helmed adroitly by her conductor, Buddy Cole, Miss Clooney delivers a touching "Danny Boy," and her three biggest hits: "Come On-a My House," "Botch-A-Me," and last summer's "Mambo Italiano." The ovation at the conclusion of her stint brings the headliner back to dedicate her final selection to her new baby son, "Brahms Lullaby."

(*Variety*, May 18, 1955)

June 27. In London, records a show with the BBC Show Band which is broadcast that night on the Light Programme.
July 4–9. Performs at the Glasgow Empire Theater in Scotland.
July 18–30. (6:15 and 8:45 P.M.) Appears at the London Palladium.

It is almost two years since one of the fairer sex from the school of tune-tonsils has dominated the Palladium stage as the chief headliner, but the prize for our patience is the satisfying mellow appreciation of the art of natural expression of performance. No mass hysteria or false emotions; no attempt to palpitate the pulse, but a clever Clooney showing an audience how they can be nursed, coaxed, humoured and sent home contented. How many artists would fail to include a recording hit enjoying the success of "Where Will the Dimple Be?" How many artists would fail to include one of the first big-sellers to establish them—"Half As Much"? But, in the case of Clooney, the smooth make-up of the programme was designed in a manner which refused to pander to tradition. Rarely has a Palladium audience been so unanimous in appreciation, yet without visible signs of fan hysteria from any section of the house. It was an object lesson in the art of developing a polite applause into a deafening crescendo.

(*New Musical Express*)

December. Rosemary is released from her Paramount contract at her own request.

1956

January 11. Rosemary announces that she is pregnant again.
January 20. Rosemary signs to star in 39 half-hour musical television films. Filming begins on February 2 at NBC with a schedule of two half-hours a week until a total of 39 shows is reached. The show is sold on a

syndicated basis and Foremost Dairies is the main sponsor. The series is filmed in black and white. The Hi-Lo's are regulars and Nelson Riddle leads the orchestra.

February 8/11. In Hollywood, dubs her vocals onto tracks prepared by the Duke Ellington Orchestra in New York for an album called *Blue Rose*.

March 17. The annual Emmy awards show at Pan Pacific Auditorium, Hollywood. Rosemary is nominated for best female singer but loses to Dinah Shore.

May 15. *The Rosemary Clooney Show* makes its debut and continues for 39 weeks.

July 7. *Billboard* announces that *The Rosemary Clooney Show* has won first place in the Best Music Series category of the Syndicated Film programs.

August 9. Maria Providencia Ferrer is born in St. John's Hospital, weighing six pounds.

October 1. Rosemary starts filming the remaining 13 episodes of *The Rosemary Clooney Show* which she was unable to complete because of her pregnancy.

1957

February 26. Rosemary announces that she is pregnant again.

March 14–27. Appears at the Riverside Theater Restaurant, Reno, Nevada.

April 9. Arrives in England to spend time with José Ferrer who is making a film.

April 20. (8:30–9:15 P.M.) Stars in the British ATV presentation *The Rosemary Clooney Show* and sings seven numbers. (10:15–11:15 P.M.) Records an hour-long radio show for the BBC.

April 25. Flies from London to Amsterdam, Holland, with her young son Miguel. (8:00–9:45 P.M.) Records an appearance on a Dutch radio show called *Showboat*.

August 1. Gabriel Vicente Ferrer is born in St. John's Hospital, two months early, weighing four pounds. He is placed in an incubator. Associated Press reports describe his condition as "hopeful."

September 2. Daily *Ford Road Shows* featuring Rosemary and Bing Crosby separately commence on CBS radio. The shows are of five-minute duration and Rosemary and Bing alternate with each other. Rosemary sings one or two songs in each show. The shows continue until August 31, 1958, and use songs from a library of musical items recorded with Buddy Cole and His Trio.

September 26. *The Lux Show with Rosemary Clooney*, a 30-minute program, makes its debut on NBC-TV. The series is broadcast live and in color on Thursday evenings from September 1957 through June 1958. Regulars on the program are Frank De Vol and his orchestra and the Modernaires.

October 13. Guests on *The Edsel Show*, a live television program on CBS hosted by Bing Crosby with Frank Sinatra and Louis Armstrong. The program wins the *Look* magazine TV Award for "Best Musical Show, 1957" and is nominated for an Emmy as the "Best Single Program of the Year."

1958

March 23. Rosemary announces that she is expecting her fourth child.
June 21–29. Entertains at the Riverside in Reno, Nevada.
July 2–15. Entertains at The Sands, Las Vegas.

> She appears onstage in a tent dress, explaining that she's not doing it to follow the current styles, but simply because she's pregnant. Miss Clooney's distinctive voice sounds better than ever as she effectively sells such numbers as "Give It All You've Got," "Tenderly," "I Miss New Orleans," "This Old House" (with Buddy Cole), "A Foggy Day" and "Come On-a My House."
> (*Variety*, July 9, 1958)

July 28–August 11. A pregnant Rosemary Clooney records the *Fancy Meeting You Here* album with Bing Crosby.
October 13. Monsita Teresa Ferrer is born at St. John's Hospital, Santa Monica, weighing six pounds, four ounces.
December 31. Adelia Guilfoyle, Rosemary's grandmother, dies in Maysville.

1959

January 18. Rosemary again entertains at the clambake following the Bing Crosby Pro-Am at Pebble Beach.
March 3. Appears on "Some of Manie's Friends," a tribute on NBC-TV to the late Manie Sachs.
June 3–28. Sings at Harrah's in Reno, Nevada.
September 11–13. Performs at the Kentucky State Fair with Fabian, Jimmy Dean, and the Four Lads. The takings are disappointing.
November. Rosemary announces that she is pregnant again.

1960

January. Rosemary signs a recording contract with RCA Victor.

February 29. (11:40–12:00 noon) *The Crosby–Clooney Show*, a 20-minute, five days a week radio show premieres on CBS. It continues until November 2, 1962, and uses items from a library of songs recorded with Buddy Cole and His Trio. Bing and Rosemary Clooney record new linking dialogue periodically.

March 23. Rafael Francisco Ferrer, a five-pound, six-ounce baby boy, is born in St. John's, Santa Monica.

June 6–22. Rosemary performs at Harrah's in Lake Tahoe.

September. Entertains at the Waldorf-Astoria in New York for a month.

> To the bright strains of "Clap Hands, Here Comes Rosie," Rosemary Clooney bounced up to the bandstand of the Empire Room at New York's Waldorf-Astoria last week. With hardly a pause for breath, the blond singer belted out "Ev'rything's Coming up Roses," and then moved into the seductive, husky-voiced rendition of "Tenderly," which has become her theme song. Before the roar of applause died down, she abruptly threw off the white ostrich-feather coat which had enveloped her like a tent. "I'll bet," she told the packed room, "that 50 per cent of the audience was saying 'She's pregnant again.' I fooled you, didn't I?"
>
> *(Newsweek*, October 3, 1960)

October 21. Sings at a rally for Senator John F. Kennedy at Madison Square Garden.

1961

March 1. Internal Revenue Service officials charge that Rosemary owes $52,522 in back income taxes for the years 1957–1959. A tax lien is placed on her property.

April. Entertains at the Desert Inn, Las Vegas.

July 21. Tapes a Jo Stafford TV special in London with Mel Tormé. The show is seen in the United Kingdom during September and later syndicated in the United States.

August 5. Stars in *The Rosemary Clooney Show* on the British ATV network. Bing Crosby makes an unbilled live appearance and sings "Fancy Meeting You Here" with Rosemary and Dave King.

August 9. Flies back to California and turns José Ferrer out of the house.

August 26. Nelson Riddle tells his wife he is leaving her. Within a few weeks he leaves the apartment he has rented in Malibu and returns home.

August 28–September 3. Rosemary performs at the Du Quoin State Fair, Illinois, with Nelson Eddy.

September 22. Rosemary files suit for divorce from José Ferrer in Superior Court in Santa Monica charging mental cruelty.

September 26. Pulls out of *The Bell Telephone Hour* (scheduled for September 29) after the sponsor and the show producer insist that she eliminate the song "If Love Were All."

October 8. In Toronto, Rosemary stars in the CBC-TV show *Parade–The Swingin' Sound of Nelson Riddle*. Rosemary and Nelson Riddle present music from their latest albums.

October 19. In Superior Court in Santa Monica, Rosemary and José Ferrer agree to temporary alimony of $1,500 per month pending the trial of her suit for divorce.

November 28–December 11. Appears at the Desert Inn, Las Vegas.

1962

January 20. Sings at an inaugural anniversary dinner for the Democratic Party in Washington, DC.

January 25. Opens a three-week engagement at Harrah's, Lake Tahoe.

April 10. Opens at the Copacabana in New York.

May 9. Rosemary is given a divorce from José Ferrer on grounds of infidelity. She receives $300 per month for each of the five children of the marriage, $1 per year token alimony, $22,000 in attorney's fees, and use of their Beverly Hills mansion in Roxbury Drive until she remarries. The Roxbury Drive house is put into trust for the five children.

June 9. Sings at a Democratic Party dinner in Washington, DC. Later, Rosemary is called to the White House to meet President Kennedy who cooks her scrambled eggs.

June. Rosemary makes 16 appearances in nine days in Germany, France, and Italy.

July 25. Flies into London en route to Monte Carlo and is met at the airport by José Ferrer.

July 26. In Monte Carlo where she sings at a Red Cross benefit at Princess Grace's invitation. Rosemary hints at a possible reconciliation with José Ferrer.

August. Appears at The Cave, Vancouver, British Columbia.

August 31–September 4. Performs at the World's Fair of Music and Sound at McCormick Place in Chicago.

October. Rosemary signs with the Reprise Records label.

October 29. Sings at the Royal Variety Show at the London Palladium. Other stars appearing are Bob Hope, Eartha Kitt, and Sophie Tucker.

November 27–December 23. Entertains at the Desert Inn, Las Vegas.

1963

January 14. José Ferrer returns to the matrimonial home.

January 20. Rosemary entertains at the Victory Dinner following the Crosby Pro-Am at Pebble Beach.

February 26. Press comments suggest that Rosemary is still in financial trouble.

March 14–31. Performs at the Fairmont in San Francisco.

> Rosemary Clooney bears a strong resemblance to the girl next door only she's brighter and sexier. When she's singing a love ballad there's a sly gleam in her eye that gives the lyrics a tongue in cheek quality. She lets you in on her joke by kidding a group of songs motivated by male superiority. It's a teasing game that she's been playing with the public for twenty years and they show no sign of tiring of the flirtation. . .. Her act is refreshingly natural; a few quips, a lot of personality and 19 songs. When it's over, you feel like you've known the attractive blonde singer all your life.
>
> (Barbara Bladen, *San Mateo Times*, March 16, 1963)

May 17–30. Appears at the Shamrock-Hilton in Houston.

August 9. Rosemary and José Ferrer surprise friends by telling them they have canceled their California divorce before it became final.

August 19–23. Entertains with Buster Keaton at the Iowa State Fair in Des Moines. They repeat the show the following week at the Minnesota State Fair in Minneapolis.

November 22. President Kennedy is assassinated in Dallas, Texas.

December. Rosemary is already hooked on prescription medication.

1964

January 12. Performs at the El San Juan Hotel in Puerto Rico.

March 23. Sings in a benefit in Palm Beach for the John F. Kennedy Memorial Hospital.

June 5. Rosemary Clooney files a countersuit against her former manager, Joe Shribman, who is suing her for back commissions in excess of $20,000.
July. Rosemary appears at The Cave, Vancouver, British Columbia.
August 31–September 3. Rosemary appears at the New Latin Quarter in Tokyo, Japan.

> Clooney, a top recording artist whom few people around the world actually get a chance to see in person, is a pro down the line. She's polished, self-assured and completely in control of the stage at all times. Those who are only familiar with her recordings should make it a point to catch La Rosemary in person to fully appreciate her talents. Her nicely paced repertoire is calculated to keep the customers in a nostalgic but-how-about-that mood that clicks with seasoned ease.
>
> (Al Ricketts, *Pacific Stars and Stripes*, September 2, 1964)

November 4. Opens at the *Royal Box* in the Americana Hotel, New York.
December 1. Press reports about Rosemary's income tax returns surface again.

1965

February 2–7. Entertains at the Hyatt Music Theater in Burlingame, San Francisco.
February 25–March 10. Performs at the Flamingo, Las Vegas.
September. Appears at the Park Sheraton, Chicago.
September 14. Opens at the *Royal Box* in the Americana Hotel in New York.
October 21–November 3. Performs at the Shamrock Hotel, Houston.

1966

February 24–March 2. Appears at The Vapors Club in Hot Springs, Arkansas.
April 28–May 1. Appears at the International Boat, Trailer & Sports Show at the Portland Coliseum, Washington.

> This was Miss Clooney's first Portland appearance and promoter Tom O'Laughlin found her most uncooperative. She refused interviews to radio, tv, press and declined to make any personal appearance. Trailer Show committee was disappointed with the singer since she did nothing to hypo the take despite strong transient attractions near day and date. Headliner also balked at playing the huge arena-in-the-round and only worked to part of the customers.
>
> (*Variety*, May 5, 1966)

May 26. It is announced that Rosemary and José Ferrer have separated again.

June 17–26. Appears at The Three Rivers Inn, Syracuse, New York.

August 17. Rosemary sues José Ferrer for divorce.

August 28–September 5. Appears at the Oregon State Fair.

September. Signs a recording contract with United Artists Records.

September 8. Opens at the *Royal Box* in the Americana Hotel, New York.

November. Rosemary is sued in New York by attorney Samuel Siegel for $8,500. He says she owes him the money as part of his fee for winning a tax case.

November. Appears at the Chequers nightclub in Sydney, Australia, for three weeks.

December 15–21. Rosie appears at the Chateau Madrid in Fort Lauderdale, Florida.

> Singer was not in particularly good voice or in best of moods, often sounding weak and cracking on ballads and upbraiding drummer onstage for tempo differences on one tune and publicly chastising light man for following her off-stage on first bow-off a few moments later. . . . She does long Billie Holiday medley which plays up and down, with little consistency. Medleys are well written, but pipes, either under strain from rehearsal and two sets, were below material.
>
> (*Variety*, December 21, 1966)

1967

January 24–February 12. Appears at the Century Plaza Hotel, Los Angeles.

February 23–March 15. Entertains at the Fairmont Hotel, San Francisco.

March 28. Opens at the Waldorf-Astoria in New York.

August 1–29. Entertains at the Desert Inn, Las Vegas.

September 12. Rosemary and José go to Santa Monica Superior Court. Both charge the other with "extreme cruelty."

September 13. Rosemary is granted a divorce from José Ferrer.

September 20–24. Entertains at the World Food Exposition in Madison, Wisconsin.

October 11–15. Appears at the Mississippi State Fair in Jackson, Mississippi.

1968

February 10–25. Tours Japan, Thailand, the Philippines, and Taiwan. She has difficulty sleeping and her behavior becomes very erratic. Visits the

Clark Field hospital in the Philippines where the Vietnam casualties are housed. Gives two concerts in Manila.

April 4. *Martin Luther King Jr. is assassinated in Memphis, Tennessee. Rosemary is appearing in Germany at the time.*

Has a week off in London. Appears on a TV chat show and breaks down in tears when Martin Luther King's death is discussed.

Performs in Sao Paulo, Brazil.

May 12. Arrives in New York from Brazil. Goes on to give shows in Edmonton and Calgary, Canada.

May 30. Takes part in a rally for Robert Kennedy in Oakland.

June 3. Sings at a rally in San Diego for Robert Kennedy.

June 5. *Robert Kennedy is shot at the Ambassador Hotel, Los Angeles and dies the next day.*

July 2–25. Rosemary is scheduled to perform at Harold's Club in Reno, Nevada, but walks off stage during her performance on July 8

> Rosemary Clooney Quits Night Club Show
>
> Singer Rosemary Clooney has canceled what she said would be the last night club engagement of her career due to a case of acute influenza. A spokesman for Harolds Club, Reno, Nev., said Tuesday Miss Clooney was scheduled to appear at that downtown Reno casino until July 25 but walked off stage during her performance Monday night. A week ago Miss Clooney announced she would discontinue night club performances after the Harolds Club engagement but would continue to make records and television appearances.
>
> (*Press-Telegram*, July 10, 1968)

Admitted to the psychiatric unit of Mount Sinai Hospital, Los Angeles with "drug-induced psychosis."

Undergoes therapy with Dr. J. Victor Monke, three days a week for three years.

October 25. Rosemary seeks increased alimony.

1969

March 25. Rosemary wins increased alimony from José Ferrer.

April 6–17. Entertains at the Tropicana's Blue Room in Las Vegas.

July. Again appears at the Hotel Tropicana for a two-week season ending August 8.

August 14. Open at Bimbo's 365 Theater-Restaurant, San Francisco for a two-week engagement.

October 13. Opens at the Royal York Hotel, Toronto.

November 7. Rosemary returns to the Hotel Tropicana in Las Vegas for a two-week engagement.

1970

October 24. Guests on *The Andy Williams Show* and sings "Come On-a My House."

1971

February 5. Opens at the Fremont in Las Vegas, giving two shows nightly.
April 13. Guests on *The Merv Griffin Show* on CBS-TV with Mel Tormé.

1972

February 21. Rosemary sings at the Grand Executive Inn in Sheboygan, Wisconsin.
February 23. Entertains at The Blue Moon Restaurant in Chicago.
March 5. Performs at the Kahler Hotel, Rochester, Minnesota.
May 5. Appears at the Ramada Inn, Portsmouth, Rhode Island.
May 7. Sings at the Red Coach Steak House, Portsmouth, New Hampshire.
July 1–16. Entertains at the Tivoli Gardens, Copenhagen, Denmark. After her return, Rosemary's mother, who has been looking after the children, leaves the Roxbury house at Rosemary's request.
August 6–12. Rosemary sings at the San Mateo County Fair & Floral Fiesta.

1973

December 13. Marie Frances Stone, Rosemary's mother, dies of emphysema. Rosemary and her children later attend the funeral in Maysville.
December. Meets Dante DiPaolo again.
December 31–January 1. Entertains at the Hilton Inn, Albuquerque, New Mexico.

1974

February. Performs at the Royal York Hotel, Toronto, Canada.
March 20. Sings at the National Orange Show at San Bernardino, California.

March 30. Appears in a CBS-TV show called "Grammy salutes Oscar." In an interview given around this time, Rosemary reveals that she has lost 60 pounds on a special diet from a peak of 180 pounds.

July 5. Appears at the Pheasant Run Ballroom in Chicago.

July 6. Entertains at Sawmill Creek, Lake Erie, Ohio.

August 15. Guests on *The Merv Griffin Show*. Discloses for the first time that she has had mental problems.

August 27. Rosemary's father, Andrew J. Clooney, dies at the age of 71. Rosemary and Dante go to the funeral in Milford, Ohio.

September 20–21. Performs at the Top O' The Harbor in Van Nuys, California.

September 22–October 5. Sings at Taylor's Supper Club, Denver.

October 8–13. Appears at Nero's atop the Holiday Inn, Torrance, California.

1975

January 11. Entertains on a seven-day Sitmar cruise on the *S. S. Fairsea* to Mexico.

January 30–February. Appears at the Copa Room in Brooklyn, New York.

February 25. Opens at the Centre Stage Dinner Playhouse in Milwaukee.

May 17–18. Appears with Dick Haymes at the Silver Lakes Resort, California.

May 19–25. Performs at the Town 'N' Country Cabaret in Winnipeg, Manitoba, Canada.

> After her first few numbers it was obvious why the name Rosemary Clooney was once a household reference whenever singing stars were discussed. The lady has poise, grace and class plus a singing voice that projects with purpose and a clarity that has diminished very little since the days she was flying high on the entertainment scene.
>
> (Jimmy King, *Winnipeg Free Press*, May 24, 1975)

July 12–13. Performs at Six Flags Magic Mountain in Los Angeles.

July 15. Entertains at the Orange County Fair with Bob Hope.

July 17. Performs at the Ramona Bowl in Hemet, California.

August 4–17. Appears at the *Top of the World*, the supper club in the Contemporary Hotel in Walt Disney World, Florida. Her co-star is Dante DiPaolo with son Miguel on drums,

October 3–5. Rosemary, with Miguel again on drums, performs at Valparaiso's Bridge-Vu Theater in Indiana.

October 11. Entertains at Jolly Friars Grand Ball at the Fairmont Hotel, San Francisco.

October 30. Appears with Boots Randolph and Floyd Cramer at Centennial Concert Hall, Winnipeg, Canada. They also appear at Century II Convention Hall, Wichita, Kansas, in November.

1976

February 13. Entertains at the Bayfront Center in St. Petersburg, Florida, with Floyd Cramer and Boots Randolph. Later in the year, they also appear together at Will Rogers Memorial Auditorium, Fort Worth, Texas; the Bell Auditorium, Augusta, South Carolina; and at Wolf Trap Farm Park, Virginia.

March 17. The *Bing Crosby and Friends* stage show takes place at the Dorothy Chandler Pavilion, Los Angeles.

> Rosemary Clooney . . . came out in bright, bright orange, looking and sounding better than ever. Although hampered by a slight case of nerves in the beginning of her set, maturity has added depth and richness to her singing. With Crosby, she took a fast "Slow Boat to China," and in her solo spot she showed a winning way with contemporary music with Paul Simon's "50 Ways to Leave Your Lover" and Leon Russell's "Song for You."
>
> (Robert Kemnitz, *Los Angeles Herald-Examiner*, March 19, 1976)

March 20. Appears at the Holiday Inn, Stevens Point, Wisconsin.

June 2. The *Bing Crosby and Friends* stage show, including Rosemary, is at the Masonic Auditorium, San Francisco.

June 21–July 4. The *Bing Crosby and Friends* stage show is at the London Palladium.

> Rosemary Clooney, a welcome echo of the 'fifties, features strongly in the Crosby bill, singing "Slow Boat to China" with Bing and hushing the house with a strongly felt performance of the Arthur Schwartz standard "By Myself," one of the best songs of our time.
>
> (Herbert Kretzmer, *Daily Express [UK]*)

July 1. Bing and family plus Rosemary are guests of the Duke of Edinburgh at Buckingham Palace.

July 12–13. The *Bing Crosby and Friends* stage show is at the Gaiety Theater, Dublin.

July 15–16. *Bing Crosby and Friends* stage show at Usher Hall, Edinburgh.

First Miss Clooney. Delectable. Distinctive. After dueting with Bing in Billy May's ingenious arrangement of "Slow Boat to China" from their unforgettable album "Fancy Meeting You Here," she showed her class with "By Myself" and "Just One of Those Things."

(John Gibson, Edinburgh Evening News, July 16, 1976)

August 1. Rosemary opens at the Moonraker in Virginia Beach, Virginia.

August 5. Betty Clooney dies in Las Vegas, Nevada, from a brain aneurysm. Rosemary leaves her engagement in Virginia Beach to fly to Las Vegas.

August 7. Betty Clooney's funeral. Rosemary has to leave partway through to fly back to Virginia Beach. Betty had always been a conduit between the three siblings and Rosemary and her brother Nick make a pledge to take a vacation together every year without fail.

August 19–28. Entertains at the Regency Hyatt O'Hare in Chicago.

September 14. Appears at *Farm Fest '76* at Lake Crystal in Minnesota with Boots Randolph and the Statler Brothers.

October 9. Rosemary sings with Les Brown's orchestra under London Bridge at Lake Havasu, Arizona.

November 26. The *Bing Crosby and Friends* show is at the Aladdin Theater in Las Vegas. Rosemary, Joe Bushkin, and the Crosby family take part.

December 6. Bing Crosby and Rosemary sing at New York's Avery Fisher Hall as a benefit for Fordham Prep School

December 7–18. The *Bing Crosby on Broadway* stage show is at the Uris Theater, 51st Street West. Bing is again accompanied by Rosemary, Joe Bushkin, and the Crosby family.

1977

February 18–24. The *Bing Crosby and Friends* show is at the Deauville Star Theater, Miami Beach.

The pounds have made more of a difference in Rosemary Clooney than the years: she comes on stage covered by a flowing, burnt-orange gown that contrasts strikingly with her taffy-colored hair. If you liked her during her '50s heyday, you'll enjoy her still as she offers "By Myself," "Tenderly" and the romantically beautiful "Song for You," among others.

(Christine Brown, Miami Herald, February 22, 1977)

February 26. The *Bing Crosby and Friends* package is at the San José Center for the Performing Arts in California.

> The star, whose good luck in working with leading ladies extends from Mary Pickford to Liza Minnelli, introduced one of his favorite co-stars with an a capella version of "Rosie," which brought Miss Clooney on stage. After their fast classy version of "Slow Boat to China," she provided some polished solos of oldies such as the lovely ballad "Tenderly" and new ones such as Paul Simon's "Fifty Ways to Leave Your Lover." Joining the band to back her on this family night was her son, drummer Miguel Ferrer. It's a treat to watch a pro at work and more of Miss Clooney's songs would have been welcome.
>
> (Gloria Tully, *San José News*, February 28, 1977)

April. Rosemary contributes two tracks to the Concord Jazz album *A Tribute to Duke*.

July 7. Records the *Everything's Coming up Rosie* album. This is her debut album for the Concord Jazz label.

September 6–13. Rosemary Clooney, Barbara McNair, Margaret Whiting, and Rose Marie, appear as *4 Girls 4* at Doheny Plaza, Los Angeles. Helen O'Connell later replaces Barbara McNair.

September 22. The British tour of Bing Crosby's new stage show opens in Preston, England. Rosemary, Kathryn Crosby, and Joe Bushkin are in support.

September 23. Bing Crosby and Rosemary perform at Belle Vue, Manchester.

September 26–October 8. The *Bing Crosby and Friends* show is at the London Palladium.

> Of the support, Clooney gave exceptional value and should surely be more in evidence in top international cabaret halls. Crosby and Clooney both vocally hopped the decades by showing ability to evince the nostalgic past then cope with contemporary lyrics from writers of the Carole King and Neil Sedaka school.
>
> (*Billboard*, October 22, 1977)

October 10. Bing's stage show, including Rosemary, has its final performance at the Conference Centre in Brighton.

October 14. Bing Crosby dies on a golf course in Spain.

November. Rosemary's autobiography "This for Remembrance" is published.

November 22–December 11. *4 Girls 4* at Huntington Hartford Theater, Hollywood.

December. Rosemary flies to Tokyo and gives seven concerts in nine days.

1978

January 6. Rosemary records an album for Concord called *Rosie Sings Bing*.
March 7–12. Appears at the Tierra Verde Hotel on Tierra Verde, Florida.
March 25. Stars in "Terry Wogan's Music Night" which is broadcast live on BBC Radio2 from London's Royal Festival Hall.
May. *4 Girls 4* appears at the Fairmont Hotel, New Orleans, and sets a new house record. This was the first time all four of the performers had been available since their appearance in December. They go on to appear at many locations throughout the United States during the rest of the year.
June 28. Rosemary talks with Tom Snyder about mental illness on "NBC Reports: Escape from Madness."
September. Appears at the Minnesota State Fair at St. Paul supporting Bob Hope.
October. Rosemary is signed to do television commercials for Coronet paper towels and bathroom tissue.
December 31. Performs at the Hyatt Regency, Houston, Texas.

1979

January 23. *4 Girls 4* opens in Chicago and continues to appear regularly at many locations in the United States.
January 31. Rosemary appears with Boots Randolph at Ball State University in Muncie, Indiana.
September 24–October 7. Appears at the Top of the World Supper Club in the Contemporary Hotel at Walt Disney World, Florida.
December 23. Gives three performances at Ted Hook's OnStage in West 46th Street, New York.

1980

Buys a house at 106 Riverside Drive, Augusta, Kentucky.
February 3–10. *4 Girls 4* is at Harrah's South Shore Room, Reno. Allen Sviridoff becomes road manager for the act. Bill Loeb remains as manager and the act continues to have many engagements throughout the year.
February 17–18. Rosemary appears again at Ted Hook's OnStage Supper Club in New York.
May 5–18. Appears at the Top of the World Supper Club in the Contemporary Hotel at Walt Disney World.

October. Performs at the Sahara, Las Vegas, with Don Rickles.
December. Appears again at Ted Hook's OnStage in New York.

1981

March 6–8. Sings at the Walker Theater Arts Center in Brooklyn, New York. Other performers on the bill are Kay Starr, The Four Lads, and Johnny Desmond.
March 27–28. Rose Marie and Rosemary Clooney perform at Caesar's, Atlantic City.
May. *4 Girls 4* at Westbury Music Fair, Long Island. A dispute over the contract fees leads Bill Loeb to leave and Allen Sviridoff eventually takes over as manager.
June 11–16. *4 Girls 4* at Caesars Boardwalk Regency, Atlantic City. Rose Marie decides to leave the act.
July 10. Rosemary appears at the North Sea Jazz Festival at The Hague in Holland with the Concord All Stars.
September 15–20. Sings with Mel Tormé and the Glenn Miller Orchestra at Valley Forge Music Fair, Pennsylvania. They repeat the show the following week at Westbury Music Fair, Long Island.
September 29–October 10. Appears at Rick's Cafe Americain in Chicago.
October 23–25. Stars with Milton Berle in Caesar's Cabaret Theater, Atlantic City.
November 17–29. Rosemary and Margaret Whiting appear twice nightly at the New Ballroom at West 28th Street, New York.
December 2. A *New 4 Girls 4* act makes its debut at the American Theater in St. Louis. Kay Starr has replaced Margaret Whiting.

1982

January 17. The *New 4 Girls 4* act appears in Phoenix and continues to perform at many locations for the rest of the year.
March 21. Rosemary is in London and takes part in BBC Radio2's *Saturday Night Is Gala Night* at the Fairfield Hall in Croydon, London.
Summer. Rosemary, Dante, Nick, and Nina Clooney go on the Orient Express to Venice.
November 22–26. Entertains with Tony Bennett and the Count Basie Orchestra at Valley Forge Music Fair in Pennsylvania. They repeat the show the following week at Westbury Music Fair, Long Island.

December 8. *Rosie: The Rosemary Clooney Story*, a two-hour biopic starring Sondra Locke is shown on CBS-TV.

1983

January 10–14. Entertains at the Fontainebleau in Miami Beach.

February. Rose Marie is persuaded to rejoin *New 4 Girls 4* in place of Martha Raye. They join the *Rotterdam* cruise ship in Los Angeles and sail to Honolulu and then Hong Kong giving performances en route.

May 6. Rosemary is in Cincinnati for "Rosemary Clooney Day." At 6:30 P.M. she sings for 50 minutes at a free concert at the Serpentine Wall in front of a crowd estimated at 5,000.

May. Entertains at Charley's in Washington, DC.

May 27–29. Rosemary and Tony Bennett perform at the Sands Hotel and Casino, Atlantic City. In June, they appear together at Caesars Boardwalk Regency in Atlantic City before going on to entertain in Reno, Nevada.

July 28–29. The *New 4 Girls 4* act comprising Rosemary, Helen O'Connell, Kay Starr, and Rose Marie is at the Palace Theater, Philadelphia. Rosemary subsequently leaves the act.

August 3. Rosemary, Lionel Hampton, and Les Brown and His Band of Renown entertain at the Hollywood Bowl.

August 7. Performs at the Concord Jazz Festival.

August 29. Leaves for Japan with Les Brown and His Band of Renown. They give concerts in Budokan, Tokyo; at Osaka Stadium, Osaka; and at Yokohama Stadium, Yokohama.

October 29. Appears with Mel Tormé and the Concord All Stars at Jones Hall, Houston, Texas.

November 17. Featured in a concert called "Swing Greats" with Vic Damone, Kay Starr, and Buddy Greco at the Barbican Hall, London.

1984

January 12–14. Rosemary performs at the Fontainebleau, Miami Beach.

July. Appears at the Hollywood Bowl in a tribute to Harry James.

July 20. Sings with the Cincinnati Pops Orchestra at the Riverbend Music Center in Cincinnati.

July 21. Performs with Tony Bennett at the Capitol Center, Concord, New Hampshire.

July 28. Gives a free concert at the downtown AmphiTheater, Long Beach.

August 28. Performs at the New York State Fair at Syracuse, New York.

September 1. Appears in the Harborlights Music Festival at Baltimore with Joe Williams and the Duke Ellington Orchestra.

September 2. Appears at the Montreux Detroit Kool Jazz Festival at the Palms / State Theater, Detroit.

September 15–16. Entertains at Hershey Park, Pennsylvania.

October 16–24. Appears with Vic Damone and Artie Shaw and his band at the Westbury Music Fair.

December 2. Stars in her *White Christmas Party* show at the Hershey Theater, Pennsylvania. This is a celebration of the 30th anniversary of the film.

December 23. Rosemary is the headliner at the Paper Mill Playhouse, Millburn, New Jersey.

1985

May 1. Serves as grand marshal of the Kentucky Derby Festival Pegasus Parade in Louisville, Kentucky.

May 7–25. Appears at Park Ten, Park Avenue, New York.

May 9. Performs at a benefit in Carnegie Hall, New York, with Skitch Henderson and the New York Pops.

June. Entertains with Tony Bennett at the Lions International convention in the Dallas Reunion Arena before a crowd of 14,500.

August. In San Francisco, films the part of Sarah, a Bible-toting murderess, in *Sister Margaret and the Saturday Night Ladies*. This is shown on CBS-TV in January 1987.

August 21–22. Performs with Alan King at Harrah's, Tahoe, Nevada.

August 25. Entertains with the Hi-Lo's at the Concord Jazz Festival held in the Concord Pavilion, California.

August 27–September 1. Stars with Vic Damone and the Artie Shaw Orchestra at the Valley Forge Music Fair in Pennsylvania. In September they repeat the show at the South Shore Music Circus in Cohasset, Massachusetts.

September 26. Rosemary is presented with the St. Vincent's Hospital Award. The award is presented in recognition of outstanding contributions to the field of mental health.

October 6*. Nelson Riddle dies*.

October 10–16. Appears with Alan King at Harrah's, Reno, Nevada.

November 25. Sings at Westbury Music Fair with Tony Bennett and the Artie Shaw Orchestra.

December 3. Performs with Tony Bennett at Heinz Hall, Pittsburgh. A few days later, they go on to entertain at the Front Row Theater in Highland Heights, Cleveland, Ohio.

1986

January 6. Appears in *Hardcastle and McCormick* on ABC-TV playing a psychic housekeeper who predicts McCormick's death.

January 24. Performs with Tony Bennett at the Ohio Theater, Columbus, Ohio. During the year, Rosemary and Tony also appear at Riverbend, Cincinnati; the Fox Theater in Atlanta; the Coliseum Theater, Latham, New York; Cape Cod Melody Tent in Hyannis; and at the Meadow Brook Music Festival in Toledo, Ohio.

April 7. Hosts *Singers' Salute to the Songwriter*, a concert to aid the Betty Clooney Foundation for the Brain Injured at the Dorothy Chandler Pavilion in Los Angeles.

April 29–May 17. Entertains at Michael's Pub, East 55th Street, New York.

May 30–June 1. Sings at Trump Casino Hotel, Atlantic City.

June 14–15. Entertains at Disney's Epcot Center.

October. Appears at Harrah's Reno with Jim Nabors until October 8.

October 10–19. Entertains at Vine St. Bar, Los Angeles.

November 4. Opens at the Fairmont Hotel in San Francisco for a two-week stay.

November 29. In "A Tribute to Irving Berlin" with the Florida Orchestra, under the direction of Skitch Henderson, at McKay Auditorium, Tampa, Florida. Stars in similar tributes in Clearwater and St. Petersburg, Florida, in the following days.

1987

February 3–15. Appears at the Fairmont Hotel, Dallas.

March 17–22. Sings at the Blue Note, West Third Street, New York.

April 6. Hosts *Singers' Salute to the Songwriter*, a concert to aid the Betty Clooney Foundation at the Dorothy Chandler Pavilion in Los Angeles.

April 14–May 2. Entertains at the Ritz-Carlton Hotel in Washington, DC.

May 5–9. Appears with Michael Feinstein at the Ritz-Carlton in Chicago.

June 10–14. Entertains with Bob Hope at Valley Forge Music Fair, Pennsylvania, and they go on to the Westbury Music Fair, Long Island, the following week.

October 6–11. Opens for Bob Hope at the Chicago Theater.

November 23. Rosemary sings at the Royal Variety Performance held at the London Palladium in the presence of Queen Elizabeth.

November 28. *Rosemary Clooney's White Christmas Party* is at Centre East, Skokie, Illinois, and at the Riverside, Milwaukee, the next day.

December 6. Rosemary performs at the Kennedy Center Honors held at the John F. Kennedy Center with President and Nancy Reagan in attendance.

December 31. Appears at the Paper Mill Playhouse in Millburn, New Jersey.

1988

January 19–24. Appears at the Blue Note club in New York.

　　March 3–13. Entertains at the Fairmont Hotel, San Francisco.

　　March 30. Hosts *Singers' Salute to the Songwriter*, a concert to aid the Betty Clooney Foundation at the Dorothy Chandler Pavilion in Los Angeles.

April 8–9. Appears with Bob Hope at the Showboat Hotel Casino, Atlantic City.

April 12. *The Betty Clooney Center* opens in Long Beach

April 26–May 6. Appears at the Fairmont Hotel, Dallas.

June 24. Takes part in *Command Performance—An All-Star Tribute to the President*. President and Nancy Reagan are in attendance.

July 15. Appears at the Hollywood Bowl with Michael Feinstein in a "Tribute to Irving Berlin."

September 13–25. Performs at the Fairmont Hotel, Chicago.

October 30–November 2. Entertains at Harrah's, Reno, with Jim Nabors.

November 27. *Rosemary Clooney's White Christmas Party* is at the Riverside, Milwaukee, and is also performed at other locations throughout December.

1989

February 7–25. Appears at the Rainbow and Stars club, New York.

April 7–8. Entertains at the Showboat in Atlantic City with Bob Hope

April 25. Hosts *Singers' Salute to the Songwriter*, a concert to aid the Betty Clooney Foundation at the Dorothy Chandler Pavilion, Los Angeles.

May 12–13. Performs with the New York Pops Orchestra at Carnegie Hall.

June 7–11. Appears at the Valley Forge Music Fair in Pennsylvania with Bob Hope and they go on to Westbury Music Fair on Long Island the following week.

June 27. Appears at Carnegie Hall in a concert as part of the JVC Jazz Festival New York.

July 28. Rosemary executes her Last Will and Testament. She states:

> I DIRECT that I be buried near my Father in my Mother's family plot in the St. Patrick's Cemetery in Washington, Kentucky, and that the tombstone marking my grave be in the same approximate size, style and prominence as my parents' tombstones, without reference to my career or fame. It is my wish that a funeral service be conducted for me as near to the Cemetery as practicable.

She makes bequests of various personal items to her children and to Dante DiPaolo (he receives her cars), Gail Darley (her half sister), Michael Feinstein, Debby Boone, Jackie Rose and Mark Sendroff. The residue of the estate is to be divided equally among her five children. Allen Sviridoff and Mark Sendroff are named as co-executors.

August 18–19. Entertains at the Hollywood Bowl, presenting a Gershwin selection of nearly two dozen songs. The audience is counted at 15,933 on Friday and 17,818 on Saturday.

November–December. *Rosemary Clooney's White Christmas Party* is presented at various locations from California to Long Island. Debby Boone co-stars.

1990

January 30–February 24. Appears at Rainbow and Stars, New York.

April 24. Hosts *Singers' Salute to the Songwriter*, a concert to aid the Betty Clooney Foundation at the Dorothy Chandler Pavilion, Los Angeles.

May 5. Arrives in West Berlin with Bob Hope and others. They go on to give several shows including one at Rhein Main Air Base, Frankfurt, and one for US Embassy staff in Moscow.

June 15. Sings with the Cincinnati Pops Orchestra at the Riverside Music Centre, Cincinnati.

October 6. Performs with the Virginia Symphony Pops in Chrysler Hall, Norfolk, Virginia.

November 3. Sings with the Richmond Symphony Pops at the Mosque, Richmond, Virginia.

November 19–24. Entertains at Blues Alley, Tokyo, Japan.
December. Is selected one of the six best living singers of American popular song.

> It was just one man's opinion, but Rosemary Clooney's still very pleased about being selected one of the six best living singers of American popular song by writer Daniel Okrent in this month's *Life* magazine. Asked if she feels she belongs on the list with Frank Sinatra, Carmen McRae, Tony Bennett, Ella Fitzgerald and Mel Tormé, Clooney laughs loudly and says, "If I don't belong in there, you think I'm gonna tell."
>
> (*St. Paul Pioneer Press* (MN)—December 14, 1990)

December 14–16. Rosemary presents her *White Christmas Party* with Debby Boone at Orchestra Hall, Minneapolis, and later in the month at Westbury Music Fair, Long Island, and at Valley Forge Music Fair, Pennsylvania.

1991

February 5. Opens at Rainbow and Stars, New York.
March 22–24. Rich Little and Rosemary entertain at TropWorld, Atlantic City.
April 29. Hosts *Singers' Salute to the Songwriter*, a concert to aid the Betty Clooney Foundation at the Dorothy Chandler Pavilion, Los Angeles.
June 8. Appears at Wolf Trap, Virginia, with Michael Feinstein. The show is videotaped by PBS for later transmission.
July 3. Takes part in a ceremony at Mount Rushmore when the monument is formally dedicated by President Bush. Rosemary sings "America the Beautiful."
August 27. In Chicago, Rosemary tapes an appearance on *Michael Feinstein & Friends* for national broadcast on PBS on October 11.
October 12. Appears at Carnegie Hall in a show called *Rosemary Clooney and the Arrangers*.
October 17–20. Entertains with Michael Feinstein at Westbury Music Fair, New York, and they go on to perform at Valley Forge Music Fair, Pennsylvania, the following week.
December 7. Takes her *White Christmas* show to the Niagara Falls Convention and Civic Center. Debby Boone appears with her.
December 11. Opens at the Curran Theater, San Francisco, with Michael Feinstein.

1992

January 26. *José Ferrer dies at the age of 80.*
February 5–29. Appears at Rainbow and Stars, New York
March 5. Sings at the Smithsonian in Washington, DC, and is presented with the James Smithson Bicentennial Medal.
April 28. Hosts *Singers' Salute to the Songwriter*, a concert to aid the Betty Clooney Foundation at the Dorothy Chandler Pavilion, Los Angeles.
May 29–31. Sings with the Indianapolis Symphony Orchestra at the Circle Theater, Indianapolis.
July 2–4. Appears at the Hollywood Bowl with Michael Feinstein.
September 4–5. Sings with the Dallas Symphony Pops in Dallas, Texas.
October 20–November 8. Performs at the Shubert Theater, Chicago, with Michael Feinstein.
December. *Rosemary Clooney's White Christmas Party*, with Debby Boone, appears at various locations throughout the month
December 31–January 2, 1993. Rosemary performs at the Jupiter Theater in Florida.

1993

January 8. Is nominated for a Grammy for her *Girl Singer* album. She loses out to Tony Bennett's *Perfectly Frank* album.
February 10–27. Appears at Rainbow and Stars, New York.
February 10. Rosemary is rushed to the New York Hospital by ambulance about 10 P.M. after becoming ill during her Rainbow and Stars act. She is kept under observation in the emergency room for several hours and released early the next day.
March 22. Receives her second MAC award for her engagement in 1992 at Rainbow and Stars.
April 20. Hosts *Singers' Salute to the Songwriter*, a concert to aid the Betty Clooney Foundation at the Dorothy Chandler Pavilion, Los Angeles.
May 12. Hosts *The Singers' Salute to the Country Songwriter* at the Dorothy Chandler Pavilion to raise funds for the Betty Clooney Foundation.
May 22. Rosemary and Linda Ronstadt sing with the Boston Pops Orchestra conducted by John Williams at Symphony Hall, Boston. The show is taped and shown on PBS-TV in August.

June 18. Takes part in a celebration of the Newport Jazz Festival at the White House in Washington, DC. The show is taped for broadcast on PBS stations on September 12.

June 25–28. Performs with the Pittsburgh Symphony Pops at Heinz Hall, Pittsburgh.

July 1–4. Entertains at Merv Griffin's Resorts, Atlantic City.

July 26–31. Rosemary entertains at the North Shore Music Theater, Beverly, Massachusetts.

August 13. Sings at the Newport Casino as part of the JVC Newport Jazz Festival in Rhode Island.

November 1. Presents a major tribute to Bing Crosby at Carnegie Hall, New York.

November 11–13. Joins the Baltimore Symphony Orchestra for three performances.

December. *Rosemary Clooney's White Christmas Party*, with Debby Boone again supporting Rosemary, appears at various locations during the month.

1994

February 2–26. Appears at Rainbow and Stars, New York.

July 8–9. Entertains with the Cincinnati Pops Orchestra at the Riverbend Music Center in Cincinnati, Ohio.

July 12–17. Sings with Disney's All-American College Big Band at Epcot '94.

July 20–25. Rosemary entertains at TropWorld Casino, Atlantic City.

August 10. Entertains in the *Jazz at the Bowl* concert at the Hollywood Bowl.

September 20. Enters Lenox Hill Hospital in New York and has a kidney stone removed. Goes home two days later.

September 29. Appears in *ER* playing "Mary Cavanaugh/Madame X" in the episode: "Going Home."

November / December. Rosemary has bronchial pneumonia and withdraws from the *Rosemary Clooney White Christmas Party* shows planned for various locations during late November/early December.

December 15. Again appears in *ER* in an episode called "The Gift." Is nominated for an Emmy for her performance.

1995

January 20–21. Appears at Orchestra Hall, Minneapolis.

February 8–March 4. Appears at Rainbow and Stars, New York.

May 29–31. Rosemary performs at the Trump Taj Mahal, Atlantic City.
June 6. Receives the Pied Piper Award from ASCAP at the Washington Court Hotel, Washington, DC.
July 26. Sings at Carnegie Hall in a concert celebrating the music of Frank Sinatra.
July 29. Appears at the Concord Pavilion.

> Still weakened and hobbling as the result of major knee and leg surgery and bone replacement, Clooney delivered a mellow batch of songs, chatted about her new lifestyle ("I've quit my three-pack-a-day smoking habit and given up two stiff martinis before dinner," she said. "So I asked my doctor at the Mayo Clinic, 'How about my weight?' and she answered, 'You've given up enough for now'").
>
> (Philip Elwood, *San Francisco Examiner*, July 31, 1995)

August 4–5. Rosemary appears with the Hollywood Bowl Orchestra at the Hollywood Bowl.
August 11–13. Appears with the All-American College Jazz Band at the America Gardens Theater, Epcot, Florida.
August 17. At the Pleasure Island Jazz Company club in Disney World, tapes "Rosemary Clooney's Demi-Centennial: A Girl Singer's Golden Anniversary." The show is broadcast on the A&E channel on November 11.
November 25. Presents her *White Christmas Party* show, with daughter-in-law Debby and various family members, at Pueblo's State Fair Events Center, Colorado. The show goes on to Toronto, Canada, and other locations in the United States.
December 28. Rosemary attends the funeral of Dean Martin.

> Dean Martin wanted it His Way—his funeral Thursday evening at Pierce Brothers cemetery in Westwood. . . . Rosemary Clooney closed the services singing "Everybody Loves Somebody Sometime." There wasn't a dry eye in the house, mine included.
>
> (*Variety*, December 29, 1995)

1996

February 6–March 2. Appears at Rainbow and Stars, New York.
May 26. Rosemary performs with the St. Louis Symphony Orchestra at Powell Symphony Hall, St. Louis.
June 14. Receives an award at the International Jazz Hall of Fame awards event at the Tampa Bay Performing Arts Center, Florida.

June 23. Rosemary commences recording an album for Concord called *Mothers & Daughters*. It is nominated for a Grammy but loses out to a Tony Bennett album.

August 1. Performs with the San Francisco Symphony Pops in Davies Hall, San Francisco.

August 4. Rosemary and Michael Feinstein appear at the Riverbend Music Centre, Cincinnati, Ohio.

> "I'm really glad to be here," Rosemary Clooney told the audience at Riverbend Music Center Sunday night. "Of course I say that 364 nights a year, but I really mean it. I've got a house right up the river and I slept in my own bed last night!" she explained. Yes, Maysville, Ky.'s Rosemary Clooney came home Sunday—and it was a family affair. She dedicated one of her first selections to "THE nephew—George Timothy Clooney." The song: "We're in the money."
>
> (*The Cincinnati Post*, August 5, 1996)

September 19. Performs in a tribute to Nelson Riddle at Carnegie Hall as part of the Fujitsu Concord Jazz Festival.

December 2–19. Entertains at the Sands Hotel and Casino, Atlantic City. Her show is called *Rosemary Clooney's White Christmas Party*.

December 20. Tapes a show with the Boston Pops in Boston which is televised in December 1997.

1997

January 24. Rosemary and Dolores Hope sell out the 1,129-seat McCallum Theater in Palm Desert. The proceeds go to a charity.

April. Rosemary and Dante visit Rome and have an audience with the Pope.

May 11–24. Appears with Dolores Hope at the Rainbow and Stars club.

July 18. Appears with Vic Damone in the Concord Pavilion, California, as part of the Fujitsu Concord Jazz Festival.

October 14–25. Sings at Rainbow and Stars, New York.

November 7. Marries Dante DiPaolo at St. Patrick Church, Maysville, Kentucky.

December 1–19. Appears at the Sands Hotel and Casino, Atlantic City. The show is called *Rosemary Clooney's White Christmas Party*.

January 16–17. Performs in a tribute to Nelson Riddle at Abravanel Hall, Salt Lake City.

February 11. Because of illness, Rosemary has to postpone a concert due to take place at Carnegie Hall that night.

February 13. Is due to perform at Stamford Palace, Connecticut, but this has to be canceled too. She goes to New York and is admitted to Lenox Hill Hospital. A spinal tap shows viral meningitis that has reached the brain. Rosemary is in a coma for three days before recovering.

May 12–23. Entertains at Rainbow and Stars. Has to cancel her shows on May 21 and 22 due to laryngitis. Dolores Hope guests on May 23.

June 1. Gives a concert with the Count Basie Orchestra and her own sextet in Carnegie Hall.

June 19–20. Rosemary returns to Cincinnati to celebrate what she calls "the big 7-0" with Erich Kunzel and the Cincinnati Pops at Riverbend.

July 22. Stars with the Count Basie Orchestra at the Hollywood Bowl.

August 28. Rosemary, Linda Ronstadt, and Michael Feinstein perform together at Harrah's, Las Vegas.

October 5. Is presented with the Society of Singers' prestigious Ella Lifetime Achievement Award at the Beverly Hilton Hotel.

November 1. Cardinal Mahony presents the *Catholics in Media Lifetime Achievement Award* to Rosemary.

December 7. Rosemary cancels a benefit appearance at Avery Fisher Hall due to physical exhaustion. Michael Feinstein takes her place.

December 11–12. Appears with the National Symphony Orchestra Pops at the John F. Kennedy Center for the Performing Arts in Washington, D.C.

April 17–18. Appears at Blaisdell Concert Hall in Honolulu with the Honolulu Symphony Pops.

July 16. Gives a concert in Stuttgart, Germany, with Matt Catingub's Big Kahuna & The Copa Cat Pack. The concert is broadcast by PBS in November as a special called "Swing It!" which is also narrated by Rosemary.

August 6. Entertains at the Concord Pavilion in California at the Fujitsu Concord Jazz Festival with the Count Basie Orchestra.

September 25. Goes to Maysville to headline "The Rosemary Clooney Music Festival" to save the Russell Theater, where her first film, *The Stars*

Are Singing, premiered in 1953. She performs on a covered outdoor stage on Third Street at 9 P.M.

October 5–16. Performs at Feinstein's at the Regency in New York.

November 22. The Patsy's Restaurant Family in New York hosts a spectacular party for Rosemary to publicize her book, *Girl Singer*, co-authored with Joan Barthel.

December 9–12. Plays four nights at Dover Downs, Delaware. These are the only holiday shows she does this year.

2000

February 6. Entertains at the Beverly Hilton at the Society of Singers' lifetime achievement event which sees the Ella award given to Tony Bennett.

April 14 / 16. Rosemary and Michael Feinstein entertain at the Westbury Music Festival, Long Island.

May 30–June 10. Performs at Feinstein's at the Regency in New York.

September 30. Entertains at the Second Annual "Rosemary Clooney Music Festival" in Maysville.

November 27–December 3. Appears at Feinstein's at the Regency in New York. Her show is called "Rosemary Clooney's White Christmas Party."

2001

March 27–April 7. Performs at Feinstein's at the Regency in New York. Her show is called "Sentimental Journey."

April 1. Is presented with the MAC Lifetime Achievement Award by the Manhattan Association of Cabarets and Clubs.

April 25. Sings at the Annual Ella Award dinner at the Beverly Hilton Hotel which honors Julie Andrews.

May 31. The A & E Biography channel screens an hour-long tribute to Rosemary.

June 18. Appears with Michael Feinstein at Festival Hall, London.

June 20. Entertains with Michael Feinstein at the National Concert Hall, Dublin, Ireland.

September 10. Sings at the Southern Governors' Conference in Lexington, Kentucky. Nick Clooney is the emcee. Vice-President Dick Cheney is in attendance and leaves for Washington, DC after Rosemary's performance.

September 15. Appears with the Evansville Philharmonic Orchestra at The Centre, Evansville.

September 29. Appears at the third "Rosemary Clooney Music Festival" in Maysville with Michael Feinstein.

October. Rosemary appears on *The View* on ABC-TV with Barbara Walters. This was probably Rosemary's last appearance on national television.

November 16. Appears at the Blaisdell Concert Hall in Honolulu. The performance is subsequently issued on a CD "Rosemary Clooney: The Last Concert."

December. It is announced that Rosemary is one of the recipients of the 2002 Lifetime Achievement Award to be presented by the National Academy of Recording Arts and Sciences.

December. Goes to the Mayo Clinic where it is discovered that she has a shadow on her left lung.

December 14. Appears at Orchestra Hall, Minneapolis.

December 15. Appears at the Count Basie Theater, Red Bank, New Jersey. Rosemary has recently been diagnosed with lung cancer but it is kept secret.

2002

January 9. Rosemary announces that a recent routine physical examination has revealed that she is suffering from lung cancer.

January 11. Rosemary has the upper lobe of her left lung removed at the Mayo Clinic in Rochester, Minnesota.

February 27. Rosemary Clooney's oldest son, Miguel Ferrer, accepts her Lifetime Achievement Award at the Annual Grammy Awards.

Rosemary remains hospitalized at the Mayo Clinic until early May, at which time she is able to go home to Beverly Hills and share Mother's Day and her birthday with her family, which includes five children, 10 grandchildren, brother and sister-in-law Nick and Nina Clooney, sister Gail Stone Darley, and their and Betty's children

Singer Rosemary Clooney Suffers Cancer Relapse

Rosemary Clooney was briefly hospitalized this month and is undergoing treatment at home for a recurrence of lung cancer, her publicist said on Wednesday.

"She's comfortable and she's surrounded by her family," spokeswoman Linda Dozoretz said of the 74-year-old entertainer, who also is the aunt of actor George Clooney. She declined to discuss the singer's prognosis but added, "She's an eternal optimist, she really is."

(Reuters, June 26, 2002)

June 29. About 6 P.M. Rosemary Clooney dies at her Beverly Hills home.

July 3. Family members and celebrities from the entertainment world attend a funeral Mass at Good Shepherd Catholic Church, Beverly Hills.

July 5. A funeral Mass is held at a packed St. Patrick Church, Maysville, Kentucky. Among those attending are her husband Dante DiPaolo, Rosemary's children, her grandchildren, her brother Nick and his wife Nina, Rosemary's sister Gail, her nephew George Clooney, Kathryn Crosby, and Al Pacino. A reception to celebrate Rosemary's life is held at the riverside home of Nick and Nina Clooney in Augusta following graveside rites at the cemetery.

NOTES

CHAPTER 1

1. *Fresh Air*, interview with Terry Gross, National Public Radio, January 18, 1997.
2. *Rosemary Clooney—Demi-Centennial*, Concord CCF-4633, sleeve note.
3. Paul A. Tenkotte and James C. Claypool, eds., *The Encyclopedia of Northern Kentucky*, University of Kentucky Press, Lexington, 2010.
4. Nick Clooney, author interview, May 16, 2011.
5. Nick Clooney, author interview.
6. Virginia Bird, "Hollywood's Favorite Songbird," *Saturday Evening Post*, January 1955.
7. Rosemary Clooney with Joan Barthel, *Girl Singer*, Doubleday, New York, 1999.
8. *Fresh Air*, National Public Radio, January 18, 1997.
9. In a newspaper interview in 1953, Rosemary indicated that her Christian names came from the operetta *Rose Marie*, that her parents had seen shortly before her birth; Kirtley Baskette, "What Makes Rosie Glow?" *Redbook*, September 1953.
10. Rosemary Clooney with Raymond Strait, *This for Remembrance*, Simon & Schuster, New York, 1977.
11. Nick Clooney, author interview.
12. Whitney Balliett, "The Heart, the Head, and the Pipes," *The New Yorker*, August 3, 1992.
13. *Up Close with Tom Cottle*, syndicated TV, 1982.
14. Gene Cipriano, author interview 2, May 10, 2011.
15. Nick Clooney, author interview.
16. Uncredited article from *Middlesboro Daily News*, August 19, 1933.
17. Extracted from St. Patrick's High School Alumni News, 2002, and quoted by Nick Clooney, *Cincinnati Post*, December 4, 2002.
18. Nick Clooney, author interview.
19. The State of Ohio required children to stay in school until age 18. In other states it was 16.
20. Frances Kish, "Her Life Is a Song," *TVRadio Mirror*, August 1955.

CHAPTER 2

1. Quoted by George T. Simon in *The Big Bands*, Macmillan, New York, 1967.
2. Rosemary Clooney, with Joan Barthel, *Girl Singer*, Doubleday, New York, 1999.
3. Evelyn Harvey, "Everything's Rosy for Clooney," *Collier's*, November 15, 1952.
4. George T. Simon, *The Big Bands*, Macmillan, New York, 1967.
5. Christopher Popa, Big Band Library, http://www.bigbandlibrary.com/, April 2009.

6. Rosemary Clooney, with Raymond Strait, *This for Remembrance*, Simon & Schuster, New York, 1977.
7. Henry Riggs, author interview, November 4, 2010.
8. Gene Cipriano, author interview 1, April 30, 2011.
9. Quoted by Denis Norden, *Clips for a Life*, Harper Perennial, London, 2008.
10. Rosemary said in *Girl Singer* that the Sister's opening number was the Peggy Lee-Dave Barbour song "It's a Good Day," although it was not published until 1947, the year after the Clooneys joined the Pastor band.
11. Kirtley Baskette, "What Makes Rosie Glow?" *Redbook*, September, 1953.
12. "Song of the South—Tony Pastor," *Billboard*, January 18, 1947.
13. Rosemary often quoted this comment and in *This For Remembrance*, attributed it to *Downbeat*. Search of the *Downbeat* archives, however, does not reveal the relevant article and it may be that it originates from another, unidentified journal.
14. "Bread and Butter Woman," *Billboard*, September 16, 1950,
15. Alan Fischter, "Tony Pastor," *Billboard*, May 31, 1947,
16. Lubbock's anonymity ended of course with the rise to stardom and immortality of Buddy Holly, who was born there in 1936.
17. Henry Riggs, author interview.
18. "Grieving for You" *Billboard*, January 15, 1949.
19. Interview by Johnny Green, *World of Music*, KRHM, June 1961.
20. Clooney with Barthel, *Girl Singer*.
21. Tony Bennett in concert at Birmingham Symphony Hall, July 3, 2010.
22. Henry Riggs, author interview.
23. *Billboard* news item, November 27, 1948.
24. Malcolm Macfarlane and Ken Crossland, *Perry Como, A Biography and Complete Career Chronicle*, McFarland, Jefferson, NC, 2009.
25. Russell Sanjek, *American Popular Music and Its Business: The First Four Hundred Years*, Oxford University Press, New York, 1988.
26. Nick Clooney, author interview, May 16, 2011.
27. *The Hour Magazine*, syndicated TV, March 1986.
28. Nick Clooney, author interview.
29. Nick Clooney, author interview.
30. *Fresh Air*, interview with Terry Gross, National Public Radio, January 18, 1997.

CHAPTER 3
1. Joel Whitburn, *Billboard Pop Hits 1940–54*, Record Research, Menomonee Falls, WI, 1994.
2. There are various spellings of his name. "Manny" is not uncommon, nor "Sacks."
3. Sachs was reportedly offered a salary of between $50,000 and $75,000 to join RCA, more than double his take at Columbia.
4. Quoted by Albin J. Zak III, *I Don't Sound Like Nobody: Remaking Music in 1950s America*, University of Michigan Press, Ann Arbor, 2010.
5. Will Friedwald, "They Sang Along with Mitch," *Wall Street Journal*, August 4, 2010.
6. Archive of American Television, http://www.emmytvlegends.org/. Mitch Miller interviewed by Karen Herman, July 24, 2004.
7. John S. Wilson, *New York Times Magazine*, December 8, 1957, quoted by Albin J. Zak, *I Don't Sound Like Nobody: Remaking Music in 1950s America*, University of Michigan Press, Ann Arbor, 2010.
8. Mark Myers, All About Jazz, http://www.allaboutjazz.com/, August 8, 2010.

9. Richard Severo, "Mitch Miller, Maestro of the Singalong, Dies at 99," *New York Times*, August 2, 2010.
10. "Rosemary Clooney—Why Fight the Feeling," *Billboard*, August 12, 1950.
11. John Crosby, *Pittsburgh Post-Gazette*, July 11, 1950.
12. Tony Bennett, *The Good Life: The Autobiography of Tony Bennett*, Simon & Schuster, New York, 1998.
13. Nick Clooney, "Hanging out with Rosie on Early TV," *Cincinnati Post*, January 8, 2003.
14. Virginia Bird, "Hollywood's Favorite Songbird," *Saturday Evening Post*, January 1955.
15. Ibid.
16. Rosemary Clooney, with Joan Barthel, *Girl Singer*, Doubleday, New York, 1999.
17. Quoted in *Fresh Air*, interview with Terry Gross, National Public Radio, January 18, 1997.
18. James Kaplan, *Frank: The Voice*, Doubleday, New York, 2010.
19. Russell Nype and Ethel Merman sang the song together in the Broadway production of the show.
20. Bird, "Hollywood's Favorite Songbird."
21. Peter Reilly, "You've Got to Learn to Take Care of Yourself," *Stereo Review*, October 1981.
22. *Prime Time Live* interview, ABC, January 16, 1992.
23. Michael Feinstein, author interview, April 9, 2011.
24. Allen Sviridoff by email, March 21, 2012.
25. Deborah Grace Winer, *Come On-a My House*, Bear Family Records, Hambergen, Germany, 1997.
26. Ibid.
27. "Rosemary Clooney—Come On-a My House," *Billboard*, June 23 and 30, 1951.
28. Quoted by Matt Schudel, *Washington Post*, August 3, 2010.
29. Michael Feinstein's 2009 series for PBS-TV featured an interesting anecdote about the writing of the song. Lyricist Jack Lawrence said "the tune haunted me and the lyric practically wrote itself during my waking and sleeping hours. Words came so easily that I decided to wait a while before calling Walter (Gross) for fear that he might think I'd written an off-the-cuff lyric. Literally, I waited about ten days. Then feigning great excitement, I called Walter and said, "I've got it, Walter! I've got it!" In a rather deadpan tone, he asked, "What's the title?" I took a deep breath and practically sang out, "TEN-der-LY!" There was a long pause at his end. Then he sneered, "That's no title! That's what you put at the top of the sheet music: Play Tenderly!"
30. Rosemary Clooney, with Raymond Strait, *This for Remembrance*, Simon & Schuster, New York, 1977.
31. "Rosemary Clooney—Percy Faith Ork—Tenderly," *Billboard*, February 9, 1952.
32. Whitburn, *Billboard Pop Hits 1940–54*.
33. Clooney with Barthel, *Girl Singer*.

CHAPTER 4
1. Bing Crosby to Pat Duggan, Paramount Studios, August 20, 1951.
2. Tony Bennett with Will Friedwald, *The Good Life: The Autobiography of Tony Bennett*, Simon & Schuster, New York, 1998.
3. Alistair Cooke, *Letter from America*, BBC, December 23, 1977.
4. Bing Crosby with Pete Martin, *Call Me Lucky*, Simon & Schuster, New York, 1953.

5. "There's Only One Bing," *TV Radio Mirror*, October 1954.
6. Ibid.
7. Ibid.
8. Virginia Bird, "Hollywood's Favorite Songbird," *Saturday Evening Post*, January, 1955.
9. "Girl in the Groove," unattributed, *Time*, February 23, 1953.
10. Kirtley Baskette, "What Makes Rosie Glow?" *Redbook*, September 1953.
11. Bird, "Hollywood's Favorite Songbird."
12. Ibid.
13. "Girl in the Groove."
14. "Clooney Smash – Botch-a-Me," *Billboard*, June 21, 1952.
15. "Columbia Pop-Disk Primacy apparent in Billboard Charts," *Billboard*, April 19, 1952.
16. Deborah Grace Winer, *Come On-A My House*, Bear Family Records, Hambergen, Germany, 1997.
17. "The Wholesome Type," *Time*, September 8, 1952.
18. *Fresh Air*, interview with Terry Gross, National Public Radio, January 18, 1997.
19. Louella Parsons syndicated column, September 27, 1952.
20. Gilbert Millstein, "Fabulous Joe Ferrer," *Collier's*, December 25, 1953.
21. Ibid.
22. *Up Close with Tom Cottle*, syndicated TV, December 1982.
23. Hedda Hopper syndicated column, December 1952.
24. Bosley Crowther, "Movie Review: The Stars Are Singing," *New York Times*, March 12, 1953.
25. James Bacon, nationally syndicated column, September 1, 1952.
26. "Here Come the Girls," *Variety*, October 21, 1953.
27. Crowther, "Movie Review: Here Come the Girls."
28. "Here Come the Girls," *Time*, December 28, 1953.
29. Rosemary Clooney, with Joan Barthel, *Girl Singer*, Doubleday, New York, 1999.
30. Hy Gardner, syndicated column, December 19, 1952.
31. "Girl in the Groove."
32. *Red Garters* publicity pack, Paramount Pictures, 1954.
33. Bosley Crowther, "Movie Review: Red Garters," *New York Times*, March 27, 1954.
34. *Fresh Air*, interview with Terry Gross.
35. Millstein, "Fabulous Joe Ferrer."

CHAPTER 5

1. In January 1949, Columbia also introduced 7" 33-rpm singles, a number of which featured Rosemary Clooney.
2. *Perry Como Sings Merry Christmas Music*, recorded in August 1946 and released by RCA as a 4x78 "Musical Smart Set" was one of the earliest examples.
3. "There's Only One Bing," *TV Radio Mirror*, October 1954.
4. Virginia Bird, "Hollywood's Favorite Songbird," *Saturday Evening Post*, January 1955.
5. *White Christmas*, Paramount Home Video DVD, Retrospective interview with Rosemary Clooney.
6. There is considerable conjecture as to the reasons for Astaire's unavailability, with temporary retirement, dislike of the script, or a feeling that he was, at 54, too old for the part, the ones most commonly cited.
7. Some sources suggest that Rosemary provided both voices for the "Sisters" duet, but the soundtrack recording clearly contains Stevens's voice.

8. John G. Ekizian, "Me, Bing & the Best Christmas Film Ever," *New York Post*, December 14, 2001.
9. "Bingle All The Way," *Life* Magazine, October 11, 1954.
10. *White Christmas*, Paramount Home Video DVD.
11. Ibid.
12. Bosley Crowther, "Movie Review—White Christmas," *New York Times*, October 15, 1954.
13. "White Christmas," *Variety*, September 1, 1954 (review was based on a critics' preview of the film on August 27 in Hollywood).
14. "Rosemary's Old Kentucky Home," *White Christmas*, Paramount Home Video DVD.
15. Todd S. Purdum, "The Street Where They Lived," *Vanity Fair*, April 1999.
16. Ibid.
17. When Crosby appeared on *The Joe Franklin Show* in New York, December 3, 1976, the host asked him about "the battle of the baritones" and whether it was a straight fight between Crosby and Columbo. "[Rudy] Vallee was in there somewhere," Crosby said, typically using horseracing parlance. "I think he ran third, but it was a photo between Russ and me."
18. The circumstances relating to Columbo's death made the national news throughout the United States and were widely reported. Contemporary accounts clearly state that the shooting occurred at Brown's home, not Columbo's.
19. Michael Feinstein, author interview, April 9, 2011.
20. Rosemary Clooney, with Joan Barthel, *Girl Singer*, Doubleday, New York, 1999.
21. Ibid.
22. Rosemary Clooney, "Putting My Visit on Record," *Picturegoer*, February 20, 1954.
23. Crosby lived his life believing that his birth date was May 2, 1904. It was discovered from baptismal certificates, after his death, that the true date of his birth was May 3, 1903.
24. "While We're Young," *Billboard*, September 18, 1954.
25. Kirtley Baskette, "What Makes Rosie Glow?" *Redbook*, September 1953.

CHAPTER 6
1. *Marian McPartland's Piano Jazz*, National Public Radio, October 14, 1991.
2. Quoted in *Fresh Air*, interview with Terry Gross, National Public Radio, January 18, 1997.
3. *The Late Late Show with Tom Snyder*, CBS-TV, February 16, 1999.
4. Rosemary Clooney, with Joan Barthel, *Girl Singer*, Doubleday, New York, 1999.
5. "Girl in the Groove," *Time Magazine*, February 23, 1953.
6. "The Rosemary Clooney Story," *Prevue*, May 1954.
7. Jimmy Watson, "Clooney's Sensational Glasgow Opening," *New Musical Express* (UK), July 8, 1955.
8. London Palladium concert, July 1976.
9. Expressed in 2013 prices, the cost would range from $10 to $60.
10. "London Palladium: Rosemary Clooney," *The Times*, London, July 19, 1955.
11. *Primetime Live*, Diane Sawyer interview, January 16, 1992.
12. Nick Clooney, author interview, May 16, 2011.
13. *An Interview with Dinah!* The Nashville Network, September 1, 1989.
14. *The Late Late Show with Tom Snyder*.
15. Ian Bernard, author interview, March 24, 2011.

16. Bob Foster, *San Mateo Times*, October 5, 1956. See also Michael Feinstein's sleeve notes to *The Rosemary Clooney Show*, CD, Concord Jazz, 2004.
17. Erskine Johnson, syndicated column, March 27, 1956.
18. Robert L. Sokolsky, *Syracuse Herald Journal*, September 12, 1956.
19. "TV Program & Talent Awards," *Billboard*, July 29, 1957.
20. *Fresh Air*, interview with Terry Gross.
21. Peter J. Levinson, *September in the Rain: The Life of Nelson Riddle*, Taylor Trade Publishing, Lanham, MD, 2005.
22. Will Friedwald, *Sinatra! The Song Is You*, Da Capo, New York, 1997.
23. Riddle's birthday was June 1, Rosemary's May 23.
24. Levinson, *September in the Rain*.
25. Ibid.
26. Deborah Grace Winer, *Memories of You*, Bear Family Records, Hambergen, Germany, 1998.
27. Whitney Balliett, "Recording Reports; Jazz on LPs," *Saturday Review*, February 1956.
28. John Fass, *Backstory in Blue: Ellington at Newport '56*, Rutgers University Press, Piscataway, NJ, 2008.
29. Will Friedwald, unpublished essay in authors' possession, 2011.
30. Ken Vail, *Duke's Diary: Part Two: The Life of Duke Ellington 1950–1974*, Scarecrow Press, Lanham, MD, 1999.
31. "Swee' Pea is Still Amazed at Freedom Allowed in Writing for Ellington Orchestra," *Downbeat*, May 30, 1956.
32. David Hajdu, *Lush Life, A Biography of Billy Strayhorn*, Farrar, Straus and Giroux, New York, 1996.
33. Interview by Marian McPartland, *Marian McPartland's Piano Jazz*, National Public Radio, October 14, 1991.
34. Friedwald, unpublished essay.
35. Ibid.
36. Ibid.
37. Gary Giddins, *Visions of Jazz*, Oxford University Press, New York, 1998.
38. "Rosemary Clooney—An American Treasure," National Public Radio, Jazz Profile, December 3, 2008.
39. When Rosemary shared a guest spot on *The Perry Como Show* with Nat "King Cole" around this time, Como could slip his hand around her waist during one duet whereas Rosemary had to maintain clear daylight between herself and Cole on another.
40. Friedwald, unpublished essay.
41. Ibid.

CHAPTER 7

1. Bob Foster, *San Mateo Times*, October 5, 1956.
2. "Sing, Little Birdie" by Joe Shapiro and Lou Stallman is a different song from "Sing, Little Birdie" by Syd Cordell and Stan Butcher that was a 1959 hit in the United Kingdom for the husband and wife team of Pearl Carr and Teddy Johnson.
3. Bob Bernstein, "Miss Clooney Blooms in her New TV Show, *Billboard*, September 30, 1957.
4. "Television: Review," *Time*, October 7. 1957.
5. Rosemary Clooney, with Joan Barthel, *Girl Singer*, Doubleday, New York, 1999.

6. *The Pat Sajak Show*, CBS-TV, April 18, 1989.
7. *The Rosie O'Donnell Show*, syndicated TV, September 17, 1996.
8. Whitney Balliett, "The Head, the Heart and the Pipes," *New Yorker*, August 3, 1992.
9. Bob Foster, *San Mateo Times*, March 20, 1958.
10. "Oh Captain," *Billboard*, May 5, 1958.
11. "Sands, Reno: Rosemary Clooney," *Variety*, July 9, 1958.
12. Quoted by Gary Giddins in notes to Mosaic Records "The Bing Crosby CBS Radio Recordings 1954–56," 2009.
13. Buddy Cole in taped message to English collector, Stan White, published in *The Crosby Post*, August 1962.
14. Deborah Grace Winer, *Many A Wonderful Moment*, Bear Family Records, Hambergen, Germany, 1999.
15. Clooney, with Barthel, *Girl Singer*.
16. Interview included in *Girl Singer—The Rosemary Clooney Show*, Concord Records DVD, 2004.
17. Bing Crosby in sleeve notes to album, *Fancy Meeting You Here*.
18. Adam Sweeting, Billy May obituary, *The Guardian* (UK), January 27, 2004.
19. Winer, *Many A Wonderful Moment*.
20. "Fancy Meeting You Here," *The Gramophone* (UK), April 1959.
21. "Fancy Meeting You Here," *Time*, January 12, 1959.
22. Will Friedwald, *A Biographical Guide to the Great Jazz and Pop Singers*, Pantheon, New York, 2010.
23. "Johnny Green's World of Music," KRHM, June 1961.

CHAPTER 8

1. Peter Hugh Reed, *American Record Guide*, Vol. 27, July 1960.
2. *The Pat Sajak Show*, CBS-TV, April 18, 1989.
3. Gary Giddins, author interview, March 16, 2011.
4. Murray Schumach, *New York Times*, October 8, 1961.
5. Ibid.
6. Billy May had put together an item called "Solving the Riddle" for an album in 1958.
7. Peter J. Levinson, *September in the Rain: The Life of Nelson Riddle*, Taylor Trade Publishing, Lanham, MD, 2005.
8. "Rosie Solves the Swingin' Riddle," *Billboard*, December 31, 1960.
9. *Rosie Solves the Swingin' Riddle*, sleeve notes to CD release, Peter J. Levinson, 2004.
10. Quoted by James Gavin in sleeve notes to 1995 CD reissue of *Love*.
11. Ian Bernard, author interview, March 24, 2011.
12. Levinson, *September in the Rain*.
13. Bruce Eder, "Love," *All Music Guide*, http://www.allmusic.com/album/love-mw0000176922.
14. Joel Selvin, *San Francisco Chronicle*, November 5, 1995.
15. *Associated Press*, September 23, 1961.
16. *Associated Press*, October 20, 1961.
17. All quotations taken from *Associated Press* reports, May 1–3, 1962.
18. Ibid.
19. Rosemary Clooney, with Joan Barthel, *Girl Singer*, Doubleday, New York, 1999.
20. Levinson, *September in the Rain*.
21. Whitney Balliett, "The Heart, the Head, and the Pipes," *New Yorker*, August 3, 1992.

22. "Rosemary Clooney, Copacabana, NY, with Bob Thompson," *Variety*, April 11, 1962.
23. "Rosemary Clooney Sings Country Hits from the Heart," *Billboard*, February 16, 1963.
24. *Associated Press*, July 26, 1962.
25. Dorothy Manners, syndicated column, *Cedars Rapid Gazette*, August 3, 1962.
26. Maria Ferrer Murdock, author interview, February 3, 2010.
27. Rafael Ferrer, interview included in *Girl Singer—The Rosemary Clooney Show*, DVD, Concord Records, 2004.

CHAPTER 9
1. *The Larry King Show*, CNN, May 10, 1997.
2. *Associated Press*, September 14, 1967.
3. *Up Close with Tom Cottle*, syndicated TV, December 1982.
4. *Fresh Air*, interview with Terry Gross, National Public Radio, January 18, 1997.
5. Barbara Bladen, *San Mateo Times*, March 16, 1963.
6. *Variety*, July 15, 1964.
7. *A Conversation with Dinah*, The Nashville Network, September 1, 1989.
8. Interview for *Great Women Singers*, Kultur Films Inc., DVD, 2000.
9. *Merv Griffin Show* (syndicated), December 1982.
10. *Biography*, A&E Network, May 31, 2001.
11. Jack Russell, *San Mateo Times*, February 3, 1965.
12. Will Friedwald, *Sinatra! The Song Is You*, Da Capo, New York, 1997.
13. Tony Bennett, with Will Friedwald, *The Good Life: The Autobiography of Tony Bennett*, Simon & Schuster, New York, 1998.
14. Michael Feinstein, author interview, April 9, 2011.
15. Deborah Grace Winer, *Many a Wonderful Moment*, Bear Family Records, Hambergen, Germany, 1999.
16. Uncredited report, *The Post-Standard*, Syracuse, NY, June 23, 1966.
17. Ron Shaw, author interview, April 15, 2011.
18. Nick Clooney, author interview, May 16, 2011.
19. Hank Fox, "Rosie Clooney Cleans House with New Bag of Material," *Billboard*, October 1, 1966.
20. *Variety*, December 28, 1966.
21. Lee Hale, *Backstage at the Dean Martin Show*, Taylor Publishing, Dallas, TX, 2000.
22. Ibid.
23. Rosemary Clooney, with Raymond Strait, *This for Remembrance*, Simon & Schuster, New York, 1977.
24. Alan Ebert, "Rosemary Clooney's Saddest Song," *Ladies Home Journal*, March 1976.
25. Diane Sawyer, *Primetime Live*, ABC, January 2, 1992.
26. Maria Ferrer Murdock, author interview, February 3, 2010.
27. Ebert, "Rosemary Clooney's Saddest Song."
28. *A Conversation with Dinah*.

CHAPTER 10
1. "No Time to Be a Mom & a Fulltime Performer So Rosemary Clooney Quits," *Variety*, July 10, 1968.
2. Alan Ebert, "Rosemary Clooney's Saddest Song," *Ladies Home Journal*, March 1976.

3. *Up Close with Tom Cottle*, syndicated TV, December 1982.
4. Ibid.
5. Sherm Holvey, author interview 1, March 29, 2011.
6. Ebert, "Rosemary Clooney's Saddest Song."
7. *Tomorrow in Los Angeles*, NBC, November 23, 1977.
8. Maria Ferrer Murdock, author interview, February 3, 2010.
9. Nick Clooney, author interview, May 16, 2011.
10. Monsita Botwick, author interview, May 13, 2011.
11. Maria Ferrer Murdoch, author interview.
12. *Up Close with Tom Cottle*.
13. "Rosemary Clooney Says She'll Retire," *Press-Telegram*, Long Beach, CA, July 3, 1968.
14. Tom Snyder, *The Late Late Show*, CBS-TV, February 16, 1999.
15. Rosemary Clooney, with Raymond Strait, *This for Remembrance*, Simon & Schuster, New York, 1977.
16. Monsita Botwick, author interview.
17. *Great Women Singers*, Kultur Films Inc., DVD, 2000.
18. Diane Sawyer, *Primetime Live*, ABC-TV, January 1992.
19. Clooney, with Strait, *This for Remembrance*.
20. Monsita Botwick, author interview.
21. *The Late, Late Show*.
22. *The Sally Jessie Raphael Show*, syndicated TV, May 1985.
23. Nancy Anderson, *Copley News Service*, May 1, 1974.
24. Marilyn Beck, "Rosemary Clooney Hits the Comeback Trail," *Milwaukee Journal*, March 25, 1974.
25. Clooney, with Strait, *This for Remembrance*.
26. "Biography," A&E Network, May 31, 2001.
27. "Rosemary Clooney Revives 'Good Feeling of 50s,'" *Albuquerque Journal*, January 1, 1974.
28. Rosemary Clooney, with Joan Barthel, *Girl Singer*, Doubleday, New York, 1999.

CHAPTER 11
1. *The Late Late Show with Tom Snyder*, CBS-TV, February 16, 1999.
2. *Fresh Air*, interview with Terry Gross, National Public Radio, January 18, 1997.
3. Ibid.
4. Leonard Feather, *Los Angeles Times*, March 19, 1976.
5. Herbert Kretzmer, London *Daily Express* June 22, 1976.
6. James Green, London *Evening News*, June 22, 1976.
7. John Gibson, "Bing at His Best—Now I Can Die Happy," *Edinburgh Evening News*, July 16, 1976.
8. John Barber, "A Worthwhile Wait to Hear Bing Crosby," *Daily Telegraph* (UK), June 22, 1976.
9. Nick Clooney, author interview, May 16, 2011.
10. Maria Murdock Ferrer, author interview, February 3, 2010.
11. Rosemary Clooney, with Joan Barthel, *Girl Singer*, Doubleday, New York, 1999.
12. "Bing Crosby on Broadway," *Variety*, December 15, 1976.
13. Gary Giddins, *Riding on a Blue Note*, Oxford University Press, New York, 1981.
14. Douglas Watt, *New York News*, December 8, 1976.
15. Sara Lane, *Billboard*, March 12, 1977.
16. Malcolm Macfarlane, *Bing Crosby – Day by Day*, Scarecrow Press, Lanham, MD, 2001.

17. Bill Loeb, author interview, June 9, 2011.
18. Clooney, with Barthel, *Girl Singer*.
19. Scott Turner, "Every Bit a Lady—The Making of *Look My Way*," Serge Entertainment Group (from www.rosemaryclooney.com).
20. William Ruhlmann, www.Allmusic.com
21. Rosemary Clooney, "Nice to Be Around," *The Gramophone*, July, 1977.
22. Most accounts date the first Concord festival as January 1969, although *Billboard* (May 14, 1977) has the date as 1968.
23. Quoted by Dan Oullette, "Concord Records on a Roll with Grammy Wins," *Billboard*, May 14, 2005.
24. "Bay Area Car Dealer Enjoys Own Label, Producing Fests," *Billboard*, May 14, 1977.
25. Scott Hamilton, author interview, June 13, 2010.
26. Warren Vaché, author interview, June 12, 2010.
27. Peter Reilly, *Stereo Review*, April 1978.
28. "Everything's Coming Up Rosie," *Billboard*, December 3, 1977.
29. Warren Vaché, author interview.
30. Clooney, with Barthel, *Girl Singer*.

CHAPTER 12
1. Bill Loeb, author interview, June 9, 2011.
2. Interview with Jonathan Schwartz, Madison Square Garden Network cable channel, October, 1983.
3. Richard Houdek, "4 Girls 4 More Than Memories," *Los Angeles Times*, September 8, 1977.
4. Margaret Whiting, *It Might as Well Be Spring*, William Morrow, New York, 1987.
5. Matt Connor, "The Four Girls Phenomenon," www.Rosemaryclooney.com, 2004.
6. Ibid.
7. Ibid.
8. Whiting, *It Might as Well Be Spring*.
9. "Fairmont, San Francisco—Performance on August 12, 1978; 4 Girls 4: Margaret Whiting, Rosemary Clooney, Rose Marie, Helen O'Connell," *Variety*, August 16, 1978.
10. Diane Werts, *Dallas Morning News*, March 11, 1979.
11. *The Rosemary Clooney Show* DVD.
12. Rosemary Clooney, with Joan Barthel, *Girl Singer*, Doubleday, New York, 1999.
13. Bill Loeb, author interview.
14. Connor, *The Four Girls Phenomenon*.
15. Allen Sviridoff, author interview, May 14, 2011.
16. "*Tom Snyder*," CNBC-TV, *April* 14, 1993.
17. Michael Feinstein, author interview, April 9, 2011.
18. Ibid.
19. It was actually written by Neil Sedaka.
20. Peter Reilly, "You've Got to Learn to Take Care of Yourself," *Stereo Review*, October 1981.
21. John Burk, author interview, May 12, 2011.
22. Allen Sviridoff, author interview, May 14, 2011.
23. Allen Sviridoff interviewed by Judy Carmichael, *Jazz Inspired*, Sirius XM, August 2005.
24. Allen Sviridoff, author interview, March 5, 2010.

25. "Harrah's Reno, July 7, 1983: Tony Bennett, Rosemary Clooney, John Carleton Orch," *Variety*, July 13, 1983.
26. Allen Sviridoff, author interview, March 5, 2010.
27. Whiting, *It Might as Well Be Spring*.
28. Rose Marie, *Hold the Roses*, University Press of Kentucky, Lexington, 2003.
29. Rose Marie, author interview, September 9, 2011.
30. Whiting, *It Might as Well Be Spring*.
31. Connor, *The Four Girls Phenomenon*.
32. *Tomorrow in Los Angeles*, NBC-TV, November 23, 1977.
33. "Rosemary Clooney—An American Treasure," *Jazz Inspired*, National Public Radio, c. 2004.
34. *Tomorrow in Los Angeles*.
35. *Up Close with Tom Cottle*, syndicated TV, December 1982.
36. Deborah Grace Winer, author interview, June 15, 2011.
37. Stephen Holden, author interview, March 27, 2011.
38. *Merv Griffin Show*, December 1982.
39. Allen Sviridoff, author interview, May 14, 2011.
40. John J. O'Connor, *New York Times*, December 8, 1982.
41. "The New 4 Girls (4)," *Variety*, March 3, 1982.
42. Ibid.
43. John S. Wilson, *New York Times*, June 30, 1983.
44. Jack Hawn, *Los Angeles Times*, August 3, 1983.

CHAPTER 13

1. "Rosemary Clooney—An American Treasure," *Jazz Inspired*, National Public Radio, c. 2004.
2. Marian McPartland, *Marian McPartland's Piano Jazz*, National Public Radio, October 14, 1992.
3. *The Charles Grodin Show*, CNBC-TV, February 2, 1995.
4. *The Tom Snyder Show*, April 14, 1993.
5. John S. Wilson, *New York Times*, June 6, 1982.
6. "Rosie Sings Bing/Here's to My Lady," *Downbeat*, July 12, 1979.
7. "Rosemary Clooney—An American Treasure."
8. "Cut The Crap," *Downbeat*, June 1991 (exact date not known).
9. "Filming a Life," *New York Times*, December 5, 1982.
10. Interview with Jonathan Schwartz, Madison Square Garden Network cable channel, October, 1983.
11. Michael Feinstein, author interview, April 9, 2011.
12. Leonard Feather, *Rosemary Clooney Sings the Music of Cole Porter*, Concord Jazz, 1982, sleeve note.
13. Bucky Pizzarelli, author interview, October 26, 2010.
14. Warren Vaché, author interview, June 12, 2010.
15. Peter Reilly, *Stereo Review*, October 1982.
16. "Rosemary Clooney—An American Treasure."
17. Stephen Holden, author interview, March 27, 2011.
18. Jonathan Schwartz, WQEW, New York, September 17, 1996.
19. Eliot Tiegel, "Great Comebacks," *Pulse* magazine, May 1990.
20. John Oddo, author interview, June 7, 2011.
21. Nick Clooney, author interview, May 16, 2011.
22. John Schreiber, author interview, March 29, 2011.

23. Jay Leonhart, author interview, March 31, 2011.
24. *Demi-Centennial Video*, A&E Home Network, 1995.
25. Scott Hamilton, author interview, June 13, 2010.
26. Tiegel, "Great Comebacks."
27. "Rosemary Clooney Sings the Music of Irving Berlin," *Downbeat*, April 1985.
28. Debby Boone, author interview, May 18, 2011.
29. John Oddo, author interview, June 7, 2011.
30. Richard Williams, *The Times*, November 19, 1983.
31. Quoted in *Val Doonican Rocks*, BBC4 (UK), 2007.
32. "Charlie's: Rosemary Clooney," *Washington Post*, September 6, 1984.
33. Allen Sviridoff, author interview, May 14, 2011.
34. Philip Elwood, *San Francisco Examiner*, November 5, 1986.
35. Gerald Nachman, *San Francisco Chronicle*, November 1986.
36. John S. Wilson, *New York Times*, May 5, 1985.
37. Allen Sviridoff, author interview.

CHAPTER 14
1. Marian McPartland, *Marian McPartland's Piano Jazz*, National Public Radio, October 14, 1992.
2. Deborah Grace Winer, author interview, June 15, 2011.
3. Ron Shaw, author interview, April 15, 2011.
4. John Schreiber, author interview, March 29, 2011.
5. Deborah Grace Winer, author interview.
6. Allen Sviridoff, author interview, May 14, 2011.
7. Larry King interview, Mutual Radio, April 20, 1987.
8. Debby Boone, author interview, May 18, 2011.
9. Monsita Boswick, author interview, May 13, 2011.
10. Ian Bernard, author interview, March 24, 2011.
11. John Pizzarelli, author interview, October 26, 2010.
12. Michael Feinstein, author interview, April 9, 2011.
13. Deborah Grace Winer, *The Night and the Music*, Schirmer Books, New York, 1995.
14. Deborah Grace Winer, author interview.
15. John Pizzarelli, author interview.
16. Allen Sviridoff, author interview, May 12, 2012.
17. "Rosemary Clooney Sings Rodgers, Hart & Hammerstein," *Downbeat*, July 1990.
18. Ibid.
19. Eliot Tiegel, *"Great Comebacks," Pulse* magazine, May 1990.
20. Deborah Grace Winer, author interview.
21. Allen Sviridoff, author interview, May 14, 2011.
22. Stephen Holden, *New York Times*, February 11, 1989.
23. "Rainbow & Stars, N.Y.," *Variety*, February 15, 1989.
24. William A. Raidy, *The Star Ledger*, February 13, 1989.
25. Gary Giddins, *Village Voice*, October 29, 1991.
26. Ibid.
27. Joanne Kaufman, *New York Magazine*, April 22, 1991.
28. "New York Rainbow & Stars (90 seats); Jan. 30–Feb. 24, 1990; $35 cover. Performance January 30, 1990," *Variety*, February 7, 1990.
29. Sherm Holvey, author interview 2, May 9, 2011.
30. Dante DiPaolo, author interview, May 12, 2011.

31. Ken Peplowski, author interview, October 26, 2010.
32. *Larry King Weekend*, CNN, May 10,1997.
33. Quoted by James Gavin in sleeve note to *Do You Miss New York*.
34. Joanne Kaufman, *Wall Street Journal*, February 1994.
35. Gene Seymour, *Newsday*, February 2, 1994.
36. Allen Sviridoff, author interview, May 14, 2011
37. Matt Connor, "The Four Girls Phenomenon," www.Rosemaryclooney.com, 2004.
38. Jay Leonhart, author interview, March 31, 2011.
39. *Fresh Air*, interview with Terry Gross, National Public Radio, January 18, 1997.
40. *Demi-Centennial Video*, A&E Home Video, 1995.
41. *Larry King Weekend*.

CHAPTER 15

1. Philip Elwood, *San Francisco Examiner*, July 31, 1995.
2. Philip Elwood, *San Francisco Examiner*, July 30, 1996.
3. Allen Sviridoff, author interview, May 14, 2011.
4. *The Rosie O'Donnell Show* (syndicated TV), May 9, 1997.
5. The reply was not strictly true. Recording contracts had meant that Rosemary was unable to appear on the "official" soundtrack album for the film (see Chapter 5), but Columbia had issued Rosemary's own versions of the songs from the movie, along with other seasonal tracks on a 10" LP called *Irving Berlin's White Christmas* in 1955. In 1978, Rosemary had also recorded a collection of Christmas songs for Mistletoe Records (see Appendix A).
6. Glen Barros, author interview, March 24, 2011.
7. Allen Sviridoff, author interview.
8. Steve Eddy, *Orange County Register*, December 17, 2000.
9. Peter Watrous, *New York Times*, December 6, 1996.
10. Glen Barros, author interview.
11. Nick Clooney, author interview, May 16, 2011. "I did hear the Pope sneeze," Nick said. Others in the party heard the blessings exchange and it was part of the account of the meeting that Rosemary would tell.
12. Ibid.
13. *The Late Late Show with Tom Snyder*, CBS-TV, February 16, 1999.
14. Jim Knippenberg, *Cincinnati Enquirer*, November 8, 1997.
15. Philip Elwood, *San Francisco Examiner*, July 30, 1996.
16. *Larry King Weekend*, CNN, May 10, 1997.
17. Stephen Holden, author interview, March 27, 2011.
18. "Clooney's Crooning Past Prime, but Pleasant," *Tulsa World*, November 23, 1998.
19. Michael Feinstein, author interview, April 9, 2011.
20. Jonathan Schwarz interview, 1560 WQEW, May 10, 1998.
21. Quoted by James Barron, *New York Times*, May 27, 1998.
22. Quoted by Michael Quintanilla, *Los Angeles Times*, October 7, 1998.
23. Philip Elwood, *San Francisco Examiner*, November 9, 1998.
24. Michael Feinstein, author interview.
25. Stephen Holden, *New York Times*, October 8, 1999.
26. Stephen Holden, author interview.
27. Michael Feinstein, author interview.
28. Quoted by Jesse Hamlin, *San Francisco Chronicle*, January 20, 1997.

CHAPTER 16

1. Jeffrey Lee Puckett, *Courier-Journal*, March 4, 2001.
2. Will Friedwald, *Sentimental Journey* CD, 2001, sleeve note.
3. *The Rosie O'Donnell Show* (syndicated), March 28, 2000.
4. Matt Catingub, author interview, March 21, 2011.
5. Interview with Jonathan Schwartz, on 1560 WQEW AM, May 10, 1998.
6. Stephen Holden, *New York Times*, March 29, 2001.
7. Michael Feinstein, author interview, April 9, 2011.
8. Sherry Crawford, *Courier & Press*, September 17, 2001.
9. Ibid.
10. Quoted by Janelle Gelfand, *Cincinnati Enquirer*, July 1, 2002.
11. Nick Clooney, author interview, May 16, 2011.
12. Elysa Gardner, "Clooney Carried a Torch for Music," *USA Today*, June 30, 2002.
13. Terry Teachout, "Better With Age? Its Not That Simple," *New York Times*, July 7, 2002.
14. CBS *Sunday Gold*, November 28, 1999.

ACKNOWLEDGMENTS

Many people and many organizations have helped us prepare this biography of Rosemary Clooney. We were particularly fortunate to have the help of Allen Sviridoff who was Rosemary's manager for the last 20 years of her life. Allen could not have done more to aid us in bringing the project to fruition. He welcomed us to his home in Woodland Hills, California, for a long interview and patiently answered the host of questions with which we bombarded him over many months. Through his contacts he was able to introduce us to many others we might not have been able to access. Our thanks are also due to Allen's hard-working secretary, Kimberly Reeves, who oiled the wheels for us throughout the process.

Rosemary's daughters, Maria and Monsita, both gave us in-depth interviews as did Rosemary's brother, Nick, who consented to a long meeting at his home in Augusta, Kentucky, and generously entertained us afterward. Dante DiPaolo, Rosemary's second husband, met us in Beverly Hills for a fascinating conversation. Phyllis Holvey (Rosemary's cousin) and her husband Sherm gave us several interviews by phone and also entertained us at their home in Palm Desert.

Rosemary has always had a loyal fan base, and many of them provided invaluable assistance. Paul Barouh, in particular, deserves special mention. Paul was tireless in his support and he also generously loaned us a colossal number of items from his collection, which enabled us to see and hear many of Rosemary's radio and TV appearances that would otherwise have been unavailable to us. Kathy Brown and Rogier Rubens have also given important and substantial help in many areas. To each of them we give our heartfelt appreciation of their efforts with our project. Our thanks are also given to the following, all of whom made significant contributions to the preparation of this book: Dieter Beier, Ross Brethour, David Currington, Ian and Mavis Coleman, Matt Connor, Cheryl French, Dee Goldstein, Brian Henson, MaryLou Mattingly, Martin McQuade, Wendy Mitchell, Keith Parkinson, Graham Pascoe, Pamela S. Schlereth, Michael Schnurr, Mark Sendroff, Ron Shaw, Maureen Solomon, J. J. Tohill, and Greg Van Beek.

Those from the world of show business and entertainment who have given us tremendous assistance are (in alphabetical order) Ken Barnes, Glen Barros, Ian Bernard, Debby Boone, John Burk, Matt Catingub, Ray Charles, Gene Cipriano, Michael Feinstein (who also kindly contributed the Foreword), Will Friedwald (who also gave us access to his unpublished essay on the making of the *Blue Rose* album), Gary Giddins, Henry Riggs Guidotti, Ken Guidotti, Scott Hamilton, Stephen Holden, Leslie Ann Jones, Jay Leonhart, Rich Little, Bill Loeb, Roy Oakshott, John Oddo, Ken Peplowski, Stephen Pouliot, John Schreiber, Bonnie Sugarman, Jack Swersie, Warren Vaché, Roger Vorce, and Deborah Grace Winer. It was a pleasure and an honor to engage with these professionals.

As well as our interview program, our research also drew upon a variety of libraries and museums, plus online resources. Our primary aim was to access material that was contemporaneous with Rosemary's career. We found that online archive sources for newspapers and periodicals such as *Variety, Billboard*, and the *New York Times* were invaluable in this regard. Web-based sites including newspaperarchive.com, newslibrary.com, and TV.com, gave much useful information too. We also thank the staff of the Kentucky-Gateway Museum, Maysville, Kentucky; the Rosemary Clooney house, Augusta, Kentucky; the Los Angeles Public Library system; the main library of Cincinnati and Hamilton County; and the Atlantic City Free Public Library. In the United Kingdom, thanks go to the BBC Written Archives Centre at Caversham, the staff at the British Library in London and at the Manchester Central Public Library.

In respect of other internet-based references, pride of place must go to the Rosemary Clooney Palladium site run by Kathy Brown. This was a wonderful resource. We are indebted to Judy Carmichael's Jazzinspired.com site for her interviews with Scott Hamilton, Bucky Pizzarelli, John Pizzarelli, Mark Sendroff, Allen Sviridoff, and Warren Vaché. Other very helpful sites were 78discography.com; Allmusic.com; GOLDINdex database; the Internet Movie Database; kiddierekordking.com; Museum of Broadcast Communications, Chicago; Wikipedia; and youtube.com.

Suzanne Ryan and the staff at Oxford University Press in New York have been enthusiastic supporters of our book since we first proposed it to them, and we extend our thanks for their editorial and production work.

Last, but certainly not least, we must make special mention of our spouses, Linda and Pat, whose tolerance, love, and support we too easily take for granted! Thank you, ladies.

Ken Crossland and Malcolm Macfarlane
England, January 2013

BIBLIOGRAPHY

Reference was made to the following books and published articles.

BOOKS

Bennett, Tony, with Friedwald, Will, *The Good Life: The Autobiography of Tony Bennett*, Simon & Schuster, New York, 1998.

Clooney, Rosemary, with Strait, Raymond, *This for Remembrance*, Simon & Schuster, New York, 1977.

Clooney, Rosemary, with Barthel, Joan, *Girl Singer*, Doubleday, New York, 1999.

Crosby, Bing, with Martin, Pete, *Call Me Lucky*, Simon & Schuster, New York, 1953.

Fass, John, *Backstory in Blue: Ellington at Newport '56*, Rutgers University Press, Piscataway, NJ, 2008.

Friedwald, Will, *Jazz Singing—America's Great Voices from Bessie Smith to Bebop and Beyond*, Charles Scribner's Sons, New York, 1990.

Friedwald, Will, *A Biographical Guide to the Great Jazz and Pop Singers*, Pantheon Books, New York, 2010.

Friedwald, Will, *Sinatra! The Song Is You*, Da Capo, New York, 1997.

Giddins, Gary, *Riding on a Blue Note*, Oxford University Press, New York, 1981.

Giddins, Gary, *Visions of Jazz*, Oxford University Press, New York, 1998.

Hajdu, David, *Lush Life, a Biography of Billy Strayhorn*, North Point Press, New York, 1997.

Hale, Lee, *Backstage at the Dean Martin Show*, Taylor Publishing, Dallas, TX, 2000.

Kaplan, James, *Frank: The Voice*, Doubleday, New York, 2010.

Levinson, Peter J., *September in the Rain: The Life of Nelson Riddle*, Taylor Trade Publishing, Lanham, MD, 2005.

Macfarlane, Malcolm, *Bing Crosby—Day by Day*, Scarecrow Press, Lanham, MD, 2001.

Macfarlane, Malcolm, and Crossland, Ken, *Perry Como, a Biography and Complete Career Chronicle*, McFarland, Jefferson, NC, 2009.

Norden, Denis, *Clips for a Life*, Harper Perennial, London, 2008.

Rose Marie, *Hold the Roses*, University Press of Kentucky, Lexington, 2003.

Sanjek, Russell, *American Popular Music and Its Business: The First Four Hundred Years*, Oxford University Press, New York, 1988.

Simon, George T., *The Big Bands*, Macmillan, New York, 1967.

Simon, George T., *The Big Bands Songbook*, Barnes & Noble, New York, 1981.

Tenkotte, Paul A., and Claypool, James C., *The Encyclopedia of Northern Kentucky*, University of Kentucky Press, Lexington, 2010.

Vail, Ken, *Duke's Diary: Part Two: The Life of Duke Ellington 1950–1974*, Scarecrow Press, Lanham, MD, 1999.

Whitburn, Joel, *Billboard Pop Hits 1940–54*, Record Research, Menomonee Falls, WI, 1994.

Whiting, Margaret, *It Might as Well Be Spring*, William Morrow, New York, 1987.

Winer, Deborah Grace, *Come On-a My House*, Bear Family Records, Hambergen, Germany, 1997.

Winer, Deborah Grace, *Many a Wonderful Moment*, Bear Family Records, Germany, 1999.

Winer, Deborah Grace, *Memories of You*, Bear Family Records, Germany, 1998.

Winer, Deborah Grace, *The Night and the Music*, Schirmer Books, New York, 1995.

Zak, Albin J. III, *I Don't Sound Like Nobody: Remaking Music in 1950s America*, University of Michigan Press, Ann Arbor, 2010.

ARTICLES

Albert, Dora, "The Ring around Rosie," *TV Radio Mirror*, March 1958.

Balliett, Whitney, "The Heart, the Head, and the Pipes," *The New Yorker* August 3, 1992.

Balliett, Whitney, "Rosemary and Era," *The New Yorker*, December 2, 1996.

Barber, John, "A Worthwhile Wait to Hear Bing Crosby," *Daily Telegraph* (UK), June 22, 1976.

Baskette, Kirtley, "What Makes Rosie Glow?" *Redbook*, September 1953.

"Bay Area Car Dealer Enjoys Own Label, Producing Fests," *Billboard*, May 14, 1977.

Beck, Marilyn, "Rosemary Clooney Hits the Comeback Trail," *Milwaukee Journal*, March 25, 1974.

Bernstein, Bob "Miss Clooney Blooms in her New TV Show", *Billboard*, September 30, 1957.

"Bingle All the Way," *Life Magazine*, October 11, 1954.

Bird, Virginia, "Hollywood's Favorite Songbird," *Saturday Evening Post*, January, 1955.

Clooney, Nick, "Hanging Out with Rosie on Early TV," *Cincinnati Post*, January 8, 2003.

Clooney, Rosemary, "My Manhattan," *Where*, February 1990.

Clooney, Rosemary "Putting My Visit on Record," *Picturegoer*, February 20, 1954.

Connor, Matt, "The Four Girls Phenomenon," www.Rosemaryclooney.com, 2004.

"Clooney's Crooning Past Prime, but Pleasant," *Tulsa World*, November 23, 1998.

"Cut the Crap," *Downbeat*, June 1991.

Ebert, Alan, "Rosemary Clooney's Saddest Song," *Ladies Home Journal*, March 1976.

Ekizian, John G., "Me, Bing & the Best Christmas Film Ever," *New York Post*, December 14, 2001.

"Filming a Life," *New York Times*, December 5, 1982.

Friedwald, Will, "They Sang Along with Mitch," *Wall Street Journal*, August 4, 2010.

Gibson, John, "Bing at His Best—Now I Can Die Happy," *Edinburgh Evening News* (UK), July 16, 1976.

Giddins, Gary, "Going Our Way—Rosemary Clooney's Time Is Now," *Village Voice*, October 29, 1991.

"Girl in the Groove," *Time Magazine*, cover feature, February 23, 1953.

Harvey, Evelyn, "Everything's Rosy for Clooney," *Collier's*, November 15, 1952.

Hawn, Jack, "Clooney Cresting on New Career," *Los Angeles Times*, August 3, 1983.

Houdek, Richard, "4 Girls 4 More Than Memories," *Los Angeles Times*, September 8, 1977.

Kish, Frances, "Her Life Is a Song," *TV Radio Mirror*, August 1955.

Lauerman, Connie, "Growing Older Gracefully with Rosemary Clooney," *Chicago Tribune*, October 6, 1981.

Millstein, Gilbert, "Fabulous Joe Ferrer," *Collier's*, December 25, 1953.

Oullette, Dan, "Concord Records on a Roll with Grammy Wins," *Billboard*, May 14, 2005.

Pileggi, Sarah, "Rosemary Clooney," *People*, December 13, 1982.

Purdum, Todd S., "The Street Where They Lived," *Vanity Fair*, April 1999.

Reilly, Peter "You've Got to Learn to Take Care of Yourself," *Stereo Review*, October 1981.

"Rosemary Clooney's Household: It's Like Crazy," *TV Guide*, February 22–28, 1958.

"Rosemary Clooney Says She'll Retire," *Press-Telegram*, July 3, 1968.

Runbeck, Margaret Lee, "On Being Mrs. Jose Ferrer," *Good Housekeeping*, May 1956.

Severo, Richard, "Mitch Miller, Maestro of the Singalong, Dies at 99," *New York Times*, August 2, 2010.

Teachout, Terry, "Better with Age? It's Not That Simple," *New York Times*, July 7, 2002.

"The Wholesome Type," *Time Magazine*, September 8, 1952.

"There's Only One Bing," *TV Radio Mirror*, October 1954.

Tiegel, Eliot, "Great Comebacks," *Pulse* magazine, May 1990.

Turner, Scott, "Every Bit a Lady—The Making of Look My Way," Serge Entertainment Group (from www.Rosemaryclooney.com).

"TV Program & Talent Awards," *Billboard*, July 29, 1957.

Watson, Jimmy, "Clooney's Sensational Glasgow Opening," *New Musical Express* (UK), July 8, 1955.

Wilkie, Jane, "Our Rosie," *Our Screen*, June 1953.

INDEX